*Image of the Other and the Self
in the American and British press
during the Gulf Crisis and War*

INGRID DEWEWEIRE

# Image of the Other and the Self in the American and British press during the Gulf Crisis and War

Bibliographical Information of the Deutsche Nationalbibliothek
This publication is listed in the Deutsche Nationalbibliographie of the Deutsche
Nationalbibliothek; detailed bibliographical information can be accessed under
https://dnb.dnb.de.

© 2024 Ingrid Deweweire
Layout, Coverdesign and Publishing:
BoD – Books on Demand GmbH, In de Tarpen 42, 22848 Norderstedt

Printing and Production: Libri Plureos GmbH, Friedensallee 273, 22763
Hamburg

ISBN 978-3-7578-1964-4

# Contents

**Part V:**
**Image of the Other: The allies**
**Differences and similarities between the American press**
**and the British press during the Gulf Crisis and War**     389

# Acknowledgements

First and foremost, I am indebted to Michael Parsons,[1] former professor at the University of Pau et des Pays de l'Adour, France for his invaluable comments, criticism and suggestions.

I owe a huge debt of gratitude to Michel Morel, former professor at the University of Lorraine, France for providing helpful advice, patient support and constant encouragement. Without his expert guidance, this book could not have been written.

Likewise, I am most grateful to my friend Susan Goodwin for answering my many questions and helping me throughout the writing process. I would also like to thank my friend Frank Turpin for attentively reading the general conclusion. Any errors and shortcomings are my sole responsibility, however.

Finally, I wish to extend my heartfelt thanks to my family and especially my husband for his patience and generous support.

To all of them, my sincere thanks.

---

1    Professor Michael Parsons directed my doctoral thesis and provided helpful comments on this translation.

# Preface

On 2 August 1990 one hundred thousand Iraqi soldiers crossed the borders of Kuwait and invaded the whole country. The invasion triggered not only a large-scale military operation led by Washington, but also a huge media campaign. All the international press went to Dharan in Saudi Arabia to cover these events in the Persian Gulf.

At that time, there was of course no such thing as social media. Prior to their advent, governments and the mass media, i.e. radio, television and print media, were the main sources of information given to the public. As technology has developed quickly over the years and especially since the 1990s, the role of journalists has also radically changed in nature. The Internet, search engines such as Google and social media platforms such as Facebook and X, formerly Twitter, have forced journalists to redefine their role and even reinvent themselves. First, journalists are no longer the only people commenting on current events and important issues. Anyone can now write about anything on social media. Second, despite their controversial nature, social media bring together millions of users over the Internet and thus enable journalists to connect with their readers. Third, as the authenticity of what is being reported and facts and sources are sometimes not verified because of time pressures which could affect the quality of reporting, the risk of spreading fake news and misinformation is all the more prevalent. Not to mention the fact that this practice could be turned into pure propaganda, or deliberate disinformation.

The situation is all the more acute in times of crisis and war and in particular since technology has substantially altered war reporting. On the one hand and on a positive note, data can be transferred faster and more easily. Social media platforms enable journalists to bring conflicts to a worldwide audience and provide them with information about poorly accessible areas of war. However, according to the report published in 2016 by the Media Program South East Europe of the Konrad-Adenauer-Stiftung[2] in Berlin, war reporters face more and more challenges in reporting from conflict zones nowadays. They find it increasingly difficult to remain objective and respect "the professional and ethical standards of journalism".

Regardless of the above, at the time this study was written, official material referring to the Gulf Crisis and the subsequent war, such as classified and defence department documents, were still closed for thirty years, at least in the UK[3] and thus not accessible to the public outside the armed forces.[4] Therefore, until the official archives were opened for public scrutiny, much remained unknown about the Gulf dispute, which might seem

---

2   Darija Fabijanić, Christian Spahr, Vladimir Zlatarsky, eds., *Conflict Reporting in the Smartphone Era,* report, Berlin: Konrad-Adenauer-Stiftung, 2016, *passim.*

3   In the USA, documents are declassified after 25 years. However, there are nine narrow exemptions outlined by section 3.3 of Executive Order 13526 (see the following websites: <https://www.archives.gov/research/alic/reference/military/records-declassification.html>; <https://justice.gov/archives/open/declassification/declassification-faq>, consulted 5 September 2022).

4   Since my study was written, many documents on the Gulf War have been declassified. See, for example, the website of The National Security Archive at the George Washington University: <https://nsarchive2.gwu.edu/NSAEBB/NSAEBB39/>, consulted 17 August 2022.

surprising since this event appeared to be fought in full view of global television audiences.[5] It was, nonetheless, attempted to present as broad a picture as possible of the press reporting of the Kuwaiti Crisis and the Gulf War as this study might permit.

The Gulf War was undoubtedly a pivotal moment which has shaped events in the Middle East and beyond and has had a lasting impact on international relations. It could therefore serve as a reference to explain political trends in foreign policy in the last decades of the 20th century. One knows that studying the past can often shed light on events taking place today. The Gulf War was also a turning point in the history of war reporting and information management. Detailed study of the conflict and the way it was reported in the media can throw light on the way war is presented and discussed in the media today.

Finally, the issue of the Self and the Other, which is at the heart of this study, is still a topical subject since unfortunately even now it sparks mixed and emotional reactions in the public at large.[6] War almost necessarily polarizes, establishing a sharp divide between one side and the other, forcing combatants and non-combatants alike to choose their camp. Observers from outside often find themselves drawn inexorably into this rift. It

---

5     Philip M. Taylor, "Chapter Eleven: The Enduring Tensions of Democratic Propaganda in the Information Age", *British Propaganda in the Twentieth Century: Selling Democracy*, Edinburgh: Edinburgh UP, 1999, p. 253.

6     According to john a. powell and Stephen Menendian, "the problem of the 21st century is" that of "othering". See their article "The Problem of Othering: Towards Inclusiveness and Belonging", *Othering & Belonging: Expanding the Circle of Human Concern*, Issue 1, summer 2016, p. 14, UC Berkeley, <http://live-otheringandbelonging.pantheon.berkeley.edu/the-problem-of-othering/>, consulted 20 August 2022.

is almost a truism to recall that the enemy is usually portrayed very negatively and the actions and identity of one's own side and one's allies are shown in a very positive light. It is at any rate an arena in which the relationship between one group of people (or nation, or state) and another becomes acutely strained or tested to destruction. The Gulf War provides the material for a particularly enlightening case study in this respect. I hope that this study[7] will be both a useful contribution to the general debate about the Self and the Other and a helpful reference to anyone working in the field of conflict reporting.

7    This book is only a summary of the whole study, which is available in French on the following website: <http://www.theses.fr/178570982>. In case of discrepancy between the original text and its translation, the French text prevails. It should also be noted that quotation marks and punctuation mainly follow British English usage. In addition, the books included in the bibliography are in their original language.

# Introduction

> *You shall judge of a man by his foes as well as by his friends.*
> Joseph Conrad (1857-1924) *Lord Jim* (1900)

On 2 August 1990 the Iraqi army invaded neighbouring Kuwait annexing it as its nineteenth province on account of a dispute over a shared oil field. Not only did Iraq's invasion catch the world unawares, causing a stir all over the globe, but it also alarmed most world leaders, notably George Bush,[8] the then American president, and Margaret Thatcher,[9] the British Prime Minister at the time, who both quickly denounced the Iraqi take-over of Kuwait. In addition to imposing world-wide trade sanctions on Iraq, the United States and its European NATO allies were prompted to deploy troops in Saudi Arabia to deter a possible attack from Saddam Hussein, the Iraqi leader.[10] Several other Arab nations joined the anti-Iraq coalition by contributing troops to the military build-up, known as Operation Desert Shield. There followed a six-month deadlock between the Iraqi ruler and the United Nations sanctioned allied forces, which was interspersed with passionate rhetorical attacks and counterattacks by Bush and Hussein. The Iraqi dictator's refusal to withdraw from Kuwait by the January 15 U.N. deadline ended the tense waiting game with the outbreak of the Gulf War,[11] which lasted from 16-17 January

---

8   George Bush (1924-2018), a politician and businessman, was the 41st president of the United States from 1989 to 1993.
9   Margaret Thatcher (1925-2013), a Conservative politician, was Britain's Prime Minister from 1979 to 1990.
10  Saddam Hussein (1937-2006) was the president of Iraq from 1979 to 2003.
11  See appendix 1 for more information about the chronology of the Gulf Crisis and War.

1991 to 28 February 1991 and culminated in a decisive military victory for the multinational coalition of thirty-five countries.[12]

Iraq's power grab of oil-rich Kuwait set off the world's largest military operation since World War II, and an international press corps converged on Dharan in Saudi Arabia to cover the events unfolding in the Persian Gulf. The crisis dominated the headlines from August 1990 onwards and intensified as the threat of war drew closer. The subsequent conflict, known as Operation Desert Storm, became a major television event. The military closely supervised the reporters in the region who were assigned to "pools"[13] of journalists carefully selected and monitored for their coverage of the conflict. The U.S. military controlled and restricted access to information during the hostilities in the Persian Gulf. In addition to the difficulty for the journalist in producing an article in a state of emergency as news writing must be effective,[14] there is the specific problem of access to direct sources of information. The 1,200 accredited journalists were thus forced to stay in their hotels or attend lengthy military briefings. Many restrictions were imposed on journalists as well as press organizations, and all press articles had to be checked by military censorship before they could be released. The White House media advisors thought that "technological success should be mentioned more than the human factor". Despite protests from newspapers and television in the name of the right to information, the authorities considered

---

12    See appendix 2 for further information about the multinational coalition.
13    "Pools" are groups of journalists allowed to accompany fighting units. During the invasion of Panama in 1989, the U.S. military first tried the system of the "news pool" (Philip M. Taylor, *op.cit.*, p. 252).
14    "Saying a lot in few sentences and in an attractive way". Jacques Mouriquand, *L'Écriture journalistique*, Que sais-je?, Paris: PUF, 1997, p. 3.

that victory should to some extent be based on censorship; the American military[15] had not forgotten the spectre of Vietnam and its impact on public opinion.

Moreover, although the first amendment to the U.S. Constitution guarantees freedom of speech, this does not necessarily apply in wartime and thus poses a challenge to the very concept of freedom of the press. This situation raises a series of issues which are not only related to the possible constraints imposed by the state on the media – these constraints being as much a matter for military strategy as national policy – but also, and especially in this context, to the production of information by professionals. Journalists can report information transmitted by authorized spokespeople, but they may also present their own views of the facts developed on the basis of unofficial information. Even in a democratic state, there are undoubtedly justified *reasons of state*[16] that must ensure the best interests of the actors involved in the war. But what are their acceptable limits? Furthermore, how can one distinguish the ideological discourse of the government, which acts in its sole interest, from the legitimate wish to preserve the security of the armed forces? Their security could be compromised if there was no restriction on the release of potentially harmful information.

---

15  Michael Emery and Edwin Emery, *The Press and America. An Interpretive History of the Mass Media*, 6th ed., Englewood Cliffs, NJ: Prentice-Hall, 1988, pp. 518-519.

16  "Raison d'État" in French: "it means a reason for state action, on the grounds of the interests of that state and its territory, and the security and well-being of its population, which override other considerations, particularly international ones" (David Weigall, *International Relations. A Concise Companion*, London: Arnold, 2002, pp. 187-188).

This context provides a useful opportunity to reflect on the press and in particular to compare the American press with the British press during the crisis and war in the Gulf.[17] This study begins in the aftermath of the Iraqi invasion of Kuwait on 2 August 1990 and ends two weeks after the end of the Gulf War on 28 February 1991. This period is particularly interesting to analyse as it is situated at the crossroads of two eras. Although the end of the Cold War between the United States and its allies, on the one hand, and the Soviet Union and the countries of the Warsaw Pact, on the other, announced a period of peace and stability, the Gulf Crisis and the war itself undermined international relations in the late 20th century and upset the hope of a new era. The crisis and the Gulf War, which has been described by Jean Baudrillard as a "surgical war" in which "the enemy only appears as a target on a computer",[18] showed the military superiority and strategic role of the United States. The hostilities generated intense media coverage, which saw the triumph of television and especially the Cable News Channel – CNN. Not only did television emerge in the media as the fastest and most important source of information during the Gulf War, but it also gave the public the spectacle of a "live" war as well as the illusion of being close to the events. Perhaps for the last time, television was the primary source of information for most people. According to a report published by the Pew Research Center on 10 January 1991, "eighty-two percent of those surveyed said they [had] been getting most of

---

17    My former written papers consisted on the one hand in comparing articles published by two British newspapers, the *Times* and the *Guardian*, and on the other hand, in analysing similarities and differences between editorials and opinion articles (op-eds) of two American newspapers, the *New York Times* and the *Washington Post*.

18    Jean Baudrillard, *La Guerre du Golfe n'a pas eu lieu*, Paris: Galilée, 1991, p. 64.

their Gulf news from television, 40 percent said newspapers (some respondents gave multiple answers), 15 percent radio, 4 percent magazines".[19] Although a comparison between the controversial role of television and the print media during an international crisis is beyond the scope of this study, the fact is that television tends to communicate raw data to the viewer without standing back – especially during a time of crisis. Through images, some of which are repeated almost ad nauseam, audio-visual media can act potently on the emotions of individuals without appealing to their analytical faculties: TV shows whereas print media demonstrate.

The aim of this study is not to present a chronicle of events related by the press but rather to focus on the analysis of the news items which were communicated to American and British readers. It aims therefore to study the nature of the viewpoints set out in leading articles, opinion articles and letters to the editor. The main objective of this study is to examine the journalistic discourse of opinion as developed by the newspapers and the ways in which this discourse is produced. This essay analyses the development of ideas and representations and interpretations of current events. Through its belonging to the world of communication, the printed press, being an industrial product that is economically dependent on advertising,[20]

---

19 "Divided public focused on Gulf news: braced for bloody war", report, Pew Research Center, 10 January 1991, <https://www.pewresearch.org/politics/1991/01/10/divided-public-focused-on-gulf-news-braced-for-bloody-war/>, consulted on 3 March 2019.

20 Although the printed press also upholds intellectual and moral values, markets forces have an impact on it. The concentration of ownership and the power of the large media groups, as companies merge or are taken over, raise questions about the objectivity of newspaper reporting and opinion. It has been argued that proprietors of media organizations (i.e. Murdoch's company, News Corporation) use the media to promote their

does not merely inform the public but also conveys messages which progressively construct a world view – the latter being a key element in the context of this study. Newspapers communicate their perception of the world through their descriptions and judgments focused on events. While interpreting facts, they represent the world as they apprehend it, but although this representation is based on the observation of factual events, it is inevitably coloured by their assumptions and pre-conceptions, that is to say their interpretative framework. This theme is frequently discussed in the work of the historian Jacques Le Goff[21] who defines the concept of representation as including "any mental translation of a perceived external reality".[22] The documents on which the historian works "express more than a representation: an imagination of culture and power [...]".[23] By analogy, one could consider that a newspaper article shows the imaginative world of society as much as real situations like current events. The article therefore reflects and echoes the thoughts of society and only represents reality to the reader through a prism.

This thesis looks into the content and form of the discourse of the American and British press in connection with the events of crisis and war. It questions the nature of the enunciative positions adopted by editors and journalists. It examines in particular the way in which the Other and the Self were described, on the one hand, by the American daily papers, the *New York Times* and the *Washington Post*, and, on the other hand, by the British daily papers, the *Times* and the *Guardian* and the Sunday newspapers,

---

own commercial and political interests. Owners may thus directly interfere in editorial content (Refer to Nicholas Abercrombie and Brian Longhurst, *Dictionary of Media Studies*, London: Penguin Books, 2007, *passim*).

21 Jacques Le Goff, *Un Autre Moyen Âge*, Paris: Gallimard, 1999, 1372 p.
22 *Ibid.*, p. 423.
23 *Ibid.*, p. 425.

the *Sunday Times* and the *Observer* during the crisis and the war in the Gulf.[24] These newspapers were selected because they are representative of the "quality press" which devotes a significant amount of space to leading articles and "op-eds" in such a way as to present an exchange of ideas and opinions. Editorials, opinion articles and letters to the editor of the various newspapers have been selected for this thesis. Editorials, which are in general unsigned, are written by the editorial staff of the newspaper. They present the paper's position on current events. Opinion articles are often written by key figures that do not belong to the staff of the newspaper. They provide viewpoints that may differ substantially from the editorial line. Both editorials and opinion articles use rhetorical methods of persuasion. They also often pursue a debate initiated in articles from other sections of the newspaper or in previous issues.[25] Letters to the editor form "a type of section that is unified by the common rhetoric and demonstrative side of each contribution".[26] This section allows the newspaper to choose a number of texts representing readers' reactions to topical events.

Much has been written about the Gulf War and media coverage of war. The goal of this study is to broach this subject from a different perspective: examining the way in which the Gulf Crisis

---

24    One shall first refer to the American press and then the British press as far
        as the examples coming from the articles used in this study are concerned.
        The alphabetical order has been chosen in the American press: first the *New
        York Times* and then the *Washington Post*. As for the British press, one
        shall first refer to the daily newspapers and second to the Sunday papers
        according to the arbitrary place hereafter: the *Times*, the *Guardian*, the
        *Sunday Times* and finally the *Observer*.
25    Jacqueline Reimen (dir.), *Méthodes et sources. Manuel bilingue à l'usage
        des étudiants de civilisation américaine et britannique*, Nancy: PU de
        Nancy, 1989, p. 36.
26    *Ibid.*, p. 36.

and hostilities were presented to the readers on both sides of the Atlantic. The analytical framework is based on the work of Carl Schmitt,[27] a German jurist and philosopher (1888-1985), and Julien Freund,[28] a French political scientist and sociologist (1921-1993), who described relations between States in terms of friendship or hostility. A controversial figure because of his Nazi allegiances,[29] Carl Schmitt defined politics as the opposition between "friend and enemy"[30] in his book, *Der Begriff des Politischen*, published in 1932 and translated under the title, *The Concept of the Political*. Politics for Schmitt was based on relationships of enmity. By placing hostility at the centre of politics, Carl Schmitt defines conflict and the dialectics between friend and foe as the pivotal force in politics. He argues that in the absence of an enemy, there is no politics. The configuration of friend versus enemy thus structures the field of international relations and the concepts of peace and war.[31] According to the author, war, which is the continuation of politics[32] and has an ethical dignity,[33] depends on the characterization of both camps, i.e. allies and enemies. It implies the designation of a public enemy, that is to say the Other, the foreigner, the antagonist in terms of interests and

27    Carl Schmitt, *The Concept of the Political*, Chicago: U of Chicago Press, 2007, 126 p.
28    Julien Freund, *L'Essence du politique*, 3e éd., Paris: Dalloz, 2004, 867 p.
29    Gopal Balakrishnan, *L'Ennemi. Un portrait intellectuel de Carl Schmitt*, Paris: Amsterdam, 2006, p. 13.
30    Philippe Raynaud et Stéphane Rials (dir.), *Dictionnaire de philosophie politique*, Paris: Quadrige/PUF, 2005, p. 305; Carl Schmitt, *op.cit.*, pp. 64-68.
31    David Cumin, *Carl Schmitt. Biographie politique et intellectuelle*, Paris: Cerf, 2005, pp. 26, 46, 48-49.
32    He agreed with Clausewitz on this point. Clausewitz qualified war "as the continuation of politics by other means" (Julien Freund, *op.cit.*, p. 591).
33    Élisabeth Clément, et al., *La Philosophie de A à Z*, Paris: Hatier, 2000, p. 404.

values.[34] Similarly, Julien Freund considers that "there is no politics without a real or virtual enemy"[35] and that "politics [...] will divide communities into friends and enemies".[36] He claims that the foreign and security policy of a state is conditioned by the concept of friends and enemies[37] and that the mutual recognition of enemies is the foundation of international law. The definition of foreign and security policy refers therefore – for these authors – to the relationship with the Other and his/her designation as friend or foe.

Journalists look at the huge mass of information they receive and decide which "events" are newsworthy. Although they may endeavour to inform readers "objectively", their texts cannot rule out all subjectivity; "subjectivity, political preferences and the ideological assumptions of the editorial team are reflected in the selection of information and its presentation".[38] This is especially true for an opinion article. Judgments made by journalists on an event inevitably reflect their environment, their background and education, their sense of imagination in terms of sets of representations or images that underlie the psyche of any individual, and the whole system of representations, values and beliefs. Karl Popper considers that within the scope of the scientific process no observations are neutral, and they are all based on presuppositions. This comment could be applied to the role of journalists who are subjected to economic pressure and

---

34    Norbert Campagna, *Carl Schmitt. Eine Einführung*, Berlin: Parerga, 2004, pp. 28-31.
35    Julien Freund, *op. cit.*, p. 830.
36    *Ibid.*, p. 448.
37    *Ibid.*, pp. 448, 653.
38    Michel Rezé et Ralph Bowen, *Introduction à la vie américaine*, 2e éd., Paris: Masson, 1997, p. 143.

time constraints. Journalists, like researchers, make assumptions and hold prejudices which are bound to colour their writing. Do they not describe facts according to the "habitus"[39] defined by Pierre Bourdieu? How are ideas and interpretations developed in journalistic discourse? For Louis Althusser "ideology is when answers come before questions".[40] Any article is based on a system of underlying values and beliefs internalized by the journalist. This study is therefore based on the comparative reading of editorials and opinion articles or "op-eds",[41] and letters sent in by readers of newspapers. The objective is to detect the ideological values conveyed by journalists,[42] especially in a situation of crisis and war.

The analytical framework of this study is based on a thematic approach. The objective is to categorize viewpoints expressed in editorials, opinion articles and letters sent to the editor. Recurring themes and references related to the image of the Other and the Self that are used by each newspaper are compared. Differences as well as similarities in the treatment of information are highlighted. To review systematically all the leading articles, opinion articles and letters to the editor in all of the newspapers selected would have been excessively time-consuming if not impossible. However, particularly relevant editorials and opinion articles as

---

39  The whole work of the French sociologist tends to deal with all areas of society, which are analysed in terms of concepts, such as the habitus, i.e. a system of schemes of perceptions and internalized actions.

40  Quoted by Florence Aubenas et Miguel Benasayag, *La Fabrication de l'information. Les journalistes et l'idéologie de la communication*, Paris: La Découverte, 1999, p. 18.

41  The American abbreviation "op-ed" instead of "opinion article" is used in the footnotes for the sake of concision.

42  The word "journalist" in this paper is used in a generic way. It also includes the authors of opinion articles in addition to the journalists themselves.

well as letters relating to the crisis and the war in the Gulf were systematically and exhaustively included in the comparative study in order to observe the evolution of the image of the "enemy". The editorials, opinion articles and letters published two days per week in each newspaper from August 1990 to mid-March 1991 were systematically included: those published on Thursdays on the American side, in the *New York Times* and the *Washington Post*, and on the British side in the *Times* and the *Guardian*, and on Sundays in the *Sunday Times* and the *Observer* and in both American newspapers. Nevertheless, when a crucial event happened during the selected period, editorials and opinion articles were also included.

It is worth mentioning that this study does not deal with the receipt of the information by the reader. Moreover, however relevant it may be especially due to the numerous studies on the subject,[43] the analysis has also not chosen to tackle the issue of the forming of public opinion to the extent that I did not have the technical means to examine it. As well as the difficulty in defining the concept of public opinion, it is difficult to assess the relationship between press and readers and assess their mutual influence.

Beyond the chronological logic justifying starting this analysis on 2 August 1990, the date of the Iraqi invasion of Kuwait, it should be noted that as from August 1990, all the major protagonists of

---

43   See, for instance, the book by Hélène Duccini, *Faire voir, faire croire. L'opinion publique sous Louis XIII*, Seyssel: Champ Vallon, 2003, 533 p. "At that time public opinion was very limited and consisted of the capital and country's aristocratic elite" (p. 12). "It was formed in the melting pot of satirical tracts, lampoons and images, which were then used as a means of communication and information" (p. 59).

the Kuwaiti drama were present in the theatre of operations, and they remained there until the outbreak of the Gulf War on 16 January 1991. On 2 August 1990 the spotlight fell on a region of the Persian Gulf, which was a distant territory for the American and British reader. Like the author of a play, the media and in particular the print media, which is the material chosen for this study, staged the characters and gave the reader a story with twists and turns that kept him on tenterhooks until 28 February 1991, the date marking the end of hostilities. When the Gulf Crisis began in August 1990, few people had any detailed knowledge of Iraq's squabble with Kuwait, and it is striking how quickly war came to be seen as inevitable. Besides the complicated plot of this drama, in August 1990 American and British journalists introduced the reader to a leader who was presented as guilty and practically served a death sentence by the media right from the start. How was the character of the enemy presented by journalists to the reader? How were the actors in the drama described in editorials, opinion articles and letters in the six newspapers from August 1990 to mid-March 1991? These are just some of the questions this study seeks to answer.

The study is divided into five parts. The first part attempts to present the characteristics of the American press and the British press in general and those of the newspapers selected for this study in particular and recalls the historical background. The second and third parts study the way the enemy was described and represented in editorials, opinion articles and letters in American and British newspapers during the crisis and the war in the Gulf. The fourth part is more specifically devoted to the analysis of the representation of the image of the Self in the six newspapers over a period of seven months. The fifth part examines how the allies were presented to readers in the press on both sides of the Atlantic.

# Part I:

# Presentation of the American and British press

# Geopolitical context

# Chapter I:
# Presentation of the American press[1]

## 1.1   The features of the American press

> *"Congress shall make no law [...] abridging the*
> *freedom of speech, or of the press [...]".*
> First Amendment to the United States Constitution, 1791

The First Amendment to the Constitution gives the press the right to publish and freely inform the public. It is, as such, one of the cornerstones of American democracy.[2] In accordance with the First Amendment to the Constitution, there is no order of journalists and no federal laws restricting their freedom. Journalists see themselves as the "guardians of democracy". It is in this sense that the American press is often described as the Fourth Estate because of its influence.[3] A tradition of independence of the press with regard to political power was born out of this First Amendment, as well as, according to Robert Chesnais, "freedom of tone that can go up to libel".[4] Even though it is a priori protected from government interference, the press is dependent on the laws of the market and in most cases depends economically on

---

1   This chapter briefly presents the history and characteristics of the American press. Nevertheless, it does not focus on the challenges facing the press in the 21st century.
2   Robert S. Peck, "Constitutional Protection", *in An Unfettered Press,* Publication of the United States Information Agency, 1994, posted in April 2001, <http://usinfo.org/enus/media/overview/press02.html>, consulted 8 September 2022.
3   Michel Rezé & Ralph Bowen, *op. cit.*, p. 142.
4   Robert Chesnais, *Médias et politique. William Randolph Hearst à la conquête du pouvoir*, Paris: Dagorno, 1996, p. 43.

advertising revenues. Advertising accounts for three quarters of its source of income and also causes a steady increase in pagination.[5]

Despite its submission to economic pressures and its dependence on public taste the press is free to say, write and publish what it wants[6] as long as journalists respect the law. Moreover, journalists themselves stress the need to respect fundamental values, such as responsibility, truth, impartiality, accuracy and honesty.[7] The search for objectivity constitutes an ideal for the American press.[8] Most American newspapers try to separate information from opinion. Events are reported in a few sentences at the beginning of an article before being subsequently broken down into an accumulation of data, which, for Michel Rezé and Ralph Bowen, gives "an impression of objectivity inasmuch as the event does not seem to be artificially reconstructed".[9]

American newspapers are not subject to the federal licenses, unlike broadcast media.[10] The American press is mostly a local press. Apart from *USA Today* and the *Wall Street Journal*, only a few major local newspapers, such as the *Boston Globe*, the

---

5     Pierre Albert, *La Presse*, Que sais-je?, 10e éd., Paris: PUF, 1994, p. 110.

6     André Kaspi, *Les Américains. 2. Les États-Unis de 1945 à nos jours*, Paris: Seuil, 2002, p. 631.

7     Henri Pigeat et Jean Huteau, *Déontologie des médias. Institutions, pratique et nouvelles approches dans le monde*, Paris: Economica/Unesco, 2000, p. 163.

8     Claude-Jean Bertrand, *Les Médias aux États-Unis*, Que sais-je?, 3e éd., Paris: PUF, 1987, p. 5.

9     Michel Rezé & Ralph Bowen, *op. cit.*, p. 142.

10    Rosalie Targonski and Suzanne Dawkins, eds., "The American Press", *in An Unfettered Press*, Publication of the United States Information Agency, 1994, posted in April 2001, <http://usinfo.org/enus/media/overview/press01.html>, consulted 9 September 2022.

*Chicago Tribune*, the *New York Times* and the *Washington Post*, have a national readership. Therefore, the newspapers that pay particular attention to local communities are mainly focused on local information and devote little space to international news.[11] Besides quality newspapers there are tabloids, such as the *Star* and the *National Enquirer*, which favour sensational news.

In spite of the increased importance of and stiff competition from other broadcast media and television in particular, which have contributed to a decrease in the circulation of daily newspapers, about 64% of Americans read a newspaper regularly in the late 1980s,[12] including the popular and voluminous Sunday edition whose circulation was higher than that of daily newspapers.

Although some major newspapers and magazines have considerable editorial staff, they cannot cover all topics and events. That is why newspapers frequently use the services of global agencies for general information, such as *Reuters, Associated Press, Central Press Association* and *United Press International*, as well as domestic suppliers, *news services* or agencies, i.e. "*syndicates*".[13] These news agencies, whose role is to provide information and opinion, are organizations specialized in gathering and delivering news to newspapers. Professional editorialists working for these syndicates are published in different newspapers, as for example in the *New York Times* or in a local newspaper, hence the risk of

---

11    Michel Rezé & Ralph Bowen, *op. cit.*, p. 144.
12    Michel Rezé and Ralph Bowen, *Key Words in American Life: Understanding the United States,* 4th ed., Paris: Armand Colin, 1998, p. 225.
13    Nathalie Martinière, *Décrypter les médias américains*, Paris: PUF, 1998, pp. 17-18; Robert G. Picard and Jeffrey H. Brody, *The Newspaper Publishing Industry*, Boston, MA; London: Allyn & Bacon, 1997, pp. 77-78.

a certain uniformity of viewpoints expressed by the American press.[14]

Newspaper chains belonging to the same owner[15] form another important feature of the American press. Some 380 of more than 1,500 dailies published in the United States were independent at the end of the 20th century.[16] The others were owned by news groups. It is worth noting that more and more multimedia groups have taken control of newspapers and magazines, radio stations and television networks since the 1980s.[17]

No general survey of the American press would be complete without a reference to William Randolph Hearst (1863-1951),[18] whose career provided the inspiration for the film *Citizen Kane* (1941) by Orson Welles. Another major figure in the history of the press in the U.S. is Joseph Pulitzer (1847-1911) who gave his name to a prize awarded by the School of Journalism of Columbia University in New York[19] since 1917. These two iconic, competing figures of the media world in the U.S. founded their communication empires in the late 19th century by resorting

14    Robert G. Picard & Jeffrey H. Brody, *op. cit.*, p. 78.
15    Edward S. Herman and Noam Chomsky, *Manufacturing Consent. The Political Economy of the Mass Media*, New York: Pantheon Books, 1988, p. xiii.
16    Christine Soulas, *Les États-Unis d'aujourd'hui en QCM*, Paris: Ellipses, 2000, p. 112.
17    Alain Guët et Philippe Laruelle, *The US in a Nutshell*, Paris: PUF, 1996, p. 205; Nathalie Martinière, *op. cit.*, p. 8.
18    William Randolph Hearst, an editor and politician, created not only the first communication empire, but he was the first to consider information as a piece of merchandise and "to make its manipulation at the level of an art" (Robert Chesnais, *op. cit.*, p. 12).
19    Gérard Hocmard (dir.), *What's What. Dictionnaire culturel du monde anglophone*, Paris: Ellipses, 2004, p. 501.

to "yellow journalism",[20] or, in other words, tabloid journalism which publishes short news items to attract readers and increase circulation.

In conclusion, we should bear in mind that the American press is predominantly local. In accordance with the First Amendment to the Constitution it remains – at least in theory – independent of political power. Even though its mission is to inform and serve readers, the American press is subjected to the constraints of the market and advertising, the latter being its main source of income. Daily papers often rely on news agencies for their information. And yet freedom of tone and the search for impartiality characterize the press in the United States. Nonetheless, multimedia groups now control most American daily newspapers and hold a monopoly power which could restrict the freedom of the press. After the 1990s, the number of readers relying on newspapers as a main source of information declined as the Internet began to replace the traditional media thereby undercutting the business model of many newspapers at the same time.

What about the two American daily newspapers selected for this analysis? The *New York Times* and the *Washington Post* are both internationally recognized daily newspapers.[21] They

---

20    The expression "yellow journalism" comes from a comic strip which was published by Pulitzer with great success in New York in 1896, and then was taken up again by Hearst. The hero of the comic strip was a kid dressed in yellow who came to usually symbolize the gutter press in the public's mind in general (Robert Chesnais, *op. cit.*, p. 283).

21    Marie Agnès Combesque et Ibrahim Warde, *Mythologies américaines*, Paris: Félin, 2002, p. 117; also see "Le Guide mondial de la presse en ligne", *Courrier International*, Hors-série, octobre – novembre – décembre 2003, p. 53.

are characterized by the quality of their information and their independence. The choice of both dailies has also been motivated by their importance and influence in the United States.[22] The *New York Times* and the *Washington Post* are indeed respectively ranked third and fifth among the major American newspapers.[23]

## 1.2    American dailies: The *New York Times* and the *Washington Post*

*The Washington Post is read by people who think they are running the government; The New York Times is read by people who think they are running the country.*[24]

The *New York Times*, described as independent and politically liberal,[25] was founded by Henry Jarvis Raymond in 1851.[26] Although regional, this daily newspaper has an international readership[27] and is distributed nationwide.[28] Published in New York and often known as the "grey lady",[29] it has been awarded a large number of Pulitzer Prizes for the quality of its articles and

22    Marie Agnès Combesque & Ibrahim Warde, *op. cit.*, p. 117.
23    Alain Guët & Philippe Laruelle, *op. cit.*, p. 206. The *Wall Street Journal*, *USA Today* and the *Los Angeles Times* are among the ranks of first, second and fourth respectively and exceed one million copies.
24    This is the point of view of an unknown member of the *Department of Culture* of New York University, who is quoted by Nathalie Martinière, *op. cit.*, p. 10.
25    Pierre Albert, *op. cit.*, p. 110. The word "liberal" differs from the standard meaning in use in Europe. In the United States the word is opposed to that of "conservative" and is close to the notion of being "left-wing".
26    Robert G. Picard & Jeffrey H. Brody, *op. cit.*, p. 190.
27    Marie Agnès Combesque & Ibrahim Warde, *op. cit.*, p. 117.
28    Michel Rezé & Ralph Bowen, *op. cit.*, 1997, p. 143.
29    Robert G. Picard & Jeffrey H. Brody, *op. cit.*, p. 132.

journalists. "All the news that's fit to print"[30] appears in the *New York Times* which is considered as the newspaper of the elite.[31] In 1990 its circulation reached 1,700,000 copies on Sundays and 1,100,000 the other days of the week.[32] Every day the *New York Times* publishes a different column devoted, for example, to sports and leisure. Its numerous correspondents abroad have allowed the newspaper to set up a news service – the *New York Times News Service* – that distributes information which has been gathered by its network of numerous news agencies.

Its competitor, the *Washington Post* is a liberal daily newspaper,[33] founded by Stilson Hutchins in 1877.[34] It is published in Washington, and its investigative journalism has made its reputation. In 1994 more than 800,000 copies of the *Washington Post* were distributed every day and 1,000,000 on Sundays.[35]

---

30    Jonathan Crowther, ed., *Oxford Guide to British and American Culture*, Oxford: Oxford UP, 2001, p. 378.

31    Marie Agnès Combesque & Ibrahim Warde, *op. cit.*, p. 117.

32    Edwin Diamond, *Behind the Times. Inside the New* New York Times, New York: Villard Books, 1993, p. 71. In September 2010, the *New York Times* had an average circulation of 876,638 copies every day and 1,400,000 on Sundays (Jeremy Peters, "Newspaper Circulation Falls Broadly but at Slower Pace", 25 October 2010, <https://archive.nytimes.com/mediadecoder.blogs.nytimes.com/2010/10/25/newspaper-circulation-falls-broadly-but-at-slower-pace/>, consulted 7 September 2022).

33    Alain Guët & Philippe Laruelle, *op. cit.*, p. 206. The *Washington Post* is often accused of advocating "liberal ideas", i.e. ideas in "favour of strong state intervention in world affairs, as well as of vigorous defence of the rights of individuals".

34    "Le Guide mondial de la presse en ligne", *op. cit.*, p. 53.

35    Marilynne Rudick, "Editing the *Washington Post*", *in An Unfettered Press*, Publication of the United States Information Agency, 1994, posted in April 2001, <http://usinfo.org/enus/media/overview/press04.html>, consulted 9 September 2022. According to the Center for American Studies in Brussels, the *Washington Post* had an average daily circulation of 719,000 copies and 997,000 on Sunday in 1985. In 1990 its daily circulation amounted

The newspaper became world famous after the revelation of the Watergate scandal in 1972[36] by two of its journalists, Bob Woodward and Carl Bernstein. Like the *New York Times*, many of its reporters have been awarded the Pulitzer Prize. Similarly, the *Washington Post* has numerous correspondents worldwide, which has allowed it to set up the *News Service*.[37]

Both the *New York Times* and the *Washington Post* generate most of their financial resources from their advertising revenues.[38] Furthermore, both dailies are at the centre of press empires and multimedia groups thanks to the diversification of their activities. The *New York Times* and the *Washington Post* are read everywhere in the United States and cover all the news, whether national or international.

Moreover, in terms of similarity, it is interesting to mention the case of the Pentagon Papers published by both dailies in 1971 despite the objections of the Nixon government. The U.S. Supreme

---

to 780,582 copies. See the following website about the paid weekday circulation for the six months ending 30 September 1990 and 2008, as reported to the Audit Bureau of Circulations, <https://adage.com/images/random/0309/4-1990s-030909.pdf>, consulted 13 September 2022. Its daily circulation increased and reached 852,262 copies in 1995. In the same year the newspaper distributed 1,143,145 copies on Sundays. In September 2010, the *Washington Post* published a daily average of 545,345 copies (Jeremy Peters, "Newspaper Circulation Falls Broadly but at Slower Pace", 25 October 2010, <https://archive.nytimes.com/mediadecoder. blogs.nytimes.com/2010/10/25/newspaper-circulation-falls-broadly-but-at-slower-pace/>, consulted 8 September 2022).

36   This political scandal started in June 1972 and ended with the resignation of President Richard Nixon in August 1974 (Michael Emery & Edwin Emery, *op. cit.*, p. 601).

37   Robert G. Picard & Jeffrey H. Brody, *op. cit.*, p. 194.

38   Nathalie Martinière, *op. cit.*, p. 7.

court allowed the publication of the Pentagon Papers which were made up of confidential documents about American involvement in Vietnam.[39]

In addition to the coverage of international and national affairs, the *New York Times* and the *Washington Post* publish, on their centre page, the letters to the editor as well as unsigned editorials that reflect the views of the newspapers on current events. Opposite the editorial page is the "op-ed page" – for "opposite editorial page" – which is devoted to comments and columns written and signed by distinguished journalists, such as key figures from outside the newspaper, experts, or renowned academics whose positions sometimes differ from the editorial line of the newspaper.[40]

Finally, during the Gulf Crisis and War the editor-in-chief of the *New York Times* was Max Frankel[41] and the editor-in-chief of the *Washington Post* was Benjamin Bradlee.[42]

---

39    Michael Schudson, *The Power of News*, Cambridge, MA: Harvard UP, 1995, p. 146.
40    Michel Rezé & Ralph Bowen, *op. cit.*, 1997, p. 143; Nathalie Martinière, *op cit.*, pp. 13, 18.
41    Robert D. McFadden, "Lelyveld Will Succeed Frankel as the Times's Executive Editor", *New York Times*, 8 April 1994, <http://www.nytimes.com/1994/04/08/nyregion/lelyveld-will-succeed-frankel-as-the-times-s-executive-editor.html>, consulted 10 September 2022.
42    Robert G. Picard & Jeffrey H. Brody, *op. cit.*, p. 126.

# Chapter II:
# Presentation of the British press[43]

## 2.1 The features of the British press

> *"The Daily Mirror is read by people who think*
> *they run the country,*
> *The Guardian is read by people who think*
> *they ought to run the country,*
> *The Times is read by people who actually do run the country,*
> *The Daily Mail is read by the wives of people who run the country,*
> *The Financial Times is read by people who own the country,*
> *... And Sun readers don't care who runs the country as long as her*
> *measurements exceed 38-24-36".*[44]

The British are assiduous readers of the press: nearly 60% of over 15-year-olds read a daily newspaper and over 65% a Sunday paper.[45] Like the American press, the British press is characterized by its independence and its freedom of speech. Nevertheless, this freedom is limited and superficial according to David Scholes who thinks that the press never questions the existing order.[46] He believes that the press is a tool of the establishment and does

---

43  This chapter summarily presents the history and characteristics of the British press and does not address the issues faced by the British newspaper industry in the 21st century.

44  BBC *Yes Prime Minister.* Andrew Whittaker, ed., *Speak the Culture. Britain,* London: Thorogood Publishing, 2009, p. 265.

45  *Hutchinson: The Encyclopedia of Britain,* Oxford: Helicon Publishing, 1999, p. 633.

46  David Scholes, *La Grande-Bretagne contemporaine,* 3e éd., Rosny s/Bois: Bréal, 2000, p. 225.

nothing more than strengthen the reader's convictions "or, at best, his social status".[47]

The British press is not subjected to government interference.[48] As the government has decided not to legislate to curtail journalistic excesses, in particular those of the popular press, the British press is self-regulated and in 1991 set up an organization called the *Press Complaints Commission*[49] replacing the existing *Press Council*, founded in 1953, which had been unable to enforce its decisions and recommendations. The *Press Complaints Commission* has drawn up a code of ethics, the *Editor's Code of Practice*,[50] dealing with complaints levelled against newspapers and magazines. The *Press Complaints Commission* issues a monthly report detailing the outcome of complaints relating to the behaviour of the press such as the issue of intrusion into private life.

Unlike the American press, the British press is truly national. It is often referred to collectively as *Fleet Street*,[51] the name of a street in London which housed the seat of major newspapers before they moved to the neighbouring suburbs of the capital in the eighties.[52] The British national press is generally divided into a so-called quality press (made up of quality papers) and a popular

47    *Ibid.*, p. 235.
48    Marie-José Arquié, *A Key to Contemporary British Civilisation*, Paris: Vuibert, 1999, p. 263.
49    Anthony Sampson, *Who Runs this Place? The Anatomy of Britain in the 21st Century*, London: John Murray, 2005, p. 242.
50    Ian Hargreaves, *Journalism. A Very Short Introduction*, Oxford: Oxford UP, 2005, p. 114.
51    Jeremy Tunstall, *Newspaper Power. The New National Press in Britain*, Oxford: Clarendon Press, 1996, pp. 18-19.
52    Seven daily newspapers out of ten sold in Great Britain were printed in London in the nineties (Jeremy Tunstall, *ibid.*, p. 7).

or tabloid press whose circulation is often higher than that of the quality press. Four fifths of the readers of the majority of quality papers come from the wealthy segment of the population[53] whereas the tabloids are aimed at the general public.[54] Besides the distribution of readers into socio-professional categories, newspapers are also distinguished by their different editorial content: quality papers "want a high intellectual standard and make headlines from national or international news of major importance" while popular newspapers highlight "a preferably bloody or salacious anecdote to attract readers".[55] Their format also distinguished between the two types of newspapers: quality papers (broadsheets) were large in 1990 and popular papers were printed in a smaller format (tabloids). The distinction between broadsheets and tabloids is now outdated since the majority of quality papers have adopted the tabloid format.[56] The *Times*, the *Guardian*, the *Daily Telegraph* and the *Independent* are described

---

53    Jean-Claude Sergeant, *Les Médias britanniques*, Paris: Ophrys, 2004, p. 60.

54    *Ibid.*, p. 57.

55    Pierre Lurbe, *Le Royaume-Uni aujourd'hui*, Paris: Hachette, 2000, p. 119. However, for Michael Bromley, quoted by Pascale Villate-Compton (*in* Bertrand Lemonnier, et al., *Médias et culture de masse en Grande-Bretagne depuis 1945*, Paris: Armand Colin, 1999, *passim*), the boundary between quality newspapers and tabloids disappeared in 1996 because of the reduction of news on foreign countries, reports of Parliament and investigative journalism "for the benefit of mundane and unimportant news items", the proliferation of supplements, the growing place of photographs, the changing readership that was less interested in politics and economy, and the increased competition due to the price war launched by Rupert Murdoch in 1993.

56    The *Times* has been published since October 2004 in a reduced size like its rival *the Independent*. The *Guardian* and the *Observer* adopted both the Berliner size, the former in September 2005 and the latter in January 2006.

as quality papers. The *Daily Mail*, the *Express*, the *Mirror* and the *Sun* are among the most popular tabloids.

In addition to daily newspapers, the weekly papers published on Sundays are characterized by their extreme thickness since they consist of several specialized supplements.[57] The *Sunday Times*, the *Observer*, the *Sunday Telegraph* and the *Independent on Sunday* constitute the Sunday quality press. The *News of the World*, whose publication ceased on 10 July 2011,[58] the *People*, *Sunday Express*, *Sunday Mirror* and *Mail on Sunday* make up the Sunday popular press.

As regards the political distribution of newspapers, there are right-wing as well as left-wing newspapers in both categories[59] although the vast majority of newspapers are right-wing.[60] The Conservative quality press includes the *Times*, the *Daily Telegraph*, known humorously as the *Daily Torygraph* because of its loyalty to the Conservative Party, and the *Financial Times*. The *Guardian* is the best-known liberal (or centre-left) quality newspaper, with the *Independent* initially following a broadly similar line, though to a much less marked extent. The *Daily Express*, the *Daily Mail*, the *Daily Star*, the *Sun*[61] and *Today* represent the right-wing popular press. The *Daily Mirror* and the *Morning Star* are usually classified in the left-wing popular press.

---

57  Pierre Lurbe, *op. cit.*, p. 120.
58  The Sunday newspaper was shut down by Rupert Murdoch, the chairman of News International, after the phone hacking scandal.
59  Pierre Lurbe, *op. cit.*, p. 119.
60  *Ibid.*, p. 119; also see Jeremy Tunstall, *op. cit.*, p. 241.
61  Even the *Sun* supported Tony Blair in 1997.

Despite the dominance of the national press,[62] the regional press is also very important with a hundred or so daily newspapers and some 1,500 weeklies.[63] In addition to national and regional newspapers, there are also a number of magazines devoted to politics and current affairs. For example, the *Economist* "has made a clear commitment to economic liberalism since its inception"[64] and is listed among the most famous weeklies worldwide.

In 1990 the British press, which was faced with a decrease in circulation figures, was in the hands of a few groups representing most of the circulation. The most famous groups were that of Robert Maxwell, who died in 1992 and who was in control of the *Daily Mirror* in London. News International, belonging to the Australian businessman Rupert Murdoch, owns the *Times*, the *Sunday Times*, the *Sun,* and, until its closure, the *News of the World*, which represented 37% of the market of the British national media in 2004.[65] Lord Rothermere's group owns the *Daily Mail* and the *Mail on Sunday*. Conrad Black[66] owned the *Daily Telegraph*. Journalists, who see themselves as the guardians

---

62    Marie-José Arquié, *op. cit.*, p. 260.

63    Pierre Lurbe, *op. cit.*, p. 120.

64    Catherine Resche, "*The Economist*: discours de spécialité économique ou discours sur l'économie?", *ILCEA*, 11, p. 6, 30 April 2009, <http:// journals.openedition.org/ilcea/64>; <https://doi.org/10.4000/ilcea.64>, consulted 11 September 2022.

65    Anthony Sampson, *op. cit.*, p. 232.

66    In 2007 Conrad Black, the former *Telegraph* owner, was sentenced to six years and a half in prison for fraud. He was released on bail in July 2010. Ewen MacAskill, "Conrad Black freed on $2m bail", 21 July 2010, <http://www.guardian.co.uk/business/2010/jul/21/conrad-black-released-on-bail>, consulted 11 September 2022.

of public interest, are increasingly dependent on the political agenda and commercial priorities of the newspaper owner.[67]

The first union of journalists, called *The National Union of Journalists*, was founded in 1907. Conflicts with the printers and events in Wapping in 1986 contributed to the decline of this once powerful union[68] which was unable to obtain satisfaction for its claims despite a number of prolonged strikes.[69] There were 28,000 union members in 1991.[70]

Unlike the American press, the British press saw the emergence of the *Press Association* founded in 1868. The *Press Association* is the main news agency for Great Britain and Ireland. Its services are used by the national print and broadcast media and Sunday newspapers.[71] The British press has been one of the most important in the world.[72] It is financed by advertising, the product of the sale of subscriptions and copies of newspapers. It is an essential economic element[73] and plays an important role in

---

67    Anthony Sampson, *op. cit.*, p. 240.
68    Conflict between trade unions and the management of the *Times* over "the setting up of system of direct data capture led at the end of 1978 to the lock out of the company by Lord Thomson during eleven months" (Jean-Claude Sergeant, *op. cit.*, 2004, p. 66).
69    For example, when the News International journalists moved from Fleet Street to Wapping in January 1986 following the conflict between the National Union of Journalists and the National Graphical Association, or during the strike at the headquarters of the two Thomson daily newspapers in Aberdeen in 1989 (Jeremy Tunstall, *op. cit.*, p. 145).
70    Dennis Griffiths, ed., *The Encyclopedia of the British Press 1422-1992*, Basingstroke: Macmillan Press, 1992, p. 655.
71    *Ibid.*, p. 672.
72    Jean-Claude Sergeant, *op. cit.*, p. 52.
73    *Ibid.*, p. 23.

British society,[74] especially at election time, or when something major happens in the life of the royal family or the nation, such as the Falklands War or the Gulf Crisis and War. The circulation of many British newspapers dropped rapidly at the end of the 20th century and the early 21st century, essentially as a result of the rise of the use of the Internet by British readers.

## 2.2 The *Times*, the *Guardian*, the *Sunday Times* and the *Observer*

The daily newspapers, the *Times* and the *Guardian* and the Sunday papers, the *Sunday Times* and the *Observer*, are the four newspapers which have been selected for this study. Owing to the numerous historical references, especially to the Second World War and the Suez Crisis in the editorials and opinion pieces, it has been decided to briefly study the policy of the British daily and Sunday newspapers during these events. The circulation of each newspaper and its editor during the selected period will be mentioned too.

### 2.2.1 The daily newspapers: the *Times* and the *Guardian*

The two major dailies cater for well-educated readers of the middle class and are known for their serious news and authoritative reports as well as their informative accounts.

---

74    *Ibid.*, p. 53.

## The *Times*

The *Times* is Britain's oldest surviving daily national newspaper. It was founded by John Walter on 1 January 1785 under the name of the *London Daily Universal Register*.[75] The *Times* took its current name in January 1788.

The *Times*, which was nicknamed *"The Thunderer"* in 1841,[76] has become a newspaper of reference despite financial problems faced four times during the 20th century.[77] In 1966 the Canadian magnate Roy Thomson[78] took over the newspaper from Lord Kemsley[79] and merged it with the *Sunday Times* to form Times Newspapers Limited.[80] In 1981 Lord Thomson sold the newspaper to News International.

In the thirties Geoffrey Dawson, the *Times'* editor-in-chief, together with James Louis Garvin of the *Observer* and William Waite Hadley of the *Sunday Times* were supporters of the policy of 'appeasement' towards Adolf Hitler.[81] During the Suez Crisis in 1956 the circulation of the *Times* increased significantly. According to Roy Greenslade, the *Times* was inconsistent changing its viewpoints three times as to the need or not to resort to force in response to the nationalization of the Suez Canal by Nasser.[82]

75    Jonathan Crowther, ed., *op. cit.*, p. 538.
76    Graham Stewart, *The History of* The Times. *Volume VII 1981-2002. The Murdoch Years*, London: HarperCollins, 2005, p. 103.
77    Jeremy Tunstall, *op. cit.*, pp. 20, 96.
78    Graham Stewart, *op. cit.*, p. 8.
79    *Ibid.*, p. 19.
80    *Ibid.*, p. 19.
81    Jeremy Tunstall, *op. cit.*, p. 101.
82    Roy Greenslade, *Press Gang. How Newspapers Make Profits from Propaganda*, London: Pan Books, 2004, pp. 123, 131.

From 1978 to 1979 the *Times* was not published because of a conflict between employees of the daily newspaper and Lord Thomson, owner of the *Times* at the time.[83] In 1986 Rupert Murdoch, the new owner of the newspaper since 1981, decided to transfer the offices and print workshops of the *Times* from Fleet Street, where the offices of the major newspapers were located, to Wapping, in the east of London.[84] He thereby thwarted the strike of some journalists and many employees, such as the typographers opposed to new editing, printing and production techniques.[85] When the *Independent*, another quality newspaper, was launched on 7 October 1986, seventeen journalists left the *Times* and joined this new newspaper.[86]

The *Times*, which is characterized by rigorous standards of reporting and writing, albeit in a very conservative tone, considers itself as politically independent.[87] The newspaper is nonetheless close to the Conservative Party and is usually described as right of centre.[88] Its position is not monolithic; the *Times* supported Tony Blair's Labour Party in the general elections of 2001[89] and 2005.[90] Once qualified as the spokesman and epitome of

---

83    T. O. Lloyd, *Empire, Welfare State, Europe. History of the United Kingdom 1906-2001*, 5th ed., Oxford: Oxford UP, 2002, p. 445.

84    Jeremy Tunstall, *op. cit.*, p. 53.

85    Graham Stewart, *op. cit.* pp. 231-238, 245-253, *passim*.

86    *Ibid.*, p. 303.

87    Jonathan Crowther, ed., *op. cit.*, p. 538.

88    Marie-José Arquié, *op. cit.*, p. 257.

89    Jean Pouvelle, Mark Niemeyer et Adrian Park, *Repères de civilisation: Grande-Bretagne, États-Unis*, Paris: Ellipses, 2003, p. 102.

90    Ben Hall, Tim Burt and Fiona Symon, "Election 2005: What the papers said", *Financial Times*, 3 May 2005, <http://www.ft.com/cms/s/2/417fa1a2-ab60-11d9-893c-00000e2511c8,dwp_uuid=fdb2b318-aa9e-11d9-98d7-00000e2511c8.html>, consulted 13 September 2022.

the British 'establishment', the *Times* has evolved into a more diverse readership.[91] Nevertheless, according to a study of 2005, the *Times* was deemed to be the main British newspaper read by businessmen.[92]

Simon Jenkins was the editor-in-chief of the *Times* from March 1990 to September 1992[93] and thus during the Gulf Crisis and War. Finally, in terms of circulation, the *Times* printed 432,453 copies in 1990.[94]

## The *Guardian*

A moderate national daily newspaper, the *Guardian* was founded in 1821 as the weekly *Manchester Guardian* by John Edward Taylor.[95] It was originally a regional newspaper until 1959, when its headquarters was transferred to London and it changed its name.[96] Since 1936 the newspaper has been owned

---

91    Graham Stewart, *op. cit.*, pp. 610-613.
92    Mel Crowther and/or Nick Thomas, "Ipsos Reveals British Business Habits", *Daily Research News Online*, 11 October 2005, <http://www.mrweb.com/drno/news4670.htm>, consulted 13 September 2022.
93    Roy Greenslade, *op. cit.*, pp. 520, 590.
94    Brian McNair, *News and Journalism in the UK*, London: Routledge, 1994, p. 9. The circulation of the *Times* reached 479,107 copies in October 2010, hence an increase of 10.78% in twenty years ("Seven nationals each suffer double digit drop", *Press Gazette*, 12 November 2010, <http://pressgazette. co.uk/seven-nationals-each-suffer-double-digit-drop/>, consulted 13 September 2022).
95    David Ayerst, *Guardian. Biography of a Newspaper*, London: Collins, 1971, pp. 22-25.
96    David Scholes, *op. cit.*, p. 229.

by the Scott Trust, a non-profit making company[97] which was set up by Charles Prestwich Scott, who was both the owner and the editor-in-chief of the newspaper from 1872 to 1929.[98]

The *Guardian* did not share the enthusiasm of the Conservatives at the time of the Munich Agreement in 1938.[99] Moreover, the newspaper criticized the Eden government over the involvement of the army in the Suez Canal Crisis in 1956.[100] The *Guardian* could have merged with its rival, the *Times,* at the time of the financial crisis of 1966, but this project was rejected by the journalists of the Scott Trust.[101]

The *Guardian,* the UK's second oldest national daily newspaper, is respected for its independent liberal stance and the quality of its writing. It considers itself left of centre and a paper "which, over decades, has cherished its freedom from party affiliation and the concomitant ability to speak for a wider interest".[102] The *Guardian* is indeed renowned for being a newspaper of reference for the left-wing intelligentsia, teachers and trade unionists.[103] It is financially independent from any group, which allows the

97    Anthony Sampson, *op. cit.*, p. 237.
98    Jeremy Tunstall, *op. cit.*, p. 110.
99    David Ayerst, *op. cit.*, pp. 526-527; also refer to the article of 1 October 1938: "Return from Munich", *Guardian*, <http://www.theguardian.com/world/1938/oct/01/secondworldwar.fromthearchive>, consulted 13 September 2022.
100   David Randall, *The Universal Journalist*, 3rd ed., London: Pluto Press, 2007, p. 2.
101   Jeremy Tunstall, *op. cit.*, p. 111.
102   "The change of a nation", editorial, *Guardian*, 19 November 1990.
103   Kate Fox, *Watching the English. The Hidden Rules of English Behaviour*, London: Hodder and Stoughton, 2005, p. 223; also refer to Graham Stewart, *op. cit.*, p. 610; David Ayerst, *op. cit.*, pp. 481, 594-595.

newspaper to guarantee its freedom of expression. The *Guardian* forms a partnership with the *Manchester Evening News* whose profits balance the former's financial losses.[104] Because of its numerous typographical errors and typos made in the seventies the *Guardian* was dubbed the *Grauniad* by the magazine *Private Eye*.[105] In June 1993, the newspaper took over the *Observer*, a Sunday newspaper with the same political opinions.

Peter Preston was the editor-in-chief of the *Guardian* from 1975 to 1995 and consequently during the Gulf Crisis and War. It printed 430,458 copies[106] on average in 1990, which put it just about level with the *Times* and the *Independent* at that time.[107]

---

104    Roy Greenslade, *op. cit.*, p. 271.
105    Pierre Lurbe, *op. cit.*, p. 119. Because of technical improvements, the number of typographical errors was strongly reduced in 1990. Nevertheless, an opinion piece of 28 February 1991 mentioned that Sir John Thomson was Britain's permanent U.N. representative from "1882 [to] 1987" instead of "1982 to 1987".
106    Brian McNair, *op. cit.*, p. 9. The *Guardian* saw its sales decrease to 276,428 copies in October 2010, i.e. a 35.78% reduction in twenty years ("Seven nationals each suffer double digit drop", *Press Gazette*, 12 November 2010, <http://pressgazette.co.uk/seven-nationals-each-suffer-double-digit-drop/>, consulted 13 September 2022).
107    Jeremy Tunstall mentions a number of 420,000 copies for the three daily newspapers (Jeremy Tunstall, *op. cit.*, p. 53).

## 2.2.2 The Sunday newspapers: the *Sunday Times* and the *Observer*

### The *Sunday Times*

This right of centre weekly paper[108] was launched on 20 October 1822.[109] The *Sunday Times* belonged to the Kemsley Group and was taken over by Lord Thomson in 1959 before being bought by News International in 1981[110] along with the *Times*.

William Waite Hadley, the editor-in-chief of the *Sunday Times*, supported British Prime Minister Neville Chamberlain in the thirties and was a supporter of the policy of 'appeasement' towards Adolf Hitler.[111] On the other hand, the *Sunday Times* lent its unconditional support to the Conservative Prime Minister, Anthony Eden[112] when the British armed forces were sent to occupy the Suez Canal in 1956.

The *Sunday Times* was the first British newspaper to launch a colour magazine[113] in 1962. The *Sunday Times* and the *Times* published Hitler's fake notebooks in 1983 as they thought they were genuine.[114] Despite the criticism levelled against the *Sunday Times* the sales of the weekly paper increased slightly.[115]

---

108    Jonathan Crowther, ed., *op. cit.*, p. 523; also see Marie-José Arquié, *op. cit.*, p. 257.
109    Jeremy Tunstall, *op. cit.*, p. 47.
110    Roy Greenslade, *op. cit.*, p. 377.
111    Jeremy Tunstall, *op. cit.*, p. 16.
112    Roy Greenslade, *op. cit.*, p. 135.
113    Jonathan Crowther, ed., *op. cit.*, p. 523.
114    Richard Keeble, *The Newspapers Handbook*, 4th ed., London: Routledge, 2006, p. 61.
115    Graham Stewart, *op. cit.*, p. 180.

During the decade preceding the year 1986 the *Sunday Times* was afflicted by a wave of strikes and stoppages which prevented the sale of millions of copies and led to substantial financial losses for the weekly.[116]

The *Sunday Times* is a broadsheet for a well-off readership that is interested, among others, in politics, business, the arts and travelling abroad[117] and has published a list of well-known and richest figures in the United Kingdom and Ireland since 1988.[118] It is the thickest[119] and most profitable[120] of the "quality" Sunday papers published in Great Britain.

Andrew Neil was the editor-in-chief of the *Sunday Times* from 1983 to 1994 and consequently during the crisis and Gulf War itself.[121] As he[122] shared the liberal viewpoints of the owner of the weekly, Rupert Murdoch, Andrew Neil shaped the *Sunday Times*'s right-wing editorial policy[123] in favour of the Conservative Party of Margaret Thatcher and her firm stands before the outbreak of the Gulf War in 1991. In terms of circulation the *Sunday Times* printed 1,186,667 copies on average in 1990.[124]

---

116    *Ibid.*, pp. 218-219.
117    Brian MacArthur, *Deadline Sunday. A Life in the Week of the Sunday Times*, London: Hodder & Stoughton, 1991, p. 64.
118    Anthony Sampson, *op. cit.*, p. 340.
119    Brian MacArthur, *op. cit.*, p. 15.
120    Jeremy Tunstall, *op. cit.*, p. 48.
121    Andrew Marr, *My Trade. A Short History of British Journalism*, London: Pan Books, 2005, p. 233.
122    Jeremy Tunstall, *op. cit.*, p. 126.
123    "His hawkish attitude before the war". Brian MacArthur, *op. cit.*, p. 112.
124    Brian McNair, *op. cit.*, p. 9. The circulation of the *Sunday Times* decreased to 1,058,333 copies in October 2010, namely a reduction by 10.81% ("Seven nationals each suffer double digit drop", *Press Gazette*, 12 November 2010,

## The *Observer*

The *Observer* was published for the first time on 4 December 1791.[125] The newspaper is the oldest of the British Sunday newspapers.[126] The *Observer*, considered to be left of centre, supported the Labour Party in the 1979 and 1983[127] general elections.

The writer George Orwell worked as a journalist for the *Observer*[128] during the course of World War II. In the fifties the *Observer* supported the abolition of capital punishment[129] under the guidance of the editor-in-chief David Astor, who stated that "ethics was worth more than politics".[130] From 1964 he "urged the Western liberal democracies to help the black majority" in South Africa.[131]

The *Observer* and the *Manchester Guardian* opposed "the Suez invasion in 1956".[132] For example, in an editorial published on 4 November 1956, the Sunday newspaper invited the British Prime Minister, Anthony Eden, to step down.[133] This stance over Suez

&lt;http://pressgazette.co.uk/seven-nationals-each-suffer-double-digit-drop/&gt;, consulted 13 September 2022).

125 Joanna Anstey and John Silverlight, eds., The Observer *Observed. 200 Years of Distinguished Writing from One of the World's Great Newspapers*, London: Barrie & Jenkins, 1991, p. 13.

126 Richard Cockett, *David Astor and* The Observer, London: André Deutsch, 1991, p. ix.

127 Roy Greenslade, *op. cit.*, pp. 334, 453.

128 Jeremy Tunstall, *op. cit.*, p. 104.

129 Richard Cockett, *op. cit.*, p. 138.

130 Roy Greenslade, *op. cit.*, p. 127.

131 *Ibid.*, p. 153.

132 David Randall, *op. cit.*, p. 2.

133 Richard Cockett, *op. cit.*, p. 208.

aroused hostility in Government circles and the loss of regular advertisers.[134] That same year, the circulation of the *Observer* exceeded that of its rival, the *Sunday Times*.[135] Similarly, when the latter's publication was discontinued in November 1978 for a year, the circulation of the *Observer* increased by a million copies.[136]

Assailed by financial problems, the *Observer* was bought by the Californian corporation Atlantic Richfield, known as ARCO,[137] and then in 1981 by Outrams, a subsidiary of "Tiny" Rowland's Lonrho Group.[138] Under Rowland's leadership, the *Observer* campaigned against the Al Fayed family following their purchase of the luxury department store Harrods.[139] Finally, the Sunday weekly was acquired by the Guardian Media Group in 1993.[140]

After David Astor who was editor-in-chief from 1948 to 1975,[141] it was Donald Trelford who held this position from 1975 to 1993,[142] and so was editor during the period of the Gulf Crisis and War. This war was to have a special place for the newspaper, because in March 1990 Farzad Bazoft, one of its journalists, was convicted by Iraq of spying and hanged.[143] The number of copies sold by the

---

134   *Ibid.*, pp. 225, 232-233.
135   Jeremy Tunstall, *op. cit.*, p. 48.
136   Roy Greenslade, *op. cit.*, p. 334.
137   *Ibid.*, p. 333.
138   Graham Stewart, *op. cit.*, p. 31.
139   Richard Keeble, *op. cit.*, p. 45.
140   Jeremy Tunstall, *op. cit.*, p. 38; also see Anthony Sampson, *op. cit.*, p. 230.
141   Roy Greenslade, *op. cit.*, pp. 24, 281; also see Jeremy Tunstall, *op. cit.*, p. 103.
142   Andrew Marr, *op. cit.*, p. 234; also see Jeremy Tunstall, *op. cit.*, p. 133.
143   Roy Greenslade, *op. cit.*, p. 551.

weekly newspaper in 1990 amounted to an average of 566,854 newspapers.[144]

As explained in the introduction concerning American journalists, it is worth noting that during the pre-war period from August 1990 until mid-January 1991, British journalists on the ground requested a number of interviews and visits to the troops as the latter prepared for war. Accordingly, accredited reporters were invited to join the British Army pools known as Media Response Teams, which organized "desert tours" providing escort officers or military minders to accompany the journalists. Reporters who refused to participate in the newspool arrangements became known as "unilaterals". Official media pools, compelled to accept specific ground rules,[145] were set up by the British Ministry of Defence and organized by the military on the spot, which enabled the latter to monitor the nature of the coverage. Nonetheless, despite journalists' reporting being subject to military review, British journalists were said to "have accepted without rancour the restrictions placed upon them by the Ministry of Defence [...]"; "the British forces and the press appear to see themselves

---

144 Brian McNair, *op. cit.*, p. 9. In October 2010, the number of copies sold by the weekly newspaper amounted to 313,466, thus attesting to a 44.70% decrease over two decades ("Seven nationals each suffer double digit drop", *Press Gazette*, 12 November 2010, <http://pressgazette.co.uk/seven-nationals-each-suffer-double-digit-drop/>, consulted 13 September 2022).

145 Having suffered badly from news mismanagement during the Falklands War in 1982, as the Ministry of Defence tried to control all news coming out of the conflict, the British government had a more open policy for the Gulf Crisis. Moreover, the military and the media followed a plan worked out after the Falklands War, which dealt with media relations in time of tension and war. Refer to the Media Ground Rules in Denise Lohrey Gammal, *Relations between British Government Sources and the Media in Wartime*, Dissertation, Cambridge University, 1997, appendix F, pp. 240-242.

on the same side"[146] Moreover, it should also be mentioned that no complaints were made to the *Press Council*[147] with regard to the coverage of the pre-war crisis period.

Never is the media reporting of a crisis more significant than when a state is considering whether to wage war. Therefore, there is little doubt that the way in which the six-month build-up to war was covered by journalists and perceived by the public was of paramount importance to Downing Street, which was anxious to garner the support of public opinion when crisis turned into conflict.

---

146    David Sharrock, "Between the lines", features, *Guardian*, 14 January 1991.
147    The *Press Council*, founded in 1953, was replaced by the *Press Complaints Commission*, an independent, non-statutory body set up in 1991, which deals with complaints from members of the public about the conduct and contents of newspapers and magazines and is charged with upholding a Code of Practice agreed by editors.

# Chapter III:
# The geopolitical context

## 3.1 The economic and political situation of the United States and the United Kingdom in 1990-91

### 3.1.1 The United States

George Herbert Walker Bush, the Republican party candidate and Ronald Reagan's vice-president, was elected at the 1988 presidential elections. He got 54% of the votes, beating the Democrat Michael Dukatis. George H. W. Bush officially became the 41st president of the United States on 20 January 1989.

In the field of domestic policy his presidency was characterized by an economic downturn, excessive state debt and a budget deficit. The federal debt reached more than three billion dollars, and recession was a constant threat.[148] The unemployment rate rose from 5.6% in 1990[149] to 6.8% in 1991.[150] George H. W. Bush raised taxes, in contradiction to the commitment he had made in 1988.

However, Americans widely supported his foreign policy. In December 1989 a military intervention against General Manuel Antonio Noriega took place in Panama. Noriega was transferred to Miami to be tried for drug trafficking. George H. W. Bush signed

---

148     Éric Laurent, *La Face cachée du pétrole*, Paris: Plon, 2006, p. 67.
149     André Kaspi, *op. cit.*, p. 619.
150     See the website of the U.S. Bureau of Labor Statistics: <https://www.bls.gov/cps/cpsaat01.pdf>, consulted 15 September 2022.

treaties on the reduction in the number of nuclear weapons[151] with the Soviet president, Mikhail Gorbachev.

On 6 November 1990 the mid-term elections for the renewal of a third of the American Senate and the House of Representatives were marked by a strong recovery by the Democrats. The main event of George Bush's term in office was his victory over Iraq in the Gulf War of 1991. Despite his successes in foreign policy George H. W. Bush suffered from the consequences of economic difficulties.[152] He was defeated by Bill Clinton, the Democrat candidate at the 1992 elections. George H. W. Bush died on 30 November 2018.

### 3.1.2  The United Kingdom

As in the United States, the UK economy deteriorated from 1989 to 1991[153] and the unemployment rate increased[154] from 6.9% in 1990 to 8.8% in 1991.[155] Margaret Thatcher, the Conservative Prime Minister since 1979, developed a policy of rigour, challenging the *Welfare State*, initiating a programme of privatisation of state-

---

151  The first treaty (START I) was signed on 31 July 1991 and approved by the American Congress on 1 October 1992.

152  André Kaspi, *op. cit.*, p. 618.

153  Jeremy Tunstall, *op. cit.*, p. 34.

154  Jean-Baptiste Duroselle et André Kaspi, *Histoire des relations internationales de 1945 à nos jours*, Tome 2, 13e éd., Paris: Armand Colin, 2002, p. 547.

155  See *The World Almanac and Book of Facts 2004* (William A. McGeveran Jr., ed., New York: World Almanac Books, 2004, p. 142). The unemployment rate in the United Kingdom was 7% in August 1990 and 8% in March 1991, <https://statista.com/statistics/279898/unemployment-rate-in-the-united-kingdom-uk/>, consulted 15 September 2022.

owned industries and public services, easing the tax burden on businesses and opposing wage increases.[156]

Internationally, the good personal relationship between Margaret Thatcher and Ronald Reagan, the American president from 1980 to 1988, strengthened the "special relationship" between the United States and the United Kingdom.[157] Margaret Thatcher became increasingly unpopular in her country as well as within her own party[158] and was forced to resign on 22 November 1990. She helped John Major, then Chancellor of the Exchequer, to beat her two main rivals, Michael Heseltine and Douglas Hurd, and succeed her as Prime Minister.[159]

John Major was as determined as Margaret Thatcher in supporting the armed intervention of the United Nations in Kuwait.[160] He asserted himself as a close ally of the United States. His unwavering support for the American alliance made him a privileged interlocutor in Washington.[161] John Major, a more committed European than the former Prime Minister, who

---

156    Pierre Bezbakh et Sophie Gherardi (dir.), *Dictionnaire de l'économie*, Paris: Larousse/HER, 2000, p. 304.
157    Roland Marx, *Histoire de la Grande-Bretagne*, Paris: Perrin, 2004, p. 520. Also refer to Bernard Cottret, *Histoire de l'Angleterre. De Guillaume le Conquérant à nos jours*, Paris: Tallandier, 2007, p. 398.
158    Brian McNair, *Journalism and Democracy*, London: Routledge, 2000, p. 147.
159    Axel Delmotte, *L'Indispensable de la culture anglo-saxonne*, Levallois-Perret: Studyrama, 2003, pp. 63-64.
160    Roland Marx, *op. cit.*, p. 521.
161    *Ibid.*, p. 521. Also see Philippe Moreau Defarges, *Introduction à la géopolitique*, Paris: Seuil, 2005, p. 159. The author refers to the UK's role as "a loyal second, a trusted advisor to the United States".

fiercely defended British interests,[162] fought hard to ensure Britain ratified the Maastricht Treaty in December 1991.[163]

Although John Major followed the same economic policy as Margaret Thatcher, he replaced the *poll tax* by the *council tax*[164] in 1993. The *poll tax* was a local tax levied on each individual and was introduced by Margaret Thatcher[165] in April 1990. The Conservative Party won the general elections of 9 April 1992 with 322 seats against 276 for the Labour Party. John Major remained in office as Prime Minister until the elections in May 1997, which were won by the Labour Party under the leadership of Tony Blair.

## 3.2   The Gulf Crisis and War

The Gulf Crisis began on 2 August 1990 when Iraq invaded Kuwait. A government was put in place in Kuwait, which was annexed as the nineteenth province of Iraq. In the name of the independence of states, the United States, the Europeans and the Japanese, who wanted to safeguard their supply of energy resources,[166] rejected the claims of the Iraqi leader. On the same day the United Nations Security Council adopted Resolution 660 which called for the Iraqi armed forces to withdraw from

---

162   Michel Mourre, *Le Petit Mourre. Dictionnaire de l'Histoire*, Paris: Larousse-Bordas, 1998, p. 476.
163   Roland Marx, *op. cit.*, p. 522. Nonetheless, John Major did not sign the social chapter of the Maastricht treaty according to Axel Delmotte (*op. cit.*, p.64).
164   Jonathan Crowther, ed., *op. cit.*, p. 122.
165   Michel Mourre, *op. cit.*, p. 476. The implementation of the poll tax brought about large-scale demonstrations and riots which contributed to the political weakening of Margaret Thatcher.
166   André Kaspi, *op. cit.*, p. 615.

Kuwait immediately. Iraqi and Kuwaiti assets were frozen in all international financial institutions shortly after the invasion of Kuwait. Operation Desert Shield was launched on 8 August 1990: tens of thousands of American soldiers were sent to protect Saudi Arabia from the Iraqi threat.[167]

Saddam Hussein, who wanted to be the champion of the Arab cause,[168] issued a call to holy war and solemnly proclaimed the annexation of Kuwait by Iraq on 8 August 1990. The United Nations imposed the first economic sanctions in August 1990, the beginning of an embargo which was to continue until the Gulf War of 2003. On 18 August 1990, the Iraqi president took American and British nationals hostage and sent them to strategic sites where they would be used as "human shields" against potential bombings. The hostages were freed in small groups from November 1990, but it was only at Christmas time that all the hostages were freed.[169]

Under the aegis of the United Nations, the American president George Bush assembled a broad coalition of Arab and European countries against Saddam Hussein. Resolution 678, voted by the United Nations Security Council, authorized the use of force if the deadline of 15 January 1991 for the withdrawal of Iraqi troops from Kuwait was not respected. Despite many diplomatic initiatives by the Middle East countries, North Africa, the West

---

167    Jean-Baptiste Duroselle & André Kaspi, *op. cit.*, p. 544.
168    *Ibid.*, p. 542.
169    Éric Laurent, *op. cit.*, pp. 96, 99.

and the U.N. Secretary General, Javier Perez de Cuellar, Iraq refused to evacuate Kuwait.[170]

On 12 January 1991 the U.S. Congress authorized the American president to implement Resolution 678 and thus agreed on military intervention. The air strike against Iraq started on 16 January 1991, the day after the expiry of the United Nations ultimatum. The Gulf Crisis thus became the Gulf War. It was followed by a six-week military confrontation under U.S. command and under the name *Desert Storm*.[171]

The military offensive took place in two stages. First of all, massive bombing raids annihilated Iraq's military and economic facilities between 16 January and 23 February 1991 followed by a four-day ground war. The coalition forces encountered little resistance from Iraqi soldiers who surrendered almost without a fight.[172] Saddam Hussein was forced to approve all twelve resolutions of the United Nations Security Council.[173] Kuwait was freed on 28 February 1991. George Bush decided to end hostilities and a unilateral ceasefire was proclaimed.

The image of the enemy conveyed by the press on both sides of the Atlantic was a crucially important factor right from the start of the crisis. What was that image exactly? How did it evolve in the

---

170     Habib Ishow, "Le Koweït: un État vulnérable", *Relations internationales*, No. 66, été 1991, p. 131.
171     Axel Delmotte, *op. cit.*, p. 103.
172     André Nouschi, "Le Golfe et le pétrole: d'un impérialisme à l'autre?", *Relations internationales*, No. 66, été 1991, p. 161.
173     Mohammad-Reza Djalli, "Le Golfe Persique 1971-1991: de l'ordre colonial à un nouvel ordre mondial?", *Relations internationales*, No. 66, été 1991, p. 205.

editorials, op-eds and letters to the editor during the Gulf Crisis and War? These are the questions which we are going to address in the following two parts.

# Part II:

## Image of the Other:
## Personality of the enemy

## Differences and similarities
## between the American press
## and the British press
## during the Gulf Crisis and War

# Introduction

*Si vis pacem, para bellum.*
Vegetius, *De Re Militari*, III, foreword

The way in which the enemy was described and presented in editorials, opinion articles and letters to the editor during the Gulf Crisis and War can be analysed from five angles. The first is to focus on the way in which the American and British newspapers described Saddam Hussein. To do this we have compared the editorials in the American daily newspapers to those published in the British newspapers during the Gulf Crisis and War.

In the light of the points of view expressed by the American and British newspapers in their editorials we have noted, secondly, that certain qualifiers and arguments appeared regularly in the opinion articles to describe the Iraqi president. Identifying these highlights the similarities and differences between the editorials and opinion articles in the American and British press.

The third angle is to see how the qualifiers and arguments used by the editorialists and journalists changed over the period from August 1990 to mid-March 1991.

Fourthly, the speeches, press conferences and interventions by the American president and the British Prime Minister enable us to analyse possible correlations between official rhetoric and journalistic discourse.

The last area of reflection concerns the portrait drawn by readers in the letters sent to the newspapers and the extent to which the presentation of the Iraqi ruler in letters to the editor differs from the editorial line of each newspaper.

# Chapter I:
# Identification of the enemy

Who was the enemy? Was it Iraq and the Iraqis or only its leader? When editorials, opinion articles and letters to the editor referred to the Iraqi state during the period under study, they meant Saddam Hussein by metonymy. The analysis of published editorials shows a correspondence in the press on both sides of the Atlantic. The *New York Times* stated for instance that "Iraqis [...] are of many minds about Saddam Hussein".[1] On the British side, it was mainly the Sunday papers that distinguished the Iraqis from their president. For example, we note the change of opinion in the *Observer*[2] over a few months – between August 1990 and January 1991 – and its use of the possessive determiner "our" enabling the editorialist to include the reader and represent, in addition to the readership, the British people, or even the entire nation.

In U.S. opinion articles, most journalists highlighted the sufferings endured by the Iraqis as early as August 1990. However, in the *Washington Post*, the opinions expressed were different. For example, two journalists, Rowland Evans and Robert Novak, focused on the physical resemblance between Saddam Hussein

---

1    "Arab-Americans and Ugly Americans", editorial, *New York Times*, 9 September 1990, p. E 24.
2    "Jingoistic support within his own country for his foreign adventures". "Why this Hitler of the Gulf has to go", editorial, *Observer*, 5 August 1990, p. 12. The purpose of the question asked was not to obtain an answer, but to establish a certain complicity with the reader and win him or her over to the editorial staff's ideas. In January 1991, the Sunday paper wrote: "Our enemy is Saddam Hussein, not the Iraqi people [...]". "Keeping cool while the war hots up", editorial, *Observer*, 27 January 1991, p. 20.

and millions of Iraqis filled with resentment and hatred towards President Bush. The Iraqis' negative feelings towards George Bush were repeatedly emphasized in their column[3] and described, for instance on 27 August 1990, as "resentment, anger, fury and hatred". Why did the two journalists choose to insist on the Iraqis' state of mind in their article? The reason was certainly not insignificant. Did both journalists want the reader to believe that it was inconceivable to hate the leader of a democratic country? *A fortiori* when it was the president of their country, the United States, which, in their minds, was the epitome of a democratic country defending the values of freedom and equality. Moreover, by highlighting the physical identification of Iraqis with their leader and their resentment towards the American president, the authors of this article appeared to be denigrating the inhabitants of Iraq and considering them as a despicable people. The representation stressed that Iraqi citizens were fundamentally different from the newspaper's American readers, which at best reflects a form of simplistic ethnocentrism. All in all, by tarnishing the image of Iraqis, journalists could deliberately reinforce prejudices against the Iraqi people, thus creating a distorted view of the Other.[4]

In British opinion pieces, however, except for the *Times* which did not appear to mention it, the newspapers selected for this study clearly differentiated Saddam Hussein from the Iraqi people. Why was this issue not mentioned either in the editorials of the *Times* or in its opinion pieces? Did it consider that, as a newspaper of quality and reference, its role was to inform its readers and not, like the other newspapers, to seek to move the readership by

---

3    Rowland Evans and Robert Novak, "Bad Guy of Baghdad", op-ed, *Washington Post*, 27 August 1990, p. A 11.
4    Edward W. Said, *Orientalism*, London: Penguin Books, 2003, *passim*.

describing the poignant plight of the Iraqis? One possible reason is that the *Times* did not favour the writing of articles marked by emotion and preferred to keep a healthy distance from events.

In short, whether it was the editorials of the British Sunday press in particular or the opinion articles published on both sides of the Atlantic, what was often highlighted during the Gulf Crisis and War was the pain felt by the Iraqi people under Saddam Hussein's regime. Moreover, American and British editorialists, journalists and contributors insisted on the difference between the leader of Iraq and the Iraqis from January 1991 in British Sunday editorials, that is to say shortly before the outbreak of the armed conflict, and as early as August 1990 in American and British opinion articles. It is surprising that British Sunday editorials differentiated the Iraqis and their leader later than the other newspapers. One possible explanation is that they didn't want to appear cold-blooded towards their readers by commiserating with the Iraqis over the impending war.

In this context, it is worth remembering that the American president stated at a press conference on the Persian Gulf Crisis on 30 August 1990 that the United States had no dispute with the Iraqi people.[5] George Bush repeated this argument several times during the Gulf Crisis as well as during and after the hostilities.[6] The British Prime Minister, John Major, also made

---

5    "We have no argument with the people of Iraq" (<https://bush41library. tamu.edu/archives/public-papers/2189>, consulted 18 September 2022).

6    In particular on 30 August 1990, 6, 11, 16 and 24 September 1990, 1 October 1990, 1, 3, 22 and 30 November 1990 and 12 January 1991 as well as on 16, 25 and 28 January 1991, 5, 15, 27 and 28 February 1991 and 1, 4, 6 and 8 March 1991.

this distinction throughout the Gulf Crisis and War.[7] It should also be noted that some American and British journalists and contributors anticipated the American and British governments by highlighting the difference between Saddam Hussein and his people from the start of the Gulf Crisis.[8] Besides, focusing on the person of Saddam Hussein allowed journalists to conceal the fact that many Iraqi civilians and soldiers died during the hostilities whereas the leader of Iraq remained in power after the conflict.[9]

Several remarks are necessary here: first, the readers of the *Times* expressed their empathy for the Iraqi people whereas the British daily did not publish any editorial or opinion piece on that subject. In contrast, one may wonder why the readership of the *Sunday Times*, as expressed in letters to the editor, was not sensitive to the arguments developed in the editorial and opinion pieces published in the Sunday newspaper on the Iraqi people and the distinction between the Iraqis and their president. Second, echoing the line taken by editorials and opinion articles on both sides of the Atlantic, letters to the editor regularly described the Iraqi people as unfortunate and innocent during the Gulf Crisis and War. Third, readers, on the American side, distinguished between the Iraqi people and Saddam Hussein in the *New York*

---

7    "We have no quarrel whatsoever with ordinary Iraqi people". For example, refer to the Prime Minister's Questions in the House of Commons on 17 January 1991 (<https://hansard.parliament.uk/Commons/1991-01-17/debates/e77492a9-dee0-487f-8964-6824f654845e/The Gulf?highlight=just%20war#contribution-ce2c66f9-61bb-472e-bddd-155232931ec9>, consulted 18 September 2022).

8    For example, A. M. Rosenthal in the *New York Times* of 23 August 1990 and Roy Hattersley in the *Guardian* of 11 August 1990.

9    Douglas Kellner, "The Crisis in the Gulf and the Lack of Critical Media Discourse", *in* Bradley S. Greenberg and Walter Gantz, eds., *Desert Storm and the Mass Media*, 2nd ed., Cresskill, NJ: Hampton Press, 1997, p. 71.

*Times* and the *Washington Post* from September and October 1990. On the British side, this distinction was introduced much later by the readership of the *Times*, in January 1991, but in the *Guardian* and the *Observer* it was present from the start of the Gulf Crisis in August 1990. Did this mean that the readers of the *Times* were less reactive than those of the American press and other British newspapers? One could suggest that the readers of the *Times* gave themselves more time to think about current events especially since the daily did not publish any editorial or opinion piece on the difference between the Iraqis and their leader or on their miserable condition.

In the end, with the exception of the two *Washington Post* journalists who caricatured the Iraqis due to their resemblance to Saddam Hussein and despite the absence of articles in the *Times* and letters in the *Sunday Times*, we note that the adversary the United States, Britain and their allies were confronted with was not the Iraqi people, described as unlucky and innocent, but rather Saddam Hussein, as president of Iraq and head of the Iraqi army. In other words, the enemy was the leader of Iraq. By August 1990, the enemy or the Other was already defined in the American press and the British press: on the one hand, Saddam Hussein, as the leader of the enemy country, and on the other, the United States, Britain and their allies. So, analysis of the editorials, opinion articles and letters published in both the American and British press reveals the unbalanced nature of the presentation of the crisis: Saddam Hussein versus the American and British people.

In addition, journalists called Saddam Hussein by his first name in both the American press and the British press. But this did not occur in the editorials of the *New York Times*, and only one editorial in the *Washington Post*[10] displayed it. On the British side, Saddam Hussein was referred to simply as "Saddam" in the editorials of daily and Sunday newspapers from August 1990 onwards. One could infer that the editorialist of the *Washington Post* and those of the British press showed a more casual attitude towards Saddam Hussein than their counterparts of the *New York Times* by removing distance and respect for the Iraqi leader.

The opinion articles on both sides of the Atlantic used the Iraqi president's first name several times from August 1990 to mid-March 1991. Referring to Saddam Hussein by his first name helped build up a sense of complicity between journalists and readers and served to downplay his presidential status or even to discount it entirely. Moreover, the fact that American and British journalists did not use first names only to refer to the U.S. president and the British Prime Minister during the period confirms that the president of Iraq was referred to in ways which could be considered irreverent or even mocking. It should also be noted that, whereas Margaret Thatcher and John Major did not call the Iraqi leader by his first name, the American president did: he called the leader of Iraq "Saddam" 108 times between 14 August 1990 and mid-March 1991.[11]

Analysis of letters to the editor reveals that American readers, unlike British readers, did not call the Iraqi leader by his first name. On the basis of the letters analysed, the British readers

---

10    "Keep the Pressure on", editorial, *Washington Post*, 16 February 1991, p. A 26.

11    Refer for instance to Bush's remarks at a Republican Party fundraising luncheon in Denver, Colorado on 18 September 1990 (<https://bush41library.tamu.edu/archives/public-papers/2234>, consulted 19 September 2022).

of the *Guardian*, the *Sunday Times* and the *Observer* seemed generally to be lacking in courtesy and were more impertinent towards the president of Iraq than those of the American press. Calling Saddam Hussein by his first name in the letters published in the British press reflected not only a lack of respect for the presidential function, but also a generally pejorative portrayal of the Iraqi leader.

In essence, apart from the editorials in the *New York Times* and the letters published in the American press which did not resort to that method, the Iraqi leader was referred to by his first name throughout the Gulf Crisis and the war itself. This practice, which followed that of the American president, probably reflected a feeling of contempt on the part of American and British journalists as well as British readers towards the president of Iraq.

Beyond the irreverence for the leader of the Iraqi nation, can we not detect an attempt to infantilize the leader of the enemy country? Do we not address a child by his or her first name? If so, it may be inferred that this method of downgrading the status of the president of Iraq was part of a strategy of stigmatizing the enemy. The Other was presented to the readership and perceived by the British readers as an adult whose behaviour was that of an irresponsible child, characterized by an infantile way of thinking. According to Aurélie Lorrain, the first step in infantilizing the leader of an enemy country consists in differentiating the people of the enemy country from their leader and the second step is to present him as irresponsible.[12] This was seen in the British

---

12    Aurélie Lorrain, "Les États-Unis et la stigmatisation de l'ennemi", *in Géopolitique des États-Unis. Culture, intérêts, stratégies. Revue Française de Géopolitique*, Paris: Ellipses, 2005, p. 175.

editorials and the opinion articles published in the press on both sides of the Atlantic.

# Chapter II:
# Description of the enemy

## 2.1  Qualifiers

When reading American and British editorials, what is immediately striking is the vehemence of the terms used to describe Saddam Hussein. This vehemence remained the dominant feature throughout the period from August 1990 to March 1991. Editorialists, in their description of Saddam Hussein, regularly borrowed words and expressions from the lexical field of crime and totalitarian politics, such as aggressor, dictator, tyrant, threat, criminal, despot, ambitious, arrogant, blusterer, brutal, dangerous, ruthless, shrewd, untrustworthy, outlaw, brutal buffoon, villain, and barbarity. It is clear that by highlighting the barbarity of the Iraqi leader, editorialists inversely associated a value judgment favourable to the "civilized" world that they believed they represented.

With regard to the specificities of American and British newspapers, we noted that the *New York Times* and the *Washington Post* described the Iraqi leader as "cynical" and "defiant". The *New York Times* used a cultural allusion to describe Saddam Hussein as "Humpty Dumpty"[13] in February 1991 but

---

13  "Humpty Dumpty". "Saddam Hussein's Survival Strategy", editorial, *New York Times*, 17 February 1991, p. E 12. Lewis Caroll, in *Through the Looking Glass* published in 1871, takes up the character of Humpty Dumpty to deal with the problematic of the meaning of words. However, the network of meaning and the words of the articles do not tally with what Lewis Caroll deals with in his novel (Jonathan Crowther, ed., *op. cit.*, p. 264).

stressed that the Iraqi leader was not like Humpty Dumpty. So, the reference did not belittle him but emphasized how dangerous he was. This egg-shaped character, taken from an English nursery rhyme, falls from the low wall on which it was perched and breaks into pieces. According to the editorialist, Saddam Hussein, unlike Humpty Dumpty, would not smash because of his skill, even if the possibility of his fall existed. The *Sunday Times*, for its part, marked itself out by publishing an editorial with the evocative title "The Thief of Baghdad" on 5 August 1990. Not only did this title refer to the image of a thief in a literal sense, but it also alluded to the title of a film of the same name from 1924, adapted from the "Thousand and One Nights", which captivated the imagination of Europeans in the 18th and 19th centuries.

Both the editorials of the American press or those of the British press, and in particular the *Sunday Times* which used a register of less formal language and this cinematographic allusion, stressed the darkness of the Iraqi leader during the Gulf Crisis and War. Editorialists portrayed a terrifying and dangerous adversary, a cruel and ruthless creature whose behaviour was contrary to the rules of any civilized individual.[14] On the one hand, they thus conveyed negative stereotypes usually attributed to the enemy, underlying feelings of hostility or even hate towards the Other, and which were used in American and British editorials to shape the image of the enemy in the person of Saddam Hussein. On the other hand, editorialists implicitly defined themselves and their readers, by contrast, as just, virtuous, humble, peaceful, inoffensive, benevolent, law-abiding and above all civilized.

---

14    In classical times, the Greeks gave the name of barbarians to all people foreign to their civilization. The Romans called barbarians all people foreign to Greek civilization and their own.

With respect to the timing of the qualifiers identified in editorials on either side of the Atlantic and mentioned earlier, 80% of them appeared as early as August 1990 or at the latest in September 1990, which meant that Saddam Hussein's uncompromising portrait was firmly in place as early as August 1990. However, the situation was more contrasted with regard to the recurrence of terms, or their synonyms used from August 1990 to mid-March 1991 insofar as each newspaper seemed to follow a different logic, whether in the American press or the British press.

From the beginning of the Gulf Crisis, the main features of the Iraqi leader were thus defined in editorials. There did not seem to be any change in the perception of the enemy either. With the exception of slight semantic changes, the already clearly established portrait of the leader of Iraq was reiterated, as it were, by the use of the same qualifiers – for example, ambitious, arrogant, blusterer, brutal, dangerous, ruthless, untrustworthy and shrewd – from August 1990 to March 1991. Beyond the utilitarian and instructive function of the presentation of the protagonist responsible for the crisis, editorialists of American and British newspapers intended to persuade the readership of Saddam Hussein's malice, even to frighten it.

The vehemence of the qualifiers describing the Iraqi leader that characterized editorials of the American and British press from August 1990 to mid-March 1991 was also present, and even accentuated, in opinion articles published during the same period. We thus find the same qualifiers in the op-eds: for example, aggressor, despot, dictator, threat, tyrant, ambitious, dangerous, bully, cunning, ruthless, outlaw, etc.

In addition, journalists on both sides of the Atlantic highlighted the megalomania of the Iraqi president in opinion articles. For instance, one of A. M. Rosenthal's articles[15] was entitled "Mother of All Columns". The ironic title, substituting the word column for that of a battle, contained a pun in reference to the words of Saddam Hussein who described the Gulf War as the "mother of all battles".[16] This flash of wit from the seasoned columnist allowed to capture the critical attention of the reader, which is the primary purpose of a newspaper article.

The portrayal of the Iraqi leader was also characterized by his designation as the "Butcher of Baghdad"[17] in some opinion articles on either side of the Atlantic. This provocative phrase, "Butcher of Baghdad", illustrative of the incisive style of the American columnist, William Safire, and the two British Sunday newspapers, made the Iraqi leader appear as a fierce man with bloodthirsty instincts, thereby reinforcing his image as a murderer.

---

15    A. M. Rosenthal, executive director of the *New York Times* from 1977 to 1988 and columnist from 1987 to 1999 won the Pulitzer Prize in 1960 and was known for his conservative positions. (Robert D. McFadden, "A. M. Rosenthal, Editor of *The Times*, Dies at 84", *New York Times*, 11 May 2006, <http://www.nytimes.com/2006/05/11/nyregion/11rosenthal.html>, consulted 20 September 2022).

16    "The Persian Gulf War, the 'mother of all battles' in Saddam Hussein's worlds was intense but short [...]". George Brown Tindall and David Emory Shi, *America. A Narrative History*, 4th ed., New York; London: W.W. Norton & Co, 1997, p. 1145.

17    "Butcher of Baghdad". William Safire, "Forget about Gulfo", op-ed, *New York Times*, 6 September 1990, p. A 22; Jim Hoagland, "Saddam's Big Lie", op-ed, *Washington Post*, 9 August 1990, p. A 23; Robert Harris, "This is not our finest hour and Saddam's not Hitler", op-ed, *Sunday Times*, 23 September 1990, Sect. 3, p. 6; Chaim Bermant, "Palestinians' wild spasm of folly", op-ed, *Observer*, 26 August 1990, p. 9.

Furthermore, two terms – "ogre"[18] and "monster"[19] – were used in the American and British press to describe Saddam Hussein. By using these two words, journalists played on the register of fear, possibly arousing childhood memories in their readers. We will not enter into the debate here as to whether they managed to achieve it or not. What counts here is that the choice of this vocabulary was part of a rhetorical strategy that played on the emotional state and divided reality into two antinomical domains, namely Good on the one hand and Evil on the other. On the one hand, the terms "ogre" and "monster" were likely to increase the anguish the reader might feel when reading the description of the Iraqi leader, and on the other hand, both terms – as mentioned above – referred the reader to the stories of their childhood. The ogre, a frightening character in legends and fairy tales, is a ferocious being eager for human flesh and is feared because of its cruelty. He appears as Grendel in Beowulf[20] and is fought by the eponymous hero and his companions. But in the end, the ogre, Saddam Hussein, who caused intense fear in his country, was

---

18    "Ogre". William Raspberry, "… The Villain", op-ed, *Washington Post*, 22 August 1990, p. A 21. The journalist provided Saddam Hussein's portrayal in the title which succinctly and explicitly summarized his opinion, which was developed in the article. The *Sunday Times* also compared the Iraqi leader to an ogre in the following article: "Preparing for war", editorial, *Sunday Times*, 19 August 1990, Sect. 3, p. 5. It is worth remembering that Napoleon I was also represented as an ogre by the British.

19    "Monster". Flora Lewis, "Plug In To Moscow", op-ed, *New York Times*, 29 September 1990, p. 23; Jim Hoagland, "America's Frankenstein's Monster", op-ed, *Washington Post*, 7 February 1991, p. A 19; Paddy Ashdown, MP, "Why war may still be the least worst option", op-ed, *Guardian*, 10 January 1991, p. 19; Norman Stone, "We have the technology: let us turn it on this monster", op-ed, *Sunday Times*, 5 August 1990, Sect. 3, p. 7; Adrian Hamilton, "Iran leads merry embargo dance", op-ed, *Observer*, 23 September 1990, p. 17.

20    David Daiches, *A Critical History of English Literature*, vol. I, 2nd ed., London: Secker & Warburg, 1972, p. 9.

overcome by the United States and their allies during the Gulf War. Similarly, the designation "monster" referred to the image of a destructive and evil character inspiring terror. For instance, Jim Hoagland's article[21] published in the *Washington Post* on 7 February 1991, "America's Frankenstein's Monster", referred to the novel by Mary Shelley of 1818, *Frankenstein*.[22] Like the "creature" created by a young scientist from Geneva, Saddam Hussein became America's own Frankenstein's monster "with coaching from the CIA and the State Department".

In a nutshell, the ogre, whose symbolism approximates that of the monster designating a bloodthirsty criminal, offered the image of a creature with a terrifying appearance that represented, like Saddam Hussein, the figure of the State, war and the tyrant.[23] Not only did journalists favour pathos in a lexical choice that could be characterized as infantilizing, but, for them, the ogre and the monster constituted, in the person of the Iraqi ruler, an external threat for American and British readers.

Journalists of the two American newspapers also referred to Saddam Hussein as a "gangster".[24] In the *Washington Post*, Jim Hoagland, Charles Krauthammer, as well as Mark Shields,

---

21 Jim Hoagland, "America's Frankenstein's Monster", op-ed, *Washington Post*, 7 February 1991, p. A 19.
22 Nicola Chalton, ed., *Who Wrote What When?*, London: Simon & Schuster UK, 1999, p. 558.
23 Jean Chevalier et Alain Gheerbrant, *Dictionnaire des symboles: mythes, rêves, coutumes, gestes, formes, figures, couleurs, nombres*, Paris: Robert Laffont, 2004, pp. 645, 693.
24 "Gangster". Anthony Lewis, "Lessons of Victory", op-ed, *New York Times*, 1 March 1991, p. A 27; James Q. Wilson, "Why We Are Fighting ...", op-ed, *Washington Post*, 17 January 1991, p. A 21.

considered him a "thug".[25] In the British press, Charles Bremner of the *Times* called the Iraqi ruler an "assassin".[26] Moreover, the *New York Times*, on the American side, and the *Times*, on the British side, accused him of being a "terrorist leader"[27] and underlined the opposition between the Iraqi leader and the "civilized" world.[28] As noted earlier, journalists, by these terms, implicitly recognized the superiority of their civilization over Saddam Hussein's barbaric and savage world. They implied that, following the example of good citizens, they respected, like their readers, the laws of the city contrary to the primitive monster represented by this rogue leader. As we can see, a dualistic marking was at work in the discourse of journalists, thus reinforcing the collective norm to which the *New York Times* and the *Times* subscribed.

Opinion articles contained not only terms and expressions drawn from the lexical field of crime, such as those used in editorials, but also words pertaining to the lexical field of war. The *New York Times* and the *Washington Post*, on the American

---

25  "Thug". Jim Hoagland, "A Quick Rewrite of History", op-ed, *Washington Post*, 7 October 1990, p. D 7; Charles Krauthammer, "A Festival of Appeasement", op-ed, *Washington Post*, 3 August 1990, p. A 23; "It's Not Just Oil", op-ed, *Washington Post*, 17 August 1990, p. A 27; "The Case for Destroying Saddam", op-ed, *Washington Post*, 25 November 1990, p. C 7; Mark Shields, "What Are the Boys Fighting For?", op-ed, *Washington Post*, 28 August 1990, p. A 17.

26  "Assassin". Charles Bremner, "Saddam's psyche shows the strain", op-ed, *Times*, 17 January 1991, p. 12.

27  "Terrorist leader". A. M. Rosenthal, "Know Your Allies", op-ed, *New York Times*, 26 August 1990, p. E 19; Bernard Levin, "Preying on our minds, but only because we let them", op-ed, *Times*, 13 September 1990, p. 14.

28  "His lone wolf conflict with the entire civilized world". Robert Satloff, "Escape Route for Saddam Hussein: Jordan", op-ed, *New York Times*, 11 August 1990, p. A 25. "Iraq [is] ruled [...] beyond the constraints of any of the restraints of civilisation". Bernard Levin, "Preying on our minds, but only because we let them", op-ed, *Times*, 13 September 1990, p. 14.

side, and the *Observer*, on the British side, focused on the warlike[29] character of the Iraqi leader. To the image of a monstrous murderer was thus added the image of an implacable and terrifying warmongering enemy.

It is hardly surprising that the Iraqi leader was described as "bad"[30] on both sides of the Atlantic given the other qualifiers journalists attached to Saddam Hussein to portray him. On this subject, Anna Quindlen, in the *New York Times*, equated the Iraqi ruler with "a big bad guy with [the] sinister mustache of a James Bond villain".[31] This comparison served to reinforce the image of Saddam Hussein in his role as the stereotypical, aggressive, ruthless and fierce scoundrel in the face of the noble and fearless knight embodied by the popular character of James Bond on screen. Moreover, does the wearing of the moustache not corroborate, in the collective unconscious, the portrait of the traitor of foreign origin as characters confronting the British agent 007 are often represented? We may also point out that this opinion article, titled "The Invasion Vacation", resorted to

---

29     "Warlike leader". Tom Wicker, "Bush Stands Warned", op-ed, *New York Times*, 2 December 1990, p. E 19. "Belligerent Saddam". Jack Anderson and Dale Van Atta, "Why Arafat Backed Saddam", op-ed, *Washington Post*, 26 August 1990, p. C 7. "Belligerent enemy". Adrian Hamilton, "Palestine peace hopes founded on shifting sand", op-ed, *Observer*, 7 October 1990, p. 16.

30     "Bad". Anna Quindlen, "The Invasion Vacation", op-ed, *New York Times*, 19 August 1990, p. E 19; Rowland Evans and Robert Novak, "Message from Mubarak", op-ed, *Washington Post*, 17 August 1990, p. A 27; Michael Jones, "Mad, bad and increasingly dangerous to know", op-ed, *Sunday Times*, 3 February 1991, Sect. 1, p. 14; Helga Graham, "Mad, bad and dangerous to know", op-ed, *Observer*, 12 August 1990, p. 12.

31     Anna Quindlen, "The Invasion Vacation", op-ed, *New York Times*, 19 August 1990, p. E 19.

the rhetoric of the spoken word,[32] with all the alliterations and assonances of which the American press and the British press were fond. With its catchy and ironic presentation, this headline attracted readers' attention and coloured their reading of the whole article.

In a similar vein and with regard to the British press, the *Sunday Times* published, on 3 February 1991, an opinion piece by Michael Jones, the title of which, "Mad, bad and increasingly dangerous to know", included the adjective "bad" referred to above, and which seemed to echo that of an opinion piece by Helga Graham published in the *Observer* on 12 August 1990: "Mad, bad and dangerous to know". One might think that journalists read competing newspapers or copied each other. In addition, this title, "Mad, bad and dangerous to know", characterizing the Iraqi leader, referred to the name of the album by British pop band "Dead or Alive" released in 1986. The reader was therefore expected to have a wide-ranging general knowledge.

Thus, as a continuation of the reflection begun on editorials, the reading of opinion articles from August 1990 to mid-March 1991 confirms the unfavourable image of a violent and brutal enemy. The terms used to depict the Iraqi leader were overloaded with affects and showed an increased virulence in the sense that they fell within lexical fields not only of crime, as in editorials, but also of war. Whether it was the opinion articles of the American press or those of the British press, journalists and contributors highlighted the monstrosity of the president of Iraq and presented

---

32     Headlines were long shouted by newspaper sellers (Delphine Chartier, *La Traduction journalistique, Anglais-Français*, Toulouse: PU du Mirail, 2000, p. 32).

him as the enemy to be defeated. Even if the terms "gangster" and "thug" were used only on the U.S. side to represent Saddam Hussein and the *Times* called him "assassin", identical words were used on both sides of the Atlantic to crystallize hatred against the enemy. To that end, journalists adorned their articles with clichés, banalities, stereotyped terms to represent the Other, half-man half monster, as an opponent to beat, which, as we have seen, had the advantage of defining readers as civilized human beings devoid of all treachery, vileness, and other ignominy of which they accused the Iraqi leader.

As in the editorials, the moment when qualifiers begin to be used to describe the president of Iraq is interesting as well as the recurrence of these qualifiers, and this gives us an idea of the way the portrayal of the enemy changes over time. It can also highlight similarities and differences between editorials and opinion articles. On the basis of identical qualifiers[33] listed in editorials and opinion articles, we noted that 90% of qualifiers appeared as from August 1990 or at the latest in September 1990 in opinion articles. However, while the term "outlaw",[34] for example, was used to refer to Saddam Hussein in editorials from August 1990, it was not used in opinion articles until January 1991, which may mean that compliance with the law was a major

---

33  The sample includes the following qualifiers: "aggressor", "despot", "dictator", "outlaw", "threat", "tyrant" and "ambitious", "dangerous", "ruthless" and "cunning" leader.

34  "Outlaw". "Shoulder to Shoulder against Iraq", editorial, *New York Times*, 10 September 1990, p. A 22; Richard Nixon, "Why", op-ed, *New York Times*, 6 January 1991, p. E 19; "Saddam Hussein's Diplomacy", editorial, *Washington Post*, 22 August 1990, p. A 20; "Iraq's naked villainy", editorial, *Times*, 3 August 1990, p. 1; Paul Wilkinson, "A way to avoid the no-win war", op-ed, *Guardian*, 3 January 1991, p. 15.

issue for the editorial staff of newspapers, and in particular in the American press and in the *Times* on the British side. As for the qualifiers[35] specifically used in opinion articles, 83% of them were also found in August 1990 or September 1990. As was the case in editorials, the portrait of the Iraqi leader was defined in opinion articles as from August 1990. On the other hand, as regards the recurrence of these terms or their synonyms used from August 1990 to mid-March 1991, it seems difficult to identify any specific patterns distinguishing the American and British press.

Finally, in editorials and opinion articles, the qualifiers used to depict Saddam Hussein were repeated over and over again during the month of August, when American and British editorial writers and journalists were presenting the Iraqi leader to the reader. The repetition of terms such as tyrant, dictator, gangster or even villain reinforced and dramatized their message. Contributors or the editorial staff of each newspaper were able to construct their discourse by endless repetitions in order to hammer their message home. Like advertising slogans, the repeated descriptions of Saddam Hussein served to arouse the reader's interest.

As a corollary to this reflection, two articles in which the contributor described Saddam Hussein as a "tyrant" were particularly striking, one published in the American press and the other in the British press. The first, entitled "The Tyrants on Our Side in the Gulf",[36] was published in the *Washington Post* on 1

---

35    The qualifiers used are "bandit", "butcher of Baghdad", "gangster", "murderer", "monster", "warmonger", "warlord", "bad", "megalomaniac" and "terrorist" ruler.

36    "Tyrant". Jim Hoagland, "The Tyrants on Our Side in the Gulf", op-ed, *Washington Post*, 1 November 1990, p. A 23.

November 1990. The journalist, Jim Hoagland, strongly criticized the attitude of the Bush administration, which sought support, in the anti-Iraq coalition, from countries like China[37] and Syria, whose regimes he considered to be totalitarian. As for the title of the opinion piece published in the *Times* on 23 August 1990, "To lie, to creep, perchance to smarm, ay, there's the rub",[38] it consisted of an offbeat repetition of the verses of the famous first scene of the third act of *Hamlet*. Undoubtedly, the verses of the famous Shakespearean tirade were known by heart by every cultivated reader of the *Times*. This literary reference was bound to flatter the ego of the reader "who is insatiably waiting for pleasures"[39] in the sense that the involved distance was likely to please the sophisticated reader, capable of discerning broader cultural allusions. The art of convincing by seduction indeed constitutes one of the major rhetorical devices used in journalism.

As a reminder of what has been said of editorials, the unfavourable image of the Iraqi leader was formed in opinion articles from August 1990 by the use of qualifiers which hardly evolved during the Gulf Crisis and War. There did not seem to be any gradation of terminology relating to the depiction of the enemy from August 1990 to mid-March 1991 in the American press and the British press. Concerning the difference between

---

37   The reader should refer to the chapter on the allies and more particularly on China.

38   Bernard Levin, "To lie, to creep, perchance to smarm, ay, there's the rub", op-ed, *Times*, 23 August 1990, p. 8.

39   Michel Morel, "Howard Barker: la disposition de spectacle et de lecture mise à nu", *Études anglaises*, 2002/3, Tome 55, pp. 344-357, <http://www.cairn.info/revue-etudes-anglaises-2002-3-page-344.htm>, consulted 21 September 2022.

qualifiers used in editorials and opinion articles, they appeared more virulent in opinion articles.

In their numerous speeches and press conferences during the Gulf Crisis and War, the American president George Bush and the British Prime Minister Margaret Thatcher, from August 1990 to November 1990, and John Major, from December 1990 to mid-March 1991, repeatedly described Saddam Hussein as a "dictator"[40] and as an "aggressor".[41] Besides, George Bush and Margaret Thatcher called him inter alia "tyrant",[42] "despot"[43] and "outlaw".[44] If those who govern us seek to use the media in the hope of influencing public opinion, we must recognize that, in the present case, the political leaders of the two countries were certainly delighted that the print media resorted to the qualifiers they had used themselves, perhaps reflecting a privileged relationship between the media and government, especially in times of crisis and war. During a conflict, journalists are confronted with the problem of the degree of their freedom of expression. Between their wish to inform the public and military censorship, their room for manoeuvre can sometimes be very restricted. While it is necessary for reasons of security to protect

---

40  George Bush used the term "dictator" seventy-nine times during the Gulf Crisis and War, Margaret Thatcher twenty-two times and John Major ten times.

41  The term "aggressor" was used twenty-five times in the speeches of the American president, twenty times by Margaret Thatcher and three times by John Major.

42  George Bush and Margaret Thatcher used the word "tyrant" eight times.

43  This term was used five times by the American president and twice by Margaret Thatcher.

44  George Bush described Saddam Hussein as an "outlaw" eighteen times whereas Margaret Thatcher resorted to this term four times to depict the Iraqi leader.

the lives of soldiers engaged in combat, the freedom of the press is all the same severely limited as a result. It is moreover recognized that the first amendment to the American Constitution on freedom of expression and of the press does not apply in time of war.[45] As a reminder, journalists were, during the events in the Persian Gulf, assigned to "pools" of journalists for the coverage of hostilities. They were subject to restrictions[46] imposed by the military authorities on information that could be transmitted and published. Media control was to be one of the elements of the battlefield.[47] For example, soldiers at Saudi checkpoints were ordered to prevent journalists from going to the border if they were not part of a "pool" and had not accepted the rules of military censorship.[48] But what are the limits on military censorship? As a result of controls and limitations of access to information during a war, it seems difficult, if almost impossible, for journalists to reconcile freedom of information, necessary for the proper functioning of democracy, and the security of the armed forces engaged in the conflict. As a consequence, how can their readers, who are also citizens, be informed as objectively as possible on the basis of censored information? The reader cannot be correctly informed if the truth is filtered, and even distorted. "When war is declared, truth is the first casualty", remarked U.S. Senator Hiram Johnson and wrote Arthur Ponsonby.[49]

---

45      Claude-Jean Bertrand, *op. cit.*, p. 31; also see Robert G. Picard & Jeffrey H. Brody, *op. cit.*, p. 166.

46      Refer to the Ground Rules and Guidelines for Desert Shield *in* Hedrick Smith, ed., *The Media and The Gulf War: The Press and Democracy in Wartime*, Washington, DC: Seven Locks Press, 1992, pp. 4-12.

47      Éric Laurent, *op. cit.*, p. 66.

48      Robert Fisk, *The Great War for Civilization. The Conquest of the Middle East*, rev. ed., London: Harper Perennial, 2006, p. 759.

49      U.S. Senator Hiram Johnson is purported to have coined this sentence in 1918. Anne Morelli refers to Arthur Ponsoby in *Principes élémentaires de*

There is also the question of self-censorship by journalists, which affects the content of their articles. Journalists internalize not only the guidelines and ideological lines of their newspaper and write according to what the reader expects, but, according to Robert Fisk, journalist with the British daily the *Independent*, they also censor themselves, because of their "uncritical repetition of the statements of generals and major generals" and "on the grounds that their 'access' to senior military officials" gives them information necessary for the media coverage of the war "that might otherwise be denied [to] their readers".[50] Hence the risk of complicity, almost osmosis[51] between reporters in uniform and soldiers in the operation theatre. Painful compromises between contradictory imperatives are therefore essential for journalists: between the duty to respect the military secrecy of belligerents and the right to information of readers,[52] between the limits between military censorship and self-censorship, journalists must therefore, despite the speed of transmission techniques and dissemination of information, maintain competence, rigour and critical distance from information provided by military and governmental staff. Or at the very least they must analyse and question the reliability and accuracy of this information and seek to dismantle propagandist mechanisms and set current events in their context.

---

*propagande de guerre*, Bruxelles: Labor, 2001, pp. 5, 81. Lord Ponsonby denounced war propaganda during the First World War in *Falsehood in Wartime: Propaganda Lies of the First World War*, published in London in 1928.

50    Robert Fisk, *op. cit.*, p. 772.

51    *Ibid.*, p. 738. Robert Fisk speaks of a "symbiotic, even osmotic relationship" between journalists and soldiers. "Half the reporters in Saudi Arabia, [...], want to be soldiers. Half the soldiers want to be in the news business".

52    Élisabeth Coss-Humbert, "La Rhétorique de presse pendant la guerre du Golfe", *in* Béatrice Fleury-Vilatte (dir.), *op. cit.*, p. 15.

With regard to readers' letters published in the press on either side of the Atlantic from August 1990 to mid-March 1991, we found similar terms to those used in editorials to depict the Iraqi ruler (using terms such as dictator, aggressor, despot, monster, bully, tyrant, and adjectives like dangerous and ruthless). Should we be surprised at the use of such qualifiers in readers' letters? One can only be struck by the analogy between the designations used in editorials and opinion articles and those used in letters. According to Jean-Marie Domenach, "the average man is an essentially influential being; it has become possible to suggest opinions which he will come to consider as his own". [53] One may wonder whether what is possible in terms of advertising is also done so that newspapers can influence their readers. A possible answer to this difficult question might be suggested by analysing the composition of the readership of American and British newspapers, the assessment of which is based on the letters referred to above. First, the readership of the *New York Times* and the *Times* was international, as illustrated for example by the letter sent to the American daily by Eduard Ryabtsev, a Middle East analyst for the Novosti Information Agency, or that published in the British daily by Abdulla Y. Bishara, the General Secretary of the Gulf Cooperation Council (GCC) in Riyadh, Saudi Arabia. Many prominent figures wanted their letters published in a prestigious daily newspaper, such as the *New York Times* on the American side or the *Times* on the British side. Second, letters came mostly from the academic, political and journalistic world. For instance, the letter[54] by Mowahid H. Shah, Editor of

---

53    Jean-Marie Domenach, *La Propagande politique*, Que sais-je?, 7e éd., Paris: PUF, 1973, p. 16.

54    Mowahid H. Shah, "Iran Has Condemned the Iraqi Invasion", letters, *New York Times*, 16 August 1990, p. A 24. Vera Baudin Saeedpour, "What

the newspaper *Eastern Times*, was published in the *New York Times* on 16 August 1990, and that by Vera Baudin Saeedpour, Director of the Kurdish programme and the association "Cultural Survival", was published in the American daily on 23 September 1990. Similarly, the *Times* published a letter[55] by Tony Smythe, Director of Medical Campaign against Nuclear Weapons, on 13 August 1990, and the *Guardian* letters[56] by Fadir Faqir, a member of the department of Arabic and Islamic Studies at the University of Exeter, and Sir Frederic Bennett, President of the Anglo-Jordanian Society and a Conservative MP from 1951 to 1987. As these examples show, the readership consisted of well-known figures whose opinions were expected to provide a thoughtful contribution to the debate.

It should also be remembered that, within the framework of this study, the impact of vocabulary used by editorial writers, journalists and contributors on the readership during the Gulf Crisis and War was not assessed. Our main goal was to check whether the features of the portrait of the Iraqi leader mentioned in readers' letters tallied with the portrait presented by the editorial staff of the newspaper in editorials. As we have seen above, the list of the qualifiers in letters published in both the American and British press revealed that this was indeed the case. The fact is that the readership sent letters to newspapers in reaction to published articles, events, or even in response to a letter from other

Britain Sowed, Iraq and U.S. Now Reap", letters, *New York Times*, 23 September 1990, p. E 20.
55    Tony Smythe, "Crisis in the Gulf", letters, *Times*, 13 August 1990, p. 11.
56    Fadir Faqir, Dr, "Arab eyes", letters, *Guardian*, 21 February 1991, p. 20; Sir Frederic Bennett, "Morality and legality on trial in the Gulf crisis", letters, *Guardian*, 30 August 1990, p. 18.

readers as illustrated by the title of the letter[57] published in the *Washington Post* of 4 October 1990, "Jim Hoagland's 'Imprudent' Plan". As a general rule, the forum including readers' opinions was intended to generate an exchange of views on topical subjects in response to letters published previously, some supporting the views of the editorial staff, others opposing them. In any case, "the main objective of editors is to spark the interest of readers by publishing lively letters on current subjects".[58] Newspapers fuel democratic debate by publishing not only editorials and opinion articles whose viewpoints may differ from the editorial line of the newspaper, but also readers' reactions.

Finally, with respect to the time of occurrence of qualifiers identified in letters on either side of the Atlantic and referred to above, the majority of them appeared as early as August 1990 or at the latest in September 1990, as in editorials. These qualifiers were irregularly repeated during the Gulf Crisis and War. As was the case with editorials, what is striking is that there did not seem to be any change in the perception of the enemy inasmuch as the portrait of Saddam Hussein presented by readers was already established in August 1990.

In essence, the tone of the letters sent to the editorial staff was in agreement with the editorial line of newspapers on both sides of the Atlantic with regard to the depiction and description of the Iraqi president. All in all, the analysis of letters shows that, apart

---

57    Stephen E. Lankenau, "Jim Hoagland's 'Imprudent' Plan", letters, *Washington Post*, 4 October 1990, p. A 26.
58    Thérèse Pothier, "Lecteurs et rédactions", *in Visages de la presse britannique*, Jean-Claude Sergeant (dir.), Nancy: PU de Nancy, 1987, p. 131.

from the ambition of the Iraqi leader, which was emphasized only in letters published in the American press, readers on both sides of the Atlantic resorted to qualifiers similar to those of editorials and opinion articles to describe the Iraqi ruler, who was perceived as a brutal, dangerous and ruthless dictator. Without being able to assess the exact impact on readers of the vocabulary used in editorials, we can nonetheless assume that these readers, some of whom were prominent figures, confronted their own opinions with those of the newspapers in question. Besides, in letters as in editorials and opinion articles, the image of the enemy was determined as early as August 1990 and did not seem to evolve during the Gulf Crisis and the war itself.[59] While there seemed to be no change in the perception of the enemy with regard to the terms used from August 1990 to mid-March 1991, the vocabulary identified consisted of a range of designations reflecting the same rhetoric of persuasion. The terms used belonged to a lexical field pertaining to the emotive or even conative function, linked to the will of the author of the letter to act on the recipient and/or another reader of the published letter. Lastly, editorial writers and journalists repeated the qualifiers used by the American president and the British Prime Minister to describe the Iraqi leader. Saddam Hussein was thus perceived as a danger to the world, and therefore for both the American president and the British Prime Minister, journalists and readers, the Iraqi ruler had to be fought.

---

59    The reading of editorials, opinion articles and letters published in the American and British press in August 1990 would have sufficed to comprehend the personality of the enemy as presented and described by editorialists, journalists and contributors on both sides of the Atlantic.

## 2.2 Psychological state

In addition to the series of unflattering terms aimed at the Iraqi president, the press, on both sides of the Atlantic, addressed the issue of Saddam Hussein's alleged madness. Whereas the American press did not seem to mention it in its editorials, the British newspapers highlighted what they saw as Saddam Hussein's mental deficiency in theirs. The reference to the mental state of the Iraqi president appeared in the *Times* and the Sunday newspapers in August 1990, while the *Guardian* only alluded to it in January 1991 just before the start of the armed conflict. In other words, British editorials no longer mentioned the madness of the Iraqi leader during the Gulf War. Does this mean that the status of the president of Iraq changed in the eyes of journalists when the war broke out? The image of the mentally retarded man, who was responsible for the Gulf War by refusing to withdraw from Kuwait was followed by that of the warrior, who had to be brought to his senses by force.

While the American press did not mention Saddam Hussein's psychological state in its editorials, this was not the case in its opinion articles. References to the madness of the Iraqi leader abounded in the *New York Times* and the *Washington Post*. However, in the *Washington Post*, the situation was more mixed in that the positions of journalists diverged on this subject, reflecting the plurality of opinions published in the newspaper. It thus offered its readers a wide range of different points of view. For example, the opinion articles of Charles Krauthammer only referred to the subject of Saddam Hussein's mental features to challenge the presentation of the Iraqi leader as a madman, stating that "Saddam Hussein is not a madman" but "he is a cold and calculating thug".[60] This dual statement by the journalist that the Iraqi leader was not a "madman"[61] was also present in an article by James Schlesinger, a councellor at the Center for Strategic and International Studies at the time and a former defense secretary, energy secretary and director of the CIA. To support his claims, he compared Saddam Hussein to George Plunkitt,[62] a 19th-century American senator from New York State who, during his political career, was a skilful proponent of a wait-and-see policy. This comparison bore witness to the fact that American readers were expected to know the history and politics of their country and have a broad-ranging culture. While the analogy between George Plunkitt and Saddam Hussein served to present him as a calculating man and a corrupt opportunist, it did not represent him as being unbalanced.

As in British editorials, American journalists and contributors only mentioned Saddam Hussein's possible madness during the Gulf Crisis. This begs the question as to why this theme was no longer addressed after the outbreak of hostilities. Undoubtedly, journalists tried to make the reader believe before the war began that the crisis and the prospect of war were attributable to the

---

60    Charles Krauthammer, "It's Not Just Oil", op-ed, *Washington Post*, 17 August 1990, p. A 27.
61    "Saddam is not a madman". Charles Krauthammer, "It's Not Just Oil", op-ed, *Washington Post*, 17 August 1990, p. A 27. "He is not mad". Charles Krauthammer, "And Why Saddam Fights", op-ed, *Washington Post*, 17 January 1991, p. A 21.
62    "He is no madman. Like George Plunkitt, he took opportunities". James Schlesinger, "Innocence Shattered", op-ed, *Washington Post*, 5 August 1990, p. D 7. George Washington Plunkitt (1842-1924) was part of New York's Tammany Hall organization, known for its illegal actions and the archetype of corruption (George Brown Tindall & David Emory Shi, *op. cit.*, p. 671; Gérard Hocmard [dir.], *op. cit.*, p. 600).

brutal madness of a dictator fearing neither God nor man. After the outbreak of the conflict, it might no longer seem necessary to them to question the origin of the war and the responsibility for starting it, but to focus on the course and outcome of the armed conflict and to inform readers of events as they unfolded.

As for opinion pieces published in the British press, we observed that except for the *Guardian* which did not allude to it, some journalists elaborated on this alleged madness. For example, Helga Graham of the *Observer* expatiated on Saddam Hussein's mental disorders. Her position can be explained by the fact that in the years preceding the Iraqi invasion, the journalist had campaigned against the Iraqi leader by regularly publishing reports on bombings and other atrocities committed, among others, against the Kurds. Furthermore, she had met with Farzad Bazoft, the British journalist working for the same newspaper, who was sentenced to death in Iraq for espionage and hanged on 15 March 1990.

All in all, only a few British journalists insisted in their articles on Saddam Hussein's possible paranoia during the Gulf Crisis and War. They were Charles Bremner in the *Times*, Michael Jones and Norman Macrae in the *Sunday Times*, and Helga Graham as well as Andrew Stephen in the *Observer*. But unlike American opinion articles and especially those in the *Washington Post*, whose contributors offered the reader a range of divergent viewpoints during the Gulf Crisis, these British journalists were unanimous in highlighting the alleged mental disorders of the Iraqi ruler from August 1990 to mid-March 1991. What better way for journalists to play on the fear of the readership than to portray Saddam Hussein as a sick person, insisting on his ramblings, vices and aberrations. Not only did this approach certainly frighten readers, but moreover it also suggested to them that the Iraqi ruler was particularly disturbing because of his mental disorders. Madness, or the opposite of reason[63] has indeed been perceived since the 18th century as the enemy of civilization.[64] As for the madman, who is a sign of guilty animality[65] and is assimilated in the collective unconscious to an unstable and antisocial psychopath, he constitutes an "obstacle to order".[66] If, according to Descartes, the madman cannot think, or, if, for Foucault, he disrupts public order,[67] it is indisputable that one cannot negotiate with an unbalanced human being like the Iraqi president. In essence, the assimilation of Saddam Hussein to a madman was part, on the one hand, of the demonization of the enemy leader by American and British journalists, and, on the other, a strategy of reducing the conflict to an antagonism between the "good", namely journalists and their readers, and the "bad", i.e. the Other, the enemy, responsible for the war.

In his speeches and press conferences from August 1990 to mid-March 1991, the American president did not call the Iraqi leader crazy, but depicted him, perhaps by euphemism, as "irrational"[68] in August and September 1990 as well as in January

---

63  Alphonse De Waelhens, *La Psychose. Essai d'interprétation analytique et existentiale*, Louvain: Nauwelaerts, 1972, p. 224.
64  Frédéric Gros, *Michel Foucault*, Que sais-je?, 3e éd., Paris: PUF, 2005, p. 23.
65  *Ibid.*, p. 23.
66  Michel Foucault, *Histoire de la folie à l'âge classique*, Paris: Gallimard, 1976, pp. 69, 70, 72-73.
67  Frédéric Gros, *op. cit.*, p. 19.
68  For instance, at a Questions-and-Answer session with reporters on 25 January 1991 (<https://bush41library.tamu.edu/archives/public-papers/2652>, consulted 27 September 2022).

1991. While there were no references to the mental state of the president of Iraq in John Major's speeches, Margaret Thatcher stated during a television programme on 1 September 1990 that she did not consider that Saddam Hussein was crazy, but that he was calculating and fanatical.[69] This means that the journalists who exploited the psychological traits of the Iraqi leader really distinguished themselves from the official point of view.

Regarding readers' letters, there was only one message from a reader of the *Washington Post* who, in August 1990, assimilated the Iraqi leader to a madman.[70] Except for this example, there did not seem to be any letters on this subject in the American and British press. On the contrary, one reader explicitly distanced himself from the *Guardian* in relation to the media hype about Saddam Hussein's madness.[71]

So, while the editorials of the two American dailies did not seem to refer to the theme of the madness of the president of Iraq during the Gulf Crisis and War, the British editorials abounded with allusions to this subject. As for the opinion articles published in the American press and the British press, some journalists, apart from those of the *Guardian*, insisted on the psychological profile of the Iraqi president during this period. However, only

---

69    "I do not regard him [Saddam Hussein] as mad [...]". "Calculating, not mad, fanatical [...]". Margaret Thatcher, TV Interview for TV-AM *Frost on Sunday*, 1 September 1990, (<https://www.margaretthatcher.org/document/108186>, consulted 27 September 2022).
70    "Madmen like Saddam Hussein". Trent D. Duffy, "Hostages and Hypocrisy at the Pump", letters, *Washington Post*, 28 August 1990, p. A 16.
71    "All too frequently we are led to conclude [...] that Saddam is a "mad mullah" rather than to try to understand why Iraq has embarked on its present course of action". Stuart Simpson, "The rules that Stalin knew – and Saddam doesn't", letters, *Guardian*, 11 August 1990, p. 18.

the *Washington Post*, on the American side, offered its readers a diverse range of opinions on this subject. Given that the description of Saddam Hussein as a madman was only the work of some American and British journalists in opinion articles published during the Gulf Crisis and War and only appeared in August 1990 in a letter to the *Washington Post*, the description of the Iraqi leader as such can be considered somewhat marginal in the portrait painted by the press on both sides of the Atlantic.

## 2.3    Bestiary

Whether or not the Iraqi leader was crazy was questionable. The few journalists who described him in this way could be blamed for having lent themselves to a biased interpretation of the president of Iraq's personality to better exaggerate his portrait. In addition to this extravagant description of the enemy, there was another component to the representation. American dailies did not hesitate in their editorials to resort to animal vocabulary to define the Iraqi president by using, for example, the words "tiger", "dragon" or "gorilla". On the British side, the *Times* was the only newspaper to borrow a term from the lexical field of animals to describe the Iraqi leader. For example, in an editorial published on 16 August 1990, the British daily paper drew a parallel between Saddam Hussein and a "python".[72] However, that was Iran's comment on the president of Iraq quoted by the editorialist. Nevertheless, since the title of the editorial retained the comparison between the Iraqi leader and a snake, it can therefore be assumed that the editorial staff endorsed this analogy or at least found it worthy of

---

72    "The python's embrace", editorial, *Times*, 16 August 1990, p. 11.

comment. It should also be noted that such terms only appeared during the Gulf Crisis and in a limited number of editorials on both sides of the Atlantic. As for the opinion articles, the words "wolf", "shark", "scorpion" and "lion" were used by American and British journalists only in August 1990 and only a few journalists gave Saddam Hussein animal names.

Whereas some people consider their enemy as an animal in the sense of being inferior,[73] these terms can also be used to suggest a negative relationship between humans and animals and to see the animal as a source of evil.[74] This form of expression refers therefore to animal symbolism. Thus, in the dictionary of symbols by Jean Chevalier and Alain Gheerbrant, we can read that "the wolf is synonymous with savagery". Negatively valued, the symbolism of the wolf focuses on ferociousness and brute force. This diabolical aspect "constitutes an obstacle on the road of the Muslim pilgrim on his way to Mecca and takes on the dimensions of the Beast of Revelation".[75] The Iraqi leader was thus this beast that shook up the region's geopolitical situation by his invasion of Kuwait. Besides, if the lion, the king of animals, is, like Saddam Hussein, the very embodiment of power, its excessive pride and confidence makes it the symbol of "the Sovereign, dazzled by his own power, who becomes a tyrant".[76] As far as the scorpion is concerned, this

---

73    Änne Ostermann und Hans Nicklas, *Vorurteile und Feindbilder*, Basel: Beltz, 1984, p. 252.
74    On this subject, refer to the book by Jean Vartier, *Les Procès d'animaux du Moyen Âge à nos jours*, Paris: Hachette, 1970, 254 p. In the Middle Ages, men and beasts were all considered as God's creatures. Thus, animals could be possessed by the forces of evil. Since there was no natural explanation for the damage done by some animals, they were given a supernatural sense. Animal trials were numerous between the 15th and 18th centuries.
75    Jean Chevalier & Alain Gheerbrant, *op. cit.*, p. 584.
76    *Ibid.*, p. 575.

animal is considered evil and is ready to sting to death anyone or anything that brushes against it, and it embodies the warlike spirit, always waiting in ambush and quick to kill.[77] As for the dragon, it is described as a severe guardian or a symbol of evil and demonic tendencies. The dragon is the guardian of hidden treasures and, as such, the adversary who must be defeated to gain access to them.[78] While the treasures guarded by the Western dragon are the Golden Fleece and the Garden of Hesperides, that guarded by the Eastern dragon, symbolized in Saddam Hussein, would rather be black gold. Finally, like the shark, whose voracity makes it the dreaded enemy of sailors, and like the python, the infernal deity, Saddam Hussein was presented as a Chtonian monster, a scourge ready to descend upon the world.

In any case, by comparing Saddam Hussein, in the editorials, to a tiger, a dragon, a gorilla and a python, and, in the opinion articles, to a wolf and a shark, American and British editorialists and journalists were probably trying to impress readers and even frighten them. The choice of this animal vocabulary gave a particular intensity to their demonstration and allowed them to exaggerate the portrait of Saddam Hussein and thus highlight his primitive savagery. Describing the president of Iraq in this way seemed to be a way to express contempt for the Iraqi leader represented by journalists as a carnivore, a predator and a savage. By highlighting the animality of the Iraqi ruler, American and British editorialists and journalists might imply that, like a beast, the president of Iraq had no soul and was deprived of reason. They opposed the animal in Saddam Hussein to the Man, symbolizing

---

77    *Ibid.*, pp. 854-855.
78    *Ibid.*, p. 366.

the journalist and the reader, who are creatures endowed with intelligence, divinity, humanity and conscious of their finiteness. In classical times gods willingly took on an animal form, but, according to journalists, what the animal personified in Saddam Hussein lacks is possessed by Man. If Man has a soul and is endowed with reason, it means then that the animal, which is devoid of them, thus does not exist. Could it be inferred that the enemy, the Other in the person of Saddam Hussein, was then reduced to a state of *non-being* for some journalists? At any rate, by insisting on Saddam Hussein's animality, American and British journalists implicitly deprived him of his quality as a human being and reduced him to the status of an animal. Thus, in addition to the image of a bloodthirsty tyrant, there was that of a bestial and inhuman being manifesting cruel greed or that of a beast that the West had not been able to tame and domesticate.

As for the letters to the editor, no words belonging to the animal lexicon seemed to have been used in the letters analysed. Readers on both sides of the Atlantic appeared to have shown more reserve than American and British editorialists and journalists. The same was true of the American president and the British Prime Minister[79] who did not use the terms listed in the press on both sides of the Atlantic in their speeches from August 1990 to mid-March 1991. The contrary would have been surprising insofar as the representatives of a country or government are supposed to use a controlled vocabulary that is above all adapted to their roles.

---

79    In a speech on 5 August 1990 at the Aspen Institute in Colorado, Margaret Thatcher used the expression "dragon to slay" when she discussed the drug problem (<https://www.margaretthatcher.org/document/108174>, consulted 28 September 2022).

In conclusion, there were only a few editorials and opinion articles in the American and British press comparing the Iraqi president to wild animals. These exceptional comparisons were part of a strategy of persuasion used by editorialists and journalists to express their disdain for the president of Iraq and especially to denigrate him and tarnish his image.

## 2.4   Demonological and religious language

What was also striking was Saddam Hussein's description as the incarnation of evil. While, in the American press, the *New York Times* equated the Iraqi leader to "Satan"[80] in an editorial published in August 1990, the *Washington Post*, by contrast, did not seem to refer to this comparison in its editorials. The description of the Iraqi leader as the power of evil appeared in the *New York Times* only in August 1990. In the British press, this analogy can be found in the *Sunday Times* in August 1990, which described the Iraqi leader as "an evil despot"[81] and wrote the following month that "unless civilised people rally to the cause of freedom, wherever it is threatened, evil triumphs"[82] and in January 1991 the Sunday paper referred to "the forces of evil"[83] personified in Saddam Hussein. The comparison appeared in the *Guardian* only in January 1991 and in the *Observer* in March

---

80   "His Enemy Is the World", editorial, *New York Times*, 17 August 1990, p. A 28.
81   "The thief of Baghdad", editorial, *Sunday Times*, 5 August 1990, Sect. 3, p. 7.
82   "Lest we forget", editorial, *Sunday Times*, 16 September 1990, Sect. 3, p. 7.
83   "The war dividend", editorial, *Sunday Times*, 13 January 1991, Sect. 3, p. 7.

1991. Only the *Sunday Times* returned to this subject during the Gulf Crisis and War. To sum up, the *Washington Post*, on the American side, and the *Times*, on the British side, stood out from the other newspapers selected for this study in that they did not seem to devote editorials to Saddam Hussein's description as an Angel of Darkness.

Regarding opinion articles published in the American press, many columnists, particularly in the *Washington Post*, frequently described the Iraqi leader as the symbol of Evil during the Gulf Crisis and War. On the British side, it was mainly the Sunday newspapers that insisted on the tendency of the Iraqi leader to do evil, but more moderately than the American dailies. Interestingly, opinion articles published in the *Times* did not repeat the comparison between Saddam Hussein and the devil. The British newspaper, which considered itself as a newspaper of reference, may have considered these comparisons unworthy of its readers.

In any event, by depicting the Iraqi leader as a demon, the editorialists of the *New York Times*, on the American side, and of the *Guardian* and Sunday papers, on the British side, as well as journalists of opinion articles in American dailies, the *Guardian*[84] and British Sunday papers gave their comments a moralistic tone. Their words were also tinged with biblical imagery. In addition to likening the president of Iraq to "Satan" in the *New York Times*, he was described as the "Beast of Baghdad" in the *Washington Post*. Suggestive expressions, namely the qualifiers "harmful" and

---

84    David Hirst, "Arafat's dance with the devil", op-ed, *Guardian*, 23 August 1990, p. 19. The journalist likened Saddam Hussein to the devil in the title of his article.

"evil", were used to portray Saddam Hussein in British editorials and opinion articles. In addition, he symbolized the "forces of evil" for the *Sunday Times* and the "forces of darkness" for the *Observer*, which also compared him to a "demon". According to the translators of the Jerusalem Bible, "Satan denotes the Adversary, by antonomasia, among devils and demons".[85] Satan, leader of demons in the Jewish and Christian tradition, is the fallen Angel who transgressed God's law and thus brought about his damnation. As for the "Beast of Baghdad",[86] does it not replace the Beast of Revelation? The driving forces and purpose of the arguments of the editorialists of the *New York Times*, on the American side, the *Guardian* and Sunday newspapers, on the British side, as well as the journalists of opinion articles of American dailies, the *Guardian* and British Sunday papers were similar. Comparing the enemy to Satan or a demon highlighted his depravity and made him appear as a fundamentally evil, who had to be fought. For the purposes of demonizing Saddam Hussein, he was referred to as the "face of the devil" and the "bad guy on duty".[87] The Iraqi president was presented as the Spirit of Evil and as such had become a scourge for the world of journalists and their readers. This Prince of darkness, a source of disorder

---

85    Jean Chevalier & Alain Gheerbrant, *op. cit.*, p. 846.
86    The designation "Beast" also referred to the novel by William Golding, *Lord of the Flies*. In the book, the "Beast" is symbolized by a pig's head stuck on a stake which attracts flies and crystallizes the fears of the children left to themselves on an island. The allegorical title of the work is the translation of Beelzebud, which means in Hebrew "Lord of the flies" and is synonymous with Satan (William Golding, *Lord of the Flies*, London: Faber and Faber, 2005, 225 p.; Margaret Drabble, ed., *The Oxford Companion to English Literature*, Oxford: Oxford UP, pp. 81, 595; also see Adrian Room, rev., *Brewer's Dictionary of Phrase & Fable*, London: Cassell & Co, 2002, p. 110).
87    Anne Morelli, *op. cit*, p. 21.

and chaos and a symbol of the power of evil, represented a threat and had to be overcome by the forces of Good. They embodied civilization, namely a universe in which order reigned and to which the editorialists and journalists in question, as well as their readers, belonged. In essence, in editorials and opinion articles, the enemy, the Other, the figure of evil par excellence, and the civilized world of journalists were opposed in a simplistic, exaggerated and reductive way.

In his speeches and press conferences, George Bush also gave a Manichean vision of the situation in the Persian Gulf by opposing Good, namely the coalition, to Evil, i.e. the opposing side.[88] Similarly, Margaret Thatcher stated in November 1990 that "evil has to be stopped".[89] For John Major, the president of Iraq was "a thorough force for evil in his actions".[90]

Whereas Saddam Hussein's assimilation to an evil power was repeatedly addressed in the editorials of the *Sunday Times* during the Gulf Crisis and War, this was not the case in the readers' letters published in the Sunday paper. The readers of this newspaper or of American dailies did not seem in their letters to have subscribed

---

88   For instance, refer to Bush's remarks to officers and troops at Hickam Air Force Base in Pearl Harbor, Hawaii on 28 October 1990 (<https://bush41library.tamu.edu/archives/public-papers/2369>, consulted 29 September 2022).

89   Refer to the joint press conference with President Bush in Paris on 19 November 1990 (<https://www.margaretthatcher.org/document/108248>, consulted 29 September 2022).

90   Refer to John Major's statement on the Gulf War to the House of Commons on 15 January 1991 (<https://johnmajorarchive.org.uk/1991/01/15/mr-majors-commons-statement-on-the-gulf-war-15-january-1991/>, consulted 29 September 2022).

to this analogy, suggesting that the impact of editorials on the readership on this subject was only limited.

All in all, it should thus be remembered that, except for the *Times* and readers' letters published in the American press, which did not mention it, the editorials of the *New York Times* and the opinion articles of both American dailies and those of the *Guardian*, the *Sunday Times* and the *Observer* referred to the realm of hell where Saddam Hussein and the "Beast" served to highlight the darkness of this evil spirit. These assimilations, published from August 1990 onwards and irregularly repeated until early March 1991, gave the journalists' discourse a moralizing tone and echoed the comments of George Bush, Margaret Thatcher and John Major.

In the same vein somewhat, some editorialists and journalists' comments on both sides of the Atlantic took on a religious orientation. For example, in its editorials, the *Times* maintained that the Iraqi president "is a bad Muslim [who] has no religious authority whatever for declaring jihad"[91] referring to Saddam Hussein's call for jihad on 10 August 1990. As for opinion articles, William Safire of the *New York Times* described Saddam Hussein as an "unholy man"[92] in October 1990, and in November 1990 called him "a messianic nuclear aggressor".[93] To associate the term "aggressor" with the adjective "messianic" constituted something of an oxymoron, as the first word described an individual negatively,

---

91    "Saddam's bogus appeal", editorial, *Times*, 7 February 1991, p. 11.
92    William Safire, "Of Stones and Walls", op-ed, *New York Times*, 11 October 1990, p. A 25.
93    William Safire, "The Second Front", op-ed, *New York Times*, 1 November 1990, p. A 29.

and the second term referred to the belief in the coming of the Messiah and the birth of a better world. The association thus enabled the journalist to ridicule the president of Iraq. For its part, the *New York Times* published a letter in January 1991 describing Saddam Hussein as "a messianic ruler",[94] repeating the same term used by William Safire a few months earlier. This adjective "messianic" was neither used by the American president nor by the British Prime Minister in their speeches or communiqués during the Gulf Crisis and the war itself.

In general, there are few articles containing biblical references published during the Gulf Crisis and War. The religious allusions only served to illustrate another facet of the Iraqi leader's personality. Saddam Hussein was described as an unholy leader, which again implied his difference from journalists who would share the same values as those of their readers, namely peace and love of one's neighbour. However, what was more striking was the irony used by the journalists in question to depict Saddam Hussein. Through their moralistic and their religious-oriented discourse, they tried to impose a dualistic conception of the world with, on the one hand, the genius of evil incarnated by the Iraqi president and, on the other hand, the world of journalists and of course their readers. Once again, it was a technique, like that of the official powers, for demonizing the enemy leader. The pattern applied by the press on either side of the Atlantic followed classical mechanisms inherent to all propaganda. The question of whether or not journalists acted in good faith was not at the centre of the reflection that was initiated in this work. The fact is that the way

---

94    Leo Treitler, "Winning Is Losing", letters, *New York Times*, 27 January 1991, p. E 16.

their rhetoric and views were expressed in editorials and opinion articles was extravagant.

## 2.5    Saddam Hussein and the dictators of the past

### 2.5.1  Hitler

As has already been said, Saddam Hussein was often described in the press as a dictator; it was thus normal that newspapers tried to situate him in relation to the great dictators of the past. He was in particular compared to Adolf Hitler. Nevertheless, the analysis of the few editorials published in the American press showed that the *New York Times* and the *Washington Post* criticized this comparison of the Iraqi leader with the Nazi leader by the Bush administration[95] in November 1990. On the British side, however, the situation was more contrasted: whereas the *Times* did not use this comparison in its editorials, the *Guardian* and the Sunday newspapers did. For example, the Sunday newspapers further accentuated this interpretation of Saddam Hussein. He was not only described as a modern-day Hitler, but also referred to as the "Führer". The *Sunday Times* in particular relished describing Iraq's leader as the new Hitler from August 1990 to March

---

95    On 23 October 1990 George Bush stated that "we're dealing with Hitler revisited, a totalitarianism and a brutality that is naked and unprecedented in modern times" (<https://bush41library.tamu.edu/archives/public-papers/2352>, consulted 3 October 2022). In his speeches, the American president took up this analogy ten times in October 1990 and six times in November 1990.

1991.[96] In addition, in the catchy title of the editorial published in the *Observer* on 5 August 1990, "Why this Hitler of the Gulf has to go",[97] the simple present as well as the expression "have to" gave the utterance a peremptory tone. Not only did this editorial compare Saddam Hussein to Hitler five times, but it also referred to the occupation of Kuwait as an "Anschluss". The repetition of the Nazi leader's name in the title and text of the editorial made the article expressive and lively. This repetition, a process of dramatizing the discourse, not only aroused the reader's interest, but also emphasized the persuasive effect. By constantly holding forth on the comparison between the Iraqi leader and Hitler, the editorial thus exaggerated the portrait of Saddam Hussein to better strike the reader's mind.

The following remarks ensue from the previous paragraph. First, when the American newspapers mentioned the comparison between the Iraqi president and the Nazi leader, they did so to condemn as unworthy the attitude of their government, which paralleled Saddam Hussein and Hitler. This may be the reason why they devoted only a few editorials to this subject. Second, on the British side, the *Sunday Times* stood out from other newspapers in that it was the newspaper that most often compared Saddam Hussein to Hitler.

Concerning the opinion articles, we noted that whether in the op-eds of the *New York Times* or those of the *Washington Post*,

---

96   For instance: "From what we know of President Saddam, like Hitler before him, he will go on taking what does not belong to him until somebody stops him". "The thief of Baghdad", editorial, *Sunday Times*, 5 August 1990, Sect. 3, p. 7.

97   "He is as cunning as Hitler; the world *is* facing another Hitler". "Why this Hitler of the Gulf has to go", editorial, *Observer*, 5 August 1990, p. 12.

the comparison between the Iraqi leader and Hitler provoked a heated debate in both dailies during the Gulf Crisis and the war itself. Furthermore, the majority of opinion articles published by the *Washington Post* rejected the comparison between Saddam Hussein and Hitler used by President Bush.

In the British press, all the newspapers also debated, in their opinion pieces, the parallel drawn between Saddam Hussein and Hitler right from the start of the Gulf Crisis. For instance, in the *Guardian*, David Hirst called the Iraqi leader "the new Hitler for the West"[98] and also described the invasion of Kuwait as an "Anschluss".[99] The emphatic vocabulary with a strong dramatic connotation was above all intended to bring back to the minds of some readers the horrors of the Second World War. In both the American and British press, Saddam Hussein's identification with Hitler was magnified by multiple references to the Second World War, suggested for example by the concept of the policy of 'appeasement' or a reference to the Munich Agreement, which was intended to remind readers of historical precedents. According to Ghassan Salamé, the main purpose of this "hasty, historically false and politically dangerous assimilation with Hitler" was to prevent any negotiated solution to the conflict, since "if the Iraqi leader was a Hitler, any negotiated solution was no more

---

98    David Hirst, "Saddam's gift and his gamble", op-ed, *Guardian*, 16 August 1990, p. 19.
99    David Hirst, "A lion among the gazelles", op-ed, *Guardian*, 3 August 1990, p. 17. Like the substantives "Führer" and "Anschluss" in the editorial of the *Observer* published in August 1990, the use of German words reflected the journalist's linguistic and historical knowledge as he assumed that his reader was equally familiar with the language.

than a Munich".[100] With regard to the Sunday newspapers, the *Sunday Times* allowed journalists and contributors to express divergent views on Saddam Hussein's assimilation to the Nazi leader throughout the Crisis and the Gulf War. Like the *Sunday Times* which was the scene of a passionate debate on this point between journalists and contributors, so was the *Observer*, but to a lesser extent.

In short, opinion articles published on both sides of the Atlantic sparked a democratic debate in this area with articles expressing different opinions published from August 1990 until March 1991, apart from the *Guardian*, whose analogy was endorsed by a journalist, and of the *Observer* which was only interested in the parallel between Hussein and Hitler in October and November 1990. Regarding the editorials published in both the American and British press, we noted that whereas American dailies criticized, in a limited number of editorials, Saddam Hussein's identification with Hitler by their government, the *Guardian*, the *Sunday Times* and the *Observer* endorsed it. The British press was therefore more partisan than the American press on this point. Nevertheless, the *Times* stood out from the other British newspapers by not mentioning it in its editorials, a possible sign that it did not intend to lower itself to this type of comparison.

As regards readers' letters, we noted in essence that the readers of the *New York Times* and those of the British Sunday newspapers compared Saddam Hussein with a new Hitler right from the start

---

100    Ghassan Salamé, "Le Golfe: nuages après la tempête", *Politique étrangère*, No. 2, été 1991, p. 458.

of the crisis since these analogies were found in letters published in August and September 1990. By contrast, there did not seem to be letters referring to this question during the armed conflict. It should be remembered that the editorials of the *New York Times* and those of the *Washington Post* only briefly addressed this issue in order to discredit the attitude of the Bush administration. Given that readers whose letters were published in the *New York Times* referred to the comparison between Saddam Hussein and Hitler, it can be assumed that they had formed their own opinion on the basis of sources of information other than the editorials of these newspapers. The situation was different for the British reader of the *Sunday Times* as the Sunday newspaper returned to the analogy between the president of Iraq and Hitler over and over again. The reader might have thus been influenced by the editorials of the *Sunday Times* and subscribed to the opinion expressed in the articles published in the Sunday paper.

In summary, the comparison between the Iraqi president and the Nazi leader was the subject of discussions in numerous articles in both the American and British press. As far as editorials are concerned, the opinions expressed were clear-cut, namely, on the one hand, the criticism of American dailies against the analogy established by the Bush administration and, on the other hand, support for the comparison in British Sunday newspapers but no mention of this topic in the *Times*. As for opinion articles, Saddam Hussein's description as a new Hitler was at the centre of a controversy among journalists and contributors, some subscribing to the comparison and others criticizing it.

In this regard, one might wonder whether the analogy between an enemy leader and the Nazi dictator was not a somewhat reductive rhetoric. In addition to his representation as a model of absolute evil in the collective imagination, it was above all for those who formed the opinion an effective way to demonize the adversary "as a classical propaganda process",[101] in order to convince, *a fortiori* in a democracy, a public opinion supposedly reluctant to see its country going to war. Thus, according to Anne Morelli, the reader needs clearly identified "good" and "bad" characters, and "the most simplistic way is to treat the current "bad guy" as the new Hitler".[102]

## 2.5.2 Other dictators

In addition to the assimilation of the Iraqi leader to the German dictator, newspapers on both sides of the Atlantic referred to other statesmen who have marked the history of mankind. In this section, we deliberately chose not to follow the order defined at the beginning of the chapter, that is to say the analysis by type of articles, but rather to propose an inventory of personalities referred to in the American and British newspapers. In order to describe Saddam Hussein's personality, the American press and the British press mentioned the following statesmen:[103] Nebuchadnezzar, Saladin, Bismarck, Mao, Mussolini, Stalin, Nasser and Noriega. For the sake of consistency, the leaders who appeared in both the USA and the UK will be examined first, and then those mentioned in the press on only one side or the other of the Atlantic.

---

101    Béatrice Cormier-Rodier, "La Guerre du Golfe à la télévision", *in* Béatrice Fleury-Vilatte (dir.), *op. cit.*, p. 88.

102    Anne Morelli, *op. cit.*, p. 25.

103    The statesmen have been classified in historical order.

First, a comparison mentioned in the press on both sides of the Atlantic concerned Nebuchadnezzar, the king of Babylon whose reign marked the apogee of the neo-Babylonian Empire in the first century BC. American and British journalists expressed antagonistic viewpoints concerning the assimilation of the president of Iraq with Nebuchadnezzar. While, on the American side, the tone was moderate regarding Saddam Hussein's claimed parallel with the king of Babylon, the British press ridiculed the Iraqi leader for having made this claim. In addition, Walter Laqueur,[104] in the *Washington Post*, referred to Nebuchadnezzar II, whereas journalists[105] on the British side mentioned Nebuchadnezzar without further explanation. It is likely that it was the same king. Nevertheless, Walter Laqueur showed greater historical erudition insofar as Nebuchadnezzar I and Nebuchadnezzar II existed in the first century BC. But if the first was king of Nineveh, the second reigned over Babylon and was a king builder par excellence. In any event, this remark shows the lack of verification of this comparison by the contributors of articles published in the British press.

The identification that also appeared in the American and British press referred to Saddam Hussein's comparison of himself with Saladin, the sultan of Egypt and Syria in the 12th century. On the American side, the Israeli author, Yossi Melman,[106] as well as

---

104   "His great hero is Nebuchadnezzar II". Walter Laqueur, "Like Hitler, but Different", op-ed, *Washington Post*, 31 August 1990, p. A 27.

105   For instance: Hazhir Teimourian, "Biblical despot with chemical arms", op-ed, *Times*, 13 August 1990, p. 10. Martin Woollacott, "Now it's dawning on the people", op-ed, *Guardian*, 6 September 1990, p. 19.

106   Yossi Melman, "Why Israel May Show its Nuclear Hand", op-ed, *New York Times*, 6 August 1990, p. A 13. Yossi Melman is co-author with Dan

Rowland Evans and Robert Novak[107] were ironic, the former in the *New York Times*, and the latter in the *Washington Post*, about this analogy. Likewise, in the British press, an editorial published in the *Times* in February 1991[108] demolished this identification. Since the other British newspapers did not seem to refer to it, the daily paper was therefore the only British newspaper to repeat Margaret Thatcher's remarks. On 6 September 1990, she mocked Saddam Hussein in the House of Commons for thinking of himself as "a latter-day Saladin".[109] As for readers, we found only one letter[110] published in the *New York Times* relating to the analogy with Saladin. It may be assumed that, in view of the sultan's qualities of generosity and bravery, as well as his chivalrous personality, which earned him a great reputation in the Christian world, the reader, journalists and contributors considered this comparison inappropriate.

Concerning the comparison with Mussolini, George F. Will and Walter Laqueur[111] in the *Washington Post* highlighted the difference between the Iraqi leader's personality and that of the

Raviv of *Every Spy a Prince: The Complete History of Israel's Intelligence Community* published in 1990.

107    Rowland Evans and Robert Novak, "Overkill on Saddam", op-ed, *Washington Post*, 8 August 1990, p. A 21.

108    "Unlike Saladin, with whom he likes to compare himself, he is not chivalrous". "Saddam's bogus appeal", editorial, *Times*, 7 February 1991, p. 11.

109    Refer to the following website: <https://publications.parliament.uk/pa/cm198990/cmhansrd/1990-09-06/Debate-1.html>, consulted 4 October 2022.

110    "President Hussein does not measure up to the great Saladin". M. T. Mehdi, "The New Saladin?", letters, *New York Times*, 23 September 1990, p. E 20.

111    George F. Will, "Wolf Out of Babylon", op-ed, *Washington Post*, 3 August 1990, p. A 23; Walter Laqueur, "Like Hitler, but Different", op-ed, *Washington Post*, 31 August 1990, p. A 27.

Italian dictator whose charisma enabled him to obtain strong popular support in the 1930s. By contrast, Michael Howard[112] of the *Times* saw a similarity between the attack on Ethiopia and the invasion of Kuwait by Iraqi troops. The cultural context was different on both sides of the Atlantic: more general on the American side and more specific on the British side. In addition to this observation, it should also be noted that these articles published in both the American and British press were from internationally renowned and authoritative figures in their field.[113]

The press, on either side of the Atlantic, also compared the Iraqi leader with Stalin. For A.M. Rosenthal, Stalin was Saddam Hussein's role model.[114] In the British press, only the Sunday newspapers mentioned the analogy with the Soviet politician in their opinion pieces. It goes without saying that the president of Iraq shared many characteristics with Stalin who, in order to gain power after Lenin's death in 1924, ousted his rivals and developed the cult of personality based on repression.

As with the comparison between Mussolini and Saddam Hussein, the American view on the parallel between the president of Iraq and Gamal Abdel Nasser is more or less opposed to that

---

112 "[Mussolini's] attack on Abyssinia in 1935 provides a far more appropriate analogy". Sir Michael Howard, "Gulf: no time for sanctions to bite", op-ed, *Times*, 2 January 1991, p. 10.
113 Walter Laqueur was the chairman of the International Research Council at the Center for Strategic and International Studies in Washington until 2000, and Michael Howard was Professor of Modern History at Oxford University and Professor of Naval and Military History at Yale University.
114 A.M. Rosenthal, "Soldiers in the Sands", op-ed, *New York Times*, 12 August 1990.

of the British press.[115] Nevertheless, the reference to the Egyptian statesman was an exception in the American press (a single occurrence in an article of the *New York Times*). By contrast, it appeared in the *Guardian* and was preponderant in the *Sunday Times*, for which it was perhaps a way of highlighting its national, and even nationalistic, side. It is also true that only the British reader could find resonances of the Suez Crisis in the Gulf Crisis. The Suez Crisis had not only been disastrous for the British, "precipitating the end of Prime Minister Anthony Eden's career",[116] but it was also one of the early signs of the dissolution of the British Empire in 1956. As to why the *Sunday Times*, among other British newspapers, published several articles comparing the Iraqi leader to the Egyptian president, one could explain this by the fact that the *Sunday Times*, although moderate in its first comments on the Suez Crisis, offered stalwart support to Eden during Operation Musketeer which was launched in October 1956 following the nationalization of the Suez Canal by Nasser in July of that year.[117] The Suez Crisis also witnessed a formidable display of the British armed forces. The *Sunday Times* thus reminded the reader of Britain's once central role on the international stage and showed the Gulf Crisis through the prism of illusory and outdated grandeur.

Regarding the other references, while Saddam Hussein was compared to Nebuchadnezzar, Saladin, Mussolini, Stalin and Nasser in both the American and British press, there were

---

115   However, Paul Wilkinson (1937-2011) in the *Guardian* made moderate comments on this subject and speculated upon Saddam Hussein's beliefs when he wrote: "[Saddam Hussein] may believe that war now gives him a real chance to gain glory as a new Nasser". Paul Wilkinson, "A way to avoid the no-win war", op-ed, *Guardian*, 3 January 1991, p. 15.

116   Axel Delmotte, *op. cit.*, p. 82; also refer to Bernard Cottret, *op. cit.*, p. 393.

117   Roy Greenslade, *op. cit.*, p. 135.

references to specific politicians in the American press that were not mentioned in the British press in accordance with different cultural areas. For example, only the *New York Times* compared Saddam Hussein with Bismarck. Whereas the president of Iraq claimed to be the saviour of Arab people, Bismarck was one of the main architects of German unification in 1871. It is likely that Walter Russell Mead's deprecating allusion,[118] in the daily newspaper, to the founder of the German Empire in the 19th century was intended to mock the Iraqi leader who saw himself as "the aspiring leader of the Arab world".[119] It is strange that the British press did not compare the Iraqi ruler with the German statesman in view of the fundamental role played by Bismarck in Europe. This absence in the British newspapers could be explained by the fact that the 1870-71 war between France and Germany was of less interest to England than France.

While the reference to Bismarck appeared in the *New York Times*, that alluding to Mao and his dictatorial methods was mentioned in the *Washington Post*.[120] Although the parallel between the Iraqi leader and the president of the Chinese People's Republic until 1959 seemed to refer to the police structure of the Iraqi state, we can somewhat doubt the validity of this comparison. Mao Zedong was indeed the founder of Communist China, whereas Kurds, communists and Shia Muslims underwent a bloody and

---

118  "Saddam Hussein is nobody's candidate for the Bismarck of Arabia". Walter Russell Mead, "Germany and Japan – Dragging their Boots", op-ed, *New York Times*, 3 February 1991, p. E 19. Walter Russell Mead is an American academic.
119  Robert Fisk, *op. cit.*, p. 194.
120  "[Saddam Hussein] and the other rulers have refined a system of control and intimidation that resembles that of Stalin and Mao". Daniel Pipes, "What Kuwait Was Like", op-ed, *Washington Post*, 9 August 1990, p. A 23.

ruthless repression during Saddam Hussein's "twenty-four-year rule".[121] The allusions to the German and Chinese statesmen were an exception to the extent that only two articles, one published in the *New York Times* and the other in the *Washington Post*, referred to them.

Finally, it should be noted that the comparison between Saddam Hussein and Manuel Noriega was not used in the British press as it could only really make sense to American readers. This parallel between the Iraqi leader and the Panamanian dictator certainly reminded them of the operation "Just Cause" in December 1989 which led to the deposition of General Noriega.

In short, American journalists stood out from their British counterparts by drawing a parallel with Bismarck, but also Mao Zedong and General Noriega of Panama, who were not alluded to in the British press. By way of summary, the synthesis table on the next page also indicates the months in which the comparisons with the following statesmen were first made.

What is immediately striking in this table is that, except for a letter to the editor published in the *New York Times* relating to Saddam Hussein's designation as Saladin, there seemed to be no other readers' letters that referred to the above-mentioned personalities. Did this mean that readers were not persuaded of the relevance of these comparisons in editorials and opinion articles published in the American press and the British press? While it was certainly unlikely that readers lacked historical knowledge of these historical figures, they might not have deemed

---

121    Robert Fisk, *op. cit.*, p. 202.

it appropriate to express their views on the matter or perhaps newspapers chose not to publish letters on the subject.

We also noted that the American press did not devote editorials to the comparison of the Iraqi leader with characters from History.

| | Nebuchadnezzar | Saladin | Bismarck | Mao | Mussolini | Stalin | Nasser | Noriega |
|---|---|---|---|---|---|---|---|---|
| NYT ed | | | | | | | | |
| NYT op-ed | | August | February | | | August/November | January | August |
| NYT letters | | September | | | | | | |
| WP ed | | | | | | | | |
| WP op-ed | August | August | | August | August | August | | August |
| Times ed | | February | | | | | | |
| Times op-ed | August | | | | January | | | |
| Guardian ed | September | | | | | | | |
| Guardian op-ed | | | | | | | January | |
| ST ed | | | | | | | December | |
| ST op-ed | | | | | | August/March | August | |
| Observer ed | | | | | | | | |
| Observer op-ed | | | | | | February | | |

We may assume that the editorial staff did not find it useful to publish editorials on this topic. As for the British press, references to Saladin and Nasser in the editorials of the *Times* and the *Sunday Times* were made for the former only during the Gulf War and for the latter only at the end of the Gulf Crisis. In other words, these references seemed to hold a less prominent place in the image of the Iraqi leader presented to readers since editorialists did not refer to them in August 1990 whereas they mentioned the other facets of Saddam Hussein's personality from the beginning of the Gulf Crisis.

As regards opinion articles published on both sides of the Atlantic, the comparisons between the Iraqi leader and statesmen featured mostly in the American press in August 1990. For example, in the *Washington Post*, journalists identified Saddam Hussein with Nebuchadnezzar, Saladin, Mao, Mussolini, Stalin and Noriega only in August 1990, which meant that the portrait of the Iraqi leader was determined at the beginning of the Gulf Crisis and his image no longer evolved in the American daily about his identification with these politicians. In the British press, the situation was more nuanced in that, on the one hand, there were slightly fewer analogies with politicians than in American opinion articles, and, on the other hand, a minority of them were carried out in August 1990 and then sporadically during the Gulf Crisis, which made it impossible to reach a satisfactory conclusion by newspaper. Besides, the *Observer*, for example, was an exception since the only comparison with a statesman, i.e. with Stalin, was only mentioned in February 1991.

In conclusion, Saddam Hussein's comparisons with Nebuchadnezzar, Saladin, Mussolini, Stalin and Nasser were used in the press on both sides of the Atlantic, and those relating to Bismarck, Mao and Noriega appeared only in the American dailies. The comparison of the Iraqi leader with the Italian and Egyptian statesmen was treated differently in the American and British newspapers. Whereas American journalists highlighted the difference between Saddam Hussein and these leaders, British journalists emphasized the similarity between the invasion of Abyssinia by the Italian Duce compared to that of Kuwait and that between the Iraqi leader and the Egyptian colonel. Concerning Saddam Hussein's identification with Saladin, both the American and British press seemed to agree: the American press dealt with it ironically and only the *Times*, on the British side, underlined, like Margaret Thatcher, the difference between the Iraqi leader and the king of Babylon. As for the analogy with Mao in particular, it was the similarity between the control structures in the two countries that were highlighted. It should also be noted that the majority of parallels between the Iraqi president and the departed statesmen were mentioned in both the American and British press in August 1990, with the exception of the *Observer*, which only referred to Stalin in an opinion piece published in February 1991. Lastly, readers did not seem interested in mentioning these heads of state, since there was only one letter on the subject in the *New York Times*.

From the above, it may be inferred that, on either side of the Atlantic, editorialists, journalists and contributors resorted to the same persuasive method using cultural data tailored to the public in question. Editorialists and journalists repeatedly reminded their readers of the heads of state of past dictatorships, whether they be Stalin in the American and British press, Nasser especially in the British press, or Noriega and Mao more specifically in the

American press. They probably wanted to strike their readers and even instil fear of the Iraqi ruler in them. What was certain was that their aim was to persuade readers of Saddam Hussein's abject character and villainy, and describe him as someone who, like some of the previous tyrants, was able to stoop to the worst ignominy. All in all, after insisting on the darkest sides of the Iraqi president's personality from August 1990 onwards by comparing him to Hitler, editorialists and journalists continued to tarnish the image of the leader of Iraq by mentioning the heroes with whom Saddam Hussein identified himself to highlight the absurdity of his claims (the identification with Saladin, for example).

# Conclusion

Editorials, opinion articles and letters to the editor published in the American and British newspapers from August 1990 to mid-March 1991 showed that the enemy facing the United States and the United Kingdom was not Iraq or the Iraqis, who were described as unlucky and innocent, but Saddam Hussein, the leader of Iraq. Generally, the American and British press (apart from the *Times*) highlighted the suffering endured by the Iraqis under their president's regime and differentiated the Iraqi president from his people as early as August 1990, and even before the American and British governments did so.

The enemy identified in this way was repeatedly called by his first name during the Gulf Crisis and War in the editorials of the *Washington Post* and the British press. This was also the case in op-eds published in both countries as well as in letters sent in by British readers. This practice reflected a certain effrontery, and even an attempt to portray Saddam Hussein as a wayward child, but above all it showed a lack of respect on the part of journalists and readers for Saddam Hussein's presidential office. It was essentially a way of stigmatizing the enemy.

Journalists on both sides of the Atlantic also described him virulently with expressions from the lexical fields of crime in editorials and opinion articles and of war in opinion pieces. From editorials to op-eds, Saddam Hussein's portrait was defined as early as August 1990 and his image hardly changed until mid-March 1991 since the majority of the qualifiers used to describe the Iraqi leader appeared in August 1990. Similar designations to portray him were repeated during the Gulf Crisis and War, giving a negative image of the adversary. This image corresponded to that conveyed by the American and British authorities in their speeches. The perception of the Iraqi leader by readers of newspapers on both sides of the Atlantic echoed his presentation in editorials and op-eds. Saddam Hussein's portrait was fixed in the letters from the start of the Gulf Crisis and remained unchanged until after the end of the conflict. There was an inflationary use of vocabulary to portray the Iraqi leader as a terrifying, monstrous and dangerous enemy. Editorialists and journalists thus offered a Manichean vision of the world with, on the one hand, the "good guys" represented by journalists and their readers and, on the other hand, the "bad guy" in the person of Saddam Hussein.

Although marginal in Saddam Hussein's portrayal, his characterization as a madman appeared in the press on both sides of the Atlantic. Whereas the American press did not address this subject in its editorials, this was not the case in the British press, which referred to the Iraqi leader's alleged madness in its editorials during the Gulf Crisis. American opinion articles referred extensively to the poor mental state of the Iraqi president during the same period. On the British side, only a few journalists highlighted the Iraqi president's mental disorder from August 1990 to mid-March 1991. There were almost no letters about Saddam Hussein's psychological state in the American or British press. The question of the "madness" of the Iraqi leader was ultimately of little significance in the portrait drawn by editorialists and journalists. In fact, it was not addressed in the speeches of the American president. But when editorials in the British press and opinion articles on both sides of the Atlantic addressed the psychological profile of the Iraqi leader, their aim was to demonize the enemy. There was again the simplistic and reductive antagonism between Good on the one hand, namely "normal" and "civilized" journalists and Evil on the other hand, i.e. Saddam Hussein, the demented being responsible for the Gulf Crisis and War.

Saddam Hussein's comparison with wild animals was also anecdotal. Only a few editorials and opinion articles published in the American and British press resorted to animal vocabulary to describe the Iraqi president during the Gulf Crisis. Readers, for their part, do not seem to have used it in their letters. This was also the case with the American and British governments, which did not use an animal lexicon in their discourse. Borrowing terms from the lexical field of animals to describe Saddam Hussein was demeaning and presented him as a wild and ferocious beast. Above all, this process allowed editorialists and journalists to exaggerate the portrait of the Iraqi leader and tarnish his image. It served to strip the leader of Iraq of his presidential status and to convince the reader of the need to send troops to the Persian Gulf to conquer the dangerous beast. This strategy oversimplified reality which was divided, for journalists, into two distinct blocks, namely the intelligible world on the one hand and, on the other, the world of fierce wild animals represented by Saddam Hussein.

This caricatural and reductive opposition was amplified by Saddam Hussein's description as the embodiment of evil. Editorials in the *New York Times* and opinion articles in American newspapers and British Sunday newspapers portrayed the leader of Iraq as a demon, but the Sunday newspapers did so in a more moderate way than the American dailies. In order to demonize the Iraqi leader, editorialists and journalists assimilated the

Iraqi leader to an evil power from August 1990 until after the conflict, thereby giving their comments a moralizing and biblical tone. The goal was to persuade the reader of the evil character of Saddam Hussein and the merits of the United States and the United Kingdom entering the war. In so doing, editorialists and journalists followed in the footsteps of George Bush, Margaret Thatcher and John Major, who offered public opinion a Manichaean view of the situation in the Persian Gulf between the coalition forces representing Good and the forces of Evil led by Saddam Hussein.

In addition to the demonological terms, ironic rhetoric with religious overtones was used by a few editorialists and journalists on both sides of the Atlantic and by a reader of the *New York Times*. The objective was to denigrate the Iraqi leader described as an ungodly leader and to highlight the opposition between him and journalists and their readers. The articles in question, did not, however, reflect official statements and were an exception due to their limited number.

The portrait of the Iraqi leader reached a climax in the American and British press, which compared him to Hitler as early as August 1990. While editorials published in the two American dailies criticized the analogy drawn by the Bush administration, the situation was more contrasted on the British side: the *Times* did not address this subject and the Sunday newspapers endorsed this comparison, with the *Sunday Times* in particular repeatedly identifying the Iraqi leader as the new Hitler during the Gulf Crisis and War. Op-eds in the press on both sides of the Atlantic provided a forum for heated debate: some journalists and contributors of articles subscribed to this view while others disapproved of it. In general, Saddam Hussein's assimilation to Hitler was amplified by the use of German terms and references to the Second World War. Readers of the *New York Times* and Sunday British newspapers also portrayed the Iraqi president as the new Hitler from the beginning of the Gulf Crisis. Editorialists and journalists who chose to equate Saddam Hussein with Hitler followed the lead of the U.S. government. Their representation of Saddam Hussein, as a model of absolute evil in the collective imagination, was again a reductionist technique of demonizing the enemy.

Finally, in addition to the comparison of the Iraqi leader with Hitler, the American press and the British press, for the most part as early as August 1990, mentioned statesmen such as Nebuchadnezzar, Saladin, Bismarck, Mao, Mussolini, Stalin, Nasser and Noriega in their articles to describe Saddam Hussein's personality. However, the American press did not devote editorials to the parallel between the president of Iraq and the statesmen mentioned. The Iraqi president's analogy with the heads of state of Italy and Egypt was covered differently in American and British newspapers. The reference to Nasser was significant in the British press. Both the American and British press criticized the resemblance claimed by the Iraqi leader between himself and Saladin: American dailies were ironic about this, and the *Times* echoed the British Prime Minister's comments. Because of a different cultural context, only American op-eds drew a parallel between the Iraqi leader and Bismarck, Mao and Noriega. Readers of the newspapers selected for this study do not seem to have compared the Iraqi leader with the aforementioned statesmen. On the whole, journalists reminded their readers of these statesmen in order to colour Saddam Hussein's portrait.

The goal was to identify the personality of the enemy by referring to dictators and heads of state from the recent or distant past who were part of the collective memory. What better way than mentioning these statesmen of historical and legendary stature to persuade the reader of the magnitude of the peril represented by Saddam Hussein who, if not stopped, was likely to upset the world order.

As has already been said, the question of the analogy between Saddam Hussein and Hitler and of the mental state of the Iraqi leader sparked off fierce debate in op-eds published in the press on both sides of the Atlantic. Again, the press stimulated the democratic debate by publishing opinion articles which diverged from the editorial line of the respective newspapers and offered a plurality of points of view to readers. Similarly, the publication of readers' letters in newspapers in response to editorials, opinion articles or letters from other readers triggered the exchange of viewpoints and thus contributed to the proper functioning of the press in a democratic state. Democracy is indeed based on the existence of opponents and negotiations. The press, a pillar of democracy, is the ideal place for debate and dialogue between defenders of antagonistic positions.

As regards the specificity of newspapers, the *Times* did not devote editorials and opinion pieces to the distinction between the Iraqi leader and his people or to the likening between the president of Iraq and Satan. Likewise, the *Times* differed from other British newspapers by not dealing in its editorials with the analogy between Saddam Hussein and Hitler. Although it used animal vocabulary to portray Saddam Hussein, it is possible that the British newspaper favoured factual information free of pathos and therefore chose not to publish articles on the difference between the Iraqis and their president or those on irrational amalgams. As for the identification between the Iraqi president and Saladin, the *Times* criticized this comparison used by Saddam Hussein and, in so doing, repeated Margaret Thatcher's comments on the subject. On the other hand, the *Sunday Times* described the Iraqi leader as a madman, an evil power and as the new Hitler over and over during the Gulf Crisis and War. To this end, the Sunday newspaper used a strikingly familiar register in its articles. It also compared the Iraqi leader to Nasser on numerous occasions, fuelling a nationalist discourse as the Sunday newspaper reminded the reader of Britain's great power status in 1956.

The American and British press abounded in cultural references, whether literary, musical or cinematic, and in political allusions. In addition, the titles contained comments from editorialists, journalists and contributors. Thus, readers immediately grasped the author's reasoning and anticipated the conclusion of the article even before reading it. In other words, the title, in addition to its sensationalist role, elicited an "agnition" in the sense,[122] defined by Umberto Eco, of recognition of what the reader already knows. Moreover, in order to catch the readers' attention and gain their support, the titles of articles published in newspapers on both sides of the Atlantic used similar rhetorical devices and linguistic specificities. These included alliteration and assonance, the imperative mode and the interrogative form, puns,

---

122    Umberto Eco considers the denouement, indispensable to the detective
       novel, as a particular form of monodirectional agnition (Umberto Eco, *Il
       Superuomo Di Massa [The Mass Superman]*, Milan: Fabbri & Bompiani
       Sonzoguo, 1978). Also refer to Michel Morel, *op.cit.*, p. 356.

as well as the use of the personal pronoun and the first-person plural possessive adjective, which made it possible to include the reader and the enunciator and differentiate them from the Other.

The media discourse transformed the events into a narrative that began on 2 August 1990, following the invasion of Kuwait, and culminated in the war in January 1991. As in any story, the main character was presented to the reader. From the beginning of the Gulf Crisis, triggered by the Iraqi invasion, journalists portrayed the main character in a setting unknown to the reader. He was a stereotypical protagonist whose image was defined as early as August 1990 and hardly changed until March 1991: as the embodiment of evil, he was the object of virulent semantic attacks, animal, demonological and historical comparisons with enemies, archetypes of evil, including Hitler and Stalin. Journalists presented an adversary with an aggressive, even paranoid personality, characterized by a sense of superiority, excessive pride showing disdain for others and disrespect for human beings. In short, this enemy was not a civilized being. In addition, they also included references to atrocities committed during the Second World War. Journalistic rhetoric, which could on occasions be strikingly emphatic, often relayed the arguments and expressions of official discourse. In so doing, it reinforced the official ideology based on prejudice and a binary world view. The aim was to persuade readers of the odious personality of the main character and to guide them emotionally towards approving the sending of armed forces to the Persian Gulf. The journalistic discourse, made up of classical themes, became a caricature through repetition and exaggeration in the elaboration of the portrait of this Other, who quickly became the enemy.

# Part III:

## Image of the Other:
## Behaviour of the enemy

## Differences and similarities
## between the American press
## and the British press
## during the Gulf Crisis and War

# Chapter I:
# Abuses during the Gulf Crisis

## 1.1 The Iraqi invasion

From 2 August 1990, the event that dominated the news in editorials, opinion articles and letters to the editor published on both sides of the Atlantic was the invasion of Kuwait by the Iraqi army. The Iraqi government had never recognized the independence of Kuwait in 1961 nor the Iraqi-Kuwaiti border, which was the result of colonial divisions. It always regarded the Emirate as part of the Iraqi province of Basra. Moreover, given the location of the oilfields, Saddam Hussein maintained that Kuwait was extracting oil that belonged to Iraq.[1] But it was above all the fall in its oil revenues, following the drop in the price of a barrel of oil, which, diminishing Iraqi resources, led Iraq, after the war against Iran from 1980 to 1988, to invade Kuwait in order to avoid financial bankruptcy.[2] The Iraqi government blamed overproduction in Kuwait for falling oil prices. In addition to oil issues, Iraq asked the Kuwaiti Emirate to cancel the loans they had granted during the war between Iraq and Iran, which Kuwait refused to do. Finally, in order to improve its strategic position in the Gulf, Iraq claimed Warbah and Bubiyan Islands located in

---

1 Jean-Baptiste Duroselle & André Kaspi, *op. cit.*, p. 541.
2 Pierre-Jean Luizard, *La Question irakienne*, Paris: Fayard, 2002, pp. 143, 304. Also refer to the article by Amir Taheri: "Golfe Persique: Tempête sur l'Eldorado", *Politique internationale*, No. 49, automne 1990, p. 64. With an estimated external debt of more than 60 billion dollars, Iraq could no longer meet its current payments from its oil revenues alone.

Kuwaiti territory, the control of which would have enabled the Iraqi state to create a seaport.[3]

While Saddam Hussein justified the invasion of Kuwait for economic, historical and strategic reasons, it was presented to the American and British reader as the brutal act of an aggressor: like a criminal, the Iraqi leader was guilty of theft and a serious violation of the law. In its editorials published from August 1990 to early March 1991, the *New York Times* described the Iraqi invasion as "aggression" thirty-eight times. The *Washington Post*, for its part, used this term thirty-one times in its editorials published from August 1990 to February 1991. By describing the Iraqi invasion more often as an act of aggression, the *New York Times* was thus a little more virulent in its editorials than the *Washington Post*.

British editorials also called the Iraqi invasion of Kuwait "aggression". This designation appeared sixteen times in the *Times* from August 1990 to February 1991, six times in the *Guardian* in August and October 1990 and in January 1991, five times in the *Sunday Times* in August, September and December 1990, January and February 1991, and six times in the *Observer* in August and September 1990, January and February 1991. The *Times* therefore stood out from the other British newspapers by insisting in its editorials on the aggressive nature of Saddam Hussein's invasion of Kuwait. In general, the American press emphasized the violence of the Iraqi invasion more than the British press in its editorials because of the higher number of designations of the invasion as aggression.

---

3    Alain Gresh et Dominique Vidal, *Les 100 clés du Proche-Orient*, Paris: Hachette Littératures, 2003, p. 212.

Not only was the invasion referred to as aggression in editorials in the American and British press, but also repeatedly in opinion articles published on either side of the Atlantic. On the American side, this designation was used thirty-nine times in op-eds published in the *New York Times* from August 1990 to February 1991 and forty-five times in those of the *Washington Post* from August 1990 to early March 1991. In contrast to American editorials, journalists and contributors in the *Washington Post* were therefore slightly more scathing than those in the *New York Times*, given the greater number of times the Iraqi invasion was described as an act of aggression.

On the British side, the designation appeared twelve times in opinion pieces published in the *Times* in August and September 1990 as well as January 1991, five times in those of the *Guardian* in August 1990, January and February 1991, eight times in those of the *Sunday Times* in August 1990, October 1990 and January 1991, and four times in the *Observer* in August, September and November 1990 and January 1991. As in its editorials, the *Times* published more opinion pieces naming the invasion aggression than the *Guardian* and the Sunday papers. The *Sunday Times* differed from the *Observer* by publishing twice as many opinion pieces using this designation. The tone of journalists and contributors published in the *Times* and the *Sunday Times* was thus more caustic.

All in all, the term "aggression" was used more to describe the Iraqi army's invasion of Kuwait in the editorials and opinion articles published in the American press than in those of the British press. However, what did not change in both the American and British press was the constant repetition of this designation in editorials and op-eds published from August 1990 onwards during the Gulf Crisis and the war itself. This common characteristic reflected the editorial strategy of American and British editorialists and journalists. It enabled them to insist on the infamy of the actions of the Iraqi leader and to persuade the reader of the danger represented by this enemy. By constantly and insistently repeating the word "aggression" in their articles and sometimes several times within the same article, editorialists and journalists led the reader to become imbued with the word almost unintentionally. In the reader's mind there was thus an assimilation between "invasion" and "aggression" which, like an advertising slogan, marked the collective memory by its tone and rhythm.

As in editorials and opinion articles published on both sides of the Atlantic, the description of the Iraqi invasion as an act of aggression also dominated readers' letters in the American and British press. On the American side, for example, this designation was found in eight letters published in the *New York Times* in August, September and November 1990 as well as in February 1991, and in five letters published in the *Washington Post* in August, November and December 1990. On the British side, this designation appeared three times in letters published in the *Times* in August, September and November 1990, and in those of the *Guardian* in August 1990. A single letter referred to it in the *Sunday Times* in September 1990. The comparison was used in two letters published in the *Observer* in January 1991.

Editorialists, journalists and contributors of several opinion articles also used, in the American and British press, the expression "naked aggression" used by George Bush in his speeches on various occasions to describe the Iraqi invasion of Kuwait.[4] For example, this expression was used six times in the editorials of the *New York Times* in August and December 1990 as well as in January 1991. However, the *Washington Post* did not use the term in its editorials during the Gulf Crisis and the hostilities. On the British side, only an editorial in the *Sunday Times* on 13 January 1991 included this expression,[5] which was not mentioned by the other newspapers in their editorials.

Unlike its editorials, opinion articles in the *Washington Post* used this presidential phrase on many occasions, i.e. in August, September and November 1990. This expression was notably put in quotation marks by Charles Krauthammer, Rowland Evans and Robert Novak in their articles, which could suggest that the journalists distanced themselves from George Bush's remarks. But the analysis of the articles invalidated this hypothesis as the journalists quoting the U.S. president also shared his point of view. British newspapers did not seem to repeat George Bush's expression in their articles, except for Sir Anthony Parsons, the former British Ambassador to the United Nations from 1979 to 1982, whose article appeared in the *Times* on 3 August 1990.[6] The fact that Margaret Thatcher or John Major did not use the expression "naked aggression" in their speeches and press

---

4    For example, refer to Bush's exchange with reporters on the Iraqi invasion of Kuwait on 5 August 1990 (<https://bush41library.tamu.edu/archives/public-papers/2138>, consulted 8 October 2022). The British Prime Minister, whether it was Margaret Thatcher or John Major, did not use this expression at press conferences or in their speeches.

5    "The war dividend", editorial, *Sunday Times*, 13 January 1991, Sect. 3, p. 7.

6    Sir Anthony Parsons, "Sanctions are the world's only answer to Saddam", op-ed, *Times*, 3 August 1990, p. 10.

conferences could explain why British newspapers other than the *Times* or *the Sunday Times* did not repeat this phrase. Whether the newspapers' strategy was conscious or not, editorialists of the *New York Times* and the *Sunday Times* as well journalists and contributors of opinion articles in American dailies and the *Times*, on the British side, seemed to act as spokespersons for the U.S. government.

George Bush's expression for describing the Iraqi invasion can also be found in the letter from a reader of the *New York Times*[7] and in that from a reader of the *Observer*,[8] which shows the possible semantic impact of official speeches and the media on public opinion. Nevertheless, this observation concerns only these two examples, which does not allow us to conclude that this influence was widespread. Moreover, while the reader of the *New York Times* approved of the American president's policy and reaction towards Iraq, that of the *Observer* was ironic about George Bush's comments because of the intervention of American troops in Panama in December 1989.

Both the American and British press also compared the invasion of Kuwait to an adventure of the president of Iraq. Furthermore, American and British newspapers in editorials and opinion articles as well as many readers in the press on both sides of the Atlantic emphasized the violent and criminal nature of the Iraqi leader's invasion of Kuwait. They also insisted on the illegality of Saddam Hussein's act. So, the *New York Times* and

---

7    Michael DiGiacomo, "Negotiating an Iraqi Withdrawal Beats War. Chamberlain Lives", letters, *New York Times*, 18 November 1990, p. E 16.
8    Farzam Saleh, "Policy that gave Saddam power", letters, *Observer*, 12 August 1990, p. 42.

the *Times* in their editorials as well as some American and British journalists described the invasion repeatedly from August 1990 as a "violation of international law".[9] For example, one of Michael Ignatieff's articles stated in the *Observer* that this was "Saddam's third successive violation of international law".[10] This description also appeared in the speeches of the American president and the British Prime Minister.[11] It was true that, under the Charter of the United Nations,[12] the invasion and annexation of the Emirate were a violation of international law.

American and British newspapers also compared the invasion and occupation of Kuwait to a rape of the country, as did the U.S. president and Margaret Thatcher, who used this comparison in their speeches and press conferences.[13] The use of

---

9    For instance, "[...] to violate international law". "Iraq's naked villainy", editorial, *Times*, 3 August 1990, p. 11; "Outrageous violation of international order and decency". Tom Wicker, "Reacting to Iraq", op-ed, *New York Times*, 6 August 1990, p. A 13; "The invasion of Kuwait is a flagrant violation of international law". David Hirst, "A lion among the gazelles", op-ed, *Guardian*, 3 August 1990, p. 17.

10   Michael Ignatieff, "Mr Bush has missed an opportunity", op-ed, *Observer*, 17 February 1991, p. 19.

11   "Violation of international law". We find this phrase in George Bush's exchange with reporters on the Iraqi invasion of Kuwait on 3 August 1990 (<https://bush41library.tamu.edu/archives/public-papers/2135>), and at a joint press conference of the American president with Margaret Thatcher in Aspen, Colorado, on 2 August 1990 (<https://bush41library.tamu.edu/archives/public-papers/2124>, consulted 8 October 2022).

12   See appendix 4 for further information.

13   For example, George Bush's remarks at a Republican Campaign rally in Manchester, New Hampshire on 23 October 1990 (<https://bush41library.tamu.edu/archives/public-papers/2352>), as well as Margaret Thatcher's statement to the House of Commons on 7 November 1990 (<https://hansard.parliament.uk/Commons/1990-11-07/debates/73e4c301-ea20-4785-878d-7c744874e134/FirstDay?highlight=korea#contribution-2257c143-0c2d-4e06-b46d-c2734fb465f4>, consulted 10 October 2022).

this emotionally charged term certainly would undoubtedly have struck the reader's mind as it reinforced the image of Kuwait as a victim and emphasized the abject and transgressive nature of the invasion by the president of Iraq. In editorials published on both sides of the Atlantic and in opinion articles in American dailies and British Sunday newspapers, Saddam Hussein was thus portrayed as a criminal and a rapist and was perceived as such in two letters to the *Times* and the *Guardian*.[14] In his letter to the *Times* of 30 August 1990, the reader equated the Iraqi invasion with "a raping of an innocent state",[15] which tallied with the editorial line of the British newspaper. The writer of the letter was a Kuwaiti statesman who had been the first secretary of the Gulf Cooperation Council of Arab States from 1981. By sending a letter to the *Times* in August 1990 and another to the *Observer* in January 1991 describing the invasion as a "crime", this reader probably hoped to reach a wide audience by sending his letters to the British daily and the Sunday newspaper.[16] Apart from these letters, American and other British newspapers did not seem to have published readers' letters referring to the "rape of Kuwait". It is also possible that readers may not have found it useful to refer to it. On the American side, this would suggest that the impact of official rhetoric on readers was relative on this point. To sum up, American and British editorials as well as journalists and contributors of opinion articles in the American and British

---

14    "A Kuwait raped by his historical stepfather". John W. Deeley, "The crucial Palestinian link", letters, *Guardian*, 17 January 1991, p. 18.

15    Abdulla Y. Bishara, "UN diplomacy as Gulf option", letters, *Times*, 30 August 1990, p. 11.

16    It also shows that the British daily and the Sunday newspaper published the letters of distinguished well-known figures from all backgrounds. "The unpardonable crime of Saddam Hussein [...]". Abdulla Y. Bishara, "Just solution for the Gulf", letters, *Observer*, 13 January 1991, p. 46.

Sunday press repeated the comments of the American president and the British Prime Minister on this subject.

As a reminder of what has been said concerning the identification of Saddam Hussein with Hitler, multiple references to the Second World War punctuated articles published during the Gulf Crisis. For example, Jim Hoagland, in the *Washington Post* of 7 October 1990, described the invasion as "the Aug. 2 blitzkrieg"[17] referring to the offensive doctrine of the Third Reich at the beginning of the Second World War and in particular to Germany's invasion of Poland in 1939. In the British press, Conor Cruise O'Brien of the *Times* and an editorial in the *Guardian* compared the Iraqi invasion to the "aggression [against] Pearl Harbour".[18] The parallel between the Iraqi invasion and the attack by the Japanese air force against the American naval base at Pearl Harbor on 7 December 1941 only appeared in the British daily newspapers. Yet, it would have been legitimate to find this historical reference in the American press since this was, for American readers, a milestone in the history of their country. This air raid caused the United States to enter the Second World War. Another example of a historical reference is David Hirst's article in the *Guardian* on 3 August 1990, which likened the annexation of Kuwait to the "Anschluss",[19] that is to say Austria's annexation to Hitler's Germany on 12 March 1938. These references probably derived from readers' cultural factors to such an extent that the terms

---

17    Jim Hoagland, "A Quick Rewrite of History", op-ed, *Washington Post*, 7 October 1990, p. D 7.
18    Conor Cruise O'Brien, "Why Bush is treating Kuwait as a modern Pearl Harbour", op-ed, *Times*, 9 August 1990, p. 12; "Paying the price for past error", editorial, *Guardian*, 3 August 1990, p. 16.
19    "It is Anschluss". David Hirst, "A lion among the gazelles", op-ed, *Guardian*, 3 August 1990, p. 17.

such as "Anschluss" and "Blitzkrieg" had become part of everyday language. Journalists may also have relied on the evocative power of these expressions to resonate deeply with their readers. We can assume that they participated in the last world conflict or had a family member who took part in it. Besides, one could presume, like a reader of the *Sunday Times*, that the English were obsessed with their past and ignorant of their present.[20] Therefore, references to the Second World War may have stemmed from a colonial vision of a prestigious nation at the head of an empire in the 1930s and 1940s and which was still in the grip of imperial nostalgia in 1990-91.

Finally, we noted that, recalling the bestiary used by American editorialists and those of the *Times*, on the British side, as well as by some journalists on both sides of the Atlantic to describe Saddam Hussein, they also used verbs from the animal lexical field to depict the incursion into Kuwait by Iraq, which was personified by the Iraqi president. In this way, they painted the portrait of a human being similar to a hungry animal, having devoured its neighbour.

In this context, however, it is questionable why Iraq's invasion of Kuwait provoked a reaction of such magnitude and triggered a conflict between Iraq and a broad international coalition led by the United States. Other countries have been invaded without arousing such interest from the United States and the international community: this was the case, for example, of Lebanon by Israel, East Timor by Indonesia or during the war in

---

20    Peter Brown, "The Gulf between Iraq and Britain", letters, *Sunday Times*, 12 August 1990, Sect. 3, p. 9.

Mozambique where one of the two warring parties was supported by South Africa.[21] While, as has already been written, under the Charter of the United Nations, the invasion and annexation of the Emirate constituted a violation of international law and deserved to be punished, the war undertaken by the allies was not "a war of the United Nations,[22] [as] provided for in its Charter". Even though the primary objective was to restore Kuwait's sovereignty and independence, some claimed that the United States used the pretext of the invasion to justify a military retaliation in order to impose its supremacy and influence control over the oil resources in the Middle East.[23] According to historian Jon Wiener, it was the vagaries of domestic politics – the upcoming 1992 presidential election – that forced President Bush to decide upon the entry of the United States into the war.[24] It would appear that neither the *New York Times* and the *Washington Post* nor the British newspapers alluded to these elements in the articles analysed. By contrast, many articles published in the two American dailies highlighted the importance of oil and of Iraq's financial problems as cornerstones underlying the Iraqi incursion into Kuwait. Moreover, editorials in the *New York Times* and the *Sunday Times* as well as Fred Halliday in the *Guardian* described the grounds given by Saddam Hussein for Iraq's seizure of Kuwait as "spurious" or a "false" and "specious" pretext.[25] It should be

21    Howard Zinn, *A People's History of the United States*, New York: Harper Perennial, 2015, p. 595.

22    Expression used by Javier Perez de Cuellar, General Secretary of the United Nations and reported by Ghassan Salamé, *op. cit.*, p. 462.

23    Catherine Kaminsky, *La Géopolitique et ses enjeux*, Toulouse: Les Essentiels Milan, 2002, p. 43.

24    Howard Zinn, *op. cit.*, p. 595.

25    "The specious pretext for Iraq's invasion". "Iraq's Naked Aggression", editorial, *New York Times*, 3 August 1990, p. A 26; "spurious [grounds]". Fred Halliday, "Biting the hand that helped them", op-ed, *Guardian*, 13

noted that, on the British side, neither the *Times* nor the *Observer* seemed to address the issue of the justification for the invasion of Kuwait by its neighbour. Unlike their American and British counterparts, the journalists of the *Times* and the *Observer* may have believed that the main motives that led the Iraqi leader to invade Kuwait were not an essential topic worth mentioning or that they were self-evident.

The chart on the next page is a summary of the qualifiers of the invasion in editorials, opinion articles and letters from readers of each newspaper as well as their dates of publication.

Without going into detail on the points which have already been commented upon, this table shows that the qualifiers of the Iraqi invasion appeared mostly as early as August 1990 in editorials and opinion articles published in both the American and British press, which is hardly surprising given the importance of the media coverage given to the Iraqi invasion at that time. The situation is the same in letters to the editor. Letters describing the invasion of Kuwait were published in the American press, in particular in the *New York Times*, during the Gulf Crisis and War, and in the *Washington Post* only from August to December 1990. Letters in the British press about the description of the invasion were published in the *Times* in August, September and November 1990, in the *Guardian* and the *Observer* in August 1990 and January 1991, and in the *Sunday Times* in August and September 1990. As we have seen, the opinions expressed by readers on the Iraqi invasion largely corresponded to the editorial line of the newspapers, which

---

August 1990, p. 19; "[...] the country it [Iraq] invaded on a false pretext". "Saddam blinks", editorial, *Sunday Times*, 17 February 1991, p. V.

attested to the circularity of information between editorials, opinion articles and letters from readers in this particular case.[26]

---

26    However, it is worth remembering the letter of 12 August 1990 from a reader of the *Observer* who mocked the policy of the American president.

| | Aggression | Naked aggression | Adventure | Criminal act | Illegal act | Rape of Kuwait | References to WWII | Bestiary |
|---|---|---|---|---|---|---|---|---|
| **NYT** ed | 08/90–03/91 | 08, 12/90; 01/91 | | | 08/90 | 11, 12/90; 01/91 | | |
| **NYT** op-ed | 08/90–02/91 | 12/90 | 08/90 | | 08/90 | 10/90 | 08/90 | |
| **NYT** letters | 08, 09, 11/90; 02/91 | 11/90 | | 08/90 | | | | |
| **WP** ed | 08/90–02/91 | | | 08/90 | | 01/91 | | |
| **WP** op-ed | 08/90–03/91 | 08, 09, 11/90 | | 08/90 | | 08, 10/90 | 10/90 | 08/90 |
| **WP** letters | 08, 11, 12/90 | | | | 08/90 | | | |
| **Times** ed | 08/90–02/91 | | 08/90 | 08/90 | 08/90 | 01/91 | | |
| **Times** op-ed | 08, 09/90; 01/91 | 08/90 | | 08/90 | | | 08/90 | |
| **Times** letters | 08, 09, 11/90 | | | 09/90 | | 08/90 | | |
| **Guardian** ed | 08, 10/90; 01/91 | | | | | 10/90 | 08/90 | |
| **Guardian** op-ed | 08/90, 01–02/91 | | | | 08/90; 01/91 | | 08/90 | |
| **Guardian** letters | 08/90 | | | | 08/90 | 01/91 | | |
| **ST** ed | 08, 09, 12/90; 01–02/91 | 01/91 | | | | 08, 09, 12/90; 01/91 | | |
| **ST** op-ed | 08, 10/90; 01/91 | | | | | 10, 12/90 | 08/90 | |
| **ST** letters | 09/90 | | | | | | | |
| **Observer** ed | 08, 09/90; 01–02/91 | | | | | 10/90 | | |
| **Observer** op-ed | 08, 09, 11/90; 01/91 | | | | 02/91 | 12/90 | | 08/90 |
| **Observer** letters | 01/91 | 08/90 | | 01/91 | | | | |

All in all, the description of the invasion as aggression was indeed repeated many times in editorials and opinion articles in the American and British press during the Gulf Crisis and the war itself. In addition to the use of verbs from the lexical field of predatory animals and nouns and/or references to the Second World War, the invasion was also referred to as "the rape of Kuwait" in editorials of newspapers published on either side of the Atlantic and in the opinion articles of the two American newspapers and in those of British Sunday newspapers. As has already been said, the newspapers in question repeated the same description of the invasion of Kuwait as a "rape" used by George Bush and Margaret Thatcher in their speeches.

In a nutshell, while the British press – apart from the *Sunday Times* – did not devote editorials to the reasons for Iraq's invasion of Kuwait, editorialists, journalists and contributors of opinion articles and some readers on both sides of the Atlantic unanimously stressed the illegal, violent and criminal nature of this invasion. The president of Iraq was portrayed by journalists and perceived by readers as a bandit who had fraudulently seized the territory of his neighbour, reinforcing his image as a despicable character. Moreover, the expression "naked aggression" used by George Bush in his speeches which was repeated by a reader of the *New York Times* and the *Observer*, occurred mainly in the editorials of the *New York Times* and the *Sunday Times* as well as the opinion articles of American dailies and, on the British side, in those of the *Times*. Similarly, the terms "violation of international law" found in the speeches of the American president and the British Prime Minister appeared in the editorials of the *New York Times* and the *Times* and in the opinion articles of the American daily newspaper and the *Guardian* as well as in those of the *Observer*.

The editorialists and journalists in question thus became the spokespersons for the remarks of the American president and the British Prime Minister in describing the Iraqi invasion.

The following table correlates the expressions used by the American president and the British Prime Minister which were repeated in editorials, opinion articles and letters of each newspaper:

| | | Naked aggression (G. Bush) | Rape of Kuwait (G. Bush and M. Thatcher) | Violation of international law (G. Bush and M. Thatcher) |
|---|---|---|---|---|
| Ed | NYT | x | x | x |
| | WP | | x | |
| | Times | | x | x |
| | Guardian | | x | |
| | ST | x | x | |
| | Observer | | x | |
| Op-ed | NYT | x | x | x |
| | WP | x | x | |
| | Times | x | | |
| | Guardian | | | x |
| | ST | | x | |
| | Observer | | x | x |
| Letters | NYT | x | | |
| | WP | | | x |
| | Times | | x | |
| | Guardian | | x | x |
| | ST | | | |
| | Observer | x | | |

Without repeating what has already been said about the three expressions used by George Bush and Margaret Thatcher, the table shows the possible semantic impact of official comments on the American and British newspapers.

One may wonder whether the repetitive style of the aforementioned newspapers did not in some way hinder the reader's questioning of the information read, even though readers were supposed to be informed and educated, and the newspapers analysed belonged to the so-called quality press. This being the case, could the American and British media be accused of having been pusillanimous towards the government in power? According to the ideal of the Fourth Estate, the media and the written press in particular should inform readers, strive for objectivity and consequently try to remain neutral in all circumstances. However, the role of journalists should also enlighten and make the reader think. Journalists should scrutinise and hold to account the government, as well as question the official discourse and opinions of the established power, especially during a crisis and possible war decided by the governments that are supposed to represent the nation and the interests of its citizens. According to Trudy Lieberman,[27] conservative organizations, in particular right-wing groups, identified the constant repetition of the same messages as a key media strategy, thereby producing an "echo" or "multiplier effect", and helping "define the news and influence and shape public opinion". By repeating expressions from the speeches of George Bush and Margaret Thatcher, and although it did not take much to tarnish the image of Saddam Hussein who by his actions certainly deserved to be portrayed as a dangerous character, editorialists, journalists and contributors of the relevant articles

---

27    Trudy Lieberman, *Slanting the Story. The Forces That Shape the News*, New York: New Press, 2000, pp. 8, 13, 20, 34-35.

projected a Manichean view of the world again. They contributed to shaping a terrifying and dangerous image of the future enemy, which corresponded to that elaborated in the speeches of the coalition leader and his most loyal ally.

## 1.2    The Gulf Crisis

Descriptions in the press of the invasion of Kuwait by Saddam Hussein's army portrayed the Iraqi leader as a thief and a criminal. As the invasion triggered the Gulf Crisis, we will focus for a moment on the use of the term "crisis" in editorials, opinion articles and letters to the editor. This word, which thus described the period following the Iraqi invasion of Kuwait, was first used by George Bush at a press conference held jointly with Margaret Thatcher in Aspen, Colorado, on 2 August 1990[28] in reaction to the events in the Persian Gulf. The term "crisis" was then widely adopted by American and British editorialists and journalists. For example, the *New York Times* referred, like the American president, to an "international crisis"[29] in an editorial of 6 August 1990. Editorials in both the American and British press used the following qualifiers in their editorials: "far-reaching crisis" (the *Washington Post*, ed, 16 September 1990); "first post-cold war crisis" (the *Guardian*, ed, 3 August 1990). Opinion articles in the press on both sides of the Atlantic referred to "a grave international crisis" (the *New York Times*, op-ed, 9 August 1990); "third oil crisis" (the *Washington Post*, op-ed, 30 December

---

28    Refer to Bush's question-and-answer session with reporters on 2 August 1990 (<https://bush41library.tamu.edu/archives/public-papers/2124>, consulted 11 October 2022).

29    "The Uses of Force", editorial, *New York Times*, 6 August 1990, p. A 12.

1990); "the Kuwait crisis" (the *Times*, op-ed, 9 August 1990); "the Iraq crisis" (the *Times*, op-ed, 23 August 1990). The majority of opinion pieces published in the *Guardian* and British Sunday newspapers referred to the "Gulf crisis"[30] or simply the "crisis",[31] a term repeated over and over again in articles.

In addition to the term "crisis", editorialists and journalists on either side of the Atlantic used a more expressive, even bellicose vocabulary to describe the Gulf Crisis. For instance, an editorial in the *New York Times* described the crisis as "the [G]ulf threat" on 19 September 1990.[32] Similarly, we find the same type of expressions in both the American and British press: "the conflict with Iraq" (the *Washington Post*, ed, 23 September 1990); "the Gulf confrontation" (the *Times*, ed, 13 December 1990); "the first battle of the peaceful world" (the *New York Times*, op-ed, 27 September 1990); "the Iraq dispute" (the *Sunday Times*, op-ed, 23 September 1990); "the Persian Gulf confrontation" (the *New York Times*, letters, 14 October 1990). While Andrew Stephen from the *Observer* wrote about "the Gulf hysteria"[33] on 9 September 1990, Martin Fletcher referred in the *Times* of 23 August 1990 to "the

---

30    Hugo Young, "Fortunes of war desert the iron lady", op-ed, *Guardian*, 6 September 1990, p. 19; Ben Pimlott, "Why Labour should avoid jingoism", op-ed, *Sunday Times*, 2 September 1990, Sect. 3, p. 6; Helga Graham, "Mad, bad and dangerous to know", op-ed, *Observer*, 12 August 1990, p. 12.

31    Fred Halliday, "Belying the Euro-myths of Arabia", op-ed, *Guardian*, 14 March 1991, p. 21; Stuart Weir, "Labour puts democracy in the back", op-ed, *Sunday Times*, 9 September 1990, Sect. 3, p. 6; Michael Ignatieff, "A voice that cries in the wilderness", op-ed, *Observer*, 9 September 1990, p. 11.

32    "Is the Peace Dividend Being Engulfed?", editorial, *New York Times*, 19 September 1990, p. A 28.

33    Andrew Stephen, "Land of the free but not brave enough for art", op-ed, *Observer*, 9 September 1990, p. 16.

first act of the Kuwaiti drama",[34] suggesting that the crisis would be like a play made up of acts recounting various events until its outcome, which was not yet known in August 1990.

In the same vein, an editorial in the *New York Times* on 17 August 1990 described the crisis as a "contest between Saddam Hussein and the world".[35] In the *Guardian*, which repeated the expression used by George Bush in his speeches, we can find this notion of a binary opposition between the Iraqi leader and the world, thus reinforcing the idea that the Iraqi president was isolated from the rest of the world.[36] According to the American president, the Gulf Crisis was a global problem. Just as the Iraqi invasion was described as an act of aggression by George Bush and then by journalists, the papers once again repeated the official vocabulary, which seemed to demonstrate their conformity, and even their conscious or unconscious submission to the ideology of power.

But what is more striking was the description of the Gulf Crisis as a war by British editorialists and journalists on both sides of the Atlantic as early as August 1990. For example, the *Times*, in an editorial published on 30 August 1990, characterized the period following the Iraqi invasion as the "war of nerves"[37]

---

34     Martin Fletcher, "Glory restored, but what of the cost", op-ed, *Times*, 23 August 1990, p. 8.

35     "His Enemy Is the World", editorial, *New York Times*, 17 August 1990, p. A 28.

36     "It is a world problem". "A cause for the world, not just for the West", editorial, *Guardian*, 9 August 1990, p. 16. Refer to George Bush's Address to the Nation on 8 August 1990 announcing the deployment of U.S. armed forces to Saudi Arabia (<https://bush41library.tamu.edu/archives/public-papers/2147>, consulted 12 October 2022).

37     "A cynical gesture", editorial, *Times*, 30 August 1990, p. 11.

and the *Guardian* as the "Gulf War"[38] in an editorial dated 11 October 1990. Amy E. Schwartz wrote of "this new war"[39] in the *Washington Post* of 6 August 1990. *The Sunday Times* and the *Observer* compared the Gulf Crisis to a "phoney war",[40] thus referring readers back to the Second World War and more specifically to the period of relative inactivity on the part of the belligerents during the first months of the war.

One might wonder why American editorials did not use the word "war". Could it be because George Bush did not refer to the crisis in this way in his speeches in August 1990? The U.S. president frequently reiterated his wish for a peaceful solution to the crisis through the application of sanctions and the withdrawal of Iraqi troops from Kuwait. However, on 11 and 28 October 1990, the American president accused Saddam Hussein of waging a war of aggression[41] and, from 1 November 1990, declared that he would not rule out the military option if necessary.[42] Even though

---

38     "America's dilemma", editorial, *Guardian*, 11 October 1990, p. 20.

39     Amy E. Schwartz, "Baghdad and a Squandered Generation", op-ed, *Washington Post*, 6 August 1990, p. A 11.

40     "Lest we forget", editorial, *Sunday Times*, 16 September 1990, Sect. 3, p. 7; "Time to recall Parliament – and our goals", editorial, *Observer*, 19 August 1990, p. 10. "The Gulf phoney war". Norman Stone, "The truth behind Saddam's West Bank publicity wheeze", op-ed, *Sunday Times*, 14 October 1990, Sect. 3, p. 7. The phoney war refers to a period between September 1939 and April 1940 (David Weigall, *op.cit.*, p. 179). This expression owes its origin to the war correspondent Roland Dorgelès.

41     Cf. Bush's remarks at a White House Briefing for Representatives of Veterans Organizations on 11 October 1990 (<https://bush41library.tamu.edu/archives/public-papers/2318>), and to Officers and Troops at Hickam Air Force Base in Pearl Harbor, Hawaii on 28 October 1990 (<https://bush41library.tamu.edu/archives/public-papers/2369>, consulted 12 October 2022).

42     President's news conference in Orlando, Florida 1 November 1990 (<https://bush41library.tamu.edu/archives/public-papers/2381>, consulted

Margaret Thatcher did not call this crisis a "war", she adopted a more bellicose tone than the U.S. president when she stated as early as 29 August 1990 that the military option could not be ruled out.[43] In spite of this observation, however, it should not be concluded that American editorialists were more compliant with official language and less virulent than their British counterparts.

In a nutshell, the designation of the crisis as a war originated from British editorialists, American and British journalists and contributors who used it as early as August 1990. One may wonder whether they wished, by equating the crisis to a war, to give more weight to the events taking place in the Persian Gulf. Did they not in this way, consciously or unconsciously, make it easier for political leaders to gain public support for a possible military mobilisation and deployment of the armed forces to a distant country? In doing so, they seemed to disregard the ordinary meaning of the terms crisis and war. A crisis is not a war and, moreover, an armed conflict is very often generated only by a poorly managed crisis.[44] In fact, the equivalence between the two terms, as suggested by British editorialists as well as journalists on both sides of the Atlantic, more or less prevented any protest and/or possible discussion and surreptitiously prepared readers to de facto accept their country's entry into the war.

In any case, the Gulf Crisis, triggered by the Iraqi invasion of Kuwait, dominated media coverage from August 1990. The

12 October 2022).

43    Cf. Margaret Thatcher's press conference on the Gulf situation on 21 August 1990 (<https://www.margaretthatcher.org/document/108176>, consulted 12 October 2022).

44    Jean-Louis Dufour, *Les Crises internationales. De Pékin (1900) à Bagdad (2004)*, Bruxelles: Complexe, 2004, p. 23.

American and British press remained focused on incidents that occurred in the Persian Gulf while important events were taking place on the international scene at that time: on the one hand, the dismissal of Benazir Bhutto, the Pakistani Prime Minister, on 6 August 1990, and on the other hand, the efforts made by Nelson Mandela working with South African President Frederik de Klerk for the democratisation of the political regime. To illustrate the importance of the Gulf Crisis in the American and British press, the following three tables have been drawn up. All three show the percentage of editorials, opinion articles and letters relating to the Gulf Crisis published by each newspaper from August 1990 to mid-January 1991.

PERCENTAGE OF EDITORIALS ON THE GULF CRISIS
PUBLISHED FROM AUGUST 1990 TO MID-JANUARY 1991

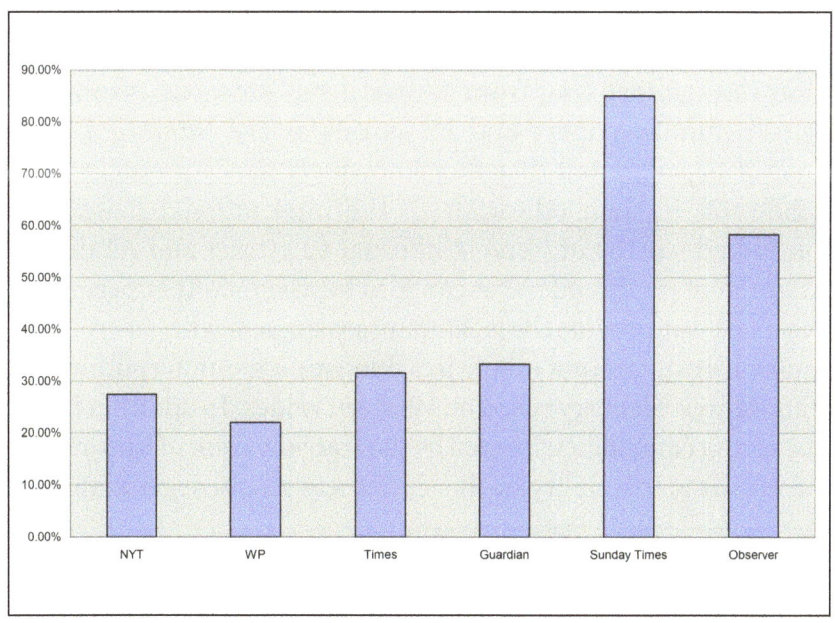

In this first table, which gives the average percentage of editorials devoted to the Gulf Crisis, 27.48%[45] of editorials published by the *New York Times* and 22.03% of editorials in the *Washington Post* during this period refer to the explosive situation in Iraq and Kuwait. The percentage of editorials published in the *Times* and the *Guardian* is slightly higher than that of the American dailies, that is to say 31.61% for the former and 33.32% for the latter. While the *Sunday Times* published a record 85% for Operation Desert Shield, the *Observer* devoted 58.32% of its editorials to it. The two British Sunday newspapers thus devoted more editorials to the salient facts in the Persian Gulf than the American and British dailies from August 1990 to mid-January 1991. In other words, American newspapers, in particular the *Washington Post*, published fewer editorials on the Gulf Crisis than British newspapers, which may seem surprising given that the United States played a leading role from the beginning of the crisis, namely that of assembling a coalition of thirty-four countries against Iraq from August 1990 onwards. As for the British Sunday papers and in particular the *Sunday Times*, could it be suggested that they knowingly gave an exaggerated dimension in their editorials to the international news they considered worthy of interest in order to attract and retain the attention of their readers? It can also be assumed that periods of crisis and war provide these Sunday newspapers with an excellent opportunity to present events in a dualistic way, underpinning an ethnocentric ideology based on Western values. In addition to the vast media campaign triggered by the Iraqi invasion of Kuwait and the resulting instability in this extremely sensitive geographical

---

45    This percentage tallies with the number of articles relating to the Gulf Crisis published on the same days in the newspapers selected for this study in relation to the total number of articles published in these newspapers.

area, it should not be forgotten that the Sunday press, with its impressive volume and numerous sections, would offer readers, according to David Scholes, "a more distanced analysis of events, impossible to have in the daily press", and "reflecting the typical British habit of spending one's Sunday reading the newspaper".[46]

Below is a histogram about opinion articles.

PERCENTAGE OF OP-EDS ON THE GULF CRISIS
PUBLISHED FROM AUGUST 1990 TO MID-JANUARY 1991

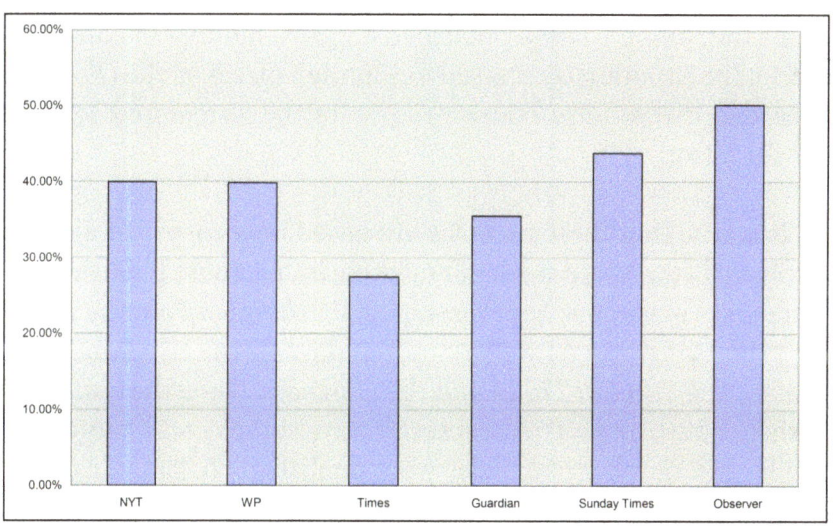

As the graph shows, both American newspapers published an equivalent number of opinion articles about what was happening in the Middle East, i.e. 39.95% in the *New York Times* and 39.83% in the *Washington Post*. In the British press, the *Times* published

---

46      David Scholes, *op. cit.*, p. 225.

27.48% of opinion pieces, and the *Guardian* 35.50% of them. By contrast, concerning the Sunday newspapers, the figure was 43.82% for the *Sunday Times* and even 50.15% for the *Observer*. As a result, there was a trend similar to that of editorials, namely the publication of a higher percentage of opinion articles in British Sunday newspapers than in American and British dailies. However, American dailies published far more opinion articles than British dailies in contrast to what has been observed for editorials published in daily newspapers on both sides of the Atlantic. On the other hand, British Sunday newspapers devoted more editorials to the Gulf Crisis than opinion articles. In addition, while the *Sunday Times* published a record number of editorials (85%), the situation is reversed for opinion pieces as the *Observer* exceeded the *Sunday Times* (50.15% for the former and 43.82% for the latter).

It is true that these remarks are based on a corpus of articles published two days a week per newspaper, i.e. those published on Thursdays in the *New York Times*, the *Washington Post*, the *Times* and the *Guardian* as well as on Sundays in the two American dailies, the *Sunday Times* and the *Observer*. Nevertheless, these articles constitute a fairly representative sample, and, moreover, the largest number of articles were published on Thursdays and Sundays, thus making it possible to draw valid conclusions. These figures also give a relatively accurate picture of a number of the media reaction at the time.

This observation, however, did not apply to the readers' letters published by both the American and British press. No information is available concerning the number of letters sent by readers and the criteria for selection may be arbitrary or questionable.

For this reason, the percentages calculated and detailed below provide only approximate data and do not allow us to draw very precise conclusions. Furthermore, not all letters sent to the editor were representative of public opinion. It is nonetheless useful to compare the figures compiled by newspaper even though the unreliability of these sources is high.

Below is a table showing the percentage of letters relating to the Gulf Crisis in relation to the total percentage of letters published by the six newspapers on the same days from August 1990 to mid-January 1991.

PERCENTAGE OF LETTERS RELATED TO THE GULF CRISIS
PUBLISHED FROM AUGUST 1990 TO MID-JANUARY 1991

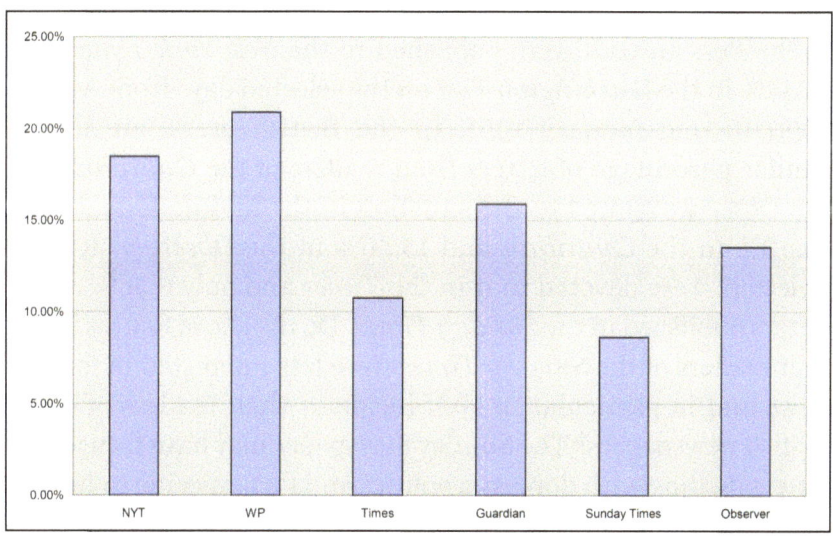

We note that, in general, American dailies published more letters about the Gulf Crisis than British newspapers in proportion to the total number of letters published. Either American dailies chose to publish a higher number of letters about the Gulf Crisis, or American readers, feeling more concerned about the events in the Persian Gulf because of the position of their country as the coalition leader, sent more letters on the subject. Nevertheless, when we compare the total number of letters published during this period by the *New York Times* and the *Washington Post*, on the American side, with that of the *Times*, the *Guardian*, the *Sunday Times* and the *Observer* on the British side, we can see that a larger number of letters were published in the British press.[47] As a reminder, the above table shows the percentage of letters about the Gulf Crisis published from August 1990 to mid-January 1991 compared to all letters published by newspapers on either side of the Atlantic. If we refine the results on the American side, we note that 18.51% of letters relating to significant events in the Persian Gulf were published in the *New York Times* and 20.91% in the *Washington Post* on the selected days from August 1990 to mid-January 1991. In the British press, an almost similar percentage of letters from readers of the *Guardian* and the *Observer* related to the situation in the Middle East, to wit 15.90% in the *Guardian* and 13.56% in the *Observer*. 10.79% of letters were devoted to it in the *Times* and only 8.56% of the letters published in the *Sunday Times*. Do the above figures imply that readers of the *Sunday Times* were less interested in foreign news and in particular in Gulf incidents than readers of other British newspapers? The Sunday newspaper may have focused on letters dealing with domestic politics and facts specific to British

---

47    From August 1990 to mid-January 1991, the American press published a total of 857 letters (the *New York Times*: 439 and the *Washington Post*: 418), and the British press 1,432 (the *Times*: 477, the *Guardian*: 341, the *Sunday Times*: 298 and the *Observer*: 316).

society. On the other hand, when we compare the two British dailies, the *Times* seemed to attach less importance to foreign policy events. However, according to Thérèse Pothier, the other national newspapers devote much less coverage to events abroad than the *Times*.[48]

In addition, the following observations should be made. On the one hand, there were leading academics and politicians among the signatories of the letters sent to the *Washington Post*. On the other hand, the majority of those who wrote to the British dailies were Conservative MPs (in the *Times*) and Labour MPs (in the *Guardian*), presidents or spokespersons of associations, academics in the Sunday press, and also ordinary readers without specific honorific titles. The letters about the Gulf Crisis published especially in the *Times* came from a plethora of personalities and members of parliament, reflecting the prestigious nature of the platform offered to the public in this daily newspaper, "a true British institution".[49]

Finally, a common feature of American and British daily newspapers was the publication of several letters under the same headline appearing in bold type. For example, there were headlines for letters dealing with a similar theme, such as: "Keeping up world pressure on Iraq",[50] the headline under which three letters were published in the *Times* of 23 August 1990.

In summary and across all types of text, British Sunday newspapers published a higher percentage of editorials and

48    Thérèse Pothier *in* Jean-Claude Sergeant (dir.), *op. cit.*, p. 137.
49    *Ibid.*, p. 136.
50    "Keeping up world pressure on Iraq", letters, *Times*, 23 August 1990, p. 9.

opinion pieces on the Gulf Crisis than American and British daily newspapers and in proportion to the total number of articles published from August 1990 to mid-January 1991. Regarding editorials in particular, the *Sunday Times* stood out from American and British newspapers by publishing an impressive number of editorials on events taking place in the Persian Gulf. While American dailies published a larger number of opinion articles on this subject than British dailies, it was the other way round for editorials. Finally, more letters were devoted to the Gulf Crisis in the American press than in the British press, with the *Sunday Times* among the six newspapers publishing the lowest percentage of letters. The Gulf Crisis thus received considerable media coverage, as evidenced by the numerous editorials and opinion articles published from August 1990 to mid-January 1991.

In essence, it should be remembered that the term "crisis", used by the American president in his speeches from the beginning of August 1990 to define the period following the invasion of Kuwait, was repeated by editorialists and journalists on both sides of the Atlantic. The editorialists of the *New York Times* and the *Guardian* also echoed George Bush's description of the crisis as a confrontation between the Iraqi leader and the world, which could demonstrate a more or less voluntary compliance of these newspapers with the official line. In both the American and British press, the Gulf Crisis was also repeatedly described in editorials and opinion articles as a battle, a conflict, and even a war, except in American editorials. The repetition and parallel of the terms crisis and war in the run-up to the hostilities served to remember and even memorize them, but also reduced any questioning of their relevance. Journalists were thus ahead of events by already talking about war in August 1990 before the outbreak of the conflict itself.

Moreover, this bellicose vocabulary was likely to plunge readers into a climate of uncertainty. Yet, uncertainty is linked to fear, which paralyses the faculties of analysis and reflection and can also give rise to doubt and anxiety. Although this study does not focus upon the reception of information, it cannot be denied that for those who want to manipulate people, nothing is easier than to stir up anxieties making public opinion more inclined to accept official and media messages. With the support of cooperative print media, it would not be exaggerated to imagine that the leader of a country like the United States, for example, could very well become a hero thanks to the annihilation of the nation's enemy and thus increase his chances of re-election.[51]

In any case, the fact that the crisis was designated as a war contributed to the denigration of the Iraqi president and reinforced his image as an enemy to be fought, since he was responsible for the outbreak of the crisis through his invasion of Kuwait. Described as a thief and criminal, Saddam Hussein was also presented as isolated from the whole world, which reinforced the antagonism between the enemy, the Other and editorialists, journalists as well as their readers.

## 1.3 The interim government

As we have seen, American and British editorials and opinion articles dealt with the conquest of Kuwait by Iraqi troops from the beginning of August 1990 and continuously until March 1991 in

---

51   However, George Bush was defeated by Bill Clinton in the presidential elections of 3 November 1992.

order to highlight its illegal, criminal and violent nature. A part of the U.S. and British press also referred to the establishment of a 'puppet' government in Kuwait by Iraqis and the claim by Iraq "that it was helping a Kuwaiti uprising against [the] Al-Sabah family".[52] During the invasion of Kuwait, Emir Sheik Jabar Ahmed al-Sabbah and his family fled the country to Saudi Arabia while Iraqi officers were installing new authorities in Kuwait.[53] As early as 5 August 1990, the American president described the Iraqi administration set up in Kuwait as a 'puppet' government, an argument he repeated on 6 and 9 August 1990.[54] Similarly, Margaret Thatcher spoke of a 'puppet' regime on 6 August and 6 September 1990.[55]

While the analysed American editorials did not refer to the establishment of this government in Kuwait, the *Times* and the *Guardian*, on the British side, addressed this subject in their editorials as of 3 August 1990.[56] With regard to opinion articles,

52    Philip M. Taylor, *War and the Media: Propaganda and Persuasion in the Gulf War*, 2nd ed., Manchester; New York: Manchester UP, 1998, p. 320.
53    Susan Jeffords and Lauren Rabinovitz, eds., *Seeing through the Media. The Persian Gulf War*, New Brunswick, NJ: Rutgers UP, 1994, pp. 307-308.
54    In his exchange with reporters on 5 August 1990 (<https://bush41library. tamu.edu/archives/public-papers/2138>). He referred to a 'puppet regime' in his Address to the Nation on 8 August 1990 (<https://bush41library. tamu.edu/archives/public-papers/2147>), and in his letter to congressional leaders on 9 August 1990 (<https://bush41library.tamu.edu/archives/ public-papers/2153>, consulted 14 October 2022).
55    Press conference, 6 August 1990 (<https://www.margaretthatcher.org/ document/108175>). See also the British Prime Minister's speech to the House of Commons on 6 September 1990 (<https://hansard.parliament. uk/Commons/1990-09-06/debates/54db6e15-456e-4257-ba864- cae4950b07f4/TheGulf?highlight=chemical#contribution-c8ad5e14-9ae7- 4882-b8c6-836ef88447b7>, consulted 14 October 2022).
56    "Creation of a puppet government". "Iraq's naked villainy", editorial, *Times*, 3 August 1990, p. 11. "The cynical promotion of a puppet regime".

Jim Hoagland of the *Washington Post*, for example, accused the Iraqi leader of "tossing aside the emirate's royal family like so much used Kleenex",[57] which, for the journalist, showed Saddam Hussein's disrespect for the legitimacy of the monarchies of the Arabian Peninsula. British newspapers did not publish opinion pieces on this issue. Like the American editorials, they may not have found it useful to take an interest in the matter. It is true that this event of lesser importance was a continuation of the invasion of Kuwait.

On 8 August 1990, Saddam Hussein annexed Kuwait, which then became an Iraqi province.[58] The American president made no further reference to this so-called government in his speeches. In essence, editorialists of British daily newspapers and American journalists[59] who alluded to the regime repeated the words of George Bush and Margaret Thatcher. Above all, their attitude served to complete, or even darken, the portrait of the Iraqi leader who appeared to be a perfidious dictator disrespectful of international law.

---

"Paying the price for past errors", editorial, *Guardian*, 3 August 1990, p. 16.

57    Jim Hoagland, "Force Hussein to Withdraw", op-ed, *Washington Post*, 7 August 1990, p. A 19.

58    Philip M. Taylor, *op. cit.*, 1998, p. 320.

59    For instance: "An Iraqi puppet regime in Kuwait". Jack Anderson and Dale van Atta, "Israel's Feeling of Vindication", op-ed, *Washington Post*, 12 August 1990, p. C 7.

## 1.4 Embassies

Like the establishment of an interim government in Kuwait by Iraq, the Iraqi injunction addressed to foreign governments on 10 August 1990 to close their embassies and consulates in Kuwait,[60] which most countries rejected,[61] showed Saddam Hussein's contempt for international law. Faced with the countries' refusal to evacuate their embassies, Saddam Hussein had them surrounded. From 14 September 1990, Iraqi soldiers entered the diplomatic precincts of several countries. In reaction to the incursion of Iraqi troops into some embassies, on 16 September 1990 the U.N. Security Council voted Resolution 667 which "strongly condemns aggressive acts perpetrated by Iraq against diplomatic premises and personnel in Kuwait [...]". As evidenced by several articles,[62] the two American dailies referred to the violation of the neutrality of embassies in August and September 1990. In so doing, they echoed the outraged words of President Bush who tackled this subject on numerous occasions in his speeches and press conferences[63] from August to December 1990.

The British press differed from the American press as these incidents were not mentioned in its editorials and opinion pieces,

---

60   Susan Jeffords & Lauren Rabinovitz, eds., *op. cit.*, p. 308.

61   Arthur H. Blair, *At War in the Gulf: A Chronology*, Texas: Texas A & M UP, 1992, pp. 18, 23, 29.

62   For example: "[...] his lawless invasion of embassies, [...]". "Iraq Swings Wild, and Low", editorial, *New York Times*, 15 September 1990, p. A 22; "In illegally ordering out the foreign embassies in Kuwait, [...] and in its harassment of the diplomats [...]". "A Rare Unity ...", editorial, *Washington Post*, 26 August 1990, p. C 6.

63   For instance, Bush's news conference on the Persian Gulf Crisis on 22 August 1990 (<https://bush41library.tamu.edu/archives/public-papers/2177>, consulted 14 October 2022).

although Margaret Thatcher referred to these events in several speeches in August, September and November 1990.[64] However, British newspapers reported on attacks on foreign embassies in Kuwait in other sections, such as on the *Times'* "Overseas News" page. The editorial staff may have decided to focus their attention in editorials and opinion pieces on other acts perpetrated by the Iraqi leader and not on the incidents in foreign embassies in the Emirate.

American and British readers did not address these events in the analysed letters. Either they did not comment on these incidents[65] or they sent letters to the editor which were not published. All in all, by publishing editorials and opinion articles on the actions undertaken by Iraqi soldiers against some foreign embassies in Kuwait, not only did American newspapers relay official statements, but they also highlighted the illegality of the Iraqi leader's actions. As with the establishment of the interim government, the American press thus insisted on Saddam Hussein's portrait as an outlaw disrespectful of the law.

---

64    For example, Thatcher's speech at Lord Mayor's banquet on 12 November 1990 (<https://www.margaretthatcher.org/document/108241>, consulted 14 October 2022).

65    Nevertheless, the *Times* of 6 September 1990 published a letter from a reader denouncing the lack of efficiency of the British embassy in Kuwait when the first hostages were released. Kirsty Norman, "Agony and anger of UK hostages", letters, *Times*, 6 September 1990, p. 11.

## 1.5 Call to Holy War

In addition to the Iraqi leader's failure to comply with international law, the press also reported on Saddam Hussein's call to Holy War on 10 August 1990, an appeal that the president of Iraq reiterated on 5 September 1990. American newspapers criticized this move in their editorials.[66] On the British side, the *Times* and the *Observer* also covered the subject in their editorials.[67] However, the *Guardian* and the *Sunday Times* did not publish editorials on the call to Holy War, which could not be fully explained by the fact that George Bush and Margaret Thatcher did not address Saddam Hussein's invocation of the Holy War in their speeches and press conferences.[68] These newspapers might have preferred to devote their editorials to other events in the Gulf Crisis.

---

66    For example: "The Month that Shook the World", editorial, *New York Times*, 2 September 1990, p. E 12; "Iraq's Isolation", editorial, *Washington Post*, 12 August 1990, p. C 6.

67    "No holy war", editorial, *Times*, 17 January 1991, p. 13. "Empty rhetoric". "Squeeze the man, not the trigger", editorial, *Observer*, 12 August 1990, p. 12.

68    However, John Major, in a statement made on 21 January 1991 about the Gulf War, criticized Saddam Hussein for wishing "to draw Israel fully into the war in the hope of inflaming Arab opinion, breaking the multinational coalition and inciting a holy war" (<https://hansard.parliament.uk/Commons/1991-01-21/debates/c80bc5e0-03fd-49fb-a838-62f4c66958e1/TheGulf?highlight=john%20major#contribution-45b223d1-b234-4128-83d8-f45ed0b23f2b>, consulted 15 October 2022). On 17 September 1990, George Bush argued during a press conference that he had been "told by some experts that he [Saddam Hussein] did not call for a jihad (<https://bush41library.tamu.edu/archives/public-papers/2231>, consulted 15 October 2022).

The American and British press also referred to Saddam Hussein's call to Holy War in their opinion articles.[69] For example, William Safire described Saddam Hussein's call to Holy War as a "[...] messianic jihad".[70] As in editorials, a reader of the *New York Times*[71] and another of the *Times*[72] condemned Saddam Hussein's exhortation to Holy War. While the expression "Holy War", related to the Crusades, refers to the wars that Christian nations waged against Muslim people in the Middle Ages to conquer the Holy Places, it also applies to wars fought by Muslims against Christians. The American dailies as well as the *Times* and the *Observer* might be blamed for not having made this distinction in their articles. But they certainly felt that their readers had sufficient knowledge to grasp the meaning of this expression.

According to Jean-Baptiste Duroselle and André Kaspi, the announcement of the Holy War by the Iraqi leader was not echoed in the Muslim world.[73] Besides, for Marcel Merle, the call

---

69    Bernard E. Trainor, "Saddam Hussein, Mideast's Noriega, Has to Go", op-ed, *New York Times*, 12 August 1990, p. E 21. For Henry Kissinger, "Saddam Hussein declared a holy war on Saudi Arabia". Henry Kissinger, "The Dangers of Stalemate", op-ed, *Washington Post*, 30 September 1990, p. D 7. On the British side, Charles Bremner stated that "his [...] statements on holy war [...] reflect a messianic belief in a destiny of martyrdom". Charles Bremner, "Saddam's psyche shows the strain", op-ed, *Times*, 17 January 1991, p. 12. Helga Graham, "The trap begins to close on Saddam", op-ed, *Observer*, 19 August 1990, p. 10.

70    William Safire, "Of Stones and Walls", op-ed, *New York Times*, 11 October 1990, p. A 25.

71    Seymour D. Reich, "The Truth Behind the Mideast's 'Great Lie'. Leader's Regret", letters, *New York Times*, 21 October 1990, p. E 18. The author sent his letter to the newspaper in reaction to an article by Anthony Lewis on 11 October 1990, entitled "The Israeli Tragedy".

72    B. S. Watson, "Conflict in the Gulf", letters, *Times*, 1 September 1990, p. 11.

73    Jean-Baptiste Duroselle & André Kaspi, *op. cit.*, p. 545.

to jihad to all Muslims and the need to defend the Holy Places of Islam in Saudi Arabia, namely Mecca and Medina, against the "defilement" of the presence of the "Infidels", made by a leader[74] at the head of a secular party, the Ba'ath, could hardly be taken seriously in the West. In any case, editorialists, journalists and contributors of articles in American newspapers and in the *Times* and the *Observer* who chose to deal with the call to jihad by the Iraqi president made it appear as a religious challenge, even a "sacrilege"[75] and showed Saddam Hussein as someone who "took God hostage, by declaring a Holy War"[76] and who above all represented a risk for the stability of the region.

## 1.6 Link with the issue of the occupied territories

While Saddam Hussein's call to Holy War was attacked in the American press and, on the British side, in the *Times* and the *Observer*, part of the press on both sides of the Atlantic also criticized the link established on 12 August 1990 by the Iraqi leader, who supported the PLO, between the evacuation of his troops from Kuwait and in particular the Israeli withdrawal of the Palestinian territories.[77] From August 1990 until the outbreak of hostilities, editorials in American newspapers, especially the

---

74 Marcel Merle, *La Crise du Golfe et le nouvel ordre international*, Paris: Economica, 1991, p. 23.
75 Élisabeth Coss-Humbert *in* Béatrice Fleury-Vilatte (dir.), *op. cit.*, p. 27.
76 *Ibid.*, p. 25.
77 Hedrick Smith, ed., *op. cit.*, p. 425. Saddam Hussein advocated a comprehensive solution for resolving all problems of occupation in the region. He linked his evacuation from Kuwait to Israeli withdrawal from the occupied territories, the disengagement of U.S. troops from Saudi Arabia and the retreat of Syria from Lebanon.

*Washington Post*, criticized Saddam Hussein's insistence on "linkage" between the settlement of the Gulf Crisis and that of the Palestinian problem.[78] According to Pierre-Jean Luizard, "Baghdad used the Palestinian question in a desperate attempt to link Palestinian issues to those of its regime".[79] Israel was Iraq's supreme enemy following, among other things, the bombing of the Osirak nuclear reactor in 1981.[80] The reaction of American editorials highlighted the special relationship between Israel and the United States: according to Ghassan Salamé, cultural, political and security links were too deep to be really called into question.[81] For Marcel Merle,[82] Israel could not therefore be put on an equal footing with Iraq even though both countries were occupying territories illegally conquered by weapons.

On this side of the Atlantic, editorials in British dailies and Sunday newspapers expressed opposing points of view concerning the Iraqi president's proposal to withdraw his troops from Kuwait subject to the Israeli withdrawal from the occupied territories and the Gaza strip. On the one hand, the *Times*[83] and the *Sunday*

---

78    "Linking that [Israeli-Palestinian talks] to the Gulf crisis would be foolish [...]". "The Siege Is Only Eight Weeks Old", editorial, *New York Times*, 1 October 1990, p. A 20; "Preposterous but revealing proposal". "Iraq's Deepening Risks", editorial, *Washington Post*, 14 August 1990, p. A 20.

79    Pierre-Jean Luizard, *op. cit.*, p. 224.

80    Sir Anthony Parsons, "La Crise du Golfe et l'avenir du Moyen-Orient", *Politique étrangère*, No. 4, hiver 1990, p. 785.

81    Ghassan Salamé, "Est/ Ouest/ (Proche) Orient", *Politique étrangère*, No. 2, été 1990, p. 261.

82    Marcel Merle, *op. cit.*, p. 96.

83    "These are two distinct conflicts". "After Jerusalem", editorial, *Times*, 11 October 1990, p. 17.

*Times*[84] criticized the link and, on the other, the *Guardian*[85] and the *Observer*[86] linked the Gulf Crisis to the Israeli-Palestinian issue.

Opinion articles published in the American press expressed a variety of opinions.[87] In the British press, the *Times* published few opinion pieces on this subject[88]. Opinion pieces in the *Guardian* and the *Sunday Times* followed the editorial line of their respective newspaper.[89] The *Observer*, among British newspapers, published the largest number of opinion pieces on the link between the Gulf Crisis and the Israeli-Palestinian problem. In addition, the Sunday

---

84    "An entirely bogus link". "The war dividend", editorial, *Sunday Times*, 13 January 1991, Sect. 3, p. 7.

85    "Does velvet line the iron glove?", editorial, *Guardian*, 1 December 1990, p. 26; "At the eleventh hour, and beyond", editorial, *Guardian,* 10 January 1991, p. 18. The newspaper believed that the idea of linkage was valid.

86    "Let the UN in", editorial, *Observer*, 14 October 1990, p. 22. The *Observer* stated that the massacres of Palestinian demonstrators in Jerusalem on 8 October 1990 made it impossible to separate the crisis from the Israeli-Palestinian question.

87    "President Bush has rightly rejected Saddam Hussein's attempt to link the Gulf crisis to the Palestinian issue". Anthony Lewis, "Happy New Year?", op-ed, *New York Times*, 31 December 1990, p. A 23; "The linkage has an ignominious origin". Jack Anderson and Dale Van Atta, "Palestinian Hopes and the Gulf Crisis", op-ed, *Washington Post*, 14 October 1990, p. C 7.

88    For example, the article by Peter Stothard, editor-in-chief, who approved of George Bush's actions and in particular those relating to the issue of "the link", and who believed in the re-election of the U.S. president because of his victory in the Gulf War. Peter Stothard, "To Bush, the spoils of war", op-ed, *Times*, 28 February 1991, p. 12.

89    For instance, the columnist Jill Tweedie, "Artful rhetoric of the new crusaders", op-ed, *Guardian*, 3 November 1990, p. 27. See also the article by Richard Falk, "A war built on grand illusions", op-ed, *Guardian*, 17 January 1991, p. 19. In the *Sunday Times*, refer to the article by Norman Macrae, "We've got the right stuff to prove dictators dead wrong", op-ed, 3 March 1991, p. VIII.

newspaper offered a plurality of viewpoints to its readers: some journalists and contributors criticized the link whereas others supported it.[90] In other words, some opinion pieces diverged from the editorial line of the *Observer* while others were in line with it.

In both the American and British press, the majority of editorials and opinion articles were published during the Gulf Crisis. While, on the American side, the *Washington Post* referred to Saddam Hussein's proposal, as early as August 1990, to withdraw his troops from Kuwait subject to the withdrawal from the occupied territories by the Israelis, the *New York Times* and the British newspapers dealt with this subject only from October 1990. It should be noted that President Bush only referred to it from September 1990.[91] George Bush refused to link the Kuwait issue to the Arab-Israeli conflict. In order to maintain the support of the Arab states within the coalition, he urged Israel not to participate in the Gulf War. According to Robert Fisk, Washington treated the Iraqi occupation of Kuwait and the Israeli occupation of the West Bank and Gaza "in so

---

90    For example, the following articles criticized the "link": Michael Ignatieff, "A voice that cries in the wilderness", op-ed, *Observer*, 9 September 1990, p. 11; Yossi Beilin, "Turning a year of war into a year of peace", op-ed, *Observer*, 10 March 1991, p. 22. On the other hand, in his article published on page 18 in the Sunday newspaper of 9 December 1990 and entitled, "Middle-East peace is indivisible", Bassam Abu-Sharif advocated the linkage "in the sense that we expect a firm commitment by the international community that it will strive to implement international law as vigorously in the Arab-Israeli conflict as it is seeking to apply in the Gulf Crisis". His opinion was not surprising given that the author was the political advisor of Yasser Arafat, the president of the PLO at that time.

91    CF. Bush's question-and-answer session on 24 September 1990 when he insisted on the absence of any link between the Palestinian issue and the Iraqi invasion of Kuwait (<https://bush41library.tamu.edu/archives/public-papers/2248>, consulted 16 October 2022).

different a fashion that" if they wanted to end the former, they were not "at all keen to end" the latter.[92] Thus, the two American dailies, which endorsed the position of the U.S. government on this issue in their editorials and numerous opinion articles, once again became the mouthpieces of official rhetoric. By focusing the reader's attention, as early as August 1990, on the correlation established by the Iraqi leader between the evacuation of Kuwait and the Palestinian question, the *Washington Post* preceded the *New York Times*, which only referred to it in October 1990. However, it is questionable whether speed or the "acceleration of information",[93] encouraged by commercial competition, is really synonymous with excellence. Rather, this "acceleration of information" seems to avoid in-depth reflection on the facts as they are highlighted by journalists. Besides, there was only one opinion article published in the *Washington Post* in February 1991 placing the Israeli-Palestinian problem in a historical context, thus attempting a little late to set the issue in its context.[94]

Margaret Thatcher did not comment on the link established by Saddam Hussein between his invasion and the Palestinian question. However, this does not explain the reason why British newspapers only covered this subject from October 1990 onwards. On 18 December 1990, John Major made a statement to the House of Commons on the European Council in Rome on 13 and 14 December 1990, explaining that "the Twelve do not accept any linkage whatsoever between Iraq's withdrawal from Kuwait and

---

92    Robert Fisk, *op. cit.*, p. 745. The author speaks of "the double standards" espoused by President Bush.
93    Thomas Ferenczi, *Le Journalisme*, Que sais-je?, Paris: PUF, 2005, p. 12.
94    See the article by Jeane Kirpatrick, "Roots of Arab Rejectionism", op-ed, *Washington Post*, 11 February 1991, p. A 9.

progress on other Middle Eastern issues". The Prime Minister also declared in the House of Commons on 15 January 1991 that "there can be no deals, no partial withdrawal and no artificial linkage".[95]

Regarding readers' letters published across the Atlantic, only the *New York Times* published, in November 1990, a reader's letter challenging the link established by the Iraqi leader.[96] It was a letter from the Chargé d'Affaires ad interim of the Embassy of Morocco, a country involved in the anti-Iraqi coalition. On the British side, it was only in the *Guardian* that a letter was published on 13 August 1990 comparing the Iraqi invasion with the Israeli occupation of the Palestinian territories and highlighting the obvious bias that underlay the disputes in the Middle East.[97] The reader's point of view was thus in line with that of the British newspaper.

The parallel with the conflict in Israel seems to be a particularly controversial and sensitive point for newspapers. On both sides of the Atlantic, the press – mostly during the Gulf Crisis – dedicated editorials and opinion articles to the link created by the Iraqi ruler between the departure of his troops from Kuwait and the Palestinian question. The American newspapers as well as the

---

95    CF. Major's statement on 18 December 1990 (<https://hansard. parliament.uk/Commons/1990-12-18/debates/d7161181-8d19-4533- a513-4054d6cc43c8/EuropeanCouncil(Rome)?highlight=sanctions#cont ribution-264644e8-5a3f-4929-8eb5-4fe587515ba5>), and on 15 January 1991 (<https://johnmajorarchive.org.uk/1991/01/15/mr-majors-commons- statement-on-the-gulf-war-15-january-1991/>, consulted 17 October 2022).

96    A. Salah Eddine Tazi, "Anti-Zionism Prevents Solution to the Palestinian Problem. No Linkage in Time", letters, *New York Times*, 1 November 1990, p. A 28.

97    R. A. Leeson, "A blimp on the Labour screen", letters, *Guardian*, 13 August 1990, p. 18.

*Times* and the *Sunday Times* criticized the Iraqi leader's position whereas the *Guardian* and the *Observer* considered in their editorials that the two cases could not be separated. The refusal of the link by the American newspapers, the *Times* and the *Sunday Times* showed the very committed and ideological side of these newspapers in that they defended Israel and above all did not want to compare it with Iraq. By relaying the official American and British positions – of George Bush and John Major – who denied the existence of the link, the American press as well as the *Times* and the *Sunday Times* appeared as the faithful interpreters of their respective governments. Finally, this subject allowed the American newspapers as well as the *Times* and the *Sunday Times* to insist on the geopolitical threat that Iraq and its leader represented for the Middle East following its invasion of Kuwait.

In August 1990 some journalists and contributors of opinion articles in the American and British press also stressed the danger posed by the Iraqi leader to Israel's security.[98] On 1 April 1990 the

---

98    "The most dramatic option available to S[addam] H[ussein], having declared an Arab holy war, is to attack Israel with chemical weapons, fulfilling his threat to scorch that country". Bernard E. Trainor, "Saddam Hussein, Mideast's Noriega, Has to Go", op-ed, *New York Times*, 12 August 1990, p. 21. "What's really at issue is a shift in the Middle East's balance of power that would [...] make a major war between the Arab states (led by Iraq) and Israel virtually inevitable. Saddam's ambition to dominate the Arab world can be best achieved by defeating Israel". Robert J. Samuelson, "Beyond the Price of Oil", op-ed, *Washington Post*, 7 August 1990, p. A 19. Like their American counterparts, British journalists and contributors of opinion pieces underlined Saddam Hussein's threat to put Israel to fire and the sword: "Saddam will want to make his threat to 'scorch' half of Israel with chemical weapons". Conor Cruise O'Brien, "Why Bush is treating Kuwait as a modern Pearl Harbour", op-ed, *Times*, 9 August 1990, p. 12. The use of quotation marks around the verb "scorch" suggests that the journalist did not agree with the words of the Iraqi leader and was therefore showing restraint. The quotation marks were probably

Iraqi president announced in a speech to the General Command of the Armed Forces that Iraq had chemical weapons and warned: "We will make sure that fire devours half of Israel if it attempts anything".[99] As we have seen, the American and British opinion articles predicted the attacks that the Iraqi leader would later commit against Israel, which enabled them to further tarnish the image of the "Master of Baghdad" and emphasize the increased risk of regional geopolitical instability, a corollary of the Iraqi leader's intentions and statements against Israel. This manoeuvre also allowed them to convince readers who might be reluctant to send armed forces to counter the president of Iraq.

## 1.7    Rapprochement with Iran

To complete the portrait of the leader of Iraq, the American press and part of the British press also dealt with the renunciation by the Iraqi leader on 15 August 1990, to win the favours of Tehran, of his meagre gains made during the conflict with Iran from 1980 to 1988.[100] This "lightning war", as the president of Iraq called it, cost the lives of about one million people and ruined the

---

derogatory, indicating the distance taken by the journalist. Also refer to the article by David Hirst, "A lion among the gazelles", op-ed, *Guardian*, 3 August 1990, p. 17: "With his blood-curdling threats against Israel". Finally, see the article by Chaim Bermant, "Palestinians' wild spasm of folly", op-ed, *Observer*, 26 August 1990, p. 9: "He might carry out his threat to destroy half Israel".

99    Alain Gresh & Dominique Vidal, *op. cit.*, p. 29.
100    *Ibid.*, p. 251. According to the authors, Saddam Hussein agreed to free prisoners, evacuate the occupied territories and return to the 1975 Algiers Agreement.

economies of both countries.[101] Unlike the *New York Times*,[102] the *Washington Post* did not mention this issue in its editorials. In British editorials, the *Times* described the Iraqi leader's peace offer to Iran as "extraordinary" and "a shrewd tactical move"[103] and the *Guardian*, in a more aggressive tone, as "the ultimate insult to the dead".[104] The *Guardian* therefore seemed as warlike as the other newspapers on this point. Unlike the *Sunday Times*,[105] the *Observer* did not publish editorials on the Iraqi leader's proposal.

Among the opinion articles published in the American and British press,[106] David Hirst of the *Guardian* noted that "Saddam Hussein's humiliating but pragmatic peace overture towards Iran is typical of his personality and politics".[107] The journalist's remark

101    Robert Fisk, *op. cit.*, p. 213; Sophie Chautard, *Guerres et conflits du XX^e siècle*, Paris: E.J.L., 2004, p. 73.
102    The *New York Times* wrote about "[Saddam Hussein's] startling overture to his archenemy, Iran". "His Enemy Is the World", editorial, *New York Times*, 17 August 1990, p. A 28.
103    "The python's embrace", editorial, *Times*, 16 August 1990, p. 11.
104    "Putting a sword through history", editorial, *Guardian*, 16 August 1990, p. 18.
105    For the *Sunday Times*, "even the few bits of land Iraq took have been handed back". "Britain at war", editorial, *Sunday Times*, 20 January 1991, Sect. 2, p. 5.
106    William Safire argued in the *New York Times* that "[Saddam Hussein] has burned his bridges in giving back his Iranian waterway conquest". "He put his people through eight years of privation in war with Iran for no gain [...]". William Safire, "Forget About Gulfo", op-ed, *New York Times*, 6 September 1990, p. A 27. For Jim Hoagland, "Saddam is suddenly willing [...] to accept Iranian control of navigation on the Shatt al Arab river". Jim Hoagland, "Saddam's Last Fantasy", op-ed, *Washington Post*, 21 August 1990, p. A 23. In the *Times*, Sir Anthony Parsons wrote about "Saddam's initiatives both propagandist and sincere [...]". Sir Anthony Parsons, "Keep the aggressor clearly in mind", op-ed, *Times*, 16 August 1990, p. 10.
107    David Hirst, "Saddam's gift and his gamble", op-ed, *Guardian*, 16 August 1990, p. 19.

thus tempered the violence of the *Guardian*'s editorial comment on this subject. Contrary to the *Observer*,[108] the *Sunday Times* did not publish opinion pieces on Saddam Hussein's peace offer to Iran.

The American and British press was interested in this issue from the beginning of the Gulf Crisis. For example, editorials in the *New York Times* in this regard were published in August 1990. American opinion articles were also published in both dailies in August 1990 and in the *New York Times* in September and October 1990. In the British press, there were also editorials and opinion pieces in August 1990 in the *Times* and the *Guardian*, which also published opinion pieces in September 1990 and January 1991. Sunday newspapers did not dwell on it much as the *Sunday Times* only covered the topic in an editorial in January 1991, and the *Observer* only published one opinion piece in August 1990. Among the letters analysed, there were no letters published on the subject of Saddam Hussein's peace offer to Iran in the U.S. and British press. Either readers did not comment on the subject, or newspapers' editors chose not to publish any letters on it.

In summary, while the Iraqi president's proposal surprised the *New York Times* in its editorial of August 1990, it was denounced in editorials in British dailies and sharply criticized by the *Guardian*. Only the *Observer* did not comment on the Iraqi ruler's initiative in its editorials. The American and British press, apart from the *Sunday Times*, published opinion articles on this subject. These editorialists and contributors did not only draw

---

108  For Helga Graham, "Saddam Hussein has made peace with the arch-enemy, Iran [...]". Helga Graham, "The trap begins to close on Saddam", op-ed, *Observer*, 19 August 1990, p. 10.

on Saddam Hussein's actions and words to write their articles and describe him, but they also referred to George Bush's and Margaret Thatcher's comments[109] on the unnecessary suffering of the Iraqi people during the Iran-Iraq war, which in their eyes was unfortunately pointless. The editorials and opinion articles analysed stressed the fact that by accepting the 1975 Algiers border Agreement on the Shatt al-Arab, which was at the origin of the conflict between Iraq and Iran, the ruler of Iraq erased eight years of war and its million deaths. The editorialists, journalists and contributors of opinion articles referred to thus highlighted the cruelty and fickle nature of the president of Iraq, who had no respect for the lives of Iraqi soldiers killed in the fighting against Iran.

## 1.8  Hostages

In addition to describing Saddam Hussein as an ambitious and cruel predator, American and British newspapers portrayed him as a despicable hostage-taker who respected neither life nor human dignity. On 18 August 1990, the Iraqi army held foreign nationals hostage and turned them into "human shields" to protect strategic areas against possible military action. The Security Council unanimously voted in favour of Resolution 664 requiring "Iraq to authorize and facilitate the immediate departure of third-State nationals [...] from Kuwait and Iraq". From 26 August

---

109   For instance, refer to Bush's news conference on 21 September 1990 (<https://bush41library.tamu.edu/archives/public-papers/2244>), and Margaret Thatcher's TV Interview for TV-AM *Frost on Sunday* on 1 September 1990 and broadcast on 9 September 1990 (<https://www.margaretthatcher.org/document/108186>, consulted 17 October 2022).

1990, several Western politicians travelled to Baghdad to plead the cause of the hostages. These included, among others, Kurt Waldheim, the Austrian president; Jesse Jackson, the former White House candidate; Edward Heath, the former British Prime Minister and Willy Brandt, the German statesman. As a result of the actions of these personalities, some hostages were released. On 29 October 1990 the Security Council adopted Resolution 674 demanding that "the Iraqi authorities and occupying forces immediately cease and desist from taking third-State nationals hostage [...]". On 6 December 1990, Saddam Hussein announced the release of all Western hostages.[110] By holding American and British citizens in captivity against their will and appearing on Iraqi television together with a group of hostages on 23 August 1990, not only did Saddam Hussein violate international law, but above all he caused widespread outrage, thereby increasing the Western world's aversion to him.

The hostages case was a hot topic in American and British newspapers.[111] The two American dailies only used the term "hostage" from 21 August 1990, the day after the U.S. president

---

110  Susan Jeffords & Lauren Rabinovitz, eds., *op. cit.*, p. 313; Hedrick Smith, ed., *op. cit.*, p. 426; Philip M. Taylor, *op. cit.*, 1998, p. 322.

111  For the *New York Times*, "Saddam Hussein violates civilized norms by segregating foreign nationals in Kuwait". "His Enemy Is the World", editorial, *New York Times*, 17 August 1990, p. A 28. Likewise, the *Washington Post* wrote that "he is using the hundreds of American civilians marooned in Iraq and the thousands of Americans caught in Iraqi-occupied Kuwait [...]. A unanimous United Nations Security Council demanded that President Hussein release all the foreign nationals he has so outrageously entrapped. [...] Hostage-taking adds to the onus on Saddam Hussein: he is the perpetrator of a double grab – not only of Kuwait but of many countries' citizens". "Iraq's Double Grab", editorial, *Washington Post*, 21 August 1990, p. A 22.

made use of that word to describe the American nationals, held in Iraq, in an exchange with reporters aboard the presidential plane, Air Force One.[112] Previously editorials had referred to "foreign nationals" and "foreign civilians" among others. It is true that the word "hostage", with its strong emotional connotations, could recall to the American reader the taking of foreign hostages by Hezbollah in Lebanon during the 1980s,[113] and especially the case of American hostages held at the U.S. embassy in Tehran after the overthrow of the Shah of Iran in 1979.

As regards the expression "foreign guests"[114] used by Saddam Hussein to describe civilians in captivity, only the *New York Times* repeated it in "quotation marks" in August 1990 to depart from the Iraqi leader's words and to show how iniquitous this expression was. In doing so, the American daily endorsed in advance the speech of the American president to Congress on 11 September 1990, in which he stated that calling the hostages "guests" was "a mockery of human decency".[115]

In the editorials of the *New York Times* or those of the *Washington Post*, the hostages were "innocent",[116] and the

---

112    See the following website: <https://bush41library.tamu.edu/archives/public-papers/2172>, consulted 18 October 2022.

113    Alain Gresh & Dominique Vidal, *op. cit.*, p. 268.

114    "Foreign guests". "Time Squeezes Iraq", editorial, *New York Times*, 21 August 1990, p. A 26.

115    Cf. Bush's address before a joint session of the Congress on the Persian Gulf Crisis and the Federal Budget Deficit (<https://bush41library.tamu.edu/archives/public-papers/2217>, consulted 18 October 2022).

116    "Innocent citizens". "Time Squeezes Iraq", editorial, *New York Times*, 21 August 1990, p. A 26. "Innocent fellow citizens". "Hussein the 'Humanitarian'", editorial, *Washington Post*, 31 August 1990, p. A 26.

*Washington Post* added that they were "helpless" and "hapless".[117] The hostage-related editorials published during the Gulf Crisis played on the reaction of solidarity and as such were likely to move readers who could identify with their compatriots held captive by Saddam Hussein. Both American newspapers constantly highlighted the leader of Iraq's lack of respect for the laws in several editorials.[118] Although Saddam Hussein's attitude confirmed this situation, it is however fair to note that by emphasizing the Iraqi ruler's contempt for the norms of the civilized world, editorialists presented the reader with a binary world in which there are civilized human beings represented by the Western world on the one hand and a cowardly, barbaric and uncivilized dictator on the other. They used a strategy of denigration which was certainly conventional but especially simplistic since it did not take into account the complexity of the world. They had also forgotten that, until his invasion of Kuwait, "the West tolerated Saddam's cruelty, his oppression and torture, his war crimes and mass murder".[119] According to Robert Fisk, Western support for the Iraqi president did not waver "even after the Israelis bombed Iraq's Osirak nuclear reactor in 1981".[120]

Concerning the differences between the two American newspapers, the *Washington Post* was cautious as it used the

---

117    "Helpless people". "Iraq's Double Grab", editorial, *Washington Post*, 21 August 1990, p. A 22. "Hapless victims". "Releasing the Hostages", editorial, *Washington Post*, 7 December 1990, p. A 22.

118    "Iraq Swings Wild, and Low", editorial, *New York Times*, 15 September 1990, p. A 22; "Three on Iraq", editorial, *Washington Post*, 17 August 1990, p. A 26.

119    Robert Fisk, *op. cit.*, p. 208.

120    *Ibid.*, p. 209.

interpolated clause "as it appears" or the adverb "apparently"[121] in its editorials three times. This distance between editorialists and the information they conveyed to the reader was underpinned by their observation and reflexion. In addition, the *New York Times* referred to Western hostages in general and to American and British citizens[122] in particular from August 1990. The *Washington Post* above all expressed its concern about American hostages[123] on many occasions and it did not give any details as to the nationality of the foreign nationals detained. Did the *Washington Post* express a stronger attachment to its own nationals than those from other countries? It can be assumed that since the American press devotes only a minority of its articles to international news, it is logical that most of the editorials referring to the hostages were dedicated to the plight of American civilians held in Iraq and Kuwait. On the basis of the articles analysed in the two American dailies, it would seem that the *New York Times* interpreted the events in a less isolationist way than the *Washington Post* in that the former also referred to the British and other Western hostages. Finally, the *New York Times* referred again to the hostages in February 1991 to remind the reader that Saddam Hussein used innocent foreigners and prisoners of war as "human shields"[124] while the *Washington Post* published editorials on the hostages

---

121 "Three on Iraq", editorial, *Washington Post*, 17 August 1990, p. A 26; "Cracks in the Gulf Alliance", editorial, *Washington Post*, 1 November 1990, p. A 22; "The Hostages' Tale", editorial, *Washington Post*, 16 December 1990, p. K 6.

122 "Britons and Americans". "His Enemy Is the World", editorial, *New York Times*, 17 August 1990, p. A 28.

123 For instance: "55 Americans". "Talk with Iraq?", editorial, *Washington Post*, 28 August 1990, p. A 16.

124 "Beyond Fury, Cool Calculation", editorial, *New York Times*, 27 February 1991, p. A 26.

from August 1990 to December 1990, that is to say during the Gulf Crisis.

Editorials in the British press reflected the disgust and contempt for Western hostage-taking, as in the *Times*, for example.[125] As in American editorials, the term "hostage" was first used by the *Guardian* on 21 August 1990,[126] the *Times* on 22 August 1990,[127] the *Observer* on 26 August 1990,[128] and the *Sunday Times* on 2 September 1990.[129] The *Observer* referred previously to "British subjects" and "hapless civilians" in an editorial of 19 August 1990.[130] In this context, it is worth recalling that Margaret Thatcher described the British held in Iraq and Kuwait as hostages on 21 August 1990 at a press conference on the situation in the Gulf.[131] Moreover, like editorials in the *Washington Post*, those published in the British press on the situation of the hostages were only published during the Gulf Crisis, which seems logical because of the release of the hostages in December 1990.

---

125  "So long as Iraq continues to hold a single civilian hostage, Saddam remains in breach of international law and affronts elementary rules of humanitarian conduct". "A cynical gesture", editorial, *Times*, 30 August 1990, p. 11.

126  "No easy options", editorial, *Guardian*, 21 August 1990, p. 14.

127  "Holding together", editorial, *Times*, 22 August 1990, p. 11.

128  "The logic of war and peace in the Gulf", editorial, *Observer*, 26 August 1990, p. 10.

129  "The Peace party", editorial, *Sunday Times*, 2 September 1990, Sect. 3, p. 7.

130  "Time to recall Parliament – and our goals", editorial, *Observer*, 19 August 1990, p. 10.

131  Cf. Margaret Thatcher's press conference on the Gulf situation (<https://www.margaretthatcher.org/document/108176>, consulted 18 October 2022).

While the editorials in the American press used the term "hostage" from 21 August 1990, Bernard E. Trainor[132] used the term in an opinion article in the *New York Times* on 12 August 1990, and therefore before the U.S. president described the American nationals as hostages. In other words, the journalist was able to anticipate the evolution of events in the Persian Gulf concerning the citizens detained there. American opinion articles devoted to the fate of the hostages were also published in the two American dailies during the Gulf Crisis: in the *New York Times* from August 1990 to November 1990 and from August 1990 to December 1990 in the *Washington Post*. At any rate, *New York Times* and *Washington Post* journalists condemned Saddam Hussein for detaining civilians. Finally, unlike the editorials in the *Washington Post* that only referred to American hostages, opinion articles in the newspaper not only mentioned American nationals, but also Europeans and other Westerners, as for example in an article published in the *Washington Post* of 22 August 1990.[133]

Lastly, Anthony Lewis, in the *New York Times*, reminded his readers of the hostage-taking that was fatal to Jimmy Carter's presidency.[134] In his article, the journalist explained that because of this historical precedent, President Bush made sure that the issue of the hostages did not limit his freedom of action. From November 1979 to January 1981, Jimmy Carter had to negotiate the release of sixty American diplomats illegally confined by

---

132   Bernard E. Trainor, "Saddam Hussein, Mideast's Noriega, Has to Go", op-ed, *New York Times*, 12 August 1990, p. 21.

133   "Up to 3,500 U.S. citizens, together with thousands of European citizens [...]". Rowland Evans and Robert Novak, "... And Reasons for Caution", op-ed, *Washington Post*, 22 August 1990, p. A 21.

134   Anthony Lewis, "Patience Is Strength", op-ed, *New York Times*, 2 November 1990, p. A 35.

Islamist students at the U.S. embassy in Tehran. The case of the hostages facilitated the election of Ronald Reagan as President in November 1980,[135] as these hostages were only released after he took office. Likewise, Richard Cohen advocated in the *Washington Post* that "the hostages should not become the Willie Horton of the Gulf crisis".[136] The journalist blamed George Bush for exaggerating the critical situation in which the hostages found themselves in order to prepare the Americans for their country's entry into the war. Willie Horton was a black, life-sentenced convict, who, on a weekend furlough granted under a programme authorized by Michael Dukakis, then Governor of Massachusetts, assaulted and raped a Maryland white woman. In the 1988 election campaign between George Bush, the Republican candidate and Michael Dukakis, his Democratic opponent, the Horton issue was the decisive factor in the voters' choice for the Republican candidate who, unlike Michael Dukakis, was in favour of the death penalty.[137] These two articles, which alluded to the impact of the hostage problem on the Bush administration's policy during the Gulf Crisis by referring to President Carter and Willie Horton, thus used arguments which could only convince American readers.

As regards opinion pieces published in the British press, two remarks are essential: firstly, it was in the *Guardian* that the largest

---

135 Michel Mourre, *op. cit.*, pp. 164, 562.

136 Richard Cohen, "Saving Face – and Lives", op-ed, *Washington Post*, 1 November 1990, p. A 23.

137 Jack W. Germond and Jules Witcover, *Whose Broad Stripes and Bright Stars? The Trivial Pursuit of the Presidency 1988*, New York: Warner Books, 1989, pp. 10-12, 163, 275. Also see the book by Tim Hope and Richard Sparks, eds., *Crime, Risk and Insecurity. Law and Order in Everyday Life and Political Discourse*, London: Routledge, 2000, pp. 242-243.

number of articles on hostages were published on Thursdays from August 1990 to December 1990.[138] It can be assumed that the *Guardian* favoured the publication of opinion pieces on stories with a human dimension such as those on hostages. Secondly, the *Sunday Times* did not publish any opinion pieces on this issue. Nonetheless, many articles on hostages were published either on the front page, or in a section created especially for the Gulf Crisis and dedicated to the events in the Persian Gulf, or also in other sections of the Sunday newspaper.[139] One might think that the *Sunday Times* chose not to publish opinion pieces for fear of exacerbating tensions during possible negotiations for the release of the hostages. Yet, this argument cannot be advanced given that the Sunday newspaper published some editorials and many articles – other than opinion pieces – on hostages during the Gulf Crisis, which, as a representative of the Fourth Estate, might have allowed it to exert some influence on political decisions. But do the media have as much power to influence a government's foreign policy as they can in terms of a country's domestic policy?

It is also worth mentioning that, like Bernard E. Trainor in the *New York Times* of 12 August 1990, Conor Cruise O'Brien, in an article in the *Times*, used the term "hostage"[140] as early as 9 August 1990 to describe Europeans and Americans detained by Iraq, whereas Margaret Thatcher did not use this term until 21 August 1990. Helga Graham from the *Observer* also preceded

---

138  For example: Hella Pick, "Sheltering behind a political fig-leaf", op-ed, *Guardian*, 21 August 1990, p. 15.

139  For instance, in the section "News Review".

140  "He [Saddam Hussein] is likely to treat as hostages at least some of the Europeans and Americans within his grasp". Conor Cruise O'Brien, "Why Bush is treating Kuwait as a modern Pearl Harbour", op-ed, *Times*, 9 August 1990, p. 12.

the Prime Minister as she referred to the Western hostages on 19 August 1990.[141] Although the *Times* journalist took discursive precautions in that he used the "be likely to" structure to express the probability that some national prisoners could be considered hostages, it is clear that these journalists did not simply report the facts, but tried to grasp their probable development: they knew what would happen to the stranded civilians in Iraq and Kuwait.

Like editorials in the *Washington Post* and the British press, as well as American opinion articles, opinion pieces published in British newspapers about the fate of the hostages only appeared during the Gulf Crisis: in the *Times* and the *Guardian* from August to December 1990, and in the *Observer* from August to October 1990. Furthermore, they mainly focused on the British hostages although they also referred to the American and European hostages. This shows that each country was self-centred and paid particular attention to those aspects of the crisis that directly affected it.

In order to highlight the emotional function and challenge, or even involve the reader, A. M. Rosenthal in a *New York Times* opinion article and, on the British side, an *Observer* editorial[142] resorted to the first-person plural possessive "our" when referring to the hostages. In contrast to the negative adjectives used to describe the Iraqi leader's actions, Westerners "in their terrible danger" were perceived, for example in the *Washington Post*, as

---

141  "Saddam's dozens of Western hostages". Helga Graham, "The trap begins to close", op-ed, *Observer*, 19 August 1990, p. 10.

142  "Our subjects". "Time to recall Parliament – and our goals", editorial, *Observer*, 19 august 1990, p. 10. "Our hostages". A. M. Rosenthal, "Iraq and Atom Bombs", op-ed, *New York Times*, 16 August 1990, p. A 25.

showing "patience and good temper"[143] and the hostages then claimed moral superiority in the eyes of the columnists and no doubt in the eyes of the reader. In addition, American and British editorialists and journalists repeatedly quoted figures representing not only the number of Americans and Britons taken hostage, but also what they evoked emotionally. This was the case of Rowland Evans and Robert Novak from the *Washington Post* who mentioned the number of "3,500 U.S. citizens"[144] or also the *Observer* that referred in an editorial of 19 August 1990 to "the threat to 4,000 of our subjects in Kuwait".[145] There can be little doubt that by making their readers feel compassionate about the hostages and portraying them as innocent victims of a brutal enemy, American and British journalists were able to convince readers of the need to deploy armed forces to fight the Iraqi president.

One last point deserves special attention. On 23 August 1990 Saddam Hussein appeared on television among British nationals. Among them was a five-year-old British child, Stuart Lockwood, whose hair was lovingly ruffled by the Iraqi president, which was, for Élisabeth Coss Humbert, a "particularly revolting and hypocritical image, that makes us fear the worst".[146] The American and British press, expressing their disapproval, made extensive reference to it in their articles. While the *Sunday Times* did not publish editorials or opinion pieces about this episode, numerous

---

143    Rowland Evans and Robert Novak, "Bad Guy of Baghdad", op-ed, *Washington Post*, 27 August 1990, p. A 11.

144    Rowland Evans and Robert Novak, "… And Reasons for Caution", op-ed, *Washington Post*, 22 August 1990, p. A 21.

145    "Time to recall Parliament – and our goals", editorial, *Observer*, 19 august 1990, p. 10.

146    Élisabeth Coss-Humbert *in* Béatrice Fleury-Vilatte (dir.), *op. cit.*, p. 27.

articles appeared in the section on the Gulf Crisis on 26 August 1990.[147] According to Richard Keeble, the press reported the meeting between the Iraqi leader and the British child as "an archetypal confrontation between good and evil",[148] a sort of epic struggle between David and Goliath.

Without denying Iraq's particularly revolting and cowardly strategy of manipulation, it must be noted that in order to convince their readers, American and British editorialists and journalists endeavoured to move readers by dramatizing the emotional nature of this event. Reports and comments on this affair were turned into an "information – show that aimed at *pathos* through the use of moving clichés".[149] To this end, American and British newspapers chose a lexicon with a strong emotional charge, such as the terms "cruel",[150] "perfidious", "gruesome"[151] and "tawdry"[152] to describe Saddam Hussein's strategy. Similarly, as

---

147 The same was true of the *Observer*, which on 26 August 1990 published an article on the issue on page 2 of the newspaper in addition to its opinion pieces. The Sunday paper did not publish any editorials on the subject.

148 Richard Keeble, *Secret State, Silent Press. New militarism, the Gulf and the modern image of warfare*, Luton: U of Luton Press, 1997, p. 76.

149 Ruth Amossy et Anne Herschberg Pierrot, *Stéréotypes et clichés*, Paris: Nathan/SEYER, 2004, p. 112.

150 "Cruel logic", "His Enemy Is the World", editorial, *New York Times*, 17 August 1990, p. A 28. "Cruel tactic". "Hussein the 'Humanitarian'", editorial, *Washington Post*, 31 August 1990, p. A 26.

151 "Iraq's perfidious hostage strategy; Saddam's gruesome hostage policy". Rowland Evans and Robert Novak, "… And Reasons for Caution", op-ed, *Washington Post*, 22 August 1990, p. A 21.

152 "Saddam's tawdry gambits with hostages". "The big picture and the side show", editorial, *Guardian*, 25 October 1990, p. 20.

mentioned above, the terms "innocent",[153] "apprehensive"[154] and "hapless"[155] were used in the press on both sides of the Atlantic to describe the hostages, who, at Saddam Hussein's hands, were "threatened",[156] "mistreated"[157] and "imperilled".[158] These hostages, who subsequently assumed the role of warriors,[159] took centre stage. From ordinary civilians, they became the heroes of a melodrama that was played out in Iraq and Kuwait. It is worth remembering that the content of the articles and the message they convey are generally interpreted by the reader according to his "horizon of expectation", hence the cardinal role of sensation, affect and emotion in the act of reading that resonates with the reader's cultural and social universe.[160] This was really the case in American and British editorials and opinion articles.

American newspapers did not publish any letters referring to the hostages. Does this mean that the American reader was not moved by the fate of his fellow citizens imprisoned in a faraway region despite the numerous editorials and opinion articles published on this issue? It is conceivable that American readers did not want to express themselves on this thorny subject or that

---

153 "Innocent foreigners as hostages". William Raspberry, "... The Villain", op-ed, *Washington Post*, 22 August 1990, p. A 21.

154 "Apprehensive British hostages". Richard Ingrams, Column, op-ed, *Observer*, 26 August 1990, p. 10.

155 "Hapless foreigners". Flora Lewis, "An Iraqi Visitor", op-ed, *New York Times*, 25 August 1990, p. E 23.

156 Fred Halliday, "Biting the hand that helped them", op-ed, *Guardian*, 13 August 1990, p. 19.

157 "Hussein the 'Humanitarian'", editorial, *Washington Post*, 31 August 1990, p. A 26.

158 Hugo Young, "The decline and recall of Parliament", op-ed, *Guardian*, 30 August 1990, p. 19.

159 Jean Baudrillard, *op. cit.*, p. 11.

160 Michel Morel, *op. cit.*, p. 344.

the two American dailies chose not to publish letters on this topic. On the British side, apart from the *Sunday Times* which did not publish letters about the civilians held in Iraq and Kuwait, the *Times*, the *Guardian*[161] and the *Observer* published letters, during the Gulf Crisis, expressing readers' empathy for the hostages. According to Richard Keeble, the British hostages became the "sudden 'victims' caught up in the drama of history" and they were "transformed into 'heroes'" by the press.[162] What is surprising is that the *Sunday Times* did not publish any letters on this subject. As already said about the letters sent to the American dailies, either readers of the *Sunday Times* did not send any letters to the Sunday paper on this subject despite the editorials published, or the Sunday newspaper decided not to publish letters about the hostages.

In summary, American and British editorials and opinion articles blamed the Iraqi leader for detaining American and British civilians in Iraq and Kuwait, whom they described as hapless and innocent. On both sides of the Atlantic, the term "hostage" was used at the end of August 1990 after its use by the American president and the British Prime Minister. Nonetheless, two journalists, one from the *New York Times* and the other from the *Times*, anticipated the course of events by using this word in early August 1990. With the exception of the *New York Times*,

---

161    For example, a Labour MP wrote in the *Guardian* that "Saddam Hussein is striking terror into the hearts of Britons [...]. Britain must now watch as he abuses British people". Ann Clwyd, MP, "Let's cast a net over the whole Middle East when seeking peace for Kuwait", letters, *Guardian*, 23 August 1990, p. 18. The female politician thus shared the feeling of repulsion towards the president of Iraq expressed in the editorials of the British newspaper.

162    Richard Keeble, *op. cit.*, 2006, p. 97.

which still referred to hostages in February 1991, articles about their fate only appeared in newspapers during the Gulf Crisis, i.e. from August to December 1990. While the *Washington Post* in its editorials was cautious in its assertions by using the adverb "apparently" and focused more on U.S. nationals, that was not the case in its opinion articles and in those of the *New York Times*. On the British side, the articles published were devoted primarily to the British hostages, but also to American and Western nationals in general. The study of the editorials and articles shows a correspondence between the American and British press regarding the treatment of the meeting between the Iraqi leader and the little British child. The two American dailies differed from British newspapers to the extent that, in opinion articles, two journalists reminded their readers of the Iranian hostage-taking under Jimmy Carter's presidency and the "Willie Horton" case. On the British side, the *Guardian* published a larger number of articles than the other British newspapers, and the *Sunday Times* did not publish any opinion pieces on hostages. Likewise, American newspapers and the *Sunday Times* did not publish any letters relating to the hostages. By contrast, letters published in the *Times*, the *Guardian* and the *Observer* reflected readers' empathy for the nationals detained in the Persian Gulf.

In the end, editorialists and journalists from the American and British press published melodramatic articles during the Gulf Crisis that were emotional in nature. Not only were these articles of interest to readers, but they were also part of a process of demonization of Saddam Hussein. On the one hand, these articles stereotypically set innocent and vulnerable victims against a tyrant who deprived them of their freedom, which certainly affected readers inclined to identify with their threatened but above all heroic compatriots. On the other hand, articles on these hostages living through a dramatic situation arguably exacerbated readers' patriotism[163] for the purpose of mobilizing against the president of Iraq. For both American and British readers, the Iraqi leader was attacking one of their own, who was a citizen representing their country or who at least was part of it. As a reminder of what has been said, American and British editorialists, journalists and contributors of opinion articles indirectly highlighted both their values and those of their readers by devaluing the adversary. All in all, they portrayed an appalling person who behaved like a barbarian to the extent that he aggravated the illegal side of his invasion by taking foreigners hostage and thus violated international conventions. In other words, he was portrayed not only as a criminal and lawbreaker, but also as an outlaw with no respect for treaties or basic humanitarian rules, i.e. the Western values common to journalists and their readers, such as the sense of justice, respect for the individual, morality and democracy among others.

## 1.9   Abuses in Kuwait

To refine Saddam Hussein's portrait as a criminal drawn up in American and British newspapers, editorialists and journalists on both sides of the Atlantic were particularly interested in the acts of barbarism and plunder perpetrated in Kuwait during the Iraqi occupation. The *New York Times* and the *Washington Post*

---

163    Richard Keeble, *op. cit.*, 1997, p. 73.

published their editorials[164] and opinion articles[165] on this issue from October 1990 and from September 1990 respectively. In the British press, editorials and opinion pieces relating to abuses committed in Kuwait were published on the whole in the dailies and the *Sunday Times* from September 1990 onwards.[166] Only the *Observer* stood out from American and British newspapers by not reporting on the misdeeds of Iraqi soldiers in its editorials and opinion pieces until February 1991.[167]

British Sunday newspapers did not publish letters relating to Saddam Hussein's depredations in Kuwait. Readers may not have commented on that. All in all, letters on Iraqi abuses in

---

164　For example: "Saddam Hussein's Threats", editorial, *Washington Post*, 25 September 1990, p. A 22; "Saddam Hussein's barbarities in Kuwait". "Israel's Friends, and Enemy", editorial, *New York Times*, 18 October 1990, p. A 24.

165　For instance: Hobart Rowen, "Americans Need Not Feel Put-Upon by their Allies", op-ed, *Washington Post*, 13 September 1990, p. A 23; William Safire, "The Phony War", op-ed, *New York Times*, 1 October 1990, p. A 21.

166　*The Times* addressed this subject in its editorials only from November 1990. "Diplomacy's last chance", editorial, *Times*, 1 November 1990, p. 15. "Saddam, and a lot of stupid things", editorial, *Guardian*, 27 September 1990, p. 18; "Lest we forget", editorial, *Sunday Times*, 16 September 1990, Sect. 3, p. 7; Marc Weller, "When Saddam is brought to court ...", op-ed, *Times*, 3 September 1990, p. 10; Norman Stone, "Heath, isolated and wrong, a clear essay in ineptitude", op-ed, *Sunday Times*, 23 September 1990, Sect. 3, p. 7.

167　"Fighting for justice, not for power", editorial, *Observer*, 24 February 1991, p. 24. Nevertheless, the Sunday newspaper dealt in August 1990 with the booty and gains that Saddam Hussein seized by force in Kuwait. See the following editorials: "Time to recall Parliament – and our goals", editorial, *Observer*, 19 August 1990, p. 10; "The logic of war and peace in the Gulf", editorial, *Observer*, 26 August 1990, p. 10. Michael Ignatieff, "Mr Bush has missed an opportunity", op-ed, *Observer*, 17 February 1991, p. 19; Michael Ignatieff, "The macho fantasy of total victory", op-ed, *Observer*, 24 February 1991, p. 23.

the Emirate were published in the *Washington Post*[168] and the *Guardian*[169] from August 1990, in the *Times*[170] from September 1990 and in the *New York Times*[171] from October 1990. The readers of the *Washington Post* and the *Guardian* were thus more responsive to the events in Kuwait in August 1990 than readers of the other dailies. This was all the more so since the editorials of these newspapers reported on the plundering and looting by the Iraqi armed forces in Kuwait from September 1990, which may mean that readers relied on other sources of information to write their letters. Finally, published letters contained arguments similar to those of editorials and opinion articles. In other words, the analysis of editorials, opinion articles and letters reveals a correspondence of the arguments used in the press on both sides of the Atlantic, which ended up establishing the portrait of Saddam Hussein as a bloodthirsty barbarian.

During the seven months of Kuwait's occupation by the Iraqi army, the country was subjected to widespread looting, and thousands of Kuwaitis were arrested, deported, tortured and executed,[172] as echoed by George Bush, Margaret Thatcher and John Major in their numerous speeches and press conferences from September 1990 to March 1991.[173] The information processing

---

168   Alexander Stolzberg, "Spelling out the Differences", letters, *Washington Post*, 22 August 1990, p. A 20.
169   J. R. Fearon-Jones, Dr, "Case for US withdrawal", letters, *Guardian*, 21 August 1990, p. 14.
170   Peter J. Pepper, "Invasion chain", letters, *Times*, 27 September 1990, p. 13.
171   Mark S. Golub, "The Truth behind the Mideast's 'Great Lie'", letters, *New York Times*, 21 October 1990, p. E 18.
172   Alain Gresh & Dominique Vidal, *op. cit.*, p. 354; Pierre-Jean Luizard, *op. cit.*, p. 230.
173   There were forty-six references to the abuses of Iraq in Kuwait in the speeches and conferences of the U.S. president from September 1990 to

thus followed a logic of interdependence and circularity: facts were repeated and commented upon over and over by American and British authorities as well as by the press. On the one hand, the American and British governments, which focused among other things on the abuses of the Iraqi leader, sought to persuade public opinion either, during the Gulf Crisis, of the need to go to war, or to justify, during and after the hostilities, the merits of their decisions. On the other hand, the media, which informed readers of Saddam Hussein's misdeeds, transformed facts – admittedly tragic – into major events, by exaggerating their scope in order to magnify the portrait of the Iraqi leader and heighten fears of him. These facts and events succeeded other events, and this was how the story of the abominable being who deserved to be killed was built during the Gulf Crisis and War. Moreover, since the media also relayed the authorities' comments, they were the sounding board for official ideas. As a result, readers received similar messages from both the governments in power and the media. Standardization of thinking was at work insofar as information, which thanks to technological prowess circulated worldwide, lived paradoxically, as it were, in a vacuum. Only one History was written, and it was that of the victors.

Whilst U.S. and British newspapers insisted on the misdeeds perpetrated by Iraqi soldiers in Kuwait, how was Kuwait represented in the press on both sides of the Atlantic? Most American and British editorials presented Kuwait in a positive

---

mid-March 1991, thirteen in those of Margaret Thatcher in October and November 1990, and four in John Major's speeches from December 1990 to mid-March 1991.

light, emphasizing the tiny and vulnerable nature of the Emirate,[174] which made the invasion by Iraqi troops even more monstrous. Only the *Times* stressed the need to restore the Emir of Kuwait to his throne.[175] What is interesting is that George Bush and Margaret Thatcher insisted in their many speeches during the Gulf Crisis and War on the necessary restoration of the Kuwaiti regime.[176] The U.S. president and the British Prime Minister also used the qualifiers "small" and "peaceful" to describe Kuwait[177] in their interventions and speeches. In other words, editorialists in

---

174    The *New York Times* wrote that "Iraq has struck at tiny Kuwait" and referred to "President Saddam Hussein's grab at a vulnerable, oil-rich neighbor". "Iraq's Naked Aggression", editorial, *New York Times*, 3 August 1990, p. A 26. The editorial of 26 August 1990 in *The New York Times* described the Emir of Kuwait as an absolute monarch. It can therefore be assumed that at the end of August 1990, the American daily did not regard Kuwait as a democratic state. "Squeeze – and Contain – Iraq", editorial, *New York Times*, 26 August 1990, p. E 18. For the *Washington Post*, Iraq attacked "its small and vulnerable Gulf neighbor". "Aggressor in the Gulf", editorial, *Washington Post*, 3 August 1990, p. A 22. The *Times* reminded his readers in March 1991 of "August 2, the day President Saddam Hussein invaded his peaceful neighbour". "Desert calm", editorial, *Times*, 1 March 1991, p. 15. The *Sunday Times* described Kuwait as "an essentially defenceless small country [...]". "War aims", editorial, *Sunday Times*, 26 August 1990, Sect. 3, p. 5. For the *Observer*, "Iraq invaded a friendly neighbouring state". "Why this Hitler of the Gulf has to go", editorial, *Observer*, 5 August 1990, p. 12.

175    "Siren voices in the Gulf", editorial, *Times*, 1 September 1990, p. 11.

176    Bush insisted on the restoration of the Kuwaiti government forty times in his speeches from August 1990 to February 1991, Margaret Thatcher alluded to it twenty times from August to November 1990 and John Major twice in December 1990 and January 1991.

177    There were twenty-four references to Kuwait described as "small" or "peaceful" in the speeches and press conferences by the American president from August 1990 to mid-March 1991, nineteen references in Margaret Thatcher's interventions from August to November 1990 and five in those of John Major in January 1991.

American and British newspapers and in the *Times* in particular relayed the content of official speeches about the Emirate.

Unlike editorialists, American journalists and contributors were rather critical of Kuwait in opinion articles.[178] In the *Washington Post*, the situation was more contrasted: some journalists drew an almost dithyrambic portrait of Kuwait. For example, Daniel Pipes, the director of the Foreign Policy Institute, stated on 9 August 1990 that:

> In a single generation, Kuwait emerged as an intellectual and cultural center of the Middle East. [...] Their newspapers, magazines and books were among the freest and most important in the region. [...] The government of Sheikh Jabir al-Sabah was the best in the Arab world. [...] Citizens exercised wide rights of freedom of speech. In short, Sheikh Jabir was the model of a benign desert autocrat. [...] Unlike many of its oil-peers, it neither supported terrorist groups nor sought to shape a new international order. [...] When Iraqi troops entered Kuwait on Aug. 2, an era of innocence abruptly came to an end. One of the few lights in the Middle East has been extinguished.[179]

Other journalists disagreed. For instance, Robert J. Samuelson reminded readers in September 1990 that Kuwait was not a democracy, but a restrictive monarchy.[180] Likewise, George F.

---

178  For example, A. M. Rosenthal described Kuwait in the *New York Times* as a feudal tyranny. A. M. Rosenthal, "Soldiers in the Sands", op-ed, *New York Times*, 12 August 1990, p. E 21.

179  Daniel Pipes, "What Kuwait Was Like", op-ed, *Washington Post*, 9 August 1990, p. A 23.

180  Robert J. Samuelson, "The Shadow of Isolationism", op-ed, *Washington Post*, 5 September 1990, p. A 19.

Will wrote the same month that Kuwait was "a boutique nation, more a country club than a country, and no democracy".[181] In the British press, opinion pieces published in the *Guardian*,[182] the *Sunday Times*[183] and the *Observer*[184] provided their readers with a variety of viewpoints in line with or contrary to the newspaper's editorial line.

The perception of Kuwait by readers whose letters were published in the American[185] and British[186] press was extensive

---

181  George F. Will, "Stuck in the Sand – For Good", op-ed, *Washington Post*, 9 September 1990, p. D 7.

182  For example, David Hirst described Kuwait as "a small and peaceful neighbour which if not exactly a democracy is one of the more liberal and intelligently-governed systems in the whole region". David Hirst, "A lion among the gazelles", op-ed, *Guardian*, 3 August 1990, p. 17. On the other hand, Fred Halliday, Professor of International Relations at the London School of Economics at the time, considered Kuwait an "undemocratic" and "corrupt" monarchy. Fred Halliday, "Biting the hand that helped them", op-ed, *Guardian*, 13 August 1990, p. 19.

183  For example, Brian Walden wrote about "peaceful Kuwait". Brian Walden, "How truth bites the dust when politicians go into the front line", op-ed, *Sunday Times*, 19 August 1990, p. 34. By contrast, Barbara Amiel referred to the "feudal regime such as that of the Emir of Kuwait". Barbara Amiel, "Letting a crocodile off the hook", op-ed, *Sunday Times*, 24 February 1991, p. IV.

184  Michael Ignatieff wrote in February 1991 that "some regimes, like Kuwait, used their own resources to give their people a high standard of living". Michael Ignatieff, "One good deed in a dirty world", op-ed, *Observer*, 10 February 1991, p. 19.

185  For example, Michael J. Clague wrote about "the anti-democratic nature and poor human-rights records" of the Kuwaiti regime. Michael J. Clague, "Crisis in the Gulf", letters, *Washington Post*, 9 august 1990, p. A 22. On the contrary, Hannah E. Schechter considered Kuwait's government "responsible, enlightened and in keeping with the history, experience and desire of its people". Hannah E. Schechter, "Spelling Out the Differences", letters, *Washington Post*, 22 August 1990, p. A 20.

186  For instance, Captain E. P. Carlisle wrote about "the ungrateful Kuwaitis, who grew fat while enjoying their protection from a militant Iran". Captain

and varied. It was essentially the *New York Times* that published the largest number of letters criticizing Kuwait and in particular the Islamic and autocratic monarchy that had become rich thanks to its oil revenues.[187]

In conclusion, editorials, in presenting Kuwait positively and compassionately, echoed the official speeches of the American president and the British Prime Minister whether they referred to the description of the Emirate as a peaceful state or a small country suffering from abuses perpetrated by the Iraqi army. It is clear that by insisting on the precarious situation in which Kuwait found itself and by presenting it as a victimized and assaulted nation, editorials and opinion articles not only reinforced the negative image of the aggressor Saddam Hussein, but also helped to prepare public opinion for the sending of troops to rescue the country illegally invaded and occupied by Iraq. This statement begs the question of how to mobilize public opinion and convince it to support a decision to go and aid a faraway country in the

---

E. P. Carlisle, "Limits of UN resolution on embargo against Iraq", letters, *Times*, 16 August 1990, p. 11. However, Abdulla Y. Bishara described Kuwait as Iraq's "peaceful neighbour" and "an innocent state". Adulla Y. Bishara, "UN diplomacy as Gulf Option", letters, *Times*, 30 August 1990, p. 11. Dennis Reid wrote in the *Sunday Times* about having been in hiding in Kuwait after the Iraqi invasion and the fact that "many Kuwaitis risked their lives to give [him] food and help". Dennis Reid, "Gas-mask children get a lesson in courage – Kuwaiti kindness", letters, *Sunday Times*, 17 February 1991, Sect. 1, p. 23. On the other hand, Charles Foster wrote about the way "the Kuwaitis have flouted their wealth while ignoring their poorer Muslim neighbours", and he described Kuwait as "a greedy and selfish state". Charles Foster, "Taking the begging bowl to Kuwait", letters, *Sunday Times*, 10 February 1991, Sect. 1, p. 20.

187    For instance, the letter by Carl Stein, "Building of U.S. Troops Alarms the Arab World – Friendly Dictators", letters, *New York Times*, 26 August 1990, p. E 18, and that by Philippa Strum, "No, We Don't Have to Go to War with Iraq", letters, *New York Times*, 8 November 1990, p. A 34.

Middle East that it knows only vaguely. If the atrocities, looting and killings committed by the Iraqi armed forces in Kuwait during their occupation of that country cannot be ignored, one may wonder why public opinion was not also informed of atrocities perpetrated in other parts of the world[188] and encouraged to react to them. But it is true that Kuwait holds about ten percent of the world's oil reserves, which could be an initial response. On the other hand, it is surprising that American and British editorials did not mention the fact, as did some opinion articles in the American and British press, that Kuwait was "a country where the notion of democracy was the most flouted and misunderstood".[189] The fact that political and military authorities tried to persuade their citizens that it was noble to help a small country that had been unjustly invaded and whose inhabitants suffered from the brutality of the Iraqi army is certainly understandable by virtue of the economic interests at stake, but that editorialists on both sides of the Atlantic, consciously or unwillingly, chose to endorse the policies and actions of their respective governments is more difficult to accept. It can certainly be assumed that due to the publication of some opinion articles with positions diametrically opposed to the editorial line of the newspapers, readers were supposed to be able to shape their own opinion thanks to the plurality of published points of view. Finally, beyond the issue of the existence or non-existence of democracy in the Emirate, which was addressed in opinion articles, it is undeniable that the victimization of Kuwait as a country unduly invaded and occupied by the local tyrant only confirmed the image of the Iraqi leader

---

188     Albert Jacquard, *Petite philosophie à l'égard des non-philosophes*, Paris: Calmann-Lévy, 1997, p. 110.
189     Anne Morelli, *op. cit.*, p. 29.

as a villain and scoundrel and increased the aversion of public opinion to him.

## 1.10 Saddam Hussein versus the civilized world

Beyond the abuses committed by Saddam Hussein from August 1990 to the outbreak of hostilities, the reference to the concept of civilization emerged as a constant element from the development of Saddam Hussein's portrait in the American press and the British press. The president of Iraq was generally depicted as a barbarian, for example in the hostage case or when we analyse the qualifiers used by editorialists and journalists to describe his personality and behaviour. Given that the antagonism between the Iraqi leader and the "civilized" world was a recurring theme in editorials and opinion articles, it is necessary to dwell upon it a little while.

On the American side, it was above all the *New York Times* which emphasized in its editorials that by taking civilians hostage and by not respecting the diplomatic immunity of embassies, Saddam Hussein trampled on the standards of civilization.[190] Similarly, opinion articles in the American newspaper referred to the "conflict" of the president of Iraq "with the civilized world".[191] While editorials and opinion articles on the subject appeared in the *New York Times* in August and September 1990 as well as January 1991, the *Washington Post* published an editorial about

---

190    For example: "His Enemy Is the World", editorial, *New York Times*, 17 August 1990, p. A 28.
191    Robert Satloff, "Escape Route for Saddam Hussein: Jordan", op-ed, *New York Times*, 11 August 1990, p. A 25.

it in August 1990 and an opinion article in March 1991, that is after the end of hostilities.

On the British side, newspapers referred to the opposition between Iraq and its ruler on the one hand and the civilized world on the other mainly in editorials in the *Guardian*[192] and the *Sunday Times*[193] as well as in opinion pieces in the *Times*[194] and especially the *Sunday Times*[195] which published many articles about it. Only the *Observer* differed from the other British newspapers by not devoting editorials or opinion pieces to this issue.[196] As in the *New York Times*, it was mainly during the Gulf Crisis that opinion pieces about the confrontation between the president of Iraq and the "civilized" nations were published in British newspapers.

Readers' letters referring to the notion of civilization were published in the *Washington Post* and the *Times* during the Gulf Crisis. For example, a reader of the *Times* accused Iraq of being "a threat to world order, to regional stability and to civilized

---

192  "Holding more than Kuwait to ransom", editorial, *Guardian*, 2 August 1990, p. 18.

193  "Lest we forget", editorial, *Sunday Times*, 16 September 1990, Sect. 3, p. 7.

194  Bernard Levin, "Preying on our minds, but only because we let them", op-ed, *Times*, 13 September 1990, p. 14.

195  For example, the following articles by Norman Macrae, "Saddam and sterling: the battles ahead", op-ed, *Sunday Times*, 26 August 1990, Sect. 3, p. 4; Norman Macrae, "Gazing in a crystal hazy with mumbo-jumbo and Gulf sand", op-ed, *Sunday Times*, 30 December 1990, Sect. 1, p. 13.

196  Nonetheless, the *Observer* published opinion pieces which questioned the American will, described as a high-tech crusade, to promote American values throughout the world. See the column by Simon Hoggart published on 3 February 1991 and the article by Andrew Stephen of the same day, entitled "A just cause, perhaps – but was it wise to get involved?".

behaviour".[197] The *New York Times*, on the American side, the *Guardian* and the *Sunday Times*, on the British side, hardly published any letters on this subject. It is difficult to explain the reasons for this as we do not know the selection criteria for the publication of letters.

On the whole, editorialists and journalists from American and British dailies as well as the *Sunday Times* consistently pointed to an opposition between the Iraqi leader and the world in which they lived and that they considered civilized. Yet, what does the term "civilization" correspond to? According to *The Cambridge Advanced Learner's Dictionary*, the term "civilization" refers to human society with its well-developed social organizations, or the culture and way of life of a society at a particular period in time. This notion is often defined as the process by which a society or place reaches an advanced stage of social and cultural development and organization. In other words, the term "civilization" can refer to the whole of cultural, political and institutional productions specific to a group of societies,[198] and it is first defined as the totality of acquisitions of human societies. Thanks to its arsenal of rules, laws and institutions, civilization would also be characterized by its opposition to violence as a regulating principle of human relations.[199] In this sense, the definition is opposed to the state of nature and barbarity, which seems to be the accepted meaning

---

197    Abdulla Y. Bishara, "UN diplomacy as Gulf option", letters, *Times*, 30 August 1990, p. 11. Since the author of the letter was the Secretary General of the Cooperation Council for the Arab States of the Gulf at that time, he could perhaps be criticized for being judge and party.

198    Frédéric Laupies (dir.), *Dictionnaire de culture générale*, 2e éd., Paris: PUF, 2005, p. 1207.

199    Alexis Chabot, *Cours particulier de culture générale*, Paris: Ellipses, 2009, p. 226.

in editorials and opinion articles. By the same token, the verb "civilize" means to educate a people or a country so that it moves from a primitive condition to a state of higher cultural, intellectual, material and social development. Examination of American and British editorials and opinion articles suggests that contributors seemed convinced of the unquestionable superiority of their world over that of the Iraqi president and thus displayed a contemptuous attitude towards Saddam Hussein. By expressing unfavourable value judgments on the world of the president of Iraq, editorialists and journalists from American and British dailies as well as from the *Sunday Times* might have considered themselves vested with a mission towards the people they described as uncivilized because they were convinced of the supremacy of Western civilization, more advanced in their eyes, and of its values, which included, among others, justice, democracy, Christian humanism and the defence of human rights. According to Claude Lévi-Strauss, the most obvious values professed by Western civilization "that are least open to question" would seem to be: on the one hand the continual increase in "the per capita supply of energy" and on the other hand the protection and prolongation of human life.[200] The existence of a dictator like Saddam Hussein therefore posed a threat to editorialists, journalists and some contributors as well as to some readers in that the Iraqi leader strove by his actions to work against these Western assumptions.

In their many speeches and at press conferences from August 1990 until January 1991, American President George Bush[201]

---

200    Claude Lévi-Strauss, *Race and History*, Paris: Unesco, 1952, p. 32.
201    There are twenty-three references to either the adjective "civilized" or the substantive "civilization" to describe the world or values not respected by

and British Prime Minister Margaret Thatcher[202] insisted on the antagonism between the president of Iraq and civilized nations such as the United States and the United Kingdom concerning, for example, the continued detention of thousands of Americans and Britons in captivity and the intrusion into foreign embassies in Kuwait. In addition, the two heads of state vilified Saddam Hussein for infringing the standards and values of civilization through his behaviour. In any case, government officials had to persuade public opinion that this was indeed a reason to send armed troops to liberate a faraway country of which it had very little knowledge.

In conclusion, although the *Observer* did not publish editorials and opinion pieces on this issue, editorialists and journalists from American and British dailies and the *Sunday Times* as well as some readers of the *Washington Post* and the *Times* relayed the official rhetoric and judged the world of Saddam Hussein – the Enemy, the Other – inferior to theirs. By this opposition, they placed themselves in a comparative and ethnocentric perspective. They emphasized the profound difference between their civilized world and that of the president of Iraq, which they regarded as dangerous, uncontrollable, uncertain and opaque. The degree of civilization or non-civilization presupposes that the society that American and British editorialists and journalists believed they represented had made some progress in the evolution of humanity in comparison with the approach of the Iraqi leader considered

---

Saddam Hussein in nineteen speeches and press conferences of the U.S. president.

202 Ten references to civilized countries or the contempt by the Iraqi president of the standards of civilization appeared in seven of Margaret Thatcher's speeches. John Major, who became Prime Minister at the end of November 1990, does not seem to have commented on the matter.

barbaric or ruthless and devoid of moral values. For Claude Lévi-Strauss, "all civilizations, one after another, recognize the superiority of [...] Western civilization".[203] However, Edward W. Said wonders how one "can today speak of 'Western civilization' except as in large measure an ideological fiction, implying a sort of detached superiority for a handful of values and ideas, none of which has much meaning outside the history of conquest, immigration, travel and the mingling of peoples that gave the Western nations their present mixed identities".[204] Be that as it may, the dualistic and unequivocal world implicitly presented to the reader in editorials and opinion articles in the press on both sides of the Atlantic – except in the *Observer* – and pitting good against evil, sheriffs against outlaws, did not exist or at least was only possible in the biased writings of American and British editorialists and journalists. However, we could defend them by repeating Claude Lévi-Strauss's argument, namely that "no culture is capable of a true judgment of any other, since no culture can lay aside its own limitations, and its appreciation is therefore inevitably relative".[205]

# Conclusion

Iraq's invasion of Kuwait on 2 August 1990 left the world in a state of shock[206] and became the most high-profile event of the summer of 1990 and the following months. The invasion marked the beginning of a media series whose every development

---

203    Claude Lévi-Strauss, *op. cit.*, p. 30.
204    Edward W. Said, *op. cit.*, p. 349.
205    Claude Lévi-Strauss, *op. cit.*, p. 30.
206    Éric Laurent, *op. cit.*, p. 204.

was relayed and amplified in the American and British press. Described as aggression, an adventure, a criminal and illegal act, even the rape of Kuwait, in some editorials and opinion articles and even by some readers, the invasion appeared as the act of a bloodthirsty barbarian.

In addition to the description of the invasion of Kuwait as an act of aggression and its comparison with a rape of the Emirate, the American press and the British press also agreed on the following points: the use of the term crisis; the designation of civilians as hostages and the condemnation of Saddam Hussein for taking foreign civilians hostage; the accusation against the Iraqi leader for the ransacking and looting committed in Kuwait. However, the British press differed from the American press by not commenting on the incursion of Iraqi troops into foreign embassies and the indignation of the British Prime Minister about it. Similarly, the American press stood out from the British press by not calling the crisis a "war" in its editorials and by being reluctant to describe the provisional government installed in Kuwait as a 'puppet' government as the American and British authorities did.

All the ingredients were thus in place to convince readers of the obligation to send troops to the Persian Gulf to stop the dictator and ultimately engage their country in conflict with Iraq. It is true that, under a dictatorship, the regime in power is free to engage its army in a military conflict without the need to seek the permission of the people, anyway deprived of freedom of expression and protest. This is, of course, not the same in a democratic country. Nevertheless, public opinion can be influenced using a variety of techniques. These include, among others, the demonization of the enemy by those in power, in this case relayed by the media. In 1990-91, it served to persuade American and British public opinion to endorse the policy being pursued, approve the dispatch of the army of the respective countries to the Persian Gulf, and above all prepare their citizens for their country's entry into war.

# Chapter II:
# Abuses during the Gulf War [207]

As we have just seen, the image of the protagonist, who quickly became the number one enemy, was firmly in place from August 1990 and changed little until the war. What was the situation like during the hostilities from mid-January to the end of February 1991? How did this portrait evolve in editorials, opinion articles and letters to the editor during this period?

## 2.1   Attempts to divide the coalition

Although of lesser importance, there was a theme in the American and British press, which had already been covered during the Gulf Crisis but which some newspapers dealt mainly with during the war itself, namely Saddam Hussein's attempts to divide the anti-Iraqi coalition. On the American side, editorials of the two newspapers[208] focused on the efforts of the president of Iraq to divide the thirty-five nations of the international coalition mandated by the U.N. and placed under U.S. command. On the British side, only the *Times*[209] and the *Observer*[210] referred in their editorials to the attempts of the president of Iraq to split the allies. Both newspapers may have been sensitive to this issue because of

---

207   For the sake of consistency, the chronological order of the most significant events that took place during the Gulf War has been followed.

208   "A Good Gulf Pep Rally", editorial, *New York Times*, 13 September 1990, p. A 26; "Iraq's Double Grab", editorial, *Washington Post*, 21 August 1990, p. A 22.

209   "Half a peace plan", editorial, *Times*, 21 February 1991, p. 11.

210   "Window of opportunity", editorial, *Observer*, 2 September 1991, p. 12.

the level of support provided to Washington by Margaret Thatcher and John Major during the Gulf Crisis and War. Whereas the *Times* approved of American policy and the entry into war of Britain as a staunch ally alongside the United States, the *Observer*, on the other hand, published numerous editorials opposing the Gulf War[211] and criticizing the attitude of the United States.[212]

American opinion articles on Iraq's endeavours were published in the two U.S. newspapers during the Gulf War.[213] In the British press, Paddy Ashdown, the Liberal MP, speculated in the *Observer* in February 1991 on Saddam Hussein's possible intention to "break the solidarity of the coalition".[214] The other British newspapers made little mention in their opinion pieces of Iraq's attempts to fracture the coalition arrayed against it. The American press differed thus from the British press by publishing more editorials and opinion articles on Saddam Hussein's endeavours to split the allied countries. Given the role of the United States as the leader of the coalition, it certainly made sense for the American press to devote many articles to this issue.

---

211 For example: "Squeeze the man, not the trigger", editorial, *Observer*, 12 August 1990, p. 12. However, there were two editorials reflecting the fatalist acceptance of the conflict by the Sunday paper: "A stark choice that can't be avoided", editorial, *Observer*, 13 January 1991, p. 14; "Remember what the victims are dying for", editorial, *Observer*, 20 January 1991, p. 18.

212 For instance: "Stand firm on sanctions", editorial, *Observer*, 28 October 1990, p. 20.

213 "Wreck the coalition". Leslie H. Gelb, "A Final Pause", op-ed, *New York Times*, 13 January 1991, p. E 19; "Iraq's attempt to fracture the coalition with Scud attacks on Israel". Charles Krauthammer, "The Ground War: Hold It Off", op-ed, *Washington Post*, 1 February 1991, p. A 21.

214 Paddy Ashdown, MP, "Just so far and no further", op-ed, *Observer*, 24 February 1991, p. 24.

Except for a reader's letter in the *New York Times* speculating, among other things, on the possible collapse of the coalition,[215] readers did not comment in the *Washington Post* and the British newspapers on the Iraqi ruler's attempts to divide the allies. Again, either the newspapers chose not to publish letters on the subject, or readers did not comment on Saddam Hussein's endeavours to wreck the coalition of countries united against him.

American and British editorialists and journalists generally based their assessment of Saddam Hussein's personality on what he was doing, such as, for example, his peace proposal to Iran or the misdeeds of his army in Kuwait. However, this time, American editorialists, journalists and contributors as well as those from the *Times* and the *Observer* interpreted the behaviour of the Iraqi leader as an attempt to divide the coalition. They speculated on the risk of collapse of the allied anti-Iraqi coalition. In doing so, they were merely relaying the views expressed by George Bush and Margaret Thatcher.[216] The American president repeatedly stressed the determination of the president of Iraq to separate the U.S.-led coalition partners. In view of the Iraqi leader's actions, it is plausible, even probable that the American president may have been right about Saddam Hussein's objective, but the fact is that, consciously or not, the American press and a part of the British press once again faithfully and loyally reproduced the official statements of their respective governments. All in all, American

---

215    Michael DiGiacomo, "Negotiating an Iraqi Withdrawal Beats War", letters, *New York Times*, 18 November 1990, p. E 16.

216    Cf. George Bush's exchanges with reporters on 27 October 1990 (<https://bush41library.tamu.edu/archives/public-papers/2364>, consulted 6 August 2021). Similarly, Margaret Thatcher shared George Bush's point of view in her interview for TV-AM on 28 October 1990 (<https://www.margaretthatcher.org/document/108232>, consulted 5 August 2021).

newspapers, in their editorials and opinion articles, as well as, on the British side, the *Times*, in its editorials, and the *Observer*, in its editorials and opinion pieces, painted the portrait of a disruptive leader, who sought to dissolve the union between the countries of the anti-Iraqi coalition, thereby reinforcing his negative image.

## 2.2 Launch of Iraqi missiles

From 18 January 1991, Iraq fired Soviet-made Scud rockets at Saudi Arabia as well as at Israel[217] to try to draw the Hebrew State into the conflict. According to Pierre-Jean Luizard, Baghdad, by firing Scuds at Israel, used the Palestinian example in order to link Palestinian issues to those of its regime.[218] Washington asked Israel not to intervene in the war. By way of solidarity with Israel, the United States provided the Hebrew state with Patriot missiles.[219] In their editorials and opinion articles,[220] the two American newspapers condemned these attacks which were described, for example in the *New York Times*, as "barbarous",[221] the Scuds being referred to as "terror weapons".[222] Unlike the American editorials that referred to Iraq's attacks of Scud missiles on both Israel and Saudi Arabia, the British press only focused on

217    Philip M. Taylor, *op. cit.*, 1998, p. 322.
218    Pierre-Jean Luizard, *op. cit.*, p. 234.
219    Max Gallo, *Les Clés de l'Histoire contemporaine*, Paris: Libraires Arthème Fayard, 2005, p. 832.
220    For instance, Hobart Rowen, "The Bottom Line in the Gulf", op-ed, *Washington Post*, 31 January 1991, p. A 19.
221    "This Aggression Will Not Stand", editorial, *New York Times*, 1 March 1991, p. A 26.
222    William Safire, "The Great Scud-Patriot Mystery", op-ed, *New York Times*, 7 March 1991, p. A 25.

Scuds targeting the Jewish state.[223] Editors of British newspapers might have preferred to highlight Iraq's aggression against a non-combatant nation.

The British press preceded the American press by publishing editorials on the launch of Scud missiles already in January 1991.[224] In addition to castigating Iraqi Scud missile attacks on civilians, American editorials and opinion articles as well as the *Observer* underlined the effectiveness of American Patriot missiles capable of intercepting and destroying Scud missiles.[225] Except for Hugo Young from the *Guardian* who blamed the Pentagon and the British Ministry of Defence for their lack of knowledge of the extent of the destruction in the enemy camp,[226] most articles praised the superiority of American technology. This enthusiasm for the Patriots limited the conflict to its technological aspect according to Chantal Bernard-Putz and contributed to boosting

---

223  For example: "Containing a war", editorial, *Times*, 17 January 1991, p. 13; "The debate and the bill", editorial, *Guardian*, 24 January 1991, p. 20; "The shame of Europe", editorial, *Sunday Times*, 27 January 1991, Sect. 1, p. 11.

224  "War in the open", editorial, *Times*, 21 January 1991, p. 11; "The debate and the bill", editorial, *Guardian*, 24 January 1991, p. 20; "The shame of Europe", editorial, *Sunday Times*, 27 January 1991, Sect. 1, p. 11; "Keeping cool while the war hots up", editorial, *Observer*, 27 January 1991, p. 20.

225  "Patriots Work. Star Wars Won't", editorial, *New York Times*, 3 February 1991, p. E 18; "The U.S. and Israel after the War", editorial, *Washington Post*, 18 February 1991, p. A 24; "Keeping cool while the war hots up", editorial, *Observer*, 27 January 1991, p. 20. The Sunday paper argued that "watching Patriot missiles rush into the night sky to explode and destroy the Iraqi Scuds was like taking part in a brilliant computer game".

226  Hugo Young, "The nightmare begins to loom", op-ed, *Guardian*, 24 January 1991, p. 20.

a patriotic impetus.[227] One may wonder why missiles fired by Iraq were fiercely criticized in the American press while those used by the allied armies drew tremendous admiration. Likewise, why did editorialists and journalists not question the destruction of infrastructure and the death of civilians and enemy soldiers?[228] No doubt it is foreseeable that, in times of war, the press, like the government in power, becomes extremely patriotic towards the allied troops engaged in combat and shows no compassion for adversaries for fear of being accused of naivety or defeatism, or even collaboration. According to Élisabeth Coss-Humbert, Patriot anti-missile missiles took on an ethical aura as defensive weapons. Contrary to the Scuds, this "sacred" weapon did not target the population but instead defended men against the weapons of Evil. For the author, it was thus the battle of the Patriots against the Scuds.[229]

On the whole, British newspapers devoted more editorials to the launch of Scuds than opinion pieces. Regarding readers' letters, the American press did not publish any letters relating

---

227    Chantal Bernard-Putz, "L'Armement et l'information scientifique et technique dans la presse quotidienne", *in* Béatrice Fleury-Vilatte (dir.), *op. cit.*, pp. 10, 51, 56. In addition to photographs, American and British newspapers resorted to sketches and drawings to present weapons used by the allies.

228    In the British press, the *Times* published an article by Mary Kaldor, author of *The Imaginary War. Understanding the East-West Conflict*, which wondered about the big bombing raids of the allies on Iraq and the hundreds of people killed "despite the precision of our high-tech weaponry" (Mary Kaldor, "Death blows to democracy too", op-ed, *Times*, 26 January 1991, p. 10).

229    Élisabeth Coss-Humbert *in* Béatrice Fleury-Vilatte (dir.), *op. cit.*, p. 22. According to Alain Gresh and Dominique Vidal, Iraq fired 93 Scuds against Israel and Saudi Arabia during the Gulf War (Alain Gresh & Dominique Vidal, *op. cit.*, p. 78).

to the subject and few letters were published in the British press. For example, a reader of the *Guardian* blamed the United States for smashing Iraq "from sewers to scuds".[230] By publishing this letter, the *Guardian* stood on the sidelines of spontaneous dualism. In the *Sunday Times*, a reader whose name and address were withheld accused Saddam Hussein of targeting the civilian population and children, in particular in Riyadh.[231] As British newspapers did not allude to the firing of Scuds on Saudi Arabia, it could be suggested that the reader of the Sunday paper had another source of information.[232]

All in all, both American and British editorials and opinion articles stressed the missile attacks on civilian populations. The rhetoric of editorialists on both sides of the Atlantic and journalists in the United States thus adopted the official announcements of the U.S. president. George Bush, in several of his conferences on the progress of the Gulf War,[233] highlighted Iraq's use of Scud missiles targeted at innocent civilians in both Israel and Saudi Arabia. Similarly, the American president praised the performance of U.S. Patriot missiles capable of striking down Iraqi Scuds,[234] which was

---

230   Howard Senter, "West's capabilities for waging the peace", letters, *Guardian*, 28 February 1991, p. 20.

231   Name and address withheld, "Gas-mask children get a lesson in courage", letters, *Sunday Times*, 17 February 1991, Sect. 1, p. 23.

232   Moreover, since neither the name nor the address of the reader was mentioned, it is possible that the letter came from a reader living in Saudi Arabia or having some knowledge and family in the region.

233   For example, refer to Bush's remarks to the Reserve Officers Association on 23 January 1991 (<https://bush41library.tamu.edu/archives/public-papers/2648>, consulted 6 August 2021).

234   For instance, see the American president's address before a joint session of the Congress on the State of the Union on 29 January 1991 (<https://bush41library.tamu.edu/archives/public-papers/2656>, consulted 6 August 2021).

a technological feat also echoed, as we have seen, by American editorialists and journalists and by *Observer* editorialists. In any case, by repeating that Iraqi Scud rockets fell mainly on civilians in Israel and Saudi Arabia, American and British editorialists and U.S. journalists exaggerated the portrait of the Iraqi leader who appeared from then on as an aggressor whose cowardly attacks on innocent people did not respect the rules of war.[235] However, in their defence, it must be said that Saddam Hussein's own behaviour and personality had already contributed to this negative portrait.

## 2.3   Captured allied soldiers

Another event caught the attention of the American and British press: seven captured airmen, their faces swollen, were shown on Iraqi television on 20 January 1991.[236] Saddam Hussein announced their detention as "human shields" in strategic locations. In so doing, the Iraqi leader flouted the Geneva Convention on the treatment of prisoners of war.

The American and British press referred to the "abuse of prisoners"[237] and "the exploitation of POWs"[238] in their editorials and opinion articles. For example, the *Times* wrote in its editorial of 22 January 1991 that "Iraq's decision to parade [the prisoners of war] clearly violates article 13 of the Third Geneva Convention of

---

235   Élisabeth Coss-Humbert *in* Béatrice Fleury-Vilatte (dir.), *op. cit.*, p. 30.
236   Hedrick Smith, ed., *op. cit.*, p. 428.
237   For example: "The Protesters, Heard", editorial, *New York Times*, 27 January 1991, p. E 16.
238   For instance: "Longer, Tougher, Costlier", editorial, *Washington Post*, 27 January 1991, p. C 6.

1949" and spoke of "inhumane treatment".[239] The *Sunday Times* was the only British newspaper that did not publish opinion pieces on this subject. Nonetheless, there were several articles on this point in the Sunday paper under the heading "News Review" focusing on the Gulf War.[240] On the whole, most journalists unanimously blamed Saddam Hussein for his treatment of the captured pilots. By contrast, Andrew Stephen in the *Observer* expressed surprise, with a touch of sarcasm, at George Bush's outrage that "the POWs are ill-treated by the Iraqi thugs".[241]

George Bush and John Major stressed Saddam Hussein's cruelty towards the prisoners of war on 21 January 1991.[242] The U.S. president and the British Prime Minister accused the president of Iraq of violating the provisions of the Geneva Convention relative to the treatment of prisoners of war. George Bush also stated on 27 February 1991 and in his victory speech to Congress on 6 March 1991 that American soldiers treated Iraqi

---

239     "Saddam's new hostages", editorial, *Times*, 22 January 1991, p. 11.

240     For example, the following articles: Bryan Appleyard, "Unattributables march to an antiquated drum", Gulf War, *Sunday Times*, 27 January 1991, Sect. 1, p. 18; The RAF Pilot, "The new stuff flies to heroic heights in its finest hour", Profile, *Sunday Times*, 27 January 1991, Sect. 1, p. 14; "Bad News and bloody surprises", Insight, *Sunday Times*, 27 January 1991, Sect. 1, p. 7.

241     Andrew Stephen, "A just cause, perhaps – but was it wise to get involved?", op-ed, *Observer*, 3 February 1991, p. 11.

242     Refer to George Bush's exchange with reporters on 21 January 1991 (<https://bush41library.tamu.edu/archives/public-papers/2638>, consulted 5 August 2021). Also see John Major's statement to the House of Commons on 21 January 1991 (<https://hansard.parliament.uk/Commons/1991-01-21/debates/c80bc5e0-03fd-49fb-a838-62f4c66958e1/TheGulf?highlight=john%20major#contribution-45b223d1-b234-4128-83d8-f45ed0b23f2b>, consulted 5 August 2021).

228

prisoners humanely and "with kindness".[243] Likewise, John Major declared on 7 February 1991 that "in no way can Iraq's behaviour be equated with that of the allies in their treatment of prisoners of war. Iraq is in gross and flagrant violation of its obligations while the allies are doing everything possible to ensure that they meet their commitments under the Geneva Convention".[244] Editorialists, journalists, and contributors – apart from Andrew Stephen of the *Observer* – echoed what their respective governments said about allied prisoners and Iraqi soldiers and repeated the official version. They joined the authorities in presenting the enemy as an amoral and inhuman monster, a paradigm of evil that did not respect the war conventions. American journalists in particular contrasted the exemplary behaviour of U.S. soldiers towards Iraqi prisoners with the barbaric acts suffered by allied prisoners at the hands of the Iraqi armed forces. Like its leader, the Iraqi army was demonized. Readers were told that by mistreating allied prisoners, Iraqi soldiers were also failing to respect the rules of war, which meant that they were not civilized, unlike the coalition forces.[245] We find here again the Manichean view between "good" and "evil" or rather between "the good guys" and

---

243    Cf. George Bush's Address to the Nation on the Suspension of Allied Offensive Combat Operations in the Persian Gulf on 27 February 1991 (<https://bush41library.tamu.edu/archives/public-papers/2746>, consulted 4 August 2021). Also refer to his address before a joint session of the Congress on the Cessation of the Persian Gulf Conflict on 6 March 1991 (<https://bush41library.tamu.edu/archives/public-papers/2767>, consulted 5 August 2021).

244    Cf. the Prime Minister's Question Time from 7 February 1991 (<https://johnmajorarchive.org.uk/1991/02/07/pmqt-7-february-1991/>, consulted 22 July 2021).

245    One might wonder why the media were not more civilized and restrained when they published images of Iraqis in their burned-out tanks and trucks fleeing from Kuwait on the "Highway of Death" (Robert Fisk, *op. cit.*, pp. 845-846).

"the bad guys". This binary reading of events, with journalists contrasting the fortitude and valour of allied soldiers[246] with the inhumanity and brutality of the Iraqi army, raises a number of questions. According to Anne Morelli, war propaganda consists in making people believe that violence is solely the work of the enemy army, composed essentially of lawless bandits while our own army is devoted to the service of the population, even the enemy population.[247] The author claims that it turned out after the Gulf War that the bruises of the Western pilots captured by the Iraqis came from their ejection from their aircraft in full flight and were not the result of mistreatment by the Iraqis.[248]

The American press and the *Observer*, on the British side, stood out from the other British newspapers by not publishing letters relating to the airmen exhibited on Iraqi television. However, the *Times* published the reaction of Conservative MP Michael Grylls demanding the removal from power of Saddam Hussein and his henchmen for their atrocities and war crimes against "our British and US prisoners of war".[249] The author's use of the possessive adjective "our" included the reader and differentiated allied soldiers from enemy combatants. This adjective thus introduced a sense of cohesion, of belonging to a group which defined its identity in terms of its relationship to itself and to the Other. On

---

246  Unfortunately, future events showed that U.S. forces were capable of wrongdoing against captured combatants and non-combatants as in the Guantanamo Bay detention camp.

247  Anne Morelli, *op. cit.*, p. 37.

248  *Ibid.*, p. 43. However, Robert Fisk wrote that "RAF crews later gave graphic accounts of their mistreatment at the hands of Iraq's security goons" (Robert Fisk, *op. cit.*, p. 851n).

249  Michael Grylls, "Wider perspective on peace and war", letters, *Times*, 21 February 1991, p. 15.

the other hand, a reader of the *Guardian* wondered ironically at the end of February 1991 about the relevance of publishing photos of Iraqi soldiers captured whereas the exhibition of allied pilots had been condemned as a breach of the Geneva Convention.[250] The reader's reaction reflected his sense of distance from current events and especially from the presentation and interpretation of events by the media in general and the written press in particular.

In summary, arguments about the allied airmen paraded on Iraqi television can be found not only in the discourse of government authorities but also in editorials and most opinion articles (except for one *Observer* journalist). Apart from this exception, there was therefore an alignment between official rhetoric and journalistic prose. The press did not offer readers a multiplicity of points of view on the issue of allied prisoners but adopted the "official" portrait of the Iraqi leader as a cruel despot ready to break the rules of war.

## 2.4   Environmental pollution

On 25 January 1991, Saddam Hussein released thousands of tons of oil into the Persian Gulf and set fire to hundreds of oil wells in Kuwait.[251] The American and British press unanimously condemned the Iraqi leader in their editorials for "the flooding of oil into the Gulf".[252] The *Sunday Times* adopted a more scathing

---

250   Mike Ellwood, "Rules bent to snapping point", letters, *Guardian*, 28 February 1991, p. 20.

251   Élisabeth Coss-Humbert *in* Béatrice Fleury-Vilatte, *op. cit.*, p. 25; George Brown Tindall & David Emory Shi, *op. cit.*, p. 1146.

252   For example: "Longer, Tougher, Costlier", editorial, *Washington Post*, 27 January 1991, p. C 6.

tone in its editorials than the American press and the other British newspapers by describing the oil slick as "an act of unparalleled environmental terrorism"[253] and "environmental vandalism".[254] This is hardly surprising given that the *Sunday Times'* articles were often more virulent in tone than those of British daily newspapers.

We find the same arguments about the oil pollution in the Gulf in the opinion articles published on both sides of the Atlantic. For example, William Safire spoke in the *New York Times* of "ecoterrorism against cormorants".[255] Matthew Parris had already referred in the *Times* to the killing of cormorants by Saddam Hussein, adding that "the monster is hurting animals".[256] Although the *Sunday Times* did not devote opinion pieces on this subject, the Sunday paper published a front-page photo of an oil-covered cormorant and described it as a "war victim".[257]

Opinion articles in the American and British newspapers repeated George Bush's multiple references to Saddam Hussein's "environmental terrorism", an expression used by the U.S. president in several exchanges with reporters or during news

253    "The shame of Europe", editorial, *Sunday Times*, 27 January 1991, Sect. 1, p. 11.
254    "Finishing Saddam", editorial, *Sunday Times*, 3 February 1991, Sect. 1, p. 11.
255    William Safire, "Don't Throw Away Victory", op-ed, *New York Times*, 31 January 1991, p. A 23. William Safire used a neologism, namely the term "ecoterrorism" that was first recorded in 1990.
256    Matthew Parris, "… and moreover", op-ed, *Times*, 28 January 1991, p. 10.
257    Sean Ryan, "Oil spillage is world's worst", *Sunday Times*, 27 January 1991, p. 1. The Sunday newspaper also published numerous articles on the subject in the section "Overseas news".

conferences.[258] Likewise, opinion pieces in the British press also echoed the statements made on this subject by John Major who deplored "Iraq's wanton destruction of the environment of the Middle East" and "deliberate pollution of the Gulf".[259] There were few letters published in the American[260] and British[261] press.

The interest shown by the American press in environmental matters such as climate issues and the protection of the environment might seem surprising given that they did not become the subject of major political concern until the mid-1990s.[262] The fact that American editorialists and journalists highlighted the oil slick undoubtedly reflected the U.S. government's willingness,

---

258     For example, see the U.S. president's address on the State of the Union on 29 January 1991 (<https://bush41library.tamu.edu/archives/public-papers/2656>), as well as his news conference on 5 February 1991 (<https://bush41library.tamu.edu/archives/public-papers/2681>, consulted 7 August 2021).

259     Refer to the Prime Minister's Question Time from 29 January and 31 January 1991 (<https://johnmajorarchive.org.uk/1991/01/29/pmqt-written-answers-29-january-1991/>), and (<https://johnmajorarchive.org.uk/1991/01/31/pmqt-written-answers-31-january-1991/>, consulted 7 August 2021).

260     For example, the *New York Times* published a letter by Andrea Sotebeer Azar from Saudi Arabia ("Gulf Oil Spill Should Come as No Surprise") on 31 January 1991. The author described the "oil spill at least 10 times that of the Exxon Valdez". Exxon Valdez was an oil tanker that struck a reef off the coast of Alaska on 24 March 1989 and spilled 10.8 million US gallons of crude oil. The oil spill affected 2,100 km of coastline.

261     For instance, the following letter by Léonie Archer and Philip Barnes, Dr, "Burning issues in the Gulf", letters, *Guardian*, 1 February 1991, p. 18. The authors referred to "the danger of marine spillage" as "millions of tonnes of crude were deliberately pumped into the sea".

262     The United States did not ratify the Kyoto Treaty, which was signed in 1997 and only came into force in 2005. It should also be noted that the European Environment Agency has only been active since 1994 (<http://www.eea.europa.eu/about-us/who>, consulted 1 July 2021).

in concert with the media, to add yet another accusation against the enemy for being guilty of an "ecological disaster" in the words of the report received by the American president on 25 January 1991 about the flooding of millions of barrels of oil into the Persian Gulf.[263] At any rate, however important environmental issues are, it should not be forgotten that in the Gulf War, as in all conflicts, the primary concern of political and military authorities and public opinion is above all to avoid the loss of life of their countries' armed forces at all costs.

In summary, the American press seemed more concerned about this issue than the British press to judge by the large number of editorials and opinion articles on Saddam Hussein's destruction of oil wells and the resulting impact on the environment. However, this perception is arguably misleading since British newspapers published numerous articles on the pollution caused by the oil spill under other headings. Among British newspapers, editorials in the *Sunday Times* were more aggressive towards the Iraqi leader in view of the environmental disaster. On the whole, editorials and opinion articles subscribed to the comments made by the U.S. president and the British Prime Minister. There is no doubt that Saddam Hussein's actions contributed to increasing public aversion to him. Nonetheless, American and British newspapers could be criticized for failing to highlight the ecological effects of the coalition-led Gulf War.[264] According to Ghassan Salamé, the U.S. Department of Energy banned the release of estimates of the

---

263 Éric Laurent, *Tempête du désert. Les secrets de la Maison-Blanche*, Paris: Olivier Orban, 1991, p. 244.

264 In this regard, it is worth referring to the article by Mary Kaldor published in the *Times* on 26 January 1991, "Death blows to democracy too", in which the author questioned the human, economic and ecological costs of the Gulf War. But this article was an exception.

environmental impact of the war.[265] In any case, for American and British editorialists, journalists and contributors and public opinion, Saddam Hussein took nature hostage[266] and through his ecological crime[267] displayed his contempt for all animal, plant or human life on the planet, which only reinforced his portrait as a threat to the world.


## 2.5    Bombing of a shelter in Amiriyah

As a corollary to the image of the Iraqi president conveyed by the American and British newspapers during the hostilities, another significant event revealed the way the conflict was covered by the press on both sides of the Atlantic, namely the bombing of an air-raid shelter in the Amiriyah neighbourhood of Baghdad on 13 February 1991. According to the Iraqi authorities, nearly 400 Iraqi civilians – mainly women and children – were killed in this attack. By contrast, the Bush administration stated that U.S. forces had identified the command and communications centre in Baghdad as a military target.[268] Press Secretary Fitzwater

---

265    Ghassan Salamé, *op. cit.*, 1991, p. 455.

266    Élisabeth Coss-Humbert *in* Béatrice Fleury-Vilatte, *op. cit.*, p. 25.

267    According to Robert Fisk, it was Saddam Hussein's greatest environmental and economic crime in the Emirate. He explains that "two million tons of carbon dioxide and five thousand tons of soot [were] spurting into the skies of Kuwait every day". In addition, "more than sixty million barrels of oil and gas a day [...] were transformed into the chemicals that were [...] poisoning the land and seas as far east as the Himalayas (Robert Fisk, *op. cit.*, pp. 857-859).

268    Arthur H. Blair, *op. cit.*, p. 99. On 14 February 1991, Prime Minister John Major declared that "there has been precision bombing, and that site was bombed because there was legitimate reason to believe that it was a military target" (<https://johnmajorarchive.org.uk/1991/02/14/pmqt-written-answers-14-february-1991/>, consulted 7 August 2021).

argued that they did not know that civilians were sheltering at the location.[269] He insisted on Saddam Hussein's failure to respect the lives of civilians and POWs who were moved to strategic military sites for use as human shields. Iraq, usually very discreet about its losses, exploited the tragedy of the destroyed bunker by announcing the number of civilian deaths in order to appeal to international opinion and generate anxiety about the horrors of war and hostility to the killing of innocent victims.[270]

The next day, this bombing, which was accidental for the American authorities, was widely commented in newspapers on both sides of the Atlantic. However, the tragic event triggered different reactions in editorials published in the American and British press. American editorials adopted a thoughtful, even pragmatic approach to the accident: while they regretted civilian casualties, they responded to the tragedy by warning the coalition in the *New York Times*[271] and the U.S. military in the *Washington Post*[272] of the danger of attacking targets where there was a risk of civilian casualties. In the British press, the situation was more

---

269   Statement by Press Secretary Fitzwater on Allied Bombing in Baghdad on 13 February 1991. See the website <https://www.presidency.ucsb.edu/node/264918> by Gerhard Peters and John T. Woolley, The American Presidency Project, consulted 7 August 2021. Also refer to Charles Reed and David Ryall, eds., *The Price of Peace. Just War in the Twenty-First Century*, Cambridge: Cambridge UP, 2007, p. 116.

270   Élisabeth Coss-Humbert *in* Béatrice Fleury-Vilatte, *op. cit.*, p. 25.

271   "The allies [...] need to consider whether it truly advances their war aims to strike so close to civilians [...]". "Damage Control – and Real Damage", editorial, *New York Times*, 14 February 1991, p. A 26.

272   "American authorities have got to pay scrupulous attention to the risks of hitting civilians, [...]". "The Soviet Peace Bid", editorial, *Washington Post*, 14 February 1991, p. A 22.

contrasted: while the *Times*[273] blamed the Iraqi leader for the deaths of Iraqi civilians in the bunker, editorials in the *Guardian*[274] and the *Observer*[275] placed the deaths of Iraqis – women and children – at the centre of their concerns. And although the editorial staff of the *Sunday Times* chose not to devote specific editorials to this subject, it published articles relating to the first "blunder" of the Gulf War.[276]

In the American press, only the *Washington Post* published opinion articles expressing a number of different views on the subject. For example, William Raspberry reflected on "the long-term political damage, caused by the raid"[277] while Charles Krauthammer denounced the Iraqi leader's "cynical strategy of broadcasting the carnage he has brought upon his own people".[278] On the British side, Martin Woollacott from the *Guardian* deplored "the massacre of innocents in a Baghdad basement, [...] [which] could become, for Arabs certainly and for

273  "President Saddam Hussein is capable of allowing civilians to be used as cover". "[...] Iraq's policy of planting military installations in civilian areas, particularly in cities". "Direct hit in Amiriya", editorial, *Times*, 14 February 1991, p. 15.

274  "Iraqi civilians are at risk, in their thousands". "The first image of the dead", editorial, *Guardian*, 14 February 1991, p. 20.

275  "[...] the appalling deaths of men, women and children in the Baghdad bunker [...]". "One eye on peace as well as one on war", editorial, *Observer*, 17 February 1991, p. 20.

276  For example, the article by James Adams and Marie Calvin, "Pentagon admits error on bunker hit", Gulf News, *Sunday Times*, 17 February 1991, Sect. 1, p. 2. This article was also about the Iraqi announcement of a possible withdrawal that was rejected by the coalition.

277  William Raspberry, "A Clean War", op-ed, *Washington Post*, 15 February 1991, p. A 21.

278  Charles Krauthammer, "Bombing Baghdad", op-ed, *Washington Post*, 14 February 1991, p. A 23.

some Westerners as well, the Guernica of the Gulf War".[279] It is noteworthy that the journalist combined biblical and historical references to describe this incident referring first to Herod's order to kill all male children under two years of age and then to the bombing of Guernica during the Spanish civil war in 1937, which killed many civilians.[280] In the *Sunday Times*, Robert Harris first described, in gruesome details and with strong emotional words, the harrowing scene of women and children burnt alive in the bomb shelter, before defending the BBC over its coverage of the destroyed bunker.[281] Until this incident, there had been no blood in journalists' articles: the Gulf War had been a war with "high technological concentration"[282] thanks to high-precision weapons. Concerning letters published, a group of readers used this deadly event in the *Guardian* to press the point that any war involved the death of non-combatant innocents.[283]

Beyond these differences in the American and British press, there is a common feature in editorials and opinion articles: the treatment of the event was immediate and emotional. Newspapers played on the feeling of shock following the bombing of the Amiriyah shelter. They dramatized reality by staging emotion. By seeking to move readers and strike their sensitive chord, journalists were able to get their message across, guide readers'

---

279  Martin Woollacott, "Iraq's lost generation", op-ed, *Guardian*, 15 February 1991, p. 19.
280  Pablo Picasso's painting "Guernica" depicted the effects of the aerial bombing on the city.
281  Robert Harris, "Don't shoot the media message", op-ed, *Sunday Times*, 17 February 1991, p. IV.
282  Jean Baudrillard, *op. cit.*, p. 41.
283  Miriam Stoppard, Dr, et al., "Easing the suffering of war", letters, *Guardian*, 14 March 1991, p. 20.

judgments and mobilise public opinion. Favouring emotion rather than reasoning is the traditional resource of rhetoric[284] to reduce the critical and analytical skills required when faced with an event of such magnitude. According to Anne Morelli, propaganda and emotion have always been two sides of the same coin.[285] Distress and emotion elicited by the death of Iraqi civilians was highlighted on both sides of the Atlantic. As we have seen, the tragic incident gave rise to different interpretations in that the *Times* in an editorial, and Charles Krauthammer, in an opinion article in the *Washington Post*, differed from the other newspapers by making Saddam Hussein take full responsibility for the tragedy and accusing him of exploiting it for propaganda purposes against the West. The bunker affair was thus presented as a blunder for which Saddam Hussein was responsible more than the allies.[286] The British newspaper and the *Washington Post* journalist adopted the official American discourse that downplayed the seriousness of the incident and the negative impact of the bombing on world public opinion.

## Conclusion

On the whole, the early portraits of Saddam Hussein were confirmed during the hostilities. The characteristic features of the enemy thus continued to be developed in most editorials and opinion articles in the press on both sides of the Atlantic both before the outbreak of the conflict and during the war. Apart from a few differences, American and British newspapers portrayed

---

284    Élisabeth Coss-Humbert *in* Béatrice Fleury-Vilatte, *op. cit.*, p. 24.
285    Anne Morelli, *op. cit.*, p. 57.
286    Élisabeth Coss-Humbert *in* Béatrice Fleury-Vilatte, *op. cit.*, p. 26.

the Iraqi leader as a disruptive element who attempted to divide the coalition united against his army and had no respect for the rules of war or for the environment. By way of summary, the following table correlates the events that took place during the Gulf War, the official rhetoric and their treatment in U.S. and British editorials.

| Editorials | | American press | | British press | | | |
|---|---|---|---|---|---|---|---|
| | | *New York Times* | *Washington Post* | *Times* | *Guardian* | *Sunday Times* | *Observer* |
| Bush & Thatcher | Saddam Hussein's attempt to divide the coalition | x | x | x | | | x |
| Bush | Launch of Iraqi missiles | x | x | x | x | x | x |
| Bush | In praise of American technological performance | x | x | | | | x |
| Bush & Major | Captured allied soldiers | x | x | x | x | x | x |
| Bush & Major | Environmental pollution | x | x | x | x | x | x |
| White House Press Secretary Fitzwater | Bombing of Amiriyah shelter | x | x | x | x | | x |

As we have seen and as shown in the table, American and British editorials unanimously condemned the Iraqi leader for the launch of Iraqi Scuds on the Israeli population, for mistreating allied soldiers who had been taken prisoner and for precipitating an environmental disaster. American editorials and those of the *Observer* differed from other British newspapers in that they praised the performance of the United States' military technology, as did the American president. The *Guardian*, unlike its sister newspaper the *Observer*, made little reference to American technological superiority. The *Sunday Times* differed from the American press, the British dailies and the *Observer* by not devoting editorials to the Iraqi leader's attempts to break the unity of the allies and the bombing of the Amiriyah bunker.

In essence, the American and British press drew a similar portrait of Saddam Hussein. Once again, the press on both sides of the Atlantic conveyed the stereotype of the enemy by giving a Manichean reading of the world. This binary vision corresponded to that of the American and British governments before and during the conflict. While it is necessary for the government of a democratic country to convince public opinion that the armed forces should be sent to war, it is also essential during and after the hostilities to persuade the people of the relevance of the armed intervention. It is therefore unsurprising that the same arguments are frequently repeated to justify the military intervention, emphasizing the enemy's faults and ultimately celebrating his defeat and welcoming the victory of the allied forces, thus increasing the citizens' confidence in their leaders and rejoicing in the greatness and power of their country.

# Chapter III:
# Abuses prior to the Iraqi invasion of Kuwait

Editorials, opinion articles and letters to the editor not only referred to Saddam Hussein's actions after the invasion of Kuwait but also recalled abuses committed by the president and his regime before the crisis began. This was true on both sides of the Atlantic.

## 3.1    Iran-Iraq War

The most important event covered by American and British newspapers was the war between Iran and Iraq from 1980 to 1988. On 22 September 1980, on the first day of the war, which was called the "Imposed War" by the Iranians and the "Whirlwind War" by Saddam Hussein, Iraq's armed forces, including thousands of tanks, crossed the border with Iran.[287] Between 28 December 1980 and 20 March 1984, sixty-three separate gas attacks were carried out by the Iraqis without any reaction from the international community.[288] On the contrary, Europe and the United States supported Iraq during the eight years of the conflict.[289] The United States "supplied the Iraqis with battlefield intelligence" and "some of the chemicals",[290] and Saudi Arabia was "Iraq's principal bankroller".[291] A United Nations-mediated

---

287    Robert Fisk, *op. cit.*, pp. 218-219.
288    *Ibid.*, p. 257.
289    Max Gallo, *op. cit.*, p. 831.
290    Robert Fisk, *op. cit.*, pp. 262, 753.
291    *Ibid.*, p. 753.

ceasefire was signed on 20 August 1988 "without a real winner".[292] The end of the conflict in 1988 left Iraq "bled dry and ruined".[293]

American and British editorials used similar arguments about atrocities committed by the Iraqi regime during this conflict. For example, the *New York Times* stressed Saddam Hussein's "hellish use of poison gas to attack Iranian troops and slaughter 5,000 Kurds",[294] and the *Observer* wrote that Saddam Hussein "caused the death over a million people in an eight-year war against Iran".[295]

This was also the case in American and British opinion articles which emphasized the use of chemical weapons by the Iraqi army against Iranian armed forces during the Iran-Iraq war and against Iraqi-Kurdish civilians in 1988. For instance, George F. Will reminded readers in the *Washington Post* that "Iraq used poison gas against Iran".[296] In the *Sunday Times*, Norman Macrae compared the conflict to "a trench-war Passchendaele",[297] drawing

---

292   Sophie Chautard, *op. cit.*, p. 94; Jean-Baptiste Duroselle & André Kaspi, *op. cit.*, p. 542.

293   Alain Gresh & Dominique Vidal, *op. cit.*, p. 273.

294   "Chief Trumpet", editorial, *New York Times*, 12 August 1990, p. E 20.

295   "A mailed fist for persuasion. Clamouring voice", editorial, *Observer*, 6 January 1991, p. 16.

296   George F. Will, "Wolf Out of Babylon", op-ed, *Washington Post*, 3 August 1990, p. A 23.

297   Norman Macrae, "Saddam and sterling: the battles ahead", op-ed, *Sunday Times*, 26 August 1990, Sect. 3, p. 4. The Battle of Passchendaele, known as the Third Battle of Ypres, Belgium, was fought by the Allies against the German armed forces "at Passchendaele in August-September 1917, when over 300,000 British troops were recorded as dead or wounded, many of them drowned in the mud of Flanders amidst torrential rain" (Kenneth O. Morgan, ed., *The Oxford History of Britain*, rev. ed., Oxford: Oxford UP, 2001, p. 526).

a parallel with the notorious battle of 1917 during which mustard gas was used for the first time.

The *Guardian* differed from other British newspapers because of the publication of a large number of editorials on the war against Iran, which reflected its commitment to convince readers of the Iraqi leader's villainy by highlighting the numerous casualties on each side and the crimes committed by the Iraqi army during the conflict. Similarly, a few readers of the *Guardian* echoed the editorial line of the newspaper and referred to Saddam Hussein's "devastating war with Iran"[298] and "the gassing of Kurdish villages".[299] As Martin Woollacott explained in the newspaper on 6 September 1990, "Iraqis fought a bloody war for eight years for, they were told, the Shatt-al-Arab. Now the President has given it away overnight".[300] A few days earlier, Margaret Thatcher had mentioned in an interview for TV-AM *Frost on Sunday* that the Iraqi leader, in the peace proposals with Iran, "gave away absolutely everything he had previously wanted and gone to war to obtain".[301]

George Bush also referred in his speeches and press conferences to the Iran-Iraq war as well as to Saddam Hussein's use of chemical weapons against his own people and the Kurds.[302] Like

---

298   Ann Clwyd, MP, "Let's cast a net over the whole Middle East when seeking peace with Kuwait", letters, *Guardian*, 23 August 1990, p. 18.
299   Tony Greenstein, "The rules that Stalin knew – and Saddam doesn't", letters, *Guardian*, 11 August 1990, p. 18.
300   Martin Woollacott, "Now it's dawning on the people", op-ed, *Guardian*, 6 September 1990, p. 19.
301   Cf. the following website: <https://www.margaretthatcher.org/document/108186>, consulted 28 October 2022.
302   For example, refer to George Bush's Address to the U.N. in New York on 1 October 1990 (<https://bush41library.tamu.edu/archives/public-papers/2280>, consulted 8 August 2021). As far as the British Prime

their respective governments, the American and British press each reminded their readers, in their editorials and opinion articles, of the bloody war launched by Saddam Hussein against Iran in 1980. These additional observations about the Iran-Iraq war made it possible to complete the portrait of the Iraqi leader as a criminal capable of leading his army to slaughter in 1990 as in 1980.

## 3.2 Saddam Hussein's regime

The dictatorial nature of Saddam Hussein's regime, described as "a rogue power"[303] in the *Washington Post*, was also castigated in the press on both sides of the Atlantic, as for example in an editorial in the *New York Times*:

> The Baghdad leadership could be held criminally accountable for Iraq's offenses. [...] These are punishable crimes:
> Crimes against humanity: [...] Iraq has executed thousands. [...]
> There is hardly a human rights convention that Iraq has not violated.[304]

---

Minister is concerned, see the parliamentary debate on 6 September 1990 (<https://publications.parliament.uk/pa/cm198990/cmhansrd/1990-09-06/Debate-1.html>), and on 13 November 1990 (<https://hansard.parliament.uk/Commons/1990-11-13/debates/3e90a680-fd1d-4752-b02b-1c3a1a0bf1df/GulfCrisis?highlight=chemical%20weapons#contribution-ec3aeedf-4612-45a4-be75-487eeaba757a>), as well as Margaret Thatcher's speech to the U.N. on 30 September 1990 (<https://www.margaretthatcher.org/document/108207>, consulted 8 August 2021).

303  "A deal with Saddam Hussein?", editorial, *Washington Post*, 24 October 1990, p. A 18.

304  "The World v. Saddam Hussein", editorial, *New York Times*, 25 August 1990, p. A 22.

On the British side, the *Guardian* referred in its editorial of 17 January 1991 to "an evil regime".[305] The *Sunday Times* blamed Iraq for being "a hellhole of repression, savagery and brutality".[306] This was also the case in the opinion articles published in the American and British press. For instance, Michael Kinsley described Iraq in the *Washington Post* as a "police state"[307] and Bernard Levin in the *Times* as a "bandit state".[308] According to Alain Gresh and Dominique Vidal, the entire policy of the Iraqi president was focused on ensuring the continued existence of the regime, creating a climate of fear and suspicion.[309] Saddam Hussein resorted to the most brutal methods to rule his country and suppress all attempts at democratic pluralism.[310]

## 3.3   Non-respect of treaties

The *Washington Post*[311] (but not the *New York Times*) and the British newspapers (except for the *Guardian*) referred to treaties that Saddam Hussein had failed to respect, stressing that the Iraqi leader was not trustworthy. For example, the *Times* argued

---

305  "Suddenly the sky turns orange", editorial, *Guardian*, 17 January 1991, p. 18.

306  "War aims", editorial, *Sunday Times*, 26 August 1990, Sect. 3, p. 5.

307  Michael Kinsley, "International Law: Only when It Suits Us?", op-ed, *Washington Post*, 13 September 1990, p. A 23.

308  Bernard Levin, "Preying on our minds, but only because we let them", op-ed, *Times*, 13 September 1990, p. 14.

309  Alain Gresh & Dominique Vidal, *op. cit.*, p. 274.

310  Élisabeth Coss-Humbert *in* Béatrice Fleury-Vilatte, *op. cit.*, p. 30.

311  "The Troops in the Desert", editorial, *Washington Post*, 5 September 1990, p. A 18; Jessica Matthews, "Saddam and the Bomb", op-ed, *Washington Post*, 7 December 1990, p. A 23.

in an editorial of 21 February 1991 that "Saddam must be regarded as totally unreliable in matters of treaties and diplomacy".[312]

In the *Sunday Times*, Barbara Amiel referred to "footage of Saddam tearing up treaties, as he did on television before the Iran-Iraq war".[313] In the title of the article, "Letting a crocodile off the hook" and the article itself, the journalist recalled Winston Churchill's speech of 20 January 1940, criticizing the policy of 'appeasement' of small countries, which he said was like feeding a crocodile attempting to postpone as long as possible the inevitable outcome when there would be no-one else left.[314]. Because of the threat posed by Saddam Hussein's regime for the Mediterranean and Europe, Barbara Amiel advised the allies in her article not to take half-measures with the Iraqi leader since "the failure of resolve would come back to haunt them".[315] In addition to the historical reference in its title, the article contained colloquial expressions, even slang, as was the case in some editorials and opinion pieces published in the *Sunday Times*. This less formal register gave a more polemical tone to the *Sunday Times*' articles.[316] Finally,

312 "Half a peace plan", editorial, *Times*, 21 February 1991, p. 11.
313 Barbara Amiel, "Letting a crocodile off the hook", op-ed, *Sunday Times*, 24 February 1991, p. IV.
314 Hereafter is the excerpt of Winston Churchill's speech, entitled "The War Situation: House of Many Mansions": "Each one hopes that if he feeds the crocodile enough, the crocodile will eat him last" (<https://winstonchurchill.org/resources/speeches/1940-the-finest-hour/the-war-situation-house-of-many-mansions/>, consulted 8 August 2021).
315 See the subheading of the article: "If the allies take half-measures with Saddam, the failure of resolve will come back to haunt them".
316 For example in the following articles : "Finishing Saddam", editorial, *Sunday Times*, 3 February 1991, Sect. 1, p. 11 including pejorative and animal vocabulary to describe the Iraqi president; or even the article by Norman Macrae, "Short and sharp, here's a case for the Falklands treatment", op-ed, *Sunday Times*, 19 August 1990, Sect. 3, p. 4 and the

the fact that the Iraqi leader had violated treaty commitments was not addressed by the U.S. president and the British Prime Minister. In other words, newspapers that denounced the Iraqi leader's disrespect for treaties did so on their own initiative to reinforce Saddam Hussein's negative image presented to their readers.

## 3.4 Other abuses by the Iraqi president prior to 2 August 1990

Among the other abuses committed by Saddam Hussein was the case of Farzad Bazoft, the *Observer* correspondent. For example, the *Guardian* in an editorial[317] as well as two journalists, one in the *Washington Post*[318] and the other in the *Sunday Times*,[319] reminded readers that the *Observer* journalist had been hanged in Iraq in March 1990 after being convicted of spying.[320] The journalists in question added this act to the range of crimes perpetrated by the Iraqi leader. But what is more curious is that it was the *Sunday Times* that mentioned this event even though the journalist was working for the *Observer*, the competing Sunday

---

article by Norman Stone, "So much for the pacifist coterie on the pink cloud", op-ed, *Sunday Times*, 3 March 1991, p. IX.

317 "Paying the price for past error", editorial, *Guardian*, 3 August 1990, p. 16.

318 Amy E. Schwartz, "Baghdad and a Squandered Generation", op-ed, *Washington Post*, 6 August 1990, p. A 11.

319 Norman Stone, "So much for the pacifist coterie on the pink cloud", op-ed, *Sunday Times*, 3 March 1991, p. IX. Norman Stone's article criticized the *Guardian*'s editorials during the Gulf Crisis. The journalist argued for instance that "over the Gulf, the *Guardian* has been Saddam Hussein's mental tepid hot-water bottle, with some editorials that ought to have known better".

320 Roy Greenslade, *op. cit.*, p. 551.

paper, at the time of his execution. The American and British governments did not refer to the *Observer* journalist in their speeches and news conferences during the Gulf Crisis and War.[321]

Moreover, among the grievances addressed to the president of Iraq, American and British newspapers[322] referred to Saddam Hussein's support of terrorism[323] and his "coddling of terrorists".[324] In August 1990 Iraq blackmailed Western countries into

---

321 On 15 March 1990, Margaret Thatcher stated in the House of Commons that "The Iraqi Government's action is an act of barbarism which is deeply repugnant to all civilised people. We extend our sympathy to Mr. Bazoft's family and colleagues" (<https://www.margaretthatcher.org/document/108037>, consulted 30 October 2022). Richard Norton-Taylor and Tracy McVeigh argued in the *Guardian* on 1 January 2017 that "Margaret Thatcher and her government decided not to take any action, against what ministers admitted was a 'ruthless' regime, for fear of jeopardising lucrative exports to Iraq". "'It would be bad for our interests': why Thatcher ignored the murder of an Observer journalist", *Guardian*, 1 January 2017, (<https://theguardian.com/world/2017/jan/01/fazad-bazoft-journalist-iraq-executed-saddam-hussein-thatcher>, consulted 30 October 2022).
322 For instance: "No End of Lessons on Iraq", editorial, *New York Times*, 23 September 1990, p. E 20; A. M. Rosenthal, "The Goals of War", op-ed, *New York Times*, 23 August 1990, p. A 23; Jack Anderson and Dale Van Atta, "Arab Americans: Suspects without Probable Cause", op-ed, *Washington Post*, 27 January 1991, p. C 7; "Containing the war", editorial, *Times*, 17 January 1991, p. 6; Peter Stothard, "Hard facts for the special relation", op-ed, *Times*, 20 December 1990, p. 10; "The debate to be sure", editorial, *Guardian*, 24 January 1991, p. 20; "Finishing Saddam", editorial, *Sunday Times*, 3 February 1991, Sect. 1, p. 11.
323 For example: Leslie H. Gelb, "A Party Derided", op-ed, *New York Times*, 10 March 1991, p. E 15; Bernard Levin, "Preying on our minds, but only because we let them", op-ed, *Times*, 13 September 1990, p. 14.
324 For instance, Michael Kinsley, "James A. Baker, Please Resign", op-ed, *Washington Post*, 18 October 1990, p. A 23.

terrorism,[325] which was echoed by the American president and the British Prime Minister in their remarks and news conferences.[326]

The American press[327] and the *Times*[328], on the British side, also referred to the firing of two missiles by an Iraqi Mirage at the American frigate *Stark* in 1987, "incinerating thirty-seven members of its crew".[329] It is logical that this tragic event was mainly mentioned in the two American newspapers since it would resonate much more powerfully with American readers. What is essential is that the U.S. papers reminded their readers of the Iraqi rocket attack on the USS *Stark* only to criticize the United States for having forgiven Saddam Hussein and continuing its collaboration with Iraq all the same.

Besides, from August 1990 to mid-March 1991, both American newspapers constantly vilified the Bush administration or, before it, that of Ronald Reagan for having turned a blind eye to the crimes of the Iraqi leader over the previous decade. For instance,

---

325  Marcel Merle, *op. cit.*, p. 30.

326  For instance, see George Bush's news conference of 21 September 1990 (<https://bush41library.tamu.edu/archives/public-papers/2244>). Also refer to Margaret Thatcher's speech at Lord Mayor's banquet on 12 November 1990 (<https://www.margaretthatcher.org/document/108241>), as well as John Major's parliamentary debate of 21 January 1991 (<https://hansard.parliament.uk/Commons/1991-01-21/debates/c80bc5e0-03fd-49fb-a838-62f4c66958e1/TheGulf?highlight=john%20major#contribution-45b223d1-b234-4128-83d8-f45ed0b23f2b>, consulted 9 August 2021).

327  "No End of Lessons on Iraq", editorial, *New York Times*, 23 September 1990, p. E 20; Jim Hoagland, "America's Frankenstein's Monster", op-ed, *Washington Post*, 7 February 1991, p. A 19.

328  "Iraq's Naked Villainy", editorial, *Times*, 3 August 1990, p. 11. The *Times* was the only British newspaper to refer to the incident, reflecting its interest in all that concerned the United States and to cater for its international readers.

329  Robert Fisk, *op. cit.*, p. 267.

Anthony Lewis blamed the Reagan Administration in the *New York Times* for lobbying against and blocking "Congressional efforts to impose sanctions on Iraq in 1988 because of the use of poison gas" since "it continued to extend $500 million a year in credit guarantees to Iraq to buy U.S. food products". The journalist also accused Ronald Reagan of having played down "human rights concerns, winking at horrendous cruelties by Saddam Hussein".[330] The *Washington Post* was also a virulent critic of U.S. policy towards Iraq in its many opinion articles, for example reviling the Reagan Administration's willingness to tolerate Saddam's use of chemical weapons and the Bush Administration's attempts to "curry favour" with the Iraqi ruler "with agricultural subsidies and other bribes"[331] despite his antidemocratic behaviour. However, this was not the case in its editorials, which only reproached the Bush administration for having sought "to find a narrow common ground" with the Iraqi leader.[332] According to Robert Fisk, the West had tolerated Saddam Hussein's cruelty, "his oppression and torture, his war crimes and mass murder" until his invasion of Kuwait because he was a "strongman", the Arab world's bastion against Islamic "extremism".[333]

In the British press, while the *Guardian* criticized the British government for standing by the Baghdad regime despite Iraqi atrocities,[334] the Sunday newspapers in their editorials and opinion

---

330    Anthony Lewis, "Paying for Reagan", op-ed, *New York Times*, 5 October 1990, p. A 37.

331    Hobart Rowen, "Principle and Necessity in U.S. Policy", op-ed, *Washington Post*, 16 August 1990, p. A 23.

332    "Aggressor in the Gulf", editorial, *Washington Post*, 3 August 1990, p. A 22.

333    Robert Fisk, *op. cit.*, pp. 208-209.

334    "Back from the beach", editorial, *Guardian*, 30 August 1990, p. 18.

pieces blamed the West for supplying Iraq with weapons and for its failure to react to Saddam Hussein's atrocities.[335] Finally, Edward W. Said, the Palestinian writer, argued in the *Observer* that "Saddam is the outcome of a short-sighted US Middle East policy".[336] Only the *Times* differed from other British newspapers in that it did not publish editorials or opinion pieces critical of the American or British government, which could be explained by Rupert Murdoch's support for Margaret Thatcher.[337]

Far from exonerating Saddam Hussein, the reproaches against the U.S. or British governments, or even the West, by American and British editorialists, journalists and contributors of opinion articles – with the exception of those of the *Times* – enabled readers not only to build a clearer picture of the personality of the Iraqi leader, but above all to comprehend some of the reasons underlying the Gulf Crisis. Journalists made their readers aware that the U.S. and British governments had failed to take any significant action despite the atrocities committed by the Iraqi leader.

In general, the majority of American editorials relating to the Iraqi president's criminal behaviour prior to the beginning of the Gulf Crisis were published before the outbreak of hostilities; some opinion articles also focused on this in February and March 1991. In the British press, most editorials and opinion pieces on the

---

335    Robert Harris, "This is not our finest hour and Saddam's not Hitler", op-ed, *Sunday Times*, 23 September 1990, Sect. 3, p. 6; "Stand firm on sanctions. Charges of hypocrisy", editorial, *Observer*, 28 October 1990, p. 20.
336    Edward W. Said, "Fuelling the Arab fire next time", op-ed, *Observer*, 12 August 1990, p. 12.
337    Graham Stewart, *op. cit.*, p. 186.

issue were published between August 1990 and the beginning of the conflict. However, as in U.S. newspapers, a small number of articles on this issue appeared during the hostilities. It is worth noting that the *Guardian* published the most editorials on abuses committed by Saddam Hussein before the Iraqi invasion compared to other British newspapers. Only the *Times* differed from other British newspapers by not devoting opinion pieces to this subject once the Gulf War had begun although it did publish editorials on this topic from August 1990 until mid-March 1991.

Concerning readers' letters, the American press published more letters on the crimes of the Iraqi leader before the invasion of Kuwait than its British counterparts.[338] On the British side, the *Guardian* published numerous letters criticizing American, British and Western governments for supporting the Iraqi regime with arms and for their indifference to Iraq's human rights abuses, in particular during the massacre of the Kurds.[339]

## Conclusion

To complete Saddam Hussein's uncompromising portrait, American and British editorials and opinion articles listed, from August 1990 onwards and as a reminder to readers, all

---

338     For example, the following letters: Richard M. Walden, "Soon Will Begin Appeals for Iraq's War Victims", letters, *New York Times*, 27 January 1991, p. E 16; Rene Espinosa, "The Arming of Saddam Hussein", letters, *Washington Post*, 27 September 1990, p. A 22; H. Weisl, "Need for patience in the Gulf", letters, *Times*, 6 December 1990, p. 13.

339     For instance, the letter by Ann Clwyd, MP, "Let's cast a net over the whole Middle East when seeking peace for Kuwait", letters, *Guardian*, 23 August 1990, p. 18.

the atrocities that Saddam Hussein had inflicted on his own people, and especially the Kurds, most notably during the war between Iran and Iraq. They thus followed the comments made by George Bush and Margaret Thatcher. Historical references to the president of Iraq's crimes perpetrated before 2 August 1990 were linked to those committed during the Gulf Crisis and War.

By way of summary, the table on the next page shows the main exactions perpetrated by the Iraqi ruler before the Gulf Crisis in the editorials and opinion articles of each newspaper.

As we have seen, similar arguments about the Iran-Iraq war, the dictatorial regime of the Iraqi leader, his support for terrorism and his unreliability in matters of treaties can be found in the press on both sides of the Atlantic.[340] The *Guardian* differed from the *Times* in that it published more articles on the war against Iran, perhaps reflecting its commitment to convince its readers of the Iraqi leader's villainy by highlighting the atrocities committed during that conflict. The American press as well as the *Times*, on the British side, stressed Iraq's attack against the USS *Stark*, which was not addressed in other British newspapers. The *Washington Post*, the *Guardian* and the *Sunday Times* reminded their readers of the execution of the *Observer* journalist. The American newspapers as well as the *Guardian* and the *Observer*, on the British side, criticized the Reagan and Bush administrations' policies and support for Saddam Hussein. In the British press, criticism was also levelled against the British government and the West, in particular

---

340    Most editorials and opinion articles were published before the start of hostilities.

in the *Guardian*, for turning a blind eye to the Iraqi leader's abuses. However, the *Times* did not criticize Britain's support for Iraq in its editorials and opinion pieces,[341] perhaps because it placed more value on *realpolitik* than any ethical foreign policy.

Reminding readers of the crimes committed by Saddam Hussein in both the American and British press before the Gulf Crisis began was an effective way to demonize the enemy. Nevertheless, tribute should be paid to editorialists, journalists and contributors who highlighted the inaction and complacency of U.S.[342] and British governments towards the Iraqi leader when he was considered a leading economic partner by Western countries.

---

341   As explained in the introduction, the *Times* considers itself politically independent even though it is close to the Conservative Party.

342   In accordance with American foreign policy, which is considered pragmatic, the aim was to preserve U.S. oil interests (Alain Frachon et Daniel Vernet, "Messianisme à l'américaine. Voyage chez les idéologues de 'W'", *Le Monde* 2, 22 Octobre 2002, p. 52).

| Abuses prior to 2/08/90 | | Iran-Iraq war | Dictatorial regime | Treaties not respected | Farzad Bazoft's execution | Sponsoring terrorism | USS Stark | Criticism against the | | |
|---|---|---|---|---|---|---|---|---|---|---|
| | | | | | | | | USA | UK | West |
| *New York Times* | ed | x | x | | | x | x | x | | |
| | op-ed | x | x | | | x | | | | |
| *Washington Post* | ed | x | x | x | | x | | x | | |
| | op-ed | x | x | | | x | x | x | | |
| *Times* | ed | x | | x | | x | x | | | x |
| | op-ed | | x | x | x | x | x | | | |
| *Guardian* | ed | x | x | | x | x | | | x | |
| | op-ed | x | x | | | | | x | | |
| *Sunday Times* | ed | x | x | | | x | | | | |
| | op-ed | x | x | x | x | | | | x | x |
| *Observer* | ed | x | | x | | | | | | x |
| | op-ed | x | x | | | | | x | | |

# Chapter IV:
# Speculations about Saddam Hussein's possible future actions

In addition to reminding readers of the abuses committed before 2 August 1990 and mentioning those perpetrated during the Gulf Crisis and War, American and British newspapers also speculated in their articles upon the crimes that the Iraqi leader was likely to commit in the future. Articles not only presented the vile deeds committed before the invasion and during the crisis, but also pointed to likely future atrocities in a way which could only further tarnish the already unattractive image of the Iraqi president. At the same time as the press on both sides of the Atlantic painted a deeply disturbing portrait of Saddam Hussein, the idea that he was a military, nuclear, economic and geopolitical threat to the world emerged repeatedly in American and British newspapers.

## 4.1  Iraqi army and military capabilities

From the beginning of the Gulf Crisis, the American and British press frequently emphasized Iraq's military power and the manifest strength of its armed forces, which therefore represented a global danger. For example, the *New York Times* stressed Saddam Hussein's million-man army,[343] described as "the world's fourth largest army"[344] in a *Times* editorial. The *Sunday Times* in particular

---

343    "Isolate Iraq", editorial, *New York Times*, 5 August 1990, p. E 18.
344    "When to stop", editorial, *Times*, 28 February 1991, p. 13.

also referred to the Second World War to emphasize the extent of Iraq's military arsenal, "with almost 1m battle-hardened troops and more tanks than Rommel, Eisenhower and Montgomery combined had in North Africa".[345] As we have seen with regard to the use of German words and references to the concept of 'appeasement' and the Munich Agreement, referring to the Second World War was likely to resonate with readers and produce historical echoes guiding their interpretation of the Gulf Crisis. Whereas Andrew Neil, the editor-in-chief of the *Sunday Times* in 1990, was known for his hawkish attitude before the Gulf War,[346] William Waite Hadley, the editor-in-chief of the Sunday paper during the 1930s, "became a leading appeaser of Hitler and political ally of Neville Chamberlain",[347] the then British Prime Minister.

Similar arguments were used in opinion articles in the American press and the British press. For instance, Henry Kissinger, the former U.S. Secretary of State under Richard Nixon and Gerald Ford, warned the Arab states in the *Washington Post* that none of them was "strong enough even in combination to defeat the Iraqi army, toughened in a 10-year war, supplied with advanced technology [...]".[348] However, although they were not representative of the opinions expressed by their respective newspapers, some contributors of opinion articles questioned the effectiveness of the Iraqi army.[349] The publication of opinions

---

345 "The thief of Baghdad", editorial, *Sunday Times*, 5 August 1990, Sect. 3, p. 7.

346 Brian MacArthur, *op. cit.*, p. 112.

347 Jeremy Tunstall, *op. cit.*, p. 16.

348 Henry Kissinger, "The Game Has Just Begun", op-ed, *Washington Post*, 19 August 1990, p. C 7.

349 For James Webb, who was the Assistant Secretary of Defense and the Secretary of the Navy in the Reagan Administration, "the Iraqi army is not

diverging from the editorial line reflected the principle of publishing a diversity of viewpoints in these newspapers. Apart from these articles, American and British newspapers generally emphasised, in their editorials and opinion articles, the power of the battle-hardened Iraqi armed forces. This was apparently motivated by a desire to persuade readers that, in the wake of the 1980-88 Iran-Iraq war, this was an army which was used to fighting, thus underpinning the idea of its proven military superiority. The argument concerning the considerable power of Iraqi troops was repeated over and over again in the press on both sides of the Atlantic during the Gulf Crisis until the end of hostilities. The *New York Times*, on the American side, as well as the *Times* and the *Sunday Times*, on the British side, still referred to it at the beginning of March 1991, no doubt to emphasize that the coalition's victory was all the more praiseworthy as it had crushed a formidable army.

The American president, in his addresses and remarks on the Persian Gulf Crisis,[350] referred to a powerful Iraqi army composed of a million men, a perception echoed by editorialists and most journalists in their articles. Readers' letters published in the U.S. press used the same rhetoric as in American editorials and opinion articles, namely the emphasis on the power of the Iraqi war

---

a very good army. It is also war-weary". James Webb, "... And the Horrors of a Desert War", op-ed, *New York Times*, 23 September 1990, p. E 21. Similarly, Norman Macrae described Iraq's military power as "inefficient and erratic". Norman Macrae, "An election platform built of straw", op-ed, *Sunday Times*, 7 October 1990, Sect. 3, p. 6.

350    For instance, refer to George Bush's Address to the Nation on 8 August 1990 (<https://bush41library.tamu.edu/archives/public-papers/2147>), and his remarks on the Persian Gulf crisis on 28 August 1990 (<https://bush41library.tamu.edu/archives/public-papers/2185>, consulted 10 August 2021).

machine.[351] On the British side, the situation was more contrasted. For example, while a *Sunday Times* reader highlighted "Saddam Hussein's enormous military build-up on the Kuwaiti border",[352] a *Guardian* reader claimed that "the Iraqi conscripts (the vast majority of the army) have no wish to fight".[353]

In summary, except for a minority of opinion articles and a *Guardian* reader, the American and British press, in their editorials, opinion articles and letters published from August 1990 to March 1991, emphasized the might of the Iraqi army, the impressive number of its soldiers and their fighting skills. Journalists on both sides of the Atlantic used adjectives such as "huge" and "powerful" to describe the Iraqi forces, thus stressing that they were a force to be reckoned with. In doing so, they modelled their comments on those of the American president on this subject. Finally, the *Sunday Times* in particular underlined the powerful Iraqi military capacity which it compared to forces deployed in the Second World War.

Despite the assertions of the newspapers on both sides of the Atlantic, it turned out after the Gulf War that American and European experts had overestimated the real strength of the Iraqi army,[354] including the fearsome National Guard which was

---

351   For example: "A battle-hardened and well-armed force of one million". Amir Soltani, "Iraq Without Hussein Would Be the Same", letters, *New York Times*, 5 August 1990, p. E 18. "A monstrous Iraqi war machine". Uzi Vishkin, "Another Monstrous War Machine?", letters, *Washington Post*, 6 September 1990, p. A 26.
352   Frederick Lowe, "The Gulf between Iraq and Britain", letters, *Sunday Times*, 12 August 1990, Sect. 3, p. 9.
353   Riadh T. Abed, "West's capabilities for waging the peace", letters, *Guardian*, 28 February 1991, p. 20.
354   Jean-Baptiste Duroselle & André Kaspi, *op. cit.*, p. 546.

entirely devoted to Saddam Hussein. In the authoritative opinion of these experts, whose comments were faithfully transcribed by journalists,[355] the Iraqi army was described as a formidable military power. According to Robert Fisk, Iraqi armed forces "were obsequiously referred to in the Western media as 'crack troops' [...]" when they invaded Iran in 1980. However, after the same army invaded Kuwait in August 1990, "they became the 'enemy'".[356] Considered as the fourth largest army in the world, unrivalled in the Middle East, the Iraqi army was supposed to pose a worrying military threat especially to its neighbour, Saudi Arabia, and therefore required many soldiers and equipment to be sent to the Persian Gulf. What is certain is that the concept of the world's fourth biggest army was a "slogan of formidable psychological efficiency"[357] on public opinion, and it increased the image of the president of Iraq as a dangerous and powerful opponent that had to be eliminated at all costs.

## 4.2    Iraqi chemical and biological weapons

In addition to the superiority and strength of Iraqi troops, American and British newspapers also highlighted Iraq's possession of chemical and biological weapons, thereby exacerbating the threat posed by Saddam Hussein. For example, Walter Laqueur, the chairman of the International Research Council at the Center for Strategic and International Studies at that time, wrote in the *Washington Post* that the Iraqi leader "has

---

355    Élisabeth Coss-Humbert *in* Béatrice Fleury-Vilatte, *op. cit.,* p. 21.
356    Robert Fisk, *op. cit.,* p. 621.
357    Éric Laurent, *op. cit.,* 1991, p. 23.

non-conventional weapons".[358] However, Edward N. Luttwak, who held a chair in strategy at the Center for Strategic and International Studies, argued in the *New York Times* that "Iraq's missiles armed with high explosives pose not much of a threat".[359] The different opinion, expressed by this prominent figure and which did not tally with the editorial line of the newspaper, shows the diversity of viewpoints published by the *New York Times*. In the *Guardian*, Paul Wilkinson, who was Professor of International Relations at St Andrews University and Director of the Research Institute for the study of conflict and terrorism in 1990, stressed Saddam Hussein's "readiness to use chemical weapons [...]".[360] The author of the article sought to amplify the feeling of insecurity of Western readers who might otherwise have remained indifferent to events taking place so far away from their country.

As in editorials and opinion articles, most readers underlined Iraq's massive chemical and biological arsenals.[361] However, two readers did not seem to be convinced by the media argument, as

---

358    Walter Laqueur, "Like Hitler, but Different", op-ed, *Washington Post*, 31 August 1990, p. A 27.

359    Edward N. Luttwak, "Iraq's Empty Threat Against Israel", op-ed, *New York Times*, 13 January 1991, p. E 19. Nevertheless, the author's opinion changed in January 1991 as he had underlined Iraq's enormous defence capacity in an article published on 9 August 1990. Refer to the following article: "Iraq Will Be Tough to Dislodge ...", op-ed, *New York Times*, 9 August 1990, p. A 23.

360    Paul Wilkinson, "Threat to Saudi's soft belly", op-ed, *Guardian*, 6 August 1990, p. 19. Hazhir Teimourian argued in the *Times* that "His missiles will soon have the range to threaten Europe". Hazhir Teimourian, "Biblical despot with chemical arms", op-ed, *Times,* 13 August 1990, p.10.

361    For instance: Stephen A. Wise, "The New Crusaders?", letters, *New York Times*, 23 September 1990, p. E 20; Hans Smit, "The Case for Holding Fire in the Gulf", letters, *Washington Post*, 30 December 1990, p. C 6; Ronnie Lewis, "Mankind on a precipice as the political war of words goes on", letters, *Guardian*, 15 November 1990, p. 20.

one reader of the *Washington Post*[362] and another of the *Sunday Times*[363] disagreed with the views expressed in these newspapers. But, on the whole, opinions voiced in readers' letters corresponded to those of editorials and opinion articles. To sum up, except for Edward Luttwak's doubts and these two readers, the press on both sides of the Atlantic referred to the danger of Iraq's possession of a chemical and biological arsenal.

In the American or British press, editorials and opinion articles on the so-called "terrifying" threat represented by Saddam Hussein's possession of unconventional weapons were published mainly during the Gulf Crisis and thus before the outbreak of hostilities. The possible use of these weapons gave rise to speculation among some editorialists and journalists from August 1990 to mid-January 1991.[364] These assumptions were expressed, among other things, by the use of modal auxiliaries of probability and possibility or the conjunction "if".[365] No doubt the danger of bacteriological

---

362 Rene Espinosa, "The Arming of Saddam Hussein", letters, *Washington Post*, 27 September 1990, p. A 22. The reader blamed a lot of nations, including Britain and the United States, for having provided "all sorts of weapons and technology with military application to Saddam Hussein".

363 John Whitbeck, "Gotcha and jingoism – Aggression", letters, *Sunday Times*, 2 September 1990, Sect. 3, p. 8. The reader commented ironically on the Iraqi threat because of its possession of non-conventional weapons which were also held by the United States and Israel.

364 For example: Ann Lewis, "Squelch Iraq's Nuclear Ambitions", op-ed, *New York Times*, 20 December 1990, p. A 31; James Q. Wilson, "Why We Are Fighting ...", op-ed, *Washington Post*, 17 January 1991, p. A 21; "The Peace party", editorial, *Sunday Times*, 2 September 1990, Sect. 3, p. 7; Norman Macrae, "Better to lose soldiers now than win a coward's peace in the Gulf", op-ed, *Sunday Times*, 6 January 1991, Sect. 3, p. 6; "Why this Hitler of the Gulf has to go", editorial, *Observer*, 5 August 1990, p. 12.

365 For example: Jim Hoagland, "America's Mettle", op-ed, *Washington Post*, 2 September 1990, p. B 7; Hazhir Teimourian, "Biblical despot with chemical arms", op-ed, *Times*, 13 August 1990, p. 10; Julie Flint, "Desert

weapons held by the Iraqi president was very real, as testified by their use during the Iran-Iraq war and against the Kurds in 1988, a point recalled by some journalists.[366] This represented a very effective scare tactic employed against readers and served to persuade the public of the validity of sending armed forces and of the coalition's entry into the war to reduce Iraq's military arsenal. What is important is that newspapers again echoed what the U.S. president and the British Prime Minister – Thatcher and then Major – said about the threat posed by the Iraqi leader's possession and potential use of chemical and biological weapons.[367]

As we have seen, American and British newspapers emphasized the tremendous power of the Iraqi army during the Gulf Crisis

---

Storm script has no happy ending", op-ed, *Observer*, 10 February 1991, p. 10.

366 For instance: A. M. Rosenthal, "Iraq and Atom Bombs", op-ed, *New York Times*, 16 August 1990, p. A 25; Andrew Stephen, "Bush's diplomatic army gets 'bombed' before a shot is fired", op-ed, *Observer*, 16 September 1990, p. 11.

367 For example, refer to George Bush's news conferences on 8 August 1990 (<https://bush41library.tamu.edu/archives/public-papers/2148>), and 30 August 1990 (<https://bush41library.tamu.edu/archives/public-papers/2189>). Also refer to Margaret Thatcher's joint conference with George Bush on 2 August 1990 (<https://www.margaretthatcher.org/document/108170>), or the parliamentary debate on 6 September 1990 (<https://publications.parliament.uk/pa/cm198990/cmhansrd/1990-09-06/Debate-1.html>), and her speech to UN World Children's Summit on 30 September 1990 (<https://www.margaretthatcher.org/document/108207>). Also see Major's parliamentary debates on the Gulf on 15 January 1991 (<https://hansard.parliament.uk/Commons/1991-01-15/debates/3498d88e-f437-47bc-bdc6-cd0c78a0fee8/TheGulf?highlight=chemical#contribution-93c27615-93f1-43c2-b05e-395509d2>), and 21 January 1990 (<https://hansard.parliament.uk/Commons/1991-01-21/debates/c80bc5e0-03fd-49fb-a838-62f4c66958e1/TheGulf?highlight=john%20major#contribution-45b223d1-b234-4128-83d8-f45ed0b23f2b>, consulted 12 August 2021).

and War. Likewise, following the official rhetoric, they stressed the risks inherent in Iraq's possession of chemical and biological weapons from August 1990 and until the beginning of the conflict. These weapons helped American and British editorials and opinion articles to paint a portrait of Saddam Hussein as a military threat which had to be annihilated. One wonders how the reader, subjected to the same arguments over and over again, could escape being convinced, or even frightened, by the official rhetoric relayed by the press.

## 4.3    Iraq's nuclear arsenal

Not only did the issue of chemical and biological weapons take centre stage in the press on both sides of the Atlantic from August 1990 to mid-January 1991, but the Iraqi leader's nuclear arsenal was also a key point in the arguments of American and British newspapers to make their readers intensely aware of the threat Saddam Hussein presented to the world. For example, Saddam Hussein's arsenal of nuclear weapons was, according to editorials in the *New York Times* and the *Times*, a nightmare.[368] It is surprising that the *Observer*, which had "called for unilateral

---

368    Refer to the following editorials: "The prospect of Saddam Hussein brandishing an arsenal of nuclear weapons is the nightmare of all who oppose him". "Taking out Iraq's Nukes", editorial, *New York Times*, 25 November 1990, p. E 10; "Saddam presents the nightmare scenario of nuclear/chemical warfare strategists". "Anti-war, Pro-war", editorial, *Times*, 10 September 1990, p. 13.

nuclear disarmament"[369] in the run-up to the 1959 election, did not publish editorials on the possible use of Iraqi nuclear power.[370]

In general, both American and British editorials and opinion articles drew the reader's attention to the deadlines Saddam Hussein had set himself to achieve his nuclear ambitions, implying the danger he represented to the planet in the long run. Nevertheless, the press on both sides of the Atlantic mentioned different deadlines. For instance, while a *Washington Post* editorial argued in September 1990 that Iraq could develop "nuclear weapons in perhaps five years",[371] the *Sunday Times* suggested 24 months.[372] Similarly, Hazhir Teimourian claimed in the *Times* that "his nuclear researchers may be within two years of making atomic bombs".[373] Irrespective of the different time frames mentioned, the American and British press, whose editorials and opinion articles were mainly published from August 1990 until the outbreak of hostilities,[374] fuelled speculation on the risks entailed by Iraq's nuclear ambitions. However, newspapers on both sides of the Atlantic were cautious in their assertions in that they often

---

369   Roy Greenslade, *op. cit.*, p. 126.

370   However, Simon Hoggart claimed in his column of 13 January 1991 that "Iraq will soon have the ability to make a bomb in the six months between inspection" (Simon Hoggart, Column, op-ed, *Observer*, 13 January 1991, p. 14).

371   "The Troops in the Desert", editorial, *Washington Post*, 5 September 1990, p. A 18.

372   "Preparing for war", editorial, *Sunday Times*, 19 August 1990, Sect 3, p. 5.

373   Hazhir Teimourian, "Biblical despot with chemical arms", op-ed, *Times*, 13 August 1990, p. 10.

374   Nevertheless, a few articles were published in the American press in March 1991. For example: Joseph R. Egan, "O.K., Saddam, Where's the Uranium?", op-ed, *New York Times*, 14 March 1991, p. A 25; John Keegan, "How the War Was Won", op-ed, *Washington Post*, 3 March 1991, p. C 7.

hid behind American sources and used conditional sentences containing if-clauses and modal auxiliary verbs expressing possibility or risk. In other words, they made certainly plausible but above all alarmist assumptions and fed their readers with disaster scenarios.

The American press differed from the British press by publishing editorials and articles calling for the need to reduce the proliferation of nuclear weapons.[375] Few readers[376] commented on the Iraqi nuclear threat in the American and British press, perhaps because of the lack of detailed and evidence-based information and opinion in the papers.

In essence, American and British newspapers agreed that Iraq represented a nuclear threat to the world. They highlighted the possible security danger due to the advancement of Iraq's nuclear programme and gave rise to speculation about Saddam Hussein's probable acquisition and/or possession of nuclear weapons or even their possible use. While on 22 November 1990 the U.S. president stressed Saddam Hussein's goal of acquiring a nuclear weapon arsenal,[377] Margaret Thatcher stated on 1 September 1990 that

---

375 For example, the following editorial: "Pakistan's Bomb: Proliferating Excuses", editorial, *New York Times*, 7 October 1990, p. E 18, as well as opinion articles published in U.S. newspapers: Jerome Wiesner, "Why Don't We Stop Testing the Bomb?", op-ed, *New York Times*, 23 December 1990, p. E 11; Richard Cohen, "Heading Off Iraq's Bomb", op-ed, *Washington Post*, 23 August 1990, p. A 25.

376 For example, George Chapline, a senior scientist at the Lawrence Livermore National Laboratory, feared "the possible use by Iraq of nuclear weapons". George Chapline, "Is Victory over Iraq Really a Sure Thing?", letters, *New York Times*, 10 February 1991, p. E 16.

377 Refer to his remarks to allied armed forces in Saudi Arabia on 22 November 1990 (<https://bush41library.tamu.edu/archives/public-papers/2485>).

the Iraqi leader might have a nuclear weapon within five years.[378] Editorialists, journalists and contributors of opinion articles had thus preceded the official narrative as early August 1990.[379]

Although the Bush Administration claimed that Iraq would soon have its first atomic bomb, Western intelligence services had estimated before the Gulf Crisis that "it would take Iraq three to ten years to build a nuclear weapon".[380] According to Gadi Wolfsfeld, the Bush administration was "extremely successful in using the news media to establish" Saddam Hussein as a genuine threat to world order[381] by producing stories about Iraq's powerful war machine. The description of the fearsome weapons that the Iraqi army was likely to use on the battlefield and which it had already used in Iraq in 1983[382] certainly confirmed Saddam Hussein's image as a demonic killer. Furthermore, the controversy over the nuclear threat and Iraq's possession of bacteriological weapons had a significant psychological impact at the very least

However, on 2 August 1990, George Bush had already announced his administration's efforts to control the spread of chemical and nuclear weapons (<https://bush41library.tamu.edu/archives/public-papers/2128>). On 28 August 1990, the American president argued that they had stopped "the export of furnaces that had the potential to contribute to Iraq's nuclear capabilities" (see his remarks at a White House Briefing for Members of Congress on the Persian Gulf Crisis on 28 August 1990 (<https://bush41library.tamu.edu/archives/public-papers/2185>, consulted 13 August 2021).

378    Refer to Margaret Thatcher's TV interview for TV-AM on 1 September 1990 (<https://www.margaretthatcher.org/document/108186>, consulted 13 August 2021).

379    However, the *Observer* only published opinion pieces on this subject from September 1990.

380    Howard Zinn, *op. cit.*, p. 595.

381    Gadi Wolfsfeld, *Media and Political Conflict. News from the Middle East*, Cambridge: Cambridge UP, 1997, p. 177.

382    Pierre-Jean Luizard, *op. cit.*, p. 293.

as it brought back the memory of the Great War[383] in 1915 when asphyxiating gases were used by the Germans for the first time. By highlighting the Iraqi nuclear risk, American and British editorialists, journalists and contributors undoubtedly gripped and even worried some of the readers as they played on emotion and particularly fear. Their alarming comments thus aimed to convince the reader of the need to intervene before Iraq became a nuclear power. Fearful public opinion is indeed likely to more easily accept ideas, arguments or the course of action presented to it. All in all, the paranoia induced by the idea of chemical and biological weapons and the Iraqi nuclear programme heightened the risk of war and justified, among other things, the military intervention of the United States and its allies against Iraq.

## 4.4   The oil issue

In addition to highlighting Iraqi military supremacy and Iraq's possession of biological, chemical and nuclear weapons, American and British newspapers, from August 1990 to early March 1991, stressed the fact that Saddam Hussein, following his invasion of Kuwait, "might hold oil reserves larger than those of Saudi Arabia"[384] and thus a substantial part of the world's oil reserves. If, for Louis Blin, the Gulf War should not be reduced to a war for oil,[385] although some used this expression[386] or argued that

---

383   Élisabeth Coss-Humbert *in* Béatrice Fleury-Vilatte, *op. cit.*, p. 21.
384   Robert Fisk, *op. cit.*, p. 1116.
385   Louis Blin, *Le Pétrole du Golfe. Guerre et paix au Moyen-Orient*, Paris: Maisonneuve et Larose, 1996, p. 117.
386   Étienne Gernelle, *Les Nouveaux défis du pétrole*, Toulouse: Les Essentiels Milan, 2006, p. 31.

"this was about oil rather than democracy"[387] or even spoke of an economic war,[388] it is clear that oil played a vital role during the events in the Persian Gulf and was used as an argument to mobilize public opinion against Iraq.[389] Oil, omnipresent in everyday life[390] and the world's main source of primary energy,[391] is a major strategic issue in relations between states and a specific source of tensions.[392] Moreover, the Middle East, a region of political instability[393] and the main supplier of hydrocarbons,[394] accounts for two-thirds of the world's known reserves.[395]

In his many speeches, George Bush highlighted the threat that Iraq posed to oil reserves in the Persian Gulf[396] and the collateral

---

387  Robert Fisk, *op. cit.*, p. 745.

388  Albert Jacquard, *op. cit.*, p. 110.

389  Gérard de Selys et Bogdan van Doninck (dir.), *La Guerre du pétrole*, Bruxelles: EPO, 1991, p. 49.

390  Sophie Chautard, *Géopolitique et pétrole*, Lavallois-Perret: Studyrama, 2007, p. 149.

391  Gérard Chaliand et Annie Jafalian (dir.), *La Dépendance pétrolière. Mythes et réalités d'un enjeu stratégique*, Paris: Encyclopaedia Universalis, 2005, p. 15.

392  Pascal Boniface (dir.), *Atlas des relations internationales*, Paris: Hatier, 2003, p. 52.

393  Sophie Chautard, *op. cit.*, 2007, p. 149. The term "Middle East" is used in this study to refer to the Persian Gulf. The terms "Middle East" and "Near East" have almost become synonymous and are used interchangeably to refer to the same regions (Iraq, Turkey, Iran, Saudi Arabia, Kuwait, Lebanon, the United Arab Republic, Jordan and Israel). The term "Middle East" only appeared at the beginning of the 20th century to refer to the middle area between the Near and Far East.

394  André Nouschi, *Pétrole et relations internationales depuis 1945*, Paris: Armand Colin, 1999, p. 239.

395  Philippe Moreau Defarges, *op. cit.*, p. 178; also refer to Étienne Gernelle, *op. cit.*, p. 19, as well as Gérard de Selys & Bogdan van Doninck (dir.), *op. cit.*, p. 50.

396  For example, refer to the American president's address before a joint session of the Congress on 11 September 1990 (<https://bush41library.tamu.edu/

economic consequences. Likewise, the American press drew the reader's attention in its editorials[397] and opinion articles to the danger that Iraq's stranglehold on oil could represent to U.S. interests and the American economy. For instance, Flora Lewis from the *New York Times* argued in September 1990 that "the main objective, to prevent any tyrant from controlling over half the world's oil, remains valid".[398] Similarly, Les Aspin, a Democratic representative from Wisconsin, stated in the *Washington Post* on 10 August 1990 that because of the occupation of Kuwait by Iraq,

> "Saddam threatens to control half the world's oil reserves. [...] If we allow Saddam to control half the world's oil reserves, he will control our economy – determining our rate of inflation, our interest rates, our rate of growth. That cannot be permitted".[399]

Les Aspin used the first-person plural pronoun "we" in his argument. The pronoun "we" is frequently used collectively to refer to the entire country and thus to readers in general. From this example, it can be inferred that the personal pronoun includes the enunciator and readers and therefore represents the entire nation. The personal pronoun "we" differentiates "us"

archives/public-papers/2217>), or his remarks to U.S. army troops in Saudi Arabia on 22 November 1990 (<https://bush41library.tamu.edu/archives/public-papers/2483>, consulted 14 August 2021).

397    For instance: "Other powers seem to recognize they must act, before Iraq's megalomaniac warlord gains control of nearly half the world's oil". "Isolate Iraq", editorial, *New York Times*, 5 August 1990, p. E 18. "[...] get a grip on crucial world oil supplies in the Persian Gulf". "Resistance and Appeasement", editorial, *Washington Post*, 7 August 1990, p. A 18.

398    Flora Lewis, "Plug in To Moscow", op-ed, *New York Times*, 29 September 1990, p. 23.

399    Les Aspin, "Define Our Goals in the Gulf", op-ed, *Washington Post*, 10 August 1990, p. A 15.

from "them" and thus distinguishes between the opposing sides. It is used to unite a group into an identity that is the opposite of that of the Other.[400] This ethnocentric conception of a binary world was accentuated by the first-person plural possessive "our" used by the author to involve the nation and to persuade the public of the relevance of his argument. Moreover, the repetition, in the excerpt, of the possessive pronoun four times and of the noun "rate", which focused on the economic consequences of the invasion, gave more expressive force and reinforced the politician's message. The repetition hammers home the idea developed in this passage, and, like an advertising slogan, makes skilful use of this rhetorical device. Furthermore, as previously mentioned, calling the Iraqi leader by his first name gave a familiar and at the very least disrespectful tone to the author's discourse against the president of Iraq.

On the British side, the press also emphasized the issue of the Iraqi leader's control of oil reserves and the subsequent economic risks in its editorials[401] and opinion pieces.[402] For instance,

---

400    The personal pronoun is also found in the titles of the following articles published on both sides of the Atlantic: James Q. Wilson, "Why We Are Fighting ...", op-ed, *Washington Post*, 17 January 1991, p. A 21; "Lest we forget", editorial, *Sunday Times*, 16 September 1990, Sect. 3, p. 7.

401    For example: "Iraq has gained control of a fifth of the world's oil reserves and 7 per cent of current production". "Iraq's naked villainy", editorial, *Times*, 3 August 1990, p. 11; "If the Iraqi dictator is allowed to get a hold on two-thirds of the world's oil supply, [...]. That is reason enough to stop him". "Preparing for war", editorial, *Sunday Times*, 19 August 1990, Sect. 3, p. 5. "[...] Iraq's invasion of a neighbouring state [...] has also threatened [...] the world's most valuable raw material". "Why this Hitler of the Gulf has to go", editorial, *Observer*, 5 August 1990, p. 12.

402    For instance: Sir Anthony Parsons, "Sanctions are the world's only answer to Saddam", op-ed, *Times*, 3 August 1990, p. 12; Alex Brummer, "World over a barrel", op-ed, *Guardian*, 20 September 1990, p. 19; Michael

Norman Stone speculated in the *Sunday Times* that "Saddam, taking not just Kuwait but Saudi Arabia and the Gulf states, would control nearly half the world's oil supply. With that he could dictate world prices".[403] Like the American president, Margaret Thatcher also stressed the importance of oil reserves to global economic stability.[404]

Contrary to the claims of American and British editorialists, journalists and contributors that Saddam Hussein would have controlled 50% of the world's oil reserves once Kuwait was annexed, Iraq, which alone owned 10% of these reserves, would have only held 20% of oil reserves, that is to say twice as many. The fall in American oil production forced the United States as early as 1990 to increase the volume of Arab oil imports, which was then equivalent to 50% of their total consumption.[405] With an unemployment rate close to 10%, a double trade and budget deficit, and a looming recession, economic issues were emerging as the number one foreign policy priority for the United States.[406]

---

Ignatieff, "Questions the Arabs must ask themselves", op-ed, *Observer*, 3 February 1991, p. 17.

403    Norman Stone, "How trendy pacifism edged out truth on our TV screens", op-ed, *Sunday Times*, 20 January 1991, Sect. 2, p. 5.

404    Refer to Margaret Thatcher's speech in Helsinki on 30 August 1990 (<https://www.margaretthatcher.org/document/108183>), and the parliamentary debate on 6 September 1990 (<https://hansard.parliament. uk/Commons/1990-09-06/debates/54db6e15-456e-4257-ba864-cae4950b07f4/TheGulf?highlight=chemical#contribution-c8ad5e14-9ae7-4882-b8c6-836ef88447b7>, consulted 15 August 2021).

405    William B. Quandt, "L'Amérique et le conflit israélo-arabe", *Politique étrangère*, No. 2, été 1990, p. 301. Also refer to the editorial of 2 August 1990 arguing that "imports accounted for a record 50% of the oil consumed by the U.S. during the first half of 1990". "America's Neck and a New Noose", editorial, *New York Times*, 2 August 1990, p. A 20.

406    Charles William Maynes, "Les Défis de l'Administration Bush", *Politique étrangère*, No. 1, printemps 1989, p. 17.

As a result, the Bush administration could not live with an inflationary policy caused by rising prices of imported goods, such as oil, for example. As the world's largest consumer and importer of oil,[407] the United States attached particular importance to its energy security,[408] which was one of its foreign policy priorities too.[409] According to André Nouschi, the United States dominates the world of oil,[410] the cornerstone of its way of life. On the one hand, American hegemony, in the field of hydrocarbons, could be explained by the fact that their oil companies are amongst the most important capitalist companies in the world.[411] On the other hand, not only does world oil trade take place in dollars, but in the game of international relations since 1945, the United States and oil have played an important role.[412] For Louis Blin, there is an "oil culture" in the United States. In 1990 the transport sector absorbed more than 60% of oil consumption, 42% of which was accounted for by passenger cars.[413] Henry Kissinger once stressed the importance of petroleum by saying: "Control energy and you control the nations".[414] President Carter declared in his State of the Union address to Congress on 23 January 1980 that:

> "An attempt by any outside force to gain control of the Persian Gulf region will be regarded as an assault on the vital interests of the

---

407     Gérard de Selys & Bogdan van Doninck (dir.), *op. cit.*, p. 50.

408     Gérard Chaliand & Annie Jafalian (dir.), *op. cit.*, p. 8.

409     *Ibid.*, p. 10.

410     André Nouschi, *op. cit.*, 1999, p. 233.

411     *Ibid.*, p. 241.

412     *Ibid.*, p. 239.

413     Louis Blin, *op. cit.*, p. 9.

414     Quoted by William Engdahl, *A Century of War: Anglo-American Oil Politics and the New World Order*, rev. ed., London: Pluto Press, 2004, p. xi.

United States of America, and such force will be repelled by any means necessary, including military force".[415]

We should also not forget that, before entering politics, President Bush had been a successful businessman in "the Texas oil patch",[416] hence his undeniable ability to grasp the crucial importance of oil problems.

It should also be noted that the *Washington Post* differed from the *New York Times* by arguing in several editorials that there was no oil shortage.[417] In so doing, the American newspaper repeated the remarks of the U.S. president on this subject.[418] In addition, many editorials, particularly in the *New York Times*, and opinion articles published in the American press criticized the Bush administration's lack of an energy policy.[419]

---

415   Refer to the "Carter Doctrine". David Weigall, *op. cit.*, p. 39.

416   William B. Quandt, *Peace Process. American Diplomacy and the Arab-Israeli Conflict since 1967*, 3rd ed., Washington, DC: Brookings Institution Press, 2005, p. 290.

417   For example: "The Oil Shortage that Isn't", editorial, *Washington Post*, 10 December 1990, p. A 14.

418   For instance, refer to Bush's question-and-answer sessions with reporters in New York on 1 October 1990 (<https://bush41library.tamu.edu/archives/public-papers/2283>), and in Uruguay on 4 December 1990 (<https://bush41library.tamu.edu/archives/public-papers/2526>, consulted 16 August 2021).

419   For example, "An Administration Still Hooked on Oil", editorial, *New York Times*, 17 February 1991, p. E 12; Alex Molnar, "If My Marine Son is Killed …", op-ed, *New York Times*, 23 August 1990, p. A 23. In the article, the author asked the U.S. president the following question: "Is the American 'way of life' that you say my son is risking his life for the continued 'right' of Americans to consume 25 to 30 percent of the world's oil?". Robert J. Samuelson, "Conserve Energy – Tax It", op-ed, *Washington Post*, 24 January 1991, p. A 21.

In numerous editorials and opinion articles, the two American newspapers also specified the means that should be used to reduce the United States' economic vulnerability to imported oil and thus be able to face the risks of supply disruption. These included encouraging Americans to save energy by, for example, reducing their oil consumption, developing and diversifying alternative fuels and sources of energy,[420] adopting a national energy policy, or imposing higher energy taxes, as well as increasing oil production in Latin America and using the *Strategic Petroleum Reserve*, created in 1975 after the 1973 oil crisis.[421] Journalists' arguments must, however, be put into perspective as they only emanated from a fringe of public opinion. Furthermore, even though President Bush in his speeches[422] suggested launching new initiatives to increase energy efficiency and conservation, the United States had refused according to Louis Blin to adopt a long-term energy strategy that could free it from over-dependence on Gulf oil.[423] A poll conducted on 23 August 1990 in the *Wall Street Journal* and on *NBC News* and quoted by the author indicated that 62% of Americans were opposed to taxing gasoline.[424]

---

420    For instance, the article by Tom Wicker: "The U.S. must develop alternative energy sources". Tom Wicker, "Reacting to Iraq", op-ed, *New York Times*, 6 August 1990, p. A 13.

421    "America created its *Strategic Petroleum Reserve* in 1975 after the 1973 oil crisis". "America's Neck and a New Noose", editorial, *New York Times*, 2 August 1990, p. A 20.

422    For example, refer to George Bush's remarks at a Republican Party Fundraising Breakfast in Massachusetts on 1 November 1990 (<https://bush41library.tamu.edu/archives/public-papers/2379>, consulted 17 August 2021).

423    Louis Blin, *op. cit.*, p. 117.

424    *Ibid.*, p. 10. However, the conditions of this survey are not known in terms of the questions asked, criteria for representative sample and selection as well as the method used.

On the British side, the *Sunday Times* in particular suggested reducing Britain's dependence on imported oil.[425] However, the Sunday paper did not detail the measures to be taken, unlike the American newspapers. Journalists may have believed that Britain was less dependent on the Middle East for oil supplies than the United States. In this regard, it should be noted that the *Guardian* was the only British newspaper to argue in its editorial of 3 August 1990 entitled "Future shock?" that "Britain has become self-sufficient in oil since the 70s".[426] The use of the question mark in the title of the article was not intended to receive an answer but rather encourage readers to question the arguments developed in the editorial and summarized in its title. The editorialist was able to express his or her opinion through the question and develop some bond with readers. In addition, the title, consisting of a noun and an adjective, was likely to strike readers, or at least attract their attention, because of its conciseness. In this context, we should recall that the 1973 oil price shock caused a fourfold increase in the price of Middle East oil and led Britain to exploit the oil reserves in the North Sea,[427] thus ensuring a certain degree of oil autonomy. According to Louis Blin and from a more general point of view, Britain's energy policy dominated the European oil industry and acted as a "Trojan Horse" for the United States. The author argued that Britain had always thwarted the efforts of the

---

425  For example, the article by Brian Walden: "Arab aspirations cry out for constant care and attention", op-ed, *Sunday Times*, 12 August 1990, Sect. 3, p. 4.

426  "Future shock?", editorial, *Guardian*, 3 August 1990, p. 16.

427  The oil reserves were discovered in 1969, and the first oil was extracted in 1975. Kenneth O. Morgan, ed., *op. cit.*, p. 585; also refer to his previous book: *Twentieth-Century Britain: A Very Short Introduction*, Oxford: Oxford UP, 2000, p. 79.

Brussels Commission to reduce the European Community's oil dependence.[428]

Many editorials and opinion articles published on both sides of the Atlantic[429] also highlighted the West's energy dependence on Middle Eastern oil, as the U.S. president and the British Prime Minister repeated on numerous occasions.[430] Moreover, numerous editorials, published especially in the *New York Times*, and many opinion articles in the American press emphasized the heavy dependence of Japan[431] and Europe[432] on imported

---

428    Louis Blin, *op. cit.*, p. 30.
429    For instance, the *New York Times* spoke about an "increasing dependence". "America's Neck and a New Noose", editorial, *New York Times*, 2 August 1990, p. A 20. The *Times* referred to "the danger of over-dependence on oil". "Taxing gas guzzlers", editorial, *Times*, 21 February 1991, p. 15. Likewise, the *Sunday Times* spoke of "the West's dependence upon oil". Robert Harris, "Eerie echoes of Suez debacle as Bush dons Eden mantle", op-ed, *Sunday Times*, 12 August 1990, Sect. 3, p. 4.
430    For example, refer to the American president's Address to the Nation on 8 August 1990 (<https://bush41library.tamu.edu/archives/public-papers/2147>), and to Margaret Thatcher's speech on 30 August 1990 (<https://www.margaretthatcher.org/document/108183>, consulted 17 August 2021).
431    For example, "Tokyo's Share of World Leadership", editorial, *New York Times*, 31 August 1990, p. A 26; Jim Sasser, "Is Uncle Sam Getting Stiffed?", op-ed, *New York Times*, 19 December 1990, p. A 25; "Paying for Desert Shield", editorial, *Washington Post*, 2 September 1990, p. B 6; Robert J. Samuelson, "Tired of Being the Superpower", op-ed, *Washington Post*, 19 December 1990, p. A 23. Nevertheless, the *Times* and the *Guardian* also published articles about Japan's oil dependence ("Japanese Jitters", editorial, *Times*, 23 August 1990, p. 9; Larry Elliott, "Déjà vu of the dark, dark days seven years ago", op-ed, *Guardian*, 9 August 1990, p. 17).
432    For instance, "Where's their Fair Share?", editorial, *New York Times*, 6 September 1990, p. A 26; Tom Wicker, "A Collective Effort", op-ed, *New York Times*, 2 September 1990, p. E 13; "Paying for Desert Shield", editorial, *Washington Post*, 2 September 1990, p. B 6; Robert J. Samuelson, "Beyond the Price of Oil", op-ed, *Washington Post*, 7 August 1990, p. A 19.

oil in comparison with the United States. They also stressed the fact that these countries, Japan in particular, were expected to assume, inter alia, their financial responsibilities during the Gulf Crisis and War. In doing so, American editorialists and journalists echoed Bush's remarks on 6 February 1991 that Japan, and also Germany, were both dependent on oil from the Persian Gulf.[433]

In the British press, neither the *Guardian* nor the *Observer*[434] recommended in August 1990, unlike the *Times* and the *Sunday Times*,[435] sending armed forces to restrain the president of Iraq, which was in line with the opposition of both newspapers to the dispatch and engagement of British troops in 1956 during the Suez Crisis.[436] However, during the hostilities in Iraq, the *Guardian* published opinion pieces by journalists and contributors supporting the war effort such as, for example, that of Douglas Hurd, the British Foreign Secretary, who highlighted the importance of oil supplies to British interests.[437]

---

433 Refer to Bush's remarks and question-and-answer session at a meeting of the Economic Club in New York on 6 February 1991 (<https://bush41library.tamu.edu/archives/public-papers/2691>, consulted 17 August 2021).

434 The *Guardian* and the *Observer* backed the imposition of economic sanctions against Iraq in the following editorials: "Paying the price for past errors", editorial, *Guardian*, 3 August 1990, p. 16; "Why this Hitler of the Gulf has to go", editorial, *Observer*, 5 August 1990, p. 12.

435 For example, refer to the article by Norman Macrae, "An oil scare not historically well-based", op-ed, *Sunday Times*, 12 August 1990, Sect. 3, p. 4. In his opinion piece, Norman Macrae stated that "[...] before about next December, Saddam should be either (preferably) killed by precision bombing and missilery or, alternatively, toppled by economic sanctions (which I doubt) [...]".

436 David Randall, *op. cit.*, p. 2.

437 Douglas Hurd, "Why Kuwait isn't Lithuania", op-ed, *Guardian*, 24 January 1991, p. 21.

As far as letters are concerned in the American press, readers emphasized, as did editorials and opinion articles, the dependence of the United States on imported oil.[438] Some *Washington Post* readers blamed the Iraqi leader for the increase in the price of gasoline.[439] In the British press, readers of the *Guardian*, the *Sunday Times* and the *Observer* castigated the primacy of economic interests requiring cheap oil and the sacrifice of soldiers' lives to ensure its supply.[440] Some pragmatic readers on both sides of the Atlantic, who were sensitive to ecological issues, proposed different alternatives to the use of oil.[441]

In essence, the American and British press emphasised the strategic importance of oil in their editorials, opinion articles and readers' letters. British editorials on oil were published mainly during the Gulf Crisis while American editorials on the subject appeared from August 1990 until the end of hostilities. The topics covered in the American press were repeated several

---

438 For instance, Robert L. Bard, "U.S. Doesn't Have to Go to War with Iraq on Hussein's Terms", letters, *New York Times*, 13 September 1990, p. A 26; Carl R. Henn, "More on the Iraqi Invasion", letters, *Washington Post*, 11 August 1990, p. A 20.

439 Stuart C. Schmid, "What's a Few Pennies More at the Pump?", letters, *Washington Post*, 16 August 1990, p. A 22; David Freund, "The Solution to the Energy Problem", letters, *Washington Post*, 31 August 1990, p. A 26.

440 Jeffrey A. Patterson, "The Gulf between a soldier's duty and beliefs", letters, *Guardian*, 11 October 1990, p. 20; Keith Martin, "The price of oil could be rising", letters, *Sunday Times*, 19 August 1990, Sect. 3, p. 7; George Perkin, "Mrs T and the Gulf factor", letters, *Observer*, 30 September 1990, p. 52.

441 Jonathan Lang, "All for Oil, a Fuel that Fouls Air and Water", letters, *New York Times*, 12 August 1990, p. A 20; Olivier de Messieres, "Aiding Refugees in the Middle East", letters, *Washington Post*, 13 September 1990, p. A 22; E. H. Cooke-Yarborough, "Greenhouse gamble", letters, *Times*, 13 September 1990, p. 15; Terry Moorhouse, "Moral outrage and state terror", letters, *Guardian*, 9 August 1990, p. 16.

times in various editorials published on different dates. Except for the *Times* opinion pieces which only appeared in August and September 1990, American and British newspapers published their opinion articles and readers' letters throughout the Gulf Crisis and War.

To sum up, both the American and British press speculated about likely scenarios of Saddam Hussein's possible control over oil reserves, his likely behaviour, the risks of supply disruption and contingent economic consequences. American and British newspapers constantly tried to persuade their readers of the danger posed by the Iraqi regime, following its invasion, to the supply of oil reserves, vital to Western economies. To do this, newspapers developed hypotheses and speculated by punctuating their editorials and opinion articles with modal auxiliaries of assumption, probability and condition and by the conjunction "if" as in the case of Iraq's weapons and nuclear arsenal. American and British newspapers stressed the West's oil dependence and advocated reducing oil imports from the Persian Gulf. However, only editorials and opinion articles in American newspapers and a few readers' letters published on both sides of the Atlantic recommended and detailed the various ways of reducing this dependence by developing other sources of energy, for example. The American press differed from the British press in that it claimed that the American government did not have a credible energy policy. The *Washington Post* argued in its editorials that there was no oil shortage. In the British press, only the *Guardian* highlighted Britain's self-sufficiency in oil since the 1970s. It should also be noted that American and British newspapers repeated the arguments of the American president and the British Prime Minister respectively regarding the West's energy dependence and the threat posed by Iraq to the supply of oil. Similar themes can be found in readers' letters,[442] editorials and opinion articles on both sides of the Atlantic, such as the increase in the price of oil and the inherent economic risks.

The two American newspapers and, on the British side, the *Times* and the *Sunday Times* tried to convince their readers of the need to use military force against the master of Iraq to guarantee access to cheap oil. For these newspapers, the enemy had to be fought because it threatened the energy security of Western nations. In this regard, it should be recalled that, while the objectives defined by the United Nations were the withdrawal of Iraqi troops from Kuwait and the restoration of the Emirate's sovereignty, the United States and its allies wanted above all to prevent the Baghdad regime from seizing control of Kuwait's oil and wealth. According to John B. Kelly and Amir Taheri, they wished most importantly to ensure the security of oil reserves in the Persian Gulf and their constant availability for the rest of the world.[443] In the end, Saddam Hussein was portrayed in American and British newspapers as a disruptive figure who, through his invasion, was harming Western consumers because of rising oil prices fuelling inflation and eroding their purchasing power. Saddam Hussein was thus an economic threat, which made him an adversary to be eliminated.

---

442    For example: Howard Greenlee, "Rip-off Artists", letters, *New York Times*, 12 August 1990, p. A 20; Paul F. Billingsley, "Crisis in the Gulf", letters, *Washington Post*, 9 August 1990, p. A 22; Somerset de Chair, "Control of oil and petrol prices", letters, *Times*, 4 October 1990, p. 17; Terry Moorhouse, "Moral outrage and state terror", letters, *Guardian*, 9 August 1990, p. 16.

443    John B. Kelly, "L'Après – Saddam Hussein", *Politique internationale*, No. 49, automne 1990, p. 90; Amir Taheri, *op. cit.*, p. 76.

## 4.5   Risk of geopolitical instability

As we have seen, American and British newspapers used numerous arguments to describe the different aspects of Saddam Hussein's personality and behaviour. They amplified the threat he represented to readers because of his military potential, his possible nuclear capability and his control over a large part of the oil reserves. The Iraqi president was also mainly presented as a destabilizing element in the geopolitical balance in the Persian Gulf region.

Firstly, newspapers on both sides of the Atlantic constantly promoted the idea that Saddam Hussein was a threat to world peace and order. For example, a *Times* editorial of 3 August 1990 defined Iraq as "a threat to the balance of power in the Middle East".[444] In the American press, Gary Sick from the *New York Times* asserted the day after the invasion of Kuwait that:

> "The seizure of Kuwait sends a further signal that President Saddam Hussein, the megalomaniacal leader of Iraq, must be stopped. If he is not, the consequences will be perilous for the Middle East and for the world".[445]

This passage, taken from the article of 3 August 1990, under the title "Hussein Must Be Stopped" adopted an extremely firm tone both in the title and in the text of the article, expressed in particular by the use of the modal "must".

---

444   "Iraq's naked villainy", editorial, *Times*, 3 August 1990, p. 11.
445   Gary Sick, "Hussein Must be Stopped ...", op-ed, *New York Times*, 3 August 1990, p. A 27.

As far as letters are concerned, a *Washington Post* reader stated that the Iraqi invasion of Kuwait changed the world situation drastically.[446] The *Guardian* published a letter whose reader believed that Saddam Hussein might attack other Arab nations like Saudi Arabia or Israel.[447] Only the *Observer* did not publish letters from readers expressing speculation on this subject, which does not necessarily imply that readers of the Sunday paper had not sent such letters.

Secondly, as we have seen about the link established by the Iraqi leader between his evacuation from Kuwait and the Israeli withdrawal from the occupied territories, the president of Iraq was described as a danger to Israel's security and as such having a detrimental impact on the geopolitics of the region. As a reminder, both American newspapers, in their editorials, as well as the *Times* and the *Sunday Times*, on the British side, criticized the Iraqi leader's proposal to withdraw his troops from the Emirate subject to Israel's departure. However, the *Guardian* and the *Observer* considered there was some merit in Saddam Hussein's position. In their opinion articles, some journalists and contributors in the press on both sides of the Atlantic highlighted the risks Iraq's president posed to Israel because of his threats against the Hebrew state in August 1990. They thus speculated on the attacks that Iraq could perpetrate against Israel, such as for example the possibility that the president of Iraq might use

---

446    Stuart C. Schmid, "What's a Few Pennies More at the Pump?", letters, *Washington Post*, 16 August 1990, p. A 22.

447    Ronnie Lewis, Wing Commander RAF retired, "Mankind on a precipice as the political war of words goes on", letters, *Guardian*, 15 November 1990, p. 20. The fact that the reader belonged to the British army could explain his point of view.

Scud missiles.[448] Their fears were confirmed on 18 January 1991 when Iraq did indeed fire Scuds against Israel and Saudi Arabia.

Thirdly, Saddam Hussein was also portrayed in the American press and by some British journalists[449] in the *Guardian* and the *Sunday Times* as a factor of imbalance for the unity of Arab countries. For instance, Richard Cohen stated in the *Washington Post* that "Iraq's aggression also smashed the façade of Arab unity".[450] The *New York Times*[451] differed from the *Washington Post* and British newspapers in that the newspaper was still referring on 3 March 1991 to the Iraqi leader's attempt to rally Islamic fundamentalists and the alliance he was likely to form with the Iranians. No doubt the American newspaper decided to provide a final justification for the legitimacy of the war by continuing to speculate on the actions of the president of Iraq.

Fourthly, while American and British newspapers referred to similar subjects such as the probable destabilisation of the geopolitical balance of the region following the Iraqi invasion of Kuwait, it was above all the assertion that Saddam Hussein was

---

448     For example, "Containing the war", editorial, *Times*, 17 January 1991, p. 13.

449     Only David Hirst in the *Guardian* blamed Iraq's invasion of Kuwait for having torn the Arabs asunder. David Hirst, "Arafat's dance with the devil", op-ed, *Guardian*, 23 August 1990, p. 19. Likewise, Brian Walden in the *Sunday Times* accused "Saddam's seizure of Kuwait" of having damaged the cause of Arab unity. Brian Walden, "Arab aspirations cry out for constant care and attention", op-ed, *Sunday Times*, 12 August 1990, Sect. 3, p. 4.

450     Richard Cohen, "Heading Off Iraq's Bomb", op-ed, *Washington Post*, 23 August 1990, p. A 25.

451     James E. Atkins, "Hooray?", op-ed, *New York Times*, 3 March 1991, p. E 17.

endangering vital American interests that appeared repeatedly in the two American newspapers. For Irving Kristol, a senior editorial associate of *The Public Interest*, the Iraqi invasion of Kuwait seriously challenged the U.S. national interest.[452] That was the argument advanced by the American president fifty-four times throughout the Gulf Crisis and War and which can also be found in some readers' letters.[453] In other words, the American press in most of its articles[454] as well as a certain number of readers adopted George Bush's rhetoric and denounced, mainly during the Gulf Crisis, the danger represented by the Iraqi invasion to American interests.

On the British side, the threat to Western interests following the invasion of Kuwait took centre stage. For example, the *Sunday Times* contended in an editorial dated 12 August 1990 that "President Saddam is a menace to vital Western interests in the Gulf".[455] Conor Cruise O'Brien in the *Times* and, in the *Guardian*, Paul Starr, a professor of Sociology at Princeton University in 1991, drew their readers' attention to Iraq's threat

---

452 Irving Kristol, "The Gulf: Born-Again Isolationists …", op-ed, *Washington Post*, 22 August 1990, p. A 21. *The Public Interest* was a quarterly neoconservative magazine on political economy and culture founded by Daniel Bell and Irving Kristol in 1965. Its final issue was published in spring 2005.

453 For example, the letter by Robert Schaetzel who wrote that "the crisis in the Persian Gulf, in which the interests of the United States […] are at stake". J. Robert Schaetzel, "Crisis in the Gulf: The International Response", letters, *Washington Post*, 21 August 1990, p. A 22.

454 Apart from Ted Galen Carpenter, Director of Foreign Policy Studies at the Cato Institute, who considered that "instability per se in distant regions does not threaten America's security". Ted Galen Carpenter, "America Can't Police the Planet", op-ed, *Washington Post*, 30 August 1990, p. A 23.

455 "Stopping Saddam", editorial, *Sunday Times*, 12 August 1990, Sect. 3, p. 5.

to the American economy for the former and to "liberal values and America's legitimate interests" for the latter.[456] The British daily newspapers were thus sensitive to the concerns of the American people and leaders. As far as the *Times* is concerned, the British newspaper may have wanted to align itself with the interests of its owner, Rupert Murdoch, whose News International Group was based, among others, in the United States. It could therefore be inferred that the *Times* favoured an American view on events.

In essence, American and British newspapers developed similar arguments presenting the Iraqi leader as a threat and a disruptive element in global geopolitics. The press on both sides of the Atlantic speculated on the danger posed by Iraq to Israel's security and world peace. Nevertheless, Saddam Hussein's menace was expressed in different ways, from the risk to Israel's security and the interests of the United States to a perceived global geopolitical peril. American and British editorialists, journalists and contributors thus conveyed the negative image of a formidable enemy to their readers, i.e. the image of a dangerous and powerful adversary to be defeated since he was harming world order and was therefore seen as a threat to everyone's security. In this regard, it should be noted that the noun "threat" and the verb "threaten" were used on a hundred and eighty-eight occasions by the American president during his conferences and speeches from August 1990 to mid-March 1991, eighty-eight times by Margaret Thatcher from August 1990 to November 1990, and twenty-eight times by John Major from December 1990 to mid-March 1991. As in the official rhetoric, these terms were repeated over and

---

456   Conor Cruise O'Brien, "Why Bush is treating Kuwait as a modern Pearl Harbour", op-ed, *Times*, 9 August 1990, p. 12; Paul Starr, "A liberal case for kicking ass", op-ed, *Guardian*, 7 February 1991, p. 23.

over again in the articles analysed in the American and British press in order to persuade readers of the danger represented by Saddam Hussein. The repetition of these terms reinforced the rhetorical effect of the discourse so that the contributor and/or the newspaper's editorial staff were able to build their arguments by relying on insistent repetitions in order to firmly anchor their point of view in readers' mind. The key word guided the viewpoint of the journalist who assumed the role of informing, denouncing and warning against the danger posed by the Iraqi leader.

The argumentation of the newspapers was especially important in the context of the new world order that George Bush sought to create. On 11 September 1990 the American president pleaded, in his address before a joint session of the Congress on the Persian Gulf Crisis, for the emergence of a new world order:

> "A new era, freer from the threat of terror, stronger in the pursuit of justice, and more secure in the quest for peace. An era in which the nations of the world, East and West, North and South, can prosper and live in harmony".[457]

According to Jean-Baptiste Duroselle and André Kaspi, this new world order which George Bush was referring to implied that all the problems of the Middle East, whether in Iraq, Palestine or Iran, could not be dealt with without the United States, and

---

457   See the George Bush's library website <https://bush41library.tamu.edu/archives/public-papers/2217>, consulted 19 August 2021. The American president had already referred to the new world order at a press conference on 30 August 1990 (<https://bush41library.tamu.edu/archives/public-papers/2189>), but it was not until 11 September 1990 that George Bush defined his new world order.

much less against them,[458] which thus seemed to take up the idea of the *Pax Britannica*[459] of yesteryear while strengthening the *Pax Americana*[460] of today. Robert Fisk challenged Bush's new world order by referring to an American officer who, "after only three weeks of bombing, compared his Arab enemies to insects".[461] William Engdahl argued that "Operation Desert Storm and the Bush–Thatcher Gulf War [...] had not accomplished its prime objective of reinserting Continental Europe into George Bush's and Margaret Thatcher's New World Order". He added that "the term was quickly dropped by George H.W. Bush after it drew critical attention in his 1991 State of the Union speech. It provoked too many questions as to whose order it was and what priorities it might have".[462]

In any case, while the collapse of the Soviet Union had raised hopes for a new era of peace and prosperity,[463] Saddam Hussein undoubtedly played the role of a troublemaker by invading a sovereign state, exhibiting prisoners of war, and in doing so flouting the Geneva Convention, and holding foreigners hostage

---

458  Jean-Baptiste Duroselle & André Kaspi, *op. cit.*, p. 548.
459  This Latin term for "the British Peace" was used from the 19th century to describe a large part of "the world safeguarded by British naval power" under the authority of the British Empire (David Weigall, *op. cit.*, p. 174). Britain, "the leading colonial power", dominated the world economy at that time (David Reynolds, *Britannia Overruled. British Policy and World Power in the Twentieth Century*, 2nd ed., London: Pearson Education, 2000, pp. 8, 18).
460  The Latin expression for "the American Peace" was coined during the Second World War by Henry R. Luce, an American publisher, who argued that "the Pax Americana would prevail in the second half of the 20th century" (David Weigall, *op. cit.*, p. 174).
461  Robert Fisk, *op. cit.*, p. 767.
462  William Engdahl, *op. cit.*, pp. 222, 223.
463  *Ibid.*, p. 223.

in defiance of human rights. For the American and British governments and newspapers, his exactions must therefore have reinforced the importance of Western moral values, the cornerstone of civilization in the face of barbarism.

## Conclusion

In addition to the atrocities committed by Saddam Hussein prior to 2 August 1990 and during the Gulf Crisis and War, American and British newspapers highlighted the military, nuclear, economic and geopolitical threat that the Iraqi leader represented to the world. To this end, in their editorials and opinion articles, the press on both sides of the Atlantic stressed the military power of Iraq composed of many soldiers hardened by the fighting in the war between Iraq and Iran. Like the U.S. president, American and British newspapers overall emphasized the military danger posed by Saddam Hussein. With the exception of a few opinion articles, there was therefore a large degree of correspondence between the American and British press and official U.S. discourse. Overestimating the military capabilities of the enemy's army, its equipment and its intrepid soldiers is an effective and above all classic method of frightening and ultimately convincing readers and public opinion in general of the need to send troops into combat in order to crush this allegedly invincible adversary.

The American and British press also agreed on highlighting the threat posed by Saddam Hussein's possession of chemical and biological weapons and the risk of their possible use. These chemical and biological weapons in the hands of the president of Iraq were presented in particular to the readers of the *Times* as a danger to Europe. Similar arguments relaying the official declarations of the American president and the British Prime Minister, whether Margaret Thatcher or John Major, can be found in editorials, opinion articles and letters published in the press on both sides of the Atlantic before the conflict began. Like the rhetoric about Iraq's fourth largest army in the world, highlighting the deadly peril inherent in the possession of chemical and biological weapons inevitably increased the idea of a military threat from Saddam Hussein.

In addition to this threat, the American and British press added another aspect to the worrisome portrait of the Iraqi leader by referring to Iraq's nuclear arsenal. The press on both sides of the Atlantic focused, in its editorials and opinion articles published during the Gulf Crisis, on the probable acquisition and/or possession of nuclear weapons by Iraq as well as the risk of their use. On the whole, American and British newspapers speculated on the fact that the Iraqi leader would need between two and five years to achieve his nuclear ambitions. Nevertheless, they were cautious, relying on authorized American sources and carefully hedging their claims. American newspapers differed from British newspapers in referring to the need to reduce the proliferation of nuclear weapons in general. The press on both sides of the Atlantic was ahead of the government authorities in mentioning the nuclear threat posed by Saddam Hussein as early as August 1990, whereas the U.S. president only addressed this issue in November 1990 and Margaret Thatcher in September 1990. In essence, American and British editorialists, journalists and contributors focused on Iraqi military power, the superiority of its armed forces and Iraq's possession of chemical and biological weapons and a nuclear arsenal. Their alarmist remarks undoubtedly convinced readers of the obligation to stop such a dangerous enemy.

This anxiety was reinforced by the oil issue. The press on both sides of the Atlantic echoed George Bush's and Margaret Thatcher's deep concerns about the danger presented by Saddam Hussein, following his invasion of Kuwait, for the control and supply of oil reserves and the risks of subsequent economic instability for the West. The American and British press made tentative assumptions about Iraq's stranglehold on oil reserves.

The Iraqi president was also portrayed in the American and British press as a destabilizing element in the geopolitical balance in the Persian Gulf. Firstly, editorials and opinion articles, published in the press on both sides of the Atlantic during the Gulf Crisis, highlighted the danger the Iraqi leader posed to peace and world order. Secondly, a few opinion articles in the American and British press emphasized the threat constituted by the president of Iraq to Israel's security. Thirdly, American editorials and opinion articles as well as some journalists from the *Guardian* and the *Sunday Times* accused the ruler of Iraq of breaking Arab unity through his invasion. Fourthly, American editorials and opinion articles, as well as opinion pieces in the British daily newspapers condemned the Iraqi leader for endangering American interests, as did George Bush. The *Times* and *Sunday Times* editorials highlighted the threat to Western interests following the Iraqi invasion of Kuwait. What is striking is the frequent repetition of the noun "threat" or the verb "threaten" by George Bush, Margaret Thatcher and John Major as well as in articles in the American and British press. All in all, there was a significant degree of correspondence between official statements and editorials as well as the majority of opinion articles as regards Saddam Hussein's negative image. Speculation was rife in newspapers as they were concerned, like the government authorities, about the risks the Iraqi leader posed to the Western world. As we have seen, he was thus depicted as a factor of probable imbalance in the geopolitics of the region, because of the impact on Israel's security, the breaking of Arab unity or the threat to American and Western interests.

By way of summary, the table on the next page shows the thematic correspondence between the official rhetoric and American and British editorials as regards the military, nuclear, oil, economic and geopolitical threat represented by Saddam Hussein.

This table clearly shows a high degree of convergence between editorials published in the American and British press and the official statements regarding Iraq's military power, its possession of chemical and biological weapons as well as its stranglehold on oil reserves, the question of the West's oil dependence and the geopolitical threat posed by Iraq. Except for the *Observer*, the press on both sides of the Atlantic agreed on the issue of Iraq's nuclear arsenal. Only the *Washington Post* stood out from the *New York Times* and British newspapers in relaying George Bush's assertion that there was no oil shortage. American editorials differed from those in the British press by stressing, like the American president, the geopolitical risk created by Saddam Hussein to American interests.

| Editorials | | | American press | | British press | | | |
|---|---|---|---|---|---|---|---|---|
| | | | New York Times | Washington Post | Times | Guardian | Sunday Times | Observer |
| Bush | Iraq's military power | | x | x | x | x | x | x |
| Bush, Thatcher & Major | Iraq's chemical and biological weapons | | x | x | x | x | x | x |
| Bush (11/90) & Thatcher (09/90) | Iraqi nuclear arsenal | | x | x | x | x | x | |
| Bush & Thatcher | Oil | Oil reserves held by SH and economic risk | x | x | x | x | x | x |
| Bush | | No oil shortage | | x | | | | |
| Bush & Thatcher | | The West's energy dependence | x | x | x | x | x | x |
| Bush | | Japan's energy dependence | x | x | | | | |
| Bush | Geopolitical instability | Danger to US interests | x | x | | | | |
| Bush, Thatcher & Major | | Iraq = threat | x | x | x | x | x | x |

Regarding opinion articles, American and British newspapers offered their readers, in some of their articles, a variety of viewpoints which sometimes differed from their editorial line. Likewise, the American and British press published letters whose opinions challenged or opposed those expressed in their editorials.

On the whole, in most of their editorials and opinion articles, the press on both sides of the Atlantic subscribed to the official rhetoric of the American president and the British Prime Minister. Editorialists, journalists and contributors of opinion articles speculated, through the use of conditional sentences and modals of assumption, on the military, nuclear, economic and geopolitical risk that the Iraqi ruler posed to the world. They thus exaggerated the intentions of the adversary, who had become the true Other. Yet, speculation and fear go hand in hand. By portraying the Iraqi ruler as a credible but worrisome threat, editorialists, journalists and contributors captivated their readers but above all alarmed them. Every day from August 1990 until the beginning of the war, frightening predictions about the probable and future actions of the Iraqi leader were made about the dangers involved if Saddam Hussein was not stopped. Not only did the anxiety-provoking comments aim to give readers a negative image of the enemy, but they also sought to convince them of the need to prevent Saddam Hussein from doing harm and thus accept the mobilization of armed troops in the Middle East and their country's entry into the war against Iraq.

The Iraqi leader, as a result of government declarations and with the help of the media, frightened the entire world. It was difficult for the public not to be overwhelmed by the gloom and anxiety surrounding the situation, which was relayed by newspapers. Described as a very dangerous enemy in the American and British press, Saddam Hussein was depicted as someone ready to destroy humanity with his biological and chemical weapons. Like a scourge, he was going to sweep into the world, endangering American and allied troops and perpetrating terrorist acts in countries opposed to his invasion. By fuelling the fears of readers and public opinion and spreading worrying information and news about the announced end of the world, newspapers might have thought that they could increase their circulations all the more if they frightened their readers.[464] As a general rule, the news, by focusing mainly on what is going wrong and what is frightening, causes collective anguish, which in turn generates an insatiable demand for anxiety-provoking and increasingly bad and catastrophic information through which naïve ideology is promoted due to the simplistic vision of a binary world divided into good and bad people. In this context, "conciliators" and pacifists who dare to question the dominant ideology look like unpatriotic visionaries. In a crisis or a war, the pessimistic discourse of journalists is indeed often charged with emotion and tend to be tinged with exacerbated patriotism.

---

464    However, this statement must be qualified: both American newspapers are reputable newspapers. As for the British press, the *Times* is a daily newspaper with the ambition to be a newspaper of reference and generally refrained from contributing to an atmosphere of fear during the Gulf Crisis and War. While these newspapers do appear to put journalism before profit, one can, however, wonder about the British Sunday newspapers.

# Part IV:

# Image of the Self

## Differences and similarities between the American press and the British press during the Gulf Crisis and War

# Chapter I:
# Military power

As a country's image includes, among other things, its military power, this chapter analyses the way in which the American and British armed forces as well as armaments and military equipment of both countries were represented in the press on both sides of the Atlantic. The army ensures and defends a country's security, interest and independence. It protects its citizens and its territory from potential external threats.[1] In other words, the armed forces are the cornerstone of a country's foreign and defence policy.[2] They strengthen the influence and international aura of a state[3] and consequently its image. As a corollary of the armed forces, weapons and military equipment are essential to victory in a conflict.

## 1.1　Military power of the United States

Faced with the Iraqi army, the world's fourth largest, the American press highlighted the military power of the United States in its editorials and opinion articles published between August 1990 and March 1991. For example, a *Washington Post*

---

1    Nonetheless, many disputes between countries could be resolved through diplomatic channels without resorting to arms.

2    However, some states have relatively small armed forces. They are then able to increase the budgets allocated to infrastructure, education and their citizens' health.

3    For example, the deployment of military intervention units abroad is a testament to the power of a country in the eyes of the world.

editorial stressed the "awesome expeditionary force"[4] built up by the United States in the Middle East. Editorials and opinion articles also detailed the number of troops deployed in Saudi Arabia.[5] For instance, George F. Will stated in November 1990 that "there soon may be 400,000 U.S. personnel in the Persian Gulf region".[6] By mentioning the number of troops sent to the Middle East, journalists were able not only to provide readers with factual information, but also to underline the size of the U.S. army, which certainly swelled readers with patriotic pride for the power of their country.[7]

The majority of editorialists, journalists and contributors in the two American newspapers[8] expressed their enthusiasm for the U.S. military expedition.[9] The adjectives "huge", "big" and

---

4    "Saddam Hussein's Threats", editorial, *Washington Post*, 25 September 1990, p. A 22.

5    "With its forces approaching 200,000, the United States will have more than three times as many troops in combat as all its partners put together". "Who Will Pay for the Gulf Crisis?", editorial, *New York Times*, 8 October 1990, p. A 16.

6    George F. Will, "Mobilization's Deadly Momentum", op-ed, *Washington Post*, 15 November 1990, p. A 25.

7    Over five hundred thousand American soldiers landed in Saudi Arabia and participated in Operation Desert Storm (Pierre-Jean Luizard, *op. cit.*, p. 307; also refer to Jean Baudrillard, *op. cit.*, p. 74). American forces accounted for more than 70% of seven hundred and forty thousand men mobilized against Iraq (Éric Laurent, *op. cit.*, 1991, p. 339).

8    However, a *New York Times* editorial ("Escalation, 1990 Style", editorial, *New York Times*, 27 October 1990, p. A 22) and James Webb, Assistant Secretary of Defense and Secretary of the Navy in the Reagan Administration, questioned the deployment of U.S. troops in Saudi Arabia (James Webb, "... And the Horrors of a Desert War", op-ed, *Washington Post*, 23 September 1990, p. 21).

9    Some journalists addressed societal issues in their articles about American troops. For example, Anna Quindlen from the *New York Times* referred to the situation of women in the army (Anna Quindlen, "Women Warriors",

"awesome" were legion in the American press.[10] Readers echoed the pride and support for the U.S. forces in their letters published in the *New York Times* and the *Washington Post*.[11]

The narrative on American soldiers' behaviour was the same in the articles published in both American newspapers. During the Gulf Crisis and War as well as after the hostilities, the two newspapers drew an admiring portrait of American soldiers: they were described for example as "our plucky military men and women".[12] As noted earlier, the journalist, by using the possessive adjective "our", included the reader and differentiated American soldiers from Iraqi soldiers.[13] Like editorialists and journalists,[14]

op-ed, *New York Times*, 3 February 1991, p. E 19), or of black soldiers in the armed forces (refer to A. M. Rosenthal, "Mother of All Columns", op-ed, *New York Times*, 1 March 1991, p. A 27 ; Jim Hoagland, "Race and the War", op-ed, *Washington Post*, 14 February 1991, p. A 23).

10　"A huge force". "Deployment, Fast; Procurement, Hasty", editorial, *New York Times*, 17 October 1990, p. A 26. "The biggest U.S. army". James Reston, "The President: Read His Slips", op-ed, *New York Times*, 21 October 1990, p. E 19. "An awesome expeditionary force". "Saddam Hussein's Threats", editorial, *Washington Post*, 25 September 1990, p. A 22. "The big U.S. military build-up". Rowland Evans and Robert Novak, "The Arab Solution", op-ed, *Washington Post*, 29 August 1990, p. A 25.

11　For example: Chris A. Harmon, "Pride in America", letters, *New York Times*, 3 February 1991, p. E 18; Scott A. Mills, "Containing Tyranny", letters, *Washington Post*, 25 November 1990, p. C 6.

12　George F. Will, "The Face of Violence", op-ed, *Washington Post*, 2 December 1990, p. C 7.

13　See point 2.3 in Chapter II, Part III about the virtuous behaviour of American soldiers towards Iraqi soldiers.

14　For example, Jack Anderson and Dale Van Atta, in an article titled, "Army of Rectitude", discussed the physical appearance of soldiers, described as "abstemious, clean-shaven, church-going". Their comments also had a religious dimension in that they added that the soldiers practised a religion. The two journalists lapsed into patriotic clichés, and their narrative was akin to propaganda for the U.S. military (Jack Anderson and Dale Van

readers also highlighted soldiers' bravery, their moral qualities, professionalism, motivation and dedication to duty.[15] Editorialists, journalists and contributors conveyed valuing stereotypes about American troops and fitted into a Manichean vision between the "good" American soldiers on the one hand and the "bad" Iraqi soldiers on the other. Nevertheless, it must be difficult in general, if not almost impossible, for journalists to criticize, in times of war, the soldiers of their country who are risking their lives. Whether journalists approve of the war or not, they must above all avoid arousing the wrath of their readers, whom they could lose. They therefore adopt a more or less patriotic discourse by supporting the armed forces engaged in combat for the nation. It is also likely that readers must be reassured and await comforting comments from their newspaper on the positive developments in the Gulf and the fate of their country's soldiers.

In addition to the flattering image of American troops presented by editorialists, journalists and contributors in the two newspapers, some opinion articles underlined the exemplary conduct of the war by the United States. For instance, Jim Hoagland and George F. Will explained to readers in the *Washington Post* that "the United States is concentrating on military targets and is not conducting a terror campaign against defenseless citizens". Similarly, for George F. Will, the United States was waging war by "enlisting technology in the service of a civilized sensibility".[16] This war aim was thus erected as a sacred value to be defended

---

Atta, "Army of Rectitude", op-ed, *Washington Post*, 17 February 1991, p. C 7).

15    For instance, the letter by Mike Corbett, "Soldiers Who Won't Fight", letters, *Washington Post*, 13 September 1990, p. A 22.

16    Jim Hoagland, "Simpson's Scud Attack", op-ed, *Washington Post*, 10 February 1991, p. C 7; George F. Will, "The Morality of Long-Range

against the allegedly uncivilized adversary. The opinion articles in question may have given readers the impression that the American army was waging war in an almost chivalrous manner.

Finally, a few opinion articles emphasized the heroic sacrifice[17] that the United States, a democratic nation, was willing to make to bring this conflict to a successful conclusion and come to the aid of Kuwait and Saudi Arabia, which were "both monarchies and not constitutional ones",[18] whereas it found the war "repugnant and wasteful".[19] On the one hand, the term sacrifice refers to a religious concept: like Abraham, the United States, destined for an exceptional destiny, agreed to sacrifice its sons, that is its soldiers, for a legitimate cause. On the other hand, like statesmen of countries who, before declaring war, always solemnly assure beforehand that they do not want it,[20] the United States presented itself as a peace-loving country. These journalists and contributors defined the United States as a chosen land and a democratic nation that came to the rescue of the weak. Their arguments were based on moral and religious principles that underpinned U.S. foreign policy.[21] In any case, their patriotic discourse was only used to

---

Killing", op-ed, *Washington Post*, 17 February 1991, p. C 7. These articles implied that the United States was not behaving like Saddam Hussein.

17    For instance: James Bowman, "The Worth of National Honor", op-ed, *Washington Post*, 20 January 1991, p. B 7.

18    Richard Cohen, "The Munich Metaphor", op-ed, *Washington Post*, 21 August 1990, p. A 23.

19    Jim Hoagland, "Against a Man of War ...", op-ed, *Washington Post*, 6 January 1991, p. C 7.

20    Anne Morelli, *op. cit.*, p. 7. These countries explain to their public opinion that, by virtue of their international commitments, they are forced to go to war.

21    Puritanism has contributed to the fundamental geopolitical structuring of the United States, which is expressed in and through its diplomacy (François Thual, "L'Impact du puritanisme anglais", *in Géopolitique des*

convince readers of the noble attitude of the United States and the American military in the war against Iraq and thus make them proud of the soldiers of their country.[22]

In addition to the armed forces, a nation's military power relies primarily on the possession of advanced technological weaponry. During Operation Desert Storm, the United States demonstrated its mastery of the most advanced technology, and its army had the most sophisticated weapons.[23] In the American press there was a plethora of editorials[24] and opinion articles[25] which, from August 1990 to March 1991, extolled the supremacy of U.S. high-technology weaponry in a patriotic tone. As a general rule, editorialists, journalists and contributors wanted to convince their readers, or rather confirm in their minds, that "the U.S. remains the strongest military power [...]"[26] and that "it is the

---

    *États-Unis. Culture, intérêts, stratégies. Revue Française de Géopolitique*, Paris: Ellipses, 2005, p. 124).

22    An editorial published after the hostilities spoke of "America's revived international pride" ("Good Morning, Vietnam", editorial, *New York Times*, 10 March 1991, p. E 14).

23    André Kaspi, *op. cit.*, pp. 615, 644; also refer to Jean Klein, "La Réglementation des armements après la guerre du Golfe", *Politique étrangère*, No. 3, automne 1991, p. 672.

24    For instance: "Patriots Work. Star Wars Won't", editorial, *New York Times*, 3 February 1991, p. E 18; "Paying for Desert Shield", editorial, *Washington Post*, 2 September 1990, p. B 6.

25    For example: John B. Judis, "George Bush, Meet Woodrow Wilson", op-ed, *New York Times*, 20 November 1990, p. A 21; Jack Anderson and Dale Van Atta, "High-Tech Weapons, Low-Tech Bugs", op-ed, *Washington Post*, 2 September 1990, p. B 7.

26    John B. Judis, "George Bush, Meet Woodrow Wilson", op-ed, *New York Times*, 20 November 1990, p. A 21.

only nation that can assemble and project enough power to meet any aggressor".[27]

Nonetheless, a minority of journalists and readers contested the status of the United States as a superpower, which they described as an "illusion".[28] For example, Michael Kinsley in the *Washington Post* used the film "Rambo",[29] which had been a great success in the United States some ten years earlier, to denounce the U.S. military's show of force, referring to it as a "Rambo illusion".[30] Moreover, Anna Quindlen in the *New York Times* contrasted foreign policy actions with the problematic situation of domestic policy, i.e. on the one hand the U.S. military engagement against Iraq, and, on the other hand, social problems and the weak American economy.[31] The diversity of points of view in opinion articles can also be found in readers' letters.[32]

---

27    Anthony H. Cordesman, "America's New Combat Culture", op-ed, *New York Times*, 28 February 1991, p. A 25.

28    For instance: "Superpower illusion". Tom Wicker, "War and Malaise", op-ed, *New York Times*, 30 December 1990, p. E 11.

29    This American action film, released in 1982, was based on David Morrell's novel *First Blood*. See the website: <https://www.davidmorrell.net/rambo/>, consulted 20 February 2021.

30    Michael Kinsley, "Two Myths in America", op-ed, *Washington Post*, 20 September 1990, p. A 23.

31    Anna Quindlen, "The Domestic Front", op-ed, *New York Times*, 31 January 1991, p. A 23. According to Dominique Moïsi, the U.S. budget deficit is largely attributable to the increase in defence spending (Dominique Moïsi, "Forces et faiblesses des États-Unis", *Politique étrangère*, No. 1, printemps 1989, p. 48).

32    See the letter by Gunnar Lundeberg, "U.S. Sealift Deficiencies Exposed in Gulf Crisis", letters, *New York Times*, 18 October 1990, p. A 24. The author was the president of the Sailors Union of the Pacific at that time. However, most readers praised the U.S. military technology. For instance, in the letter by Stephen A. Wise, "The New Crusaders?", letters, *New York Times*, 23 September 1990, p. E 20.

In summary, most editorials, opinion articles and readers' letters adopted a rhetoric of persuasion based on repetition of the same adjectives and laudatory arguments about U.S. military power and its supremacy over that of the enemy. In addition, the two American newspapers largely echoed the official views, as George Bush, in his speeches and conferences during the Gulf Crisis and the war itself, constantly praised the merits of U.S. soldiers and glorified cutting-edge military technology.[33] As a result, there was circularity of information between the government in power, the American press and a swathe of public opinion represented by readers celebrating the world's greatest military power in 1991.[34]

## 1.2  Britain's military power

While most articles in the American newspapers praised the military superiority of the United States, the situation on the British side was more nuanced. For example, the *Times* stated in an editorial of 13 August 1990 that "Britain has launched its

---

33  For example, refer to George Bush's remarks at a rally for senatorial candidate Lynn Martin in Chicago, Illinois on 26 September 1990 (<https://bush41library.tamu.edu/archives/public-papers/2263>), and his remarks to Raytheon missile systems plant employees in Andover, Massachusetts on 15 February 1991 (<https://bush41library.tamu.edu/archives/public-papers/2711>, consulted 11 September 2021).

34  According to René Rémond, the dissolution of the USSR rid the United States of its only competitor, allowing it to remain the only great power in the world thanks to its strategic superiority based on its scientific and technological lead (René Rémond, *Histoire des États-Unis*, Que sais-je?, 19e éd., Paris: PUF, 2003, p. 118). The United States had military means that no other power possessed (Jean-Baptiste Duroselle & André Kaspi, *op. cit.*, p. 547).

biggest military operation overseas since the Falklands campaign of 1982".[35] The editorial, entitled "In a just cause", was about the Royal Air Force units which had been sent to help U.S. forces to deter an Iraqi invasion of Saudi Arabia. The *Times* may have considered it legitimate to send British troops to the Middle East and the cause was thus deemed just.[36] The newspaper may also have referred in the title to "Operation Just Cause", a military operation undertaken by the United States against Panama in December 1989. However, it is difficult to know whether British readers remembered all U.S. military interventions even though the one referred to had taken place a few months earlier.

The *Times* editorials and opinion pieces also highlighted, on several occasions and starting in August 1990, Britain's will and determination[37] to take military action against Iraq if necessary, following its aggression. The *Times* thus portrayed Britain as a determined and combative nation. The honourable and civilized behaviour of the allied commanders – among whom were the British military – was added to the country's pugnacity. They "would be making every effort to kill as few civilians as is compatible with paralysing the Iraqi military",[38] according to an editorial on 7 February 1991. The British newspaper developed patriotic rhetoric in its editorials which became simplistic when

---

35    "In a just cause", editorial, *Times*, 13 August 1990, p. 11.

36    The issues of just cause and just war will be discussed at the end of point 1.2.

37    For instance, "Holding together", editorial, *Times*, 22 August 1990, p. 11. "Uniting the nation", editorial, *Times*, 6 September 1990, p. 11. "Britain embarked on war last week with fewer qualms than any of its allies". Daniel Johnson, "Old fires lick at Germany", op-ed, *Times*, 24 January 1991, p. 14.

38    "Saddam's bogus appeal", editorial, *Times*, 7 February 1991, p. 11.

it endowed the military authorities with moral virtues. This demagogic argument ignores the consequences of wars which are most often costly in human lives, with numerous civilian victims and soldiers described by Jean Bacon as anonymous pawns pushed towards the big slaughterhouses of honour.[39]

Finally, Michael Evans referred in March 1991 to British infantrymen who came to fight against an enemy "who seemed interested only in waving white flags".[40] As in the American newspapers, the journalist proceeded by dichotomy: on the one hand, the courageous British soldiers and on the other, the Iraqi army considered as cowards. In October 1990 a reader expressed his pride for the "Desert Rats"[41] that would be deployed in the Middle East. There was thus unanimity over time – before, during and after the Gulf War – regarding the favourable image of the British army in editorials, opinion pieces and readers' letters in the *Times*, given that the British contribution to "Operation Granby", which was the name given to the British military operations during the Gulf War, was the largest of all European contributions to the coalition.[42]

---

39    Jean Bacon, *Les Saigneurs de la guerre. Brève histoire de la guerre et de ceux qui la font*, Paris: Phébus, 2003, p. 88.
40    Michael Evans, "Yes, it really was a famous victory", op-ed, *Times*, 14 March 1991, p. 14.
41    Mark Ashley Miller, Adjutant, "Desert Rats", letters, *Times*, 1 October 1990, p. 15. The Desert Rats are the nickname of the men who served in the 7th Armoured Division in North Africa during World War II. Their shoulders or vehicles wore the Jerboa emblem (see the website <desertrats. org.uk/history.htm>, consulted 2 March 2021).
42    John Major told the House of Commons on 15 January 1991 that 35,000 service men and women were deployed in the Gulf. Refer to Hansard Parliament UK, The Gulf, vol. 183, (<https://hansard.parliament.uk/ Commons/1991-01-15/debates/3498d88e-f437-47bc-bdc6-cd0c78a0fee8/

During a crisis or conflict, a newspaper of reference such as the *Times* – and indeed most newspapers – will seek to reassure their readers and convince them of the benevolent, heroic behaviour of their country's soldiers. Readers approved of their government's actions in the Gulf Crisis and War, and above all were able to identify with the virtuous warriors depicted in the *Times*. They must therefore have had an excellent opinion of themselves. People often need to belong to a group, a community, or a country in order to build their own identity correlated to a positive self-esteem.

In contrast to the *Times*, the *Guardian* was rather ironic and critical of the British brigade, calling it a "puny force"[43] in September 1990. On the other hand, an editorial published in January 1991 referred to the British soldiers who, at the request of the U.N., had gone to set the evil regime in Iraq to rights.[44] For the *Guardian*, British soldiers were thus entrusted with a respectable and exemplary mission. The newspaper seemed to make amends by adopting a different point of view: within a few months, it blithely moved from a negative attitude, stressing the lack of military power, to laudatory remarks about British soldiers. The *Guardian* may have wanted to show its patriotism during the Gulf War.

By contrast, journalists and contributors in the *Guardian* drew a very different portrait of the British people and military. For

TheGulf?highlight=chemical#contribution-93c27615-93f1-43c2-b05e-395509d2>, consulted 8 March 2021).

43    "Europe's defence", editorial, *Guardian*, 20 September 1990, p. 18.
44    "Suddenly the sky turns orange", editorial, *Guardian*, 17 January 1991, p. 18.

instance, in February 1991, Hugo Young criticized "the phlegmatic stoicism of the British, always an ally of governments at war".[45] On the other hand, Sidney Perkowitz, a professor of condensed-matter physics at Emory University at that time, lauded "the allied forces' stated goal of minimising innocent casualties".[46] As noted in the *Times*, the professor attributed moral qualities to the coalition forces to which British officers and troops belonged. Yet, it seems difficult to be absolutely certain that so-called surgical strikes as part of a clean war strategy inflicted few or no casualties. However, the military authorities must above all sell their war to public opinion and hide the suffering of the population exposed to intensive aerial bombardments.[47] All in all, the *Guardian* published articles with a variety of positions, to which readers may or may not adhere according to their opinions;[48] journalists and contributors thus shaped a nuanced image of their country.

---

45  Hugo Young, "All quiet on the home front", op-ed, *Guardian*, 14 February 1991, p. 20.

46  Sidney Perkowitz, "The scientist at war", op-ed, *Guardian*, 7 March 1991, p. 23.

47  During the Gulf conflict, the military referred to "precision bombardment" as the effective use of terminal-guided bombs or missiles hit both strategic and tactical targets. Since war could be fought with a minimum of collateral damage, i.e. civilian deaths, modern warfare became more acceptable (François Heisbourg, "Quelles leçons stratégiques de la guerre du Golfe?", *Politique étrangère*, No. 2, été 1991, pp. 420-421). According to Jean-Baptiste Duroselle and André Kaspi, an expression summarizes the objectives of the allies: "no dead war", i.e. a war that does not kill people. The authors add that more bombs were dropped on Iraq in one week than on Germany throughout 1944 (Jean-Baptiste Duroselle & André Kaspi, *op. cit.*, p. 546). One can therefore validly question the notions of "precision bombardment" with little "collateral damage". Finally, "whereas during the Gulf War of 1991, some 7 per cent of munitions had been precision-guided (PGM), in Iraq in 2003 that percentage had increased almost by a factor of ten" (Charles Reed & David Ryall, eds., *op. cit.*, p. 183).

48  The *Guardian* was certain to meet the expectations of its readers and please them by publishing opinion pieces with contradictory viewpoints

The *Sunday Times* switched to a completely different narrative register. From the beginning of the Gulf Crisis, it recounted, in its editorials, a colourful story to the glory of its country, the British people and its British soldiers, affectionately called "our men in the Gulf" who "are the best of British".[49] For example, a *Sunday Times* editorial of 16 September 1990 stressed Britain's determination to fight because "right is on [its] side".[50] For the *Sunday Times*, there was thus a moral imperative since it was unacceptable not to react to a situation deemed unbearable,[51] namely by Iraq's invasion of Kuwait.

Most opinion pieces[52] published in the *Sunday Times* repeated and confirmed the bellicose discourse of editorials. They conveyed a favourable and ideal image of Britain and the British people. They also drew an admiring portrait of the British armed forces

---

since readers could find positions that corresponded to their own. The *Guardian* – as it were – honoured the "moral contract" that bound it to its readers (Telephone interview with Michel Morel on 6 March 2012).

49 "Christmas in the desert", editorial, *Sunday Times*, 23 December 1990, Sect. 1, p. 11.

50 "Lest we forget", editorial, *Sunday Times*, 16 September 1990, Sect. 3, p. 7. The concept of "bellum justum" or "justa causa" will be explained later.

51 Vincent Troin, "La Maîtrise de l'information: naissance et essor d'une doctrine stratégique", *in Géopolitique des États-Unis. Culture, intérêts, stratégies. Revue Française de Géopolitique,* Paris: Ellipses, 2005, p. 167.

52 For example, the articles by Norman Stone and Norman Macrae: "The British have a sound attitude to war". "An obviously outstanding professional army". Norman Stone, "How trendy pacifism edged out truth on our TV screens", op-ed, *Sunday Times*, 20 January 1991, Sect. 2, p. 5. "More than 80% of [...] Britons have cheered on the taskforce [...]". Norman Macrae, "Short and sharp, here's a case for the Falklands treatment", op-ed, *Sunday Times*, 19 August 1990, Sect. 3, p. 4. However, Robert Harris stated that "The British forces, both in place and en route, represent less than 4% of the total allied strength". Robert Harris, "This is not our finest hour and Saddam's not Hitler", op-ed, *Sunday Times*, 23 September 1990, Sect. 3, p. 6.

by highlighting the effectiveness of soldiers engaged in combat. As in the Falklands War, warlike and demagogic rhetoric was at work in the editorials and opinion pieces of the *Sunday Times*. Editorialists and journalists may have wished to share the concerns of readers who had a family member or acquaintance in the theatre of operations. In this way, their articles played to the people's patriotic tune.

By contrast, several readers rebelled against the patriotic fervour aroused by the Sunday paper. For example, one of them considered in August 1990 that "to assume that we automatically have right on our side is a recipe for war".[53] In January 1991, another reader wrote that the British attitude to war in the Gulf was jingoistic.[54] On the one hand, one may wonder whether this reader was not also attacking the extremely patriotic, and even almost fanatical, attitude of editorialists and journalists from the *Sunday Times* who were also British citizens. On the other hand, these letters, which contradicted the editorial line of the newspaper, attested to the plurality of opinions offered by the *Sunday Times* since it could very well have chosen not to publish them. In summary, however, the *Sunday Times* developed a narrative that was akin to propaganda in its editorials and opinion pieces. It can be suggested that, except for these two letters, readers may have expected their newspaper to reinforce their way of thinking. The complimentary treatment of Britain, its people and its armed forces in the *Sunday Times* editorials and opinion pieces may have been based on the psychological traits

---

53    Keith Martin, "The price of oil could be rising", letters, *Sunday Times*, 19 August 1990, Sect. 3, p. 7.

54    David Sinclair, "Europe begins to get its Gulf act together. Jingoism", letters, *Sunday Times*, 27 January 1991, Sect. 1, p. 16.

present in some of its readers. In general, readers, who live in the same country, belong to a nation sharing the same values as well as a common history, culture and way of thinking. In other words, they display the same collective identity.[55] Individuals are part of a group and as such they tend not to want their country – at war – assailed in the newspaper they buy or subscribe to.[56]

The *Observer* did not devote any editorials to the armed forces and Britain's combative attitude in the Gulf Crisis and War. It may have deemed these subjects unworthy of publication in its editorials. Nevertheless, the *Observer* published opinion pieces presenting a variety of attitudes to them. For example, Major-General Julian Thompson, who led three Commando Brigade during the Falklands campaign, argued that past planning failures had left Britain ill-prepared to fight Saddam Hussein.[57] Like Robert Harris in the *Sunday Times*, Andrew Stephen stressed the limited number of soldiers sent to the Gulf[58] and argued during the hostilities that "Britain is contributing just 5.99 per cent of the troops". By contrast, while Michael Ignatieff praised the British

---

55     Serge Paugam (dir.), *Les 100 Mots de la sociologie*, Que sais-je?, Paris: PUF, 2010, p. 72.

56     However, this statement must be kept in context, as "by the 1990s newspaper readership was much less stable" and less loyal to its chosen newspaper than the British reader in the 1960s. Besides, although "the correlation appears not to be especially strong", the people "with the most education and income do the most newspaper reading" (Jeremy Tunstall, *op. cit.*, pp. 215, 224). We should hope that educated readers question what their newspaper writes, but it is certainly possible that the views expressed by their newspaper may correspond to those of readers, whether or not they are cultivated.

57     Major-General Julian Thompson, "Making the best of a cut-price job", op-ed, *Observer*, 16 September 1990, p. 18.

58     Andrew Stephen, "Self-delusion and escapism grip America's poodle", op-ed, *Observer*, 17 February 1991, p. 15.

soldiers who were "the ones to do the dirty job",[59] Harold Evans examined the morality of publishing, in the *Observer* on 3 March 1991, the photograph of a dead Iraqi soldier, "in charred flesh and grinning skull", which "was the price of patriotism".[60] The soldier was one of many Iraqis, "whose stiffened, shabby remains" were found "lying around their burned-out tanks and trucks [...] after the American and British jets had trapped them at night in their flight from Kuwait".[61] This photograph on the "highway of death" generated outrage from readers of the Sunday newspaper.[62] Although some people were revolted by the publication of such a picture, it could be argued that it was necessary to portray the horrors of the battlefield and show what the Gulf War was really like. To all of those who advocate the concept of "clean war", it is necessary to make visible the "human cost" of war[63] and examine the notion of patriotism from all its aspects. The *Observer*'s publication of an article by Harold Evans may come as a surprise given that he was editor-in-chief[64] of the *Times* and the *Sunday Times*. Nonetheless, it was certainly interesting for

59    Michael Ignatieff, "Back to reality on the home front", op-ed, *Observer*, 3 March 1991, p. 21.
60    Harold Evans, "Necessary shock to our image of war", op-ed, *Observer*, 10 March 1991, p. 22.
61    Robert Fisk, *op. cit.*, p. 845.
62    On 10 March 1991, the *Observer* on page 50 published six letters from readers reacting to the photograph of the head of an Iraqi soldier who was charred while driving his burnt-out truck. These letters, entitled "Judgment on the face of war", were sent by the following readers: J. L. Cox, Suzanne Phillimore, Bernard and Denise Keeffe, G. Jordan, Colin Appleton and Luke Waddington. The Sunday paper may have received other letters that it did not publish, which is not possible to check.
63    Robert Fisk, *op. cit.*, p. 792.
64    Harold Evans was editor-in-chief of the *Sunday Times* from 1967 to 1981 and of the *Times* from 1981 to 1982 (Graham Stewart, *op. cit.*, pp. 17, 52-54).

the *Observer* to publish the opinion of an experienced journalist even if he had worked for rival newspapers. In any event, opinion pieces – apart from Michael Ignatieff's – that were published in the *Observer* painted a demeaning picture of the British army and an uncompromising portrait of their country.

Beyond the differences in attitude between the *Sunday Times* on the one hand and the *Guardian* and the *Observer* on the other, there was a common denominator in these newspapers, namely the use of the possessive determiner "our" when referring to British soldiers. As noticed earlier, this possessive determiner, which displays an obvious bias, not only includes the reader but also expresses a sense of national belonging. It is thus a unifying element of national identity[65] which distinguishes the side of the journalist and the reader in opposition to that of the "Other".

In addition to the armed forces, the *Times*, the *Guardian* and the *Sunday Times* also reported on the technological arsenal used. While the *Times* highlighted the "precision bombing",[66] the *Guardian* stressed "the performance of the new, hi-tech generation of weapons",[67] and the *Sunday Times* emphasized

---

65    According to Michel Serres, there is no national identity. It is more about belonging. Confusing identity and belonging leads to excesses and in particular to racism. Identity can be summed up in the DNA code, unique to each individual (Michel Serres, *Hominescence*, Paris: Le Pommier, 2001, pp. 85-86, 160-161, 196-198).

66    "Direct hit in Amiriya", editorial, *Times*, 14 February 1991, p. 15.

67    Robert J. Lifton, "Techno-bloodshed", op-ed, *Guardian*, 14 February 1991, p. 21. The author, a distinguished professor of psychiatry and psychology at the City University of New York and director of the Centre on Violence and Human Survival, argued in his article that "the performance of the new, hi-tech generation of weapons has dominated everyone's perception of the war. The communications revolution has taken us amazingly close

"our superior technology and generals".[68] The situation was more contrasted in the *Observer* as it published opinion pieces with a variety of opinions.[69]

To sum up, an editorial in the *Guardian* and opinion pieces published in the newspaper and the *Observer* drew a mixed picture of the British army as they highlighted the low number of British soldiers deployed in Saudi Arabia. Nevertheless, both newspapers from the beginning of the conflict were patriotic in their support for the troops engaged in combat. The *Times* and the *Sunday Times*, on the other hand, painted a glowing picture of the British armed forces.[70] The British soldier was almost mythologised: he embodied the brave knight armed with the moral virtues of courage and loyalty. According to the British daily newspaper

---

to the war zone but, psychologically speaking, further than ever from the war. Rather than death or suffering, we are exposed to images and technical details concerning profoundly impressive weaponry". Television makes it possible to experience war live. It magnifies fire power without the viewers feeling the suffering caused by deadly weapons. According to Arnaud Mercier, the allies promoted the technical and technological control of weapons during the Gulf conflict in order to channel the public's emotional reactions to violent images of war. The political and military authorities, on the side of the allies, thus played on the fascination for military technology (Arnaud Mercier, "Médias et violence durant la guerre du Golfe", *Cultures & Conflits*, Nos 09-10, printemps – été 1993, <http:// journals.openedition. org/conflits/296>; <https://doi.org/10.4000/conflits.296>, online since 4 March 2005, consulted 10 December 2020).

68    Barbara Amiel, "Let Iraq's true voice be heard", op-ed, *Sunday Times*, 3 March 1991, p. VIII.

69    For example: "The British do not have custom-built attack helicopters like the Apache [...]. There are insufficient troop-lift and logistic support helicopters to enable the brigade to operate in a high-intensity war". Major-General Julian Thompson, "Making the best of a cut-price job", op-ed, *Observer*, 16 September 1990, p. 18.

70    Except for Robert Harris who referred to Britain's paltry military contribution.

and the Sunday newspaper, Britain thus asserted its military power through the bravery of its army and the technological quality of its armament.[71] In doing so, the *Times* and the *Sunday Times* echoed the Prime Minister's arguments: on the one hand, Margaret Thatcher stressed the professionalism and courage of British troops on 22 November 1990,[72] and on the other, John Major praised the performance of the British forces in the Gulf as well as the important part played by RAF Tornadoes in the air campaign.[73]

One final point deserves further examination. American and British newspapers developed arguments revolving around the concept of "just cause" or "just war"[74] to justify sending their countries' troops to the Gulf region following the Iraqi invasion of Kuwait. The medieval theologian St Thomas Aquinas (1226-74) developed the notion of "just war" by specifying that it was

---

71    Opinion pieces in the *Guardian* also highlighted the technical prowess of the weapons used by the British army.

72    Refer to Margaret Thatcher's House of Commons statement on 22 November 1990 (<https://hansard.parliament.uk/Commons/1990-11-22/debates/6c776281-04cb-47fe-afdf-cadd8bb232c3/ConfidenceInHerMajestySGovernment?highlight=falklands#contribution-35208235-95ac-4621-a2f9-25c86d00e7fb>, consulted 18 July 2021).

73    For example, John Major's statements on the Gulf War to the House of Commons on 15 January 1991 (<https://hansard.parliament.uk/Commons/1991-01-15/debates/3498d88e-f437-47bc-bdc6-cd0c78a0fee8/TheGulf?highlight=chemical#contribution-93c27615-93f1-43c2-b05e-395509d2>), and on 21 January 1991 (<https://hansard.parliament.uk/Commons/1991-01-21/debates/c80bc5e0-03fd-49fb-a838-62f4c66958e1/TheGulf?highlight=john%20major#contribution-45b223d1-b234-4128-83d8-f45ed0b23f2b>, consulted 18 July 2021).

74    The Christian Church drew a distinction between just and unjust war. The just-war doctrine defines "the circumstances under which warfare is morally and legally justified" (Chris Rohmann, *The Dictionary of Important Ideas and Thinkers*, London: Arrow Books, 2002, p. 214).

necessary "that the person waging war had sufficient authority, that there was just cause and that the war was fought for peace and for the good".[75] The American press only published a few articles on this issue. For example, a *New York Times* editorial at the beginning of hostilities believed that "it is [...] a just war though not a wise one".[76] However, opinion articles published in both American newspapers offered a diversity of viewpoints. While Leslie H. Gelb stressed on 2 January 1991 that "even just wars must be measured by their costs and consequences",[77] Jim Hoagland from the *Washington Post* informed readers of the Soviet support for a just war, "even if it is led by American resolve and power".[78] The absence of letters and the small number of articles published on the subject in both newspapers may be explained by the fact that most editorialists, journalists, contributors and readers were probably convinced of the validity of the war waged by the U.S. military. The editorialists and journalists in question may have believed that everyone necessarily agreed with their opinions because of a common ideological background and thus may not have found it essential to comment on the issue in articles and letters. Moreover, for them, as for the American president who described the war in the Gulf as "a just war" eight times in a single speech[79] on 28 January 1991, war could only be just by

---

75   David Weigall, *op. cit.*, p. 129.

76   "The Protesters, Heard", editorial, *New York Times*, 27 January 1991, p. E 16.

77   Leslie H. Gelb, "To Fight in the Gulf?", op-ed, *New York Times*, 2 January 1991, p. A 17.

78   Jim Hoagland, "The Soviet's Tough New Stance", op-ed, *Washington Post*, 14 October 1990, p. C 7.

79   Cf. George Bush's remarks at the Annual Convention of the National Religious Broadcasters (<https://bush41library.tamu.edu/archives/public-papers/2653>, consulted 18 February 2021).

virtue of the moral obligation to fight against the enemy, i.e. the Other, the evil to be fought.[80]

Unlike the American press, the British press published numerous editorials and opinion pieces on the notion of "just war". For instance, a *Times* editorial of 13 August 1990, entitled "In a just cause",[81] considered the British forces' cause just. It can be assumed that the *Times* intentionally substituted the term "cause" for "war" in order to address the notion of "just war" as early as August 1990 before there was even a question of war. A *Sunday Times* editorial of 19 August 1990 went further than the *Times* in that it did not use the word "cause" in August 1990 but the term "war" and it already predicted, at the beginning of the Gulf Crisis, the outbreak of a conflict considered "a just war".[82] The two editorials in the *Times* and the *Sunday Times* thus echoed the remarks by Margaret Thatcher, who used this concept to justify the dispatch of British troops to the Gulf region and John Major, who did so to warrant Britain's involvement in the war.[83] Finally,

---

80    Vincent Troin, *op. cit.*, p. 167.

81    "In a just cause", editorial, *Times*, 13 August 1990, p. 11.

82    "Preparing for war", editorial, *Sunday Times*, 19 August 1990, Sect. 3, p. 5.

83    See Margaret Thatcher's speech at Lord Major's Banquet on 12 November 1990. The Prime Minister referred to Britain's unique qualities — "steadfastness in defence; staunchness as an ally; willingness always to give a lead" — being put to the test in a just cause (<https://www.margaretthatcher.org/document/108241>). John Major used the terms "just war" to describe the conflict in the Persian Gulf: on 15 January 1991 (<https://hansard.parliament.uk/Commons/1991-01-15/debates/3498d88e-f437-47bc-bdc6-cd0c78a0fee8/TheGulf?highlight=chemical#contribution-93c27615-93f1-43c2-b05e-395509d2>), and on 17 January 1991 (<https://hansard.parliament.uk/Commons/1991-01-17/debates/e77492a9-dee0-487f-8964-6824f654845e/The Gulf?highlight=just%20war#contribution-ce2c66f9-61bb-472e-bddd-155232931ec9>), consulted 18 February 2021).

although the *Observer* opposed Britain's entry into the war during the Gulf Crisis, it changed its mind at the start of hostilities and came to validate the legitimacy of the war.[84] It is true that in a conflict between their country's army and enemy soldiers, it is difficult for the media not to rally to government policy and support the war effort at the risk of alienating readers.

Opinion pieces in the two British daily newspapers and the *Observer* also addressed the "just war" principle.[85] While the *Sunday Times* supported the war against Iraq as a "just war" in its editorials, the Sunday paper did not devote any opinion pieces to the issue. No doubt it considered its patriotic, even nationalistic, editorials sufficient to convince its readers. The *Observer* stood out from other newspapers by publishing the largest number of opinion pieces on this subject, some of which took contradictory positions.[86] The Sunday paper thus generated an open discussion from November 1990 until the end of hostilities. This was also the case in letters sent to the *Times*,[87] the *Guardian*[88] and the

---

84    See the following editorial: "Remember what the victims are dying for", editorial, *Observer*, 20 January 1991, p. 18.

85    Refer to the following articles: Clifford Longley, "An anguished Catholic treads a careful line", op-ed, *Times*, 21 February 1991, p. 15. Rowan Williams, "Onward Christian soldiers?", op-ed, *Guardian*, 1 November 1990, p. 19.

86    For instance, the articles by Philip Crowe, Rev., "The case against a 'Just War' in the Gulf", op-ed, *Observer*, 11 November 1990, p. 22; Richard Harries, Rt Rev., "A just war, not a crusade", op-ed, *Observer*, 20 January 1991, p. 18.

87    For example, the letter by Christopher Derrick, "Right and reason in a 'just war'", letters, *Times*, 8 November 1990, p. 17.

88    For instance, Pat Grennan, "Immoral cop-out on the Gulf", letters, *Guardian*, 22 November 1990, p. 22.

*Observer.*[89] Readers questioned the notion of "just war", which became the focus of a controversy in letters published in the three British newspapers from November 1990 to January 1991.

## Conclusion

On the American side, most editorials, opinion articles and readers' letters glorified their country's military superiority, thus adopting the official rhetoric. British newspapers, on the other hand, promoted an opposite image of Britain, its military and its citizens: the *Times* and the *Sunday Times* highlighted their country's fighting spirit and British soldiers' sense of duty in their editorials and opinion pieces. By contrast, the *Guardian* and the *Observer* published opinion pieces with contradictory viewpoints, presenting a contrasting picture of Britain and its military. While it is difficult to draw conclusions about the readers' perception of their country given that only a few letters published in the newspapers were available, it is clear, however, that not all readers of the *Sunday Times* subscribed to the Sunday paper's warmongering rhetoric.

As regards the notion of "just war", editorialists, journalists and contributors as well as readers on both sides of the Atlantic who supported this doctrine were convinced of their good faith and moral superiority. Taking up the official rhetoric and convinced that their cause was just,[90] they thereby equated the

---

89    Refer to the letter by G. B. Bamford, "Morality of a just war in the Gulf", letters, *Observer*, 27 January 1991, p. 50.

90    Jean Bacon, *op. cit.*, p. 40. For David Fisher, "the First Gulf War was a just war". David Fisher, *Morality and War. Can War be Just in the Twenty-first*

enemy with a criminal. This ideological argument which involved the discrimination as well as the moral and legal disqualification of the enemy[91] was reflected in articles published in the American and British press which followed the "just war" concept. Although a large majority argued that Operation Desert Storm was based on a just cause, namely the restoration of Kuwait's sovereignty,[92] there was much debate whether the countries involved gave enough time "for sanctions and/or diplomacy to work"[93] in order to avoid conflict and thus achieve a peaceful settlement.[94]

---

*Century?*, Oxford: Oxford UP, 2011, p. 194. However, some critics accused the USA and claimed that the First Gulf War "was undertaken to secure its oil supplies from Kuwait [...]" (Richard Harries, "A British theological perspective" *in* Charles Reed & David Ryall, eds., p. 307).

91    David Cumin, "L'Ennemi dans les relations internationales. Le point de vue de Carl Schmitt", *Institut de Stratégie Comparée*, <www.stratisc.org/strat72_Cumin2-_tdm.html>, consulted 15 January 2021.

92    Marie-Claude Smouts, Dario Battistella et Pascal Venesson, *Dictionnaire des relations internationales*, 2e éd., Paris: Dalloz, 2006, p. 270.

93    David Fisher, *op. cit.*, p. 192.

94    According to Margaret MacMillan, "we like to think that war should be a last resort after all other alternatives have been exhausted" (Margaret MacMillan, *War – How Conflict Shaped Us*, London: Profile Books, 2020, p. 226).

# Chapter II:
# The role of the United States and of Britain

The power of a country is not only military but also based on the role it plays internationally and in particular during a conflict. How was the role of the United States in the American press and of Britain in the British press presented throughout the Gulf Crisis and War? It is time now to look at this important aspect of the treatment of the conflict by the newspapers concerned.

## 2.1    The role of the United States

In addition to its military power based on advanced technology and large armed forces, the United States assumed the role of coalition leader during the Gulf Crisis and hostilities, which was reflected in the American press.[95] While most editorials in the *New York Times* and the *Washington Post* agreed on the leading role played by the United States in the coalition,[96] some editorials published in both newspapers, but especially in the *New York Times*, highlighted the major burden borne by their country[97] in terms of financial costs or possible casualties. The few

---

95    The British press also addressed the military power and the role of the United States, which will be discussed in the chapter on the allies.

96    For instance: "U.S. leadership is indispensable to collective action". "The Month That Shook the World", editorial, *New York Times*, 2 September 1990, p. A 26; "The United States is the leader of the allied military coalition". "Two Plans", editorial, *Washington Post*, 23 February 1991, p. A 22.

97    "Squeeze – and Contain – Iraq", editorial, *New York Times*, 26 August 1990, p. E 18; "The War Begins", editorial, *Washington Post*, 17 January 1991, p. A 20.

editorials in the *New York Times* were more critical than those in the *Washington Post* of the consequences of U.S. leadership that brought the coalition together and sustained it for seven months.

Opinion articles in the American press addressed the same issue. However, the points of view expressed in these articles were more mixed. On the one hand, many journalists and contributors, particularly in the *Washington Post*, were strongly favourable to the U.S. leadership during the Gulf events. For example, Joshua Muravchik, in a patriotic tone, considered the United States as a model of society for other nations and announced the advent of the *Pax Americana*. On the other hand, other journalists and contributors criticized U.S. leadership as well as the unilateral nature of the Bush administration's policy.[98] For instance, Anna Quindlen, in the *New York Times*, challenged the "messiah complex"[99] of the United States, which "can no longer afford economically, psychologically or politically to be the policeman of the world". This argument implies that Americans believe they have a liberating and almost divine mission to lead people to a better world according to their way of life and values.[100] As in its editorials, the *New York Times* differed from the *Washington Post* in that more of its opinion articles disapproved of U.S. leadership.[101] Beyond this difference, articles in both newspapers

---

98    This point will be examined in more detail later.

99    Anna Quindlen, "Personally", op-ed, *New York Times*, 17 January 1991, p. A 23.

100    This messiah ideology of America's destiny took root in a culture that was shaped by the themes of the Puritan churches that arrived on the soil of the new continent in the 17th century (François Thual, *op. cit.*, p. 141).

101    52.17% of articles published in the *New York Times* and 33.33% in the *Washington Post* were against the United States' leading role in the Gulf Crisis and War.

used the same lexical and semantic field regarding the leadership role of the United States. Words, such as "leader", "cop", "guardian" or "world's policeman",[102] which were repeated over and over again from August 1990 to March 1991, were part of the rhetoric of persuasion towards readers.

There was a certain degree of plurality in letters published in the *Washington Post*.[103] However, *New York Times* readers were unanimously opposed to American leadership.[104] For example, a reader of the newspaper, referring to a TV series character, challenged the U.S. reassertion of hegemonic status and world-policeman responsibility and advised the "Lone Ranger"[105] to think seriously about becoming sheriff. In doing so, this reader did not follow the editorial line of the newspaper, which stressed the leadership role of their country.

All in all, most editorials in both American newspapers welcomed the U.S. leadership in the alliance. However, opinion

---

102 As well as the following words: "leadership" and "leading role".
103 For example, Gail Boling advised the U.S. government "to turn its badge as self-appointed policeman of the world" (Gail Boling, "More on the Iraqi Invasion", letters, *Washington Post*, 11 August 1990, p. A 20). On the other hand, other letters approved of U.S. leadership of the coalition. For example: Scott A. Mills, "Containing Tyranny", letters, *Washington Post*, 25 November 1990, p. C 6.
104 For instance, Francis Shor, Associate Professor of Humanities at Wayne State University, criticized the U.S. "policy of madness, built on arrogance of power". Francis Shor, "We Learned the Wrong lessons in Vietnam", letters, *New York Times*, 20 January 1991, p. E 18.
105 Ronald Dore, "Negotiating an Iraqi Withdrawal Beats War. Mirage of Consensus", letters, *New York Times*, 18 November 1990, p. E 16. The "Lone Ranger" is a character of fiction, who wore a mask and fought outlaws in the American Wild West (Jonathan Crowther, ed., *op. cit.*, p. 316).

articles and letters in the *Washington Post* offered a range of conflicting viewpoints. The *New York Times* appeared to be more hostile than the *Washington Post* to U.S. leadership of the coalition and military operations in a few editorials, a high number of opinion articles and letters. By publishing articles and letters opposed to its editorial line, the *New York Times* demonstrated journalistic diversity. It is however difficult to explain why it published more opinion articles opposed to its editorial line than the *Washington Post*.

Editorialists, journalists and contributors, as well as readers in the American press, who endorsed the United States' leadership role, glorified their country throughout the Gulf Crisis and War. In this way, they adopted the rhetoric of the U.S. president who, in various speeches and conferences,[106] stressed American leadership in the coalition and in standing up against Iraq's aggression. By focusing on the large American military power and the U.S. leadership role in bringing the coalition together in the theatre of operations, editorialists, journalists, contributors as well as *Washington Post* readers thus presented an idealized picture of their country. As noted in the introduction, this era marked the end of the Cold War, during which Ronald Reagan delivered many speeches about the USSR, which he called the "Evil Empire".[107] The American president's speeches reflected confidence in America's return to the forefront of the world stage. Nonetheless, American

---

106     For example, Bush's news conference of 14 August 1990 on American leadership in the world (<https://bush41library.tamu.edu/archives/public-papers/2162>), or his address before a joint session of the Congress on the Persian Gulf Crisis on 11 September 1990 (<https://bush41library.tamu.edu/archives/public-papers/2217>, consulted 3 March 2021).

107     Éric Nguyen, *La Politique étrangère des États-Unis depuis 1945*, Levallois-Perret: Studyrama, 2004, p. 125.

pragmatism, justified by the need to defend the interests of the United States, corresponds to a vision of the world marked by a political and moral responsibility to be the leading world power.[108] The United States is convinced of the universality and soundness of its model of society[109] and has a moral and sacred duty to share it with the rest of the world and to guide the world for its own good and salvation.[110] That would be its "Manifest Destiny",[111] a 19th-century belief used as moral justification for U.S. expansion, annexation and acquisition of territories. This doctrine meant that Americans had "the right and duty to spread democracy across the continent".[112] It would also underpin their expansionist foreign policy, based on moral obligation and the defence of the nation's interests. Since the fall of the Berlin Wall in 1989 and the disappearance of the Soviet Union in 1991, East-West tensions greatly eased at the time of the Gulf War.[113] The United States, with its global military, economic and technological supremacy, found itself alone in managing the world.[114] According to André Kaspi, the United States, faced with a multitude of local conflicts

---

108    Pierre-Jean Luizard, *op. cit.*, p. 319.
109    Marie-Christine Pauwels, *Civilisation américaine*, Paris: Hachette Livre, 1994, p. 141.
110    François Thual, *op. cit.*, pp. 140-141.
111    This expression was used by editor John O'Sullivan in an article in the *Democratic Review* in 1845 to describe the particular mission of the American people which was "to overspread the continent allotted by Providence for the free development of our yearly multiplying millions" (David Weigall, *op. cit.*, p. 140; George Brown Tindall & David Emory Shi, *op. cit.*, pp. 298, 395).
112    Joy Hakim, *Freedom. A History of US*, New York: Oxford UP 2003, p. 72.
113    However, the relationship between both countries has significantly deteriorated since the end of the 20th century.
114    Catherine Kaminsky, *op. cit.*, p. 26. Because of the dismemberment of the Soviet Union, the United States was then the world's only superpower (George Brown Tindall & David Emory Shi, *op. cit.*, p. 1159).

and many uncertainties, was then forced to develop a new strategy that would determine its foreign policy.[115]

Finally, it is likely that the emphasis in both American newspapers on the scale of U.S. military deployment[116] in the Gulf certainly contributed to further persuade American readers of the superpower status and special responsibilities of their country in this type of conflict to defend the national interest and world peace. The theme of national greatness and honour plus the desire to guarantee the rules of international law probably rekindled the patriotism of a part of the readership still traumatized by the humiliation of the U.S. army in the Vietnam War.

## 2.2 Britain's role

The British press highlighted the role played by Britain throughout the Gulf Crisis and War, but the four newspapers made varied comments on their country's responsibilities and action. For example, a *Times* editorial put Britain on a par with the United States in that it described the two countries and Saudi Arabia as the "leading members of the international alliance".[117] Woodrow Wyatt, however, was less neutral than the newspaper's editorial in that he emphasized, in September 1990 – and thus before the conflict – his country's importance as a pivotal player

---

115  André Kaspi, *op. cit.*, p. 641.

116  By 19 January 1991 more than half of the entire U.S. army, navy and air force were massed around Iraq and Kuwait (Éric Laurent, *op. cit.*, 1991, p. 235).

117  "Half a peace plan", editorial, *Times*, 21 February 1991, p. 11.

during the Gulf events.[118] For the journalist, the Iraqi Crisis provided Britain with an ideal opportunity to restore its national prestige and strengthen its international aura.

The *Guardian* was more nuanced on this point than the *Times*. An editorial on 20 September 1990 questioned "the relative proportions of myth and reality in our claim to Great Power status".[119] The published opinion pieces expressed different and opposing views.[120]

Unlike the *Guardian*, the *Sunday Times*, as early as September 1990 and on several occasions in its editorials during the Gulf Crisis and War, praised Britain, which, alongside the United States and in the vanguard of European countries, was determined to fight Iraq and save Kuwait.[121] It was in the *Sunday*

---

118    Woodrow Wyatt, "Resolve that impresses", op-ed, *Times*, 11 September 1990, p. 12.
119    "Europe's defence", editorial, *Guardian*, 20 September 1990, p. 18.
120    For Hella Pick, "Britain is back to its old role, as an offshore island riding the Atlantic to Washington's tune". Hella Pick, "A grave old world reborn", op-ed, *Guardian*, 13 September 1990, p. 19; on the other hand, according to Sir John Thomson, Britain's permanent UN representative from 1982-87, "Britain and France are both influential". Sir John Thomson, "How the UN could lose its American accent", op-ed, *Guardian*, 28 February 1991, p. 21.
121    For instance: "Britain is in the vanguard of the fight to rescue Kuwait [...]". "Lest we forget", editorial, *Sunday Times*, 16 September 1990, Sect. 3, p. 7. "The British are unequivocal about the need to fight and quietly resolute in their determination to win. It is [...] to Britain's great credit that it is standing shoulder-to-shoulder alongside the United States in this necessary venture [...]. Without Britain's participation, the European contribution would be derisory [...]". "Britain at war", editorial, *Sunday Times*, 20 January 1991, Sect. 2, p. 5. "Britain alone among EC countries has had the determination and foresight to commit troops [...] alongside the Americans [...]". "The shame of Europe", editorial, *Sunday Times*, 27 January 1991, Sect. 1, p. 11. "Bush and his coalition partners, with Britain in the vanguard

*Times* editorials that patriotism was most frequently praised. The journalistic rhetoric, which was based on the repetition of the same arguments, fostered a national feeling generated by the supposedly major function occupied by Britain within the coalition and above all its allegedly equal relationship with the United States. The Sunday newspaper certainly did not fail to flatter the inflated ego of its readers in times of war.

The *Observer* stood out from the other British newspapers through its sarcastic tone in its editorials[122] and opinion pieces. For instance, an editorial criticized Douglas Hurd, "stunned by a new mood of post-imperial grandeur", who "flies from capital to capital trying to orchestrate a post-war world in Britain's own image. This reflects an exaggerated idea of Britain's importance in this war [...]".[123] Likewise, Andrew Stephen castigated its country in February 1991 for "basking in nostalgic war rhetoric [...]" and suggested that "there is a collective madness, escapism and self-delusion sweeping Britain about what its role in the Gulf really is [...]".[124]

In summary, Britain's role was variously assessed in editorials and opinion pieces of the four newspapers. On the one hand, the *Times* and especially the *Sunday Times* praised their country and inflated the importance of its role in the Gulf Crisis and War, thus echoing Margaret Thatcher's and John Major's statements

---

[...]". "The defeat of Saddam", editorial, *Sunday Times*, 24 February 1991, p. V.

122   For example: "Britain isn't at the centre". "The questions that remain", editorial, *Observer*, 9 September 1990, p. 12.

123   "Major's team on trial", editorial, *Observer*, 10 February 1991, p. 20.

124   Andrew Stephen, "Self-delusion and escapism grip America's poodle", op-ed, *Observer*, 17 February 1991, p. 15.

on this point.[125] On the other hand, the *Guardian*, to a lesser extent, but especially the *Observer* expressed unfavourable opinions and downgraded Britain's position vis-à-vis the United States. According to Martin Shaw and Roy Carr-Hill, the media in general exaggerated Britain's role during the hostilities.[126] For them and the *Sunday Times*, the Gulf events enabled Britain, which had ceased to be a great power, to find itself at the forefront of nations, alongside the United States, which presumably gave it an undeniable sense of superiority. In this context, the notion of "manifest destiny", a cornerstone of the building of the United States, can be linked to the idea of "the white man's burden", which is the title of Rudyard Kipling's 1899 poem.[127] Like the poem "Recessional", it is generally regarded as an ode to British

---

125   As regards Britain's important role, refer for example to Margaret Thatcher's speech to European Democrat Union Conference on 30 August 1990 (<https://www.margaretthatcher.org/document/108183>), and her TV interview on 1 September 1990 (<https://www.margaretthatcher.org/document/108186>, consulted 11 April 2021). Also see John Major's Commons Statement on the Gulf events on 15 January 1991 (<https://hansard.parliament.uk/Commons/1991-01-15/debates/3498d88e-f437-47bc-bdc6-cd0c78a0fee8/TheGulf?highlight=chemical#contribution-93c27615-93f1-43c2-b05e-395509d2>), and the Prime Minister's Question Time from 26 February 1991 (<https://johnmajorarchive.org.uk/1991/02/26/pmqt-26-february-1991>, consulted 11 April 2021).

126   "76 percent saw [Britain] as the second most important member of the coalition [...]". Martin Shaw and Roy Carr-Hill, "Public Opinion and Media War Coverage in Britain", *in* Hamid Mowlana, George Gerbner and Herbert I. Schiller, eds., *Triumph of the Image. The Media's War in the Persian Gulf – A Global Perspective*, Boulder; San Francisco; Oxford: Westview Press, 1992, p. 152.

127   Adrian Room, *op. cit.*, p. 1265.

imperialism.[128] But as Robert Harris[129] and Norman Stone[130] in the *Sunday Times* and Michael Ignatieff[131] in the *Observer* stated at the beginning of the Gulf Crisis, it was now the United States for Robert Harris, the Americans with the help of the British for Norman Stone, and the West for Michael Ignatieff, who were in charge of shouldering responsibility and carrying this "white man's burden"[132] in the Saudi desert. The three journalists thus presented an ethnocentric conception of the mission given to the Americans and the British for Robert Harris and Norman Stone, and to the Westerners for Michael Ignatieff[133] to get rid of Saddam Hussein.

## Conclusion

In contrast to the positive image of the United States in the majority of editorials of the American newspapers regarding their country's fundamental role as the leader of the coalition, there was, in the British press, a notable divergence between the *Times* and the *Sunday Times* on the one hand, and the *Guardian* and

---

128  Rudyard Kipling's poem "Recessional" was written for Queen Victoria's Diamond Jubilee in 1897 (David Daiches, *op. cit.*, vol. IV, p. 1092). This poem reminded readers of the duties of the British Empire, but it also announced its decline (David Reynolds, *op. cit.*, p. 9).

129  Robert Harris, "Eerie echoes of Suez debacle as Bush dons Eden mantle", op-ed, *Sunday Times*, 12 August 1990, Sect. 3, p. 4.

130  Norman Stone, "We have the technology: let us turn it on this monster", op-ed, *Sunday Times*, 5 August 1990, Sect. 3, p. 7.

131  Michael Ignatieff, "A voice that cries in the wilderness", op-ed, *Observer*, 9 September 1990, p. 11.

132  The white man, called upon to bring the benefits of civilization to the whole world, was primarily Anglo-Saxon (Bernard Cottret, *op. cit.*, p. 363).

133  The journalist, however, considered shouldering the white man's burden as "the most unpalatable of historical reruns".

the *Observer* on the other, as to Britain's role. This antagonism referred to the articles published before the beginning of the conflict about the support the newspapers gave – or did not give – to Britain's entry into the war: the *Times* and the *Sunday Times* were in favour of it and the *Guardian* and the *Observer* opposed to it. Editorialists, journalists and contributors on both sides of the Atlantic who emphasized, or even overestimated, their country's role, painted, on the model of official statements, a glowing picture of their country. On the American side, they were based on an entrenched belief in the destiny of the United States to provide leadership and seemed on the British side to fall into nostalgic illusions of outdated grandeur. These editorialists, journalists and contributors in the American and British press hid behind a patriotic rhetoric that enabled them to unite readers around a common cause and perhaps help them forget, for a few months, the economic difficulties of their countries in 1990 and 1991.

By contrast, opponents reacted in a polemical tone: on the American side, in a few editorials and letters published in the *New York Times*, in numerous opinion articles in the two American newspapers, and, on the British side, in some opinion pieces in the *Guardian* and in most editorials and opinion pieces published in the *Observer*. These newspapers thus fulfilled their function as the Fourth Estate by ensuring democratic debate.

# Chapter III:
# Historical references

If a country's military power, its international influence, its behaviour in times of crisis and conflict characterize a nation, that country is also defined by its history. History undeniably shapes the national identity of a people. The historical references used by newspapers to portray the United States in the American press and Britain in the British press deserve therefore attention. The chronological order of the historical events as they unfolded in the 20th century has not been retained in this section. The analysis of references to these events has been based on their importance in the press on both sides of the Atlantic. First, the references mentioned in the American and British press will be analysed, then those that appear mostly in the American press and finally those that are specific to British newspapers.

## 3.1 Historical references in the American and British press

### 3.1.1 The Second World War

As noted earlier, there were a number of references to World War II in the press on both sides of the Atlantic whether it be comparisons of Saddam Hussein with Hitler, the use of German terms or the reference to the Munich Agreement. While this war demonstrated the moral commitment of the Allied forces to save the invaded nations, it was at the same time an example of shortcomings, i.e. the consequence of the inaction of Western governments in the face of a dictator's actions.[134]

In the American press, references to the Second World War were structured around three main themes. The first was the policy of 'appeasement'.[135] For example, a *New York Times* editorial of 3 August 1990 reminded readers of this concept to criticize the Europeans who "should understand the need to stand together against aggression".[136] In opinion articles, journalists and contributors expressed divergent points of view. They thus provoked a stormy debate between those, who, like the American president, blamed the failure of the 'appeasement' policy[137] to persuade readers of the need to stop Saddam Hussein[138] by force of arms, and those who, on the other hand, rejected the analogy made between the current situation and that of the 1930s.[139] This

---

134    The Western powers persisted in a policy of concessions as evidenced by the Munich Agreement in 1938 (Michel Mourre, *op. cit.*, p. 494).

135    As a reminder, the idea that the appeasement of an aggressor like Saddam Hussein had to be rejected and that only the use of armed force prevailed precluded any diplomatic compromise.

136    "Iraq's Naked Aggression", editorial, *New York Times*, 3 August 1990, p. A 26.

137    According to Howard Zinn, "the United States had done little about Hitler's policies of persecution" in the 1930s (Howard Zinn, *op. cit.*, p. 409).

138    For example, Alexander Haig stated that "The Munich analogy teaches us not that Saddam Hussein is already a Hitler but that we must act now to prevent him from becoming one". Alexander M. Haig Jr., "Gulf Analogy: Munich or Vietnam?", op-ed, *New York Times*, 10 December 1990, p. A 19.

139    For instance, Richard Cohen argued that "The problem with the Munich metaphor, [...] is that it suggests that something like World War II is about to be fought all over again. It's not". Richard Cohen, "The Munich Metaphor", op-ed, *Washington Post*, 21 August 1990, p. A 23.

subject was also controversial in readers' letters.[140] Secondly, a *New York Times*[141] editorial and a few opinion articles[142] in the *Washington Post* recalled the many casualties inflicted in the Second World War, in support of their deep reservations about the Gulf War. Thirdly, some opinion articles[143] published after the hostilities in both American newspapers, especially in the *New York Times*, drew a parallel between the "smashing success" for the United States in the Gulf War and the military triumph for the U.S. in World War II.

The American president also referred to the Second World War in his speeches and conferences to stress his participation in this conflict,[144] the danger of appeasing an aggressor,[145] the parallel

---

140    For example, the letter by Gustav A. Sallas, "Munich in Baghdad?", letters, *Washington Post*, 16 December 1990, p. K 6. The two American newspapers also published other letters about World War II and for instance with regard to the impact of sanctions on Iraq: Patrick Clawson, "But Does Hussein Care?", letters, *New York Times*, 3 February 1991, p. E 18.

141    "Deep Doubts about Ground War", editorial, *New York Times*, 10 February 1991, p. E 16.

142    For example, the article by William Raspberry, "A Clean War", op-ed, *Washington Post*, 15 February 1991, p. A 21.

143    For instance, the articles by Leslie H. Gelb and Richard Cohen. Leslie H. Gelb, "Dear Mr. President ...", op-ed, *New York Times*, 3 March 1991, p. E 17; Richard Cohen, "No Time for Hubris", op-ed, *Washington Post*, 28 February 1991, p. A 19.

144    See George Bush's remarks at a Republican fundraising breakfast in Des Moines, Iowa on 16 October 1990 (<https://bush41library.tamu.edu/ archives/public-papers/2331>), and his exchange with reporters on the Persian Gulf Crisis on 31 October 1990 (<https://bush41library.tamu.edu/ archives/public-papers/2377>, consulted 24 April 2021).

145    Refer to the American president's remarks at a White House Briefing for Representatives of Veterans Organizations on 11 October 1990 (<https:// bush41library.tamu.edu/archives/public-papers/2318>), and to officers and troops at Hickam Air Force Base in Pearl Harbor, Hawaii on 28 October 1990    (<https://bush41library.tamu.edu/archives/public-papers/2369>,

between Hitler's invasion of Poland in 1939 and Saddam Hussein's of Kuwait,[146] and the fact that the coalition was the "most fantastic" and the largest put together since World War II.[147] There was thus a correspondence between George Bush's arguments and those of journalists and contributors regarding the rejection of a policy of 'appeasement' to convince their readers to go to war against Iraq.

All in all, the references to the Second World War, which on the one hand concerned the attitude of the countries in question before that conflict, and on the other hand the loss of life caused by that war, enabled editorialists and journalists to communicate their approval or disapproval of the Gulf War to readers. Moreover, the *New York Times* opinion article of 3 March 1991, which reminded readers of the U.S. triumph in 1945, reinforced their victory in 1991 and painted a positive picture of a powerful country. In addition, the U.S. attitude of stepping forward "as a defender of helpless countries"[148] in World War II was akin to the American government's concern to defend Iraqi-invaded Kuwait, an idea echoed by pro-war journalists and contributors who challenged

---

consulted 24 April 2021). According to Éric Laurent, referring to World War II enabled Bush to present himself as an anti-Chamberlain who refused to compromise with a dictator (Éric Laurent, *op. cit.*, 1991, p. 80).

146    See George Bush's remarks at a Republican fundraising breakfast in Burlington, Vermont on 23 October 1990 (<https://bush41library.tamu.edu/archives/public-papers/2351>), and at a fundraising breakfast for Representative Stan Parris in Alexandria, Virginia on 31 October 1990 (<https://bush41library.tamu.edu/archives/public-papers/2376>, consulted 24 April 2021).

147    Refer to Bush's remarks to the national Italian American Foundation on 19 October 1990 (<https://bush41library.tamu.edu/archives/public-papers/2341>), and at a reception for gubernatorial candidate Pete Wilson in Thousand Oaks, California on 3 November 1990 (<https://bush41library.tamu.edu/archives/public-papers/2388>, consulted 24 April 2021).

148    Howard Zinn, *op. cit.*, p. 408.

a policy of 'appeasement' towards Saddam Hussein. Finally, the multiple references in the American press from August 1990 to March 1991 to the six-year war, which was the source of so many atrocities, bore witness to the fact that it was still strongly anchored in people's memories.[149]

On the British side, references to the Second World War evoked historical resonances in readers' mind by reminding them of Britain's victory in that war. For example, Michael Evans in the *Times* hailed the victory over Iraq in an opinion piece, entitled "Yes, it really was a famous victory".[150] The journalist also paid tribute to two British warfare strategists,[151] Sir Basil Henry Liddell Hart and Major-General John Frederick Charles Fuller whose tactics for defeating the enemy in the 1930s were "similar to the plan devised by General Norman Schwarzkopf". Michael Evans may have wanted in March 1991 to emphasize Britain's contribution to the Gulf War by providing further clarification. On the other hand, Sir Anthony Parsons argued in August 1990 that "the world is far removed from the world of 1945".[152] In other

---

149    "18 million served in the armed forces", and "25 million workers gave of their pay envelope regularly for war bonds" (*Ibid.*, p. 407).

150    Michael Evans, "Yes, it really was a famous victory", op-ed, *Times*, 14 March 1991, p. 14.

151    Captain Sir Basil Henry Liddell Hart (1895-1970) and John Frederick Charles Fuller (1878-1966) were British military historians and theorists. See the King's College London websites: <https://www.kingscollections. org/catalogues/lhcma/collection/l/li30-001/> and <https://www. kingscollections.org/catalogues/lhcma/collection/f/fu20-001/>, consulted 1 May 2021.

152    Sir Anthony Parsons, "Sanctions are the world's only answer to Saddam", op-ed, *Times*, 3 August 1990, p. 10.

words, the *Times* thus offered a plurality of viewpoints in its opinion pieces.[153]

In the *Guardian*,[154] Hugo Young, for instance, challenged the simplistic historical parallel drawn between the thirties and the current situation.[155] However, the journalist also stressed his country's past glories as he suggested that "the second world war bred a nation that is capable in some circumstances of being more warlike than many".

With regard to Sunday papers, the *Sunday Times* which, as noted earlier, referred to the Second World War to emphasize Iraqi military power, employed patriotic rhetoric by reminding readers of the Battle of Britain[156] in its editorial of 16 September 1990.[157] The editorialist drew a connection between what happened fifty years ago and the flight over Dharan in Saudi Arabia by four British Tornadoes the week before the editorial was published. In recalling this event, the *Sunday Times* evoked the resistance

---

153   The *Times* also published editorials on the Second World War. For example, an editorial of 3 January 1991, entitled "The Arab dimension", described Jordan as "the Belgium of the Middle East" and compared King Hussein of Jordan to Leopold III of Belgium who capitulated to Hitler in 1940.

154   The newspaper published some editorials and opinion pieces on the Second World War. For example: "When the masters lose control", editorial, *Guardian*, 11 January 1991, p. 20; Sidney Perkowitz, "The scientist at war", op-ed, *Guardian*, 7 March 1991, p. 23.

155   "[...] the memory of the thirties is a mixed blessing; the sneering rhetoric about appeasement, as if Saddam Hussein raised exactly the same problem as Hitler, made no contribution to serious debate". Hugo Young, "War dividend for the men of the Left", op-ed, *Guardian*, 17 January 1991, p. 19.

156   The Battle of Britain was a World War II air battle between British and German air forces over Britain in 1940.

157   "Lest we forget", editorial, *Sunday Times*, 16 September 1990, Sect. 3, p. 7. The title refers to the well-known poem "Recessional" by Rudyard Kipling.

of the Royal Air Force to German raids and paid tribute to the pilots' courage. The same editorial referred to the "Last Night of the Proms",[158] at which the patriotic songs "Rule Britannia!"[159] and "Land of Hope and Glory"[160] were – as always – performed, which the Sunday paper welcomed. The Sunday paper mainly aimed to persuade its readers not to forget the calamitous consequences of the policy of 'appeasement'[161] followed by British leaders until 1939 and incited Britain to go to war against Iraq. This argument was repeated again in the *Sunday Times* editorials of 2 December 1990[162] and 20 January 1991.[163] The Sunday paper thus echoed Margaret Thatcher's words in a speech of 18 September 1990 when she spoke of "a disastrous policy of appeasement".[164] By using nationalist rhetoric, which was underpinned by the repetition of the same arguments, the *Sunday Times* lapsed into sheer demagogy. The newspaper reminded readers of – certainly important – historical facts and military memories, but it used them to exalt the greatness of its country. The *Sunday Times*

---

158   The "Proms" is the short name for the "Promenade Concerts" which are held annually between July and September in The Royal Albert Hall, London (*Hutchinson, op. cit.*, p. 731).

159   It is a British patriotic song that is sung at the "Last Night of the Proms" (Jonathan Crowther, ed., *op. cit.*, p. 469).

160   It is the title and first line of a song sung to music by Edward Elgar. The lyrics (by C Benson) celebrate Britain's glory. The patriotic song is traditionally performed at the "Last Night of the Proms" (Jonathan Crowther, ed., *op. cit.*, p. 297).

161   Until 1939, "with British acquiescence", Hitler remilitarized the Rhineland, absorbed Austria, annexed areas of Czechoslovakia [...] (John Cannon, ed., *Dictionary of British History*, Oxford: Oxford UP, 2001, p. 579).

162   "A war and a slump", editorial, *Sunday Times*, 2 December 1990, Sect. 3, p. 7.

163   "Britain at war", editorial, *Sunday Times*, 20 January 1991, Sect. 2, p. 5.

164   Cf. Margaret Thatcher's speech of 18 September 1990 to the Czechoslovak Federal Assembly (<https://www.margaretthatcher.org/document/108194>, consulted 4 May 2021).

may have wanted to assuage its conscience given that William Waite Hadley, the editor-in-chief at the time, supported the policy of 'appeasement'.[165] Most opinion pieces[166] in the Sunday paper agreed with its editorial line.

Unlike the *Sunday Times*, the *Observer* did not resort to jingoistic discourse. For instance, an *Observer* editorial referred in a neutral tone to the Battle of Britain as "our last real solo effort".[167] A reader of the Sunday paper drew a comparison between the way the "Churchill government manipulated the media"[168] in the Second World War and the strict censorship imposed in the Gulf War. The author of the letter, Dr Ray Challinor, an expert on Marxist and Trotskyist history,[169] assumed in his letter that it would be impossible in 1991 to screen the 1943 film, "The Life and Death of Colonel Blimp",[170] whose protagonist, Colonel Blimp,[171]

---

165  Jeremy Tunstall, *op. cit.*, p. 16: "W. Hadley became a leading appeaser of Hitler and political ally of Neville Chamberlain".

166  For example, the article by Norman Stone, "Make mock of the jingoists, but they often get it right", op-ed, *Sunday Times*, 26 August 1990, Sect. 3, p. 5. However, Robert Harris criticized the parallel with the Second World War and the way in which the present crisis was portrayed. Robert Harris, "This is not our finest hour and Saddam's not Hitler", op-ed, *Sunday Times*, 23 September 1990, Sect. 3, p. 6.

167  "Deserts Rats ride again. Straining the alliance", editorial, *Observer*, 16 September 1990, p. 18.

168  Raymond Challinor, Dr, "Colonel Blimp is too hot to handle", letters, *Observer*, 3 February 1991, p. 46.

169  Refer to the obituary by Stan Newens published in the *Guardian* on 24 March 2011: <https://www.guardian.co.uk/theguardian/2011/mar/24/ray-challinor-obituary>, consulted 6 May 2021.

170  See the article by Mark Duguid, "The Life and Death of Colonel Blimp" on the website: <http://www.screenonline.org.uk/film/id/438362/>, consulted 6 May 2021.

171  It is originally a British cartoon character created by David Low in the 1930s. He represented an old British army officer, who was very patriotic

belongs to the cultural heritage of the British. This film incensed Churchill who tried unsuccessfully to ban it because he considered it unpatriotic and feared that the film would be interpreted as a satire on the British army.

In short, the *Sunday Times* looked back with nostalgia at Britain's prestigious past during the Second World War and in particular during the Battle of Britain. In several editorials, with the identical argumentation and characterized by patriotic rhetoric, as well as in a few opinion pieces, the Sunday paper painted an idealised picture of Britain as a nation determined to take on Saddam Hussein and which has learnt the lessons of its history and used them to grow in stature. This portrait was consistent with the one painted by Margaret Thatcher in her speech of 18 September 1990 about the will of the British people under Churchill to fight tyranny and oppression.[172] The daily British newspapers and the *Observer* adopted a more nuanced tone in their articles which were also patriotic but to a lesser degree than those in the *Sunday Times*.

One final point needs to be addressed. Like George Bush[173] and especially Margaret Thatcher[174] who quoted Winston Churchill

---

and traditional in his attitudes and values (Jonathan Crowther, ed., *op. cit.*, p. 59).

172   It is the same speech to which reference is made in note 164.

173   Refer to Bush's remarks at a White House Briefing for Representatives of Veterans Organizations on 11 October 1990 (<https://bush41library.tamu.edu/archives/public-papers/2318>) and his address before a joint session of the Congress on the cessation of the Persian Gulf conflict on 6 March 1991 (<https://bush41library.tamu.edu/archives/public-papers/2767>, consulted 1 May 2021).

174   See Thatcher's speech to the Aspen Institute in Aspen, Colorado on 5 August 1990 (<https://www.margaretthatcher.org/document/108174>); her

in their speeches, the American and British press also referred to the former British Prime Minister when mentioning the Second World War in their articles. For example, a *New York Times* editorial of 22 August 1990 argued that the American president did not have the same eloquence as Churchill.[175] On the British side, while Peter Stothard stated in the *Times* that "George Bush may [...] not have a Churchillian sense of destiny",[176] Robert Harris of the *Sunday Times* in contrast congratulated John Major in January 1991 on not using military jargon and being "no ersatz Churchilliana".[177] Viewpoints were therefore divided among British journalists on this subject. That the British press referred to Winston Churchill was hardly surprising since he is considered a "revered war leader".[178] It seems logical therefore that, when Britain entered a new conflict, British newspapers analysed it through the prism of the Second World War. They thus recalled the man who in 1940 was "the spirit of British resistance incarnate",[179] and embodied a sense of "patriotic unity"[180] and the determination of the British in the face of adversity, which

---

speech about the unveiling of a plaque in the Winston Churchill Square in Prague on 18 September 1990 (<https://www.margaretthatcher.org/document/108195>); her speech to the Welsh CBI on 26 September 1990 (<https://www.margaretthatcher.org/document/108206>), and her speech at the Conservative Party Conference in Bournemouth on 12 October 1990 (<https://www.margaretthatcher.org/document/108217>, consulted 1 May 2021).

175   "The President and the Hasty Hawks", editorial, *New York Times*, 22 August 1990, p. A 24.

176   Peter Stothard, "Is the real George Bush resolute enough for war?", op-ed, *Times*, 21 September 1990, p. 12.

177   Robert Harris, "Salute for the unmartial Major", op-ed, *Sunday Times*, 20 January 1991, Sect. 2, p. 4.

178   Kenneth O. Morgan, ed., *op. cit.*, 2001, p. 634.

179   John Cannon, ed., *op. cit.*, p. 146.

180   Kenneth O. Morgan, ed., *op. cit.*, 2001, pp. 622-623.

led them to victory. As such, Winston Churchill is part of the identity of the British nation.

On the other hand, it might seem odd that the two American newspapers, and in particular the *New York Times*, mentioned the British Prime Minister. Nevertheless, Winston Churchill, being half-American,[181] was a well-known and prestigious personality for Americans by virtue of the "special relationship" between the two countries, which he fervently defended,[182] and the relationship between the two political leaders – Roosevelt and Churchill[183] – in the Second World War. Winston Churchill condemned the Munich Agreement of 1938 and both leaders signed the Atlantic Charter in August 1941.[184] According to Margaret Thatcher, Winston Churchill always stressed the need to stand by the United States.[185] The U.S. president also referred the day after the

---

181    Churchill's feelings "were affected by the fact that he was half-American by birth" (David Reynolds, *op. cit.*, p. 199). He was made an honorary American citizen on 9 April 1963.

182    "The core of his policy was what he called in 1943 'the natural Anglo-American special relationship', based on his rapport with Roosevelt" (*Ibid.*, pp. 143, 173). In 1940 America was still neutral and was only ready to give Britain economic aid (*Ibid.*, p. 137; also see T. O. Lloyd, *op. cit.*, p. 195). Also refer to Jonathan Colman, *A 'special relationship'? Harold Wilson, Lyndon B. Johnson and Anglo-American relations 'at the summit'*, 1964–68, Manchester: Manchester UP, 2004, p. 2: Churchill "regarded Britain and the United States as essentially two halves of the same community".

183    "Churchill's account of his intimate collaboration with Roosevelt". Ritchie Ovendale, *Anglo-American Relations in the Twentieth Century*, Basingstoke: Macmillan Press, 1998, p. 160.

184    The Atlantic Charter was signed on 14 August 1941. It was a declaration by the two leaders of principles "on the peace settlement of a war which the Americans had not then joined" (Refer to Ritchie Ovendale, *op. cit.*, p. 44 and David Weigall, *op. cit.*, p. 17).

185    "Stand by America". Refer to the Prime Minister's acceptance speech of the Morgenthau Award in New York on 1 October 1990 (<https://www.margaretthatcher.org/document/108209>, consulted 11 May 2021).

Iraqi invasion of Kuwait to Churchill's "Iron Curtain Speech" in Fulton, Missouri on 5 May 1946 to point out that the British Prime Minister "meant to summon up a vision, a vision of strength of free nations united in defense of democracy".[186] The American press may have wished to "dress itself in the shadow of history"[187] when it recalled Winston Churchill, who was still a well-known figure for the American reader. In any case, in addition to the nostalgic references to Winston Churchill, the Gulf War thus echoed the Second World War in the American and British press since, on the one hand, George Bush and Margaret Thatcher referred to the policy of 'appeasement', and, on the other, the *New York Times* recalled the military victory of the United States and the *Sunday Times* in particular that of Britain.

## 3.1.2 The First World War

Although minor in the American and British press, the First World War is another historical reference that merits further consideration. It may be surprising that the American press

---

186  David Weigall, *op. cit.*, p. 126. See Bush's remarks at the Aspen Institute Symposium in Aspen, Colorado on 2 August 1990 (<https://bush41library.tamu.edu/archives/public-papers/2128>). Likewise, Margaret Thatcher mentioned Churchill's famous speech on 5 August and 18 September 1990. Refer to Thatcher's speech to the Aspen Institute in Aspen, Colorado on 5 August 1990 (<https://www.margaretthatcher.org/document/108174>), and her speech to Czechoslovak Federal Assembly in Prague on 18 September 1990 (<https://www.margaretthatcher.org/document/108194>, consulted 11 May 2021). Also refer to Peter Stothard's article in the *Times* published on 1 August 1990 with an unequivocal title "Thatcher rings down the curtain".

187  According to Robert Fisk, suffering from a Churchill complex is testament to "a desire to dress oneself in the shadow of history" (Robert Fisk, *op. cit.*, p. 210).

should recall the 1914-18 war. From the outbreak of hostilities in 1914, President Wilson, in agreement with most Americans, sought to "maintain strict U.S. neutrality"[188] and therefore kept his country out of the conflict.[189] But from February 1917 onwards, Germany waged all-out submarine warfare, and vessels flying the U.S. flag were sunk.[190] On 6 April 1917 the United States declared war on Germany and joined the Allies in the conflict, which gave the Allied Powers naval support, money, supplies, military equipment and especially large numbers of troops.[191] Although the United States, as in the Second World War, did not experience any fighting on its soil,[192] there is no doubt that the First World War had a profound impact because of the 53,402 American soldiers killed on the battlefields,[193] but also and above all because of the

---

188    Alan Axelrod, *Ace Your Midterms & Finals. U.S. History*, New York: McGraw-Hill, 1999, pp. 98-99. However, "most Americans (Wilson included) felt a strong cultural bond with the English".

189    Michel Mourre, *op. cit.*, p. 355.

190    André Kaspi, *Les Américains. 1. Naissance et essor des États-Unis 1607-1945*, Paris: Seuil, 1986, p. 265. On 7 May 1915, the sinking of the British liner *Lusitania* by a German U-boat, which killed 128 Americans, had already outraged American public opinion (George Brown Tindall & David Emory Shi, *op. cit.*, p. 767).

191    *Ibid.*, pp. 770-772.

192    André Kaspi, *op. cit.*, 1986, p. 337.

193    The number of 63,114 other deaths and 204,002 wounded should also be added to this figure. Refer to the report on American War and Military Operations Casualties produced by the Congressional Research Service on September 15, 2009 (<https://www.prisonlegalnews.org/media/publications/congressional_research_service_american_war_casualties_2009.pdf>, consulted 13 May 2021). The First World War took a heavy toll on France and Britain: the number of estimated soldiers killed amounted to 1,400,000 for the former and 750,000 for the latter (François Géré, *Pourquoi les guerres? Un siècle de géopolitique*, Paris: Larousse, 2003, p. 26; Michel Mourre, *op. cit.*, p. 472). Also refer to Zara S. Steiner, *Britain and the Origins of the First World War*, London: Macmillan Education, 1987, p. 256.

military victories won by American troops. Nor should Woodrow Wilson's key role be overlooked as he championed the war of law[194] and helped negotiate the peace treaties[195] and create the League of Nations.[196] This may explain why some editorialists[197] and readers[198] of the *New York Times* as well as journalists and contributors from the *Washington Post*[199] referred to this historical period. References to this conflict mainly served to show the opposition of the editorialists, journalists and readers in question to the entry of the United States into the war against Iraq, concerning either the risk of mustard gas being used during

---

194    Michel Mourre, *op. cit.*, p. 355.
195    The United States did not ratify the Treaty of Versailles, which incorporated "Fourteen Points" presented by Woodrow Wilson to Congress on 8 January 1918 as a programme for achieving lasting peace (*Ibid.*, p. 356).
196    The League of Nations was a world organization to settle international disputes. It guaranteed the political independence and territorial integrity of member states (André Kaspi, *op. cit.*, 1986, p. 272). The United States refused to join the League of Nations, which marked, among other things, the return to isolationism (George Brown Tindall & David Emory Shi, *op. cit.*, pp. 782-783).
197    For example: "Arab-Americans and Ugly Americans", editorial, *New York Times*, 9 September 1990, p. E 24.
198    For instance: Douglas Mattern, "On the Eve of Drifting into War, Once Again", letters, *New York Times*, 13 January 1991, p. E 18.
199    For example: Hussein ibn Talal, "It's Not Too Late to Prevent a War", op-ed, *Washington Post*, 23 September 1990, p. B 6; George F. Will, "Mobilization's Deadly Momentum", op-ed, *Washington Post*, 15 November 1990, p. A 25. In his article, James Bowman, the American correspondent of *The Spectator of London* stated that "it is second nature for American leaders [...] to think rather in terms of morality than of honor" and that "there is something almost un-American about the idea of war for national honor" (James Bowman, "The Worth of National Honor", op-ed, *Washington Post*, 20 January 1991, p. B 7). The author referred to Woodrow Wilson who proclaimed on taking America into World War I that the right was more precious than peace and who, according to André Kaspi, raised the moral banner of America (André Kaspi, *op. cit.*, 1986, p. 271).

the Gulf War as in the Great War,[200] or the analogy between the events in Kuwait and those in Sarajevo in June 1914,[201] which led to "the senseless slaughter of World War I".[202]

Similar topics can be found on the British side, though there are many more references than in the American press. For example, the reference to the First World War enabled one *Guardian* reader[203] and Michael Ignatieff in the *Observer* to express their opposition to a possible conflict with Iraq, and this was also the case in many other articles published in these newspapers during the Gulf Crisis.[204] Unsurprisingly, references to the First World War in articles published in the *Times* and the *Sunday Times* during the Gulf Crisis attested to their acceptance of a possible war. For instance, the two newspapers compared Iraq's invasion of Kuwait and Germany's attack on Belgium in 1914.[205] In two

200   "The Persistence of Poison Gas", editorial, *New York Times*, 3 February 1991, p. E 18.

201   Richard Cohen, "The Munich Metaphor", op-ed, *Washington Post*, 21 August 1990, p. A 23. On 28 June 1914, the Austrian Archduke Franz Ferdinand and his wife were assassinated by the Serb nationalist Gavrilo Princip at Sarajevo, which was the cause of World War I. Refer to Zara S. Steiner, *op. cit.*, pp. 42, 59, 246-247.

202   Douglas Mattern, "On the Eve of Drifting into War, Once Again", letters, *New York Times*, 13 January 1991, p. E 18.

203   "The fatal Sarajevo shot". Frank Hooley, "Let's cast a net over the whole Middle East when seeking peace for Kuwait", letters, *Guardian*, 23 August 1990, p. 18.

204   For example, Michael Ignatieff, "The itch that urges us to go to war", op-ed, *Observer*, 28 October 1990, p. 19.

205   Michael Howard, "Digging in for the duration", op-ed, *Times*, 6 September 1990, p. 10; Ben Pimlott, "Why Labour should avoid jingoism", op-ed, *Sunday Times*, 2 September 1990, Sect. 3, p. 6. The German invasion of Belgium on 4 August 1914 led Britain to go to war against Germany (Michel Mourre, *op. cit.*, p. 492). Britain also wanted to prevent Germany from dominating Europe and threatening its empire (John Cannon, ed., *op. cit.*, p. 258).

*Sunday Times* articles, Norman Stone criticized the pacifists who were against the Gulf campaign who reminded him of those of 1914-1918.[206] The journalist referred in particular to the film *Oh! What a Lovely War*[207] as he believed that it showed "the generals and jingoistic public opinion in a dreadful light". In addition to his cinematic allusion, the journalist made bellicose statements in order to convince readers of the validity of the war to be waged against Saddam Hussein. By contrast, a reader of the Sunday newspaper recalled the millions who had died by Christmas 1918 to express his opposition to the war against Iraq.[208]

These findings show firstly that the *Sunday Times* published a reader's letter whose views were contrary to those expressed in opinion pieces, which means that it did not censor letters from readers whose opinions differed from those expressed in its articles. Secondly, an *Observer* reader ironically compared "gallant little Belgium"[209] in February 1991 to "gallant little Kuwait" to

---

206  The journalist stated that "the modern anti-jingo attitudes really stem from the pacifists of that era". Norman Stone, "Make mock of the jingoists, but they often get it right", op-ed, *Sunday Times*, 26 August 1990, Sect. 3, p. 5; Norman Stone, "Doom merchants minds trapped in trench mud", op-ed, *Sunday Times*, 3 February 1991, Sect. 1, p. 11.

207  *Oh! What a Lovely War* is a 1969 British comedy and musical film, which was based on the 1963 musical satire. It depicted the lives of soldiers on the Western Front during the First World War and mocked the politicians and generals of that era (see the article "The birth of Oh! What a Lovely War" by Vincent Dowd of 12 November 2011 published on the website of the BBC: <http://www.bbc.co.uk/news/magazine-15691707>, consulted 22 May 2021).

208  Frank Allaun, "Better sanctions than shots", letters, *Sunday Times*, 13 January 1991, Sect. 3, p. 8.

209  Ernie Tory, "The world will be a safer place", letters, *Observer*, 10 February 1991, p. 46. The fact that the reader described Belgium as a "little" country referred to David Lloyd George's words, the then Chancellor of the Exchequer. On 19 September 1914, he declared at the Queen's Hall,

voice his disagreement about the Gulf War. In other words, the same historical fact can be recalled and interpreted differently depending on the purpose and the message to be conveyed. This is the case here about the comparison made by supporters or opponents of the Gulf War between the invasion of Belgium in 1914 and that of Kuwait in 1990.

To sum up, the British press referred more often to the First World War than the American press. Although the United States played a decisive role in the conflict, the U.S. army did not launch its first offensive until September 1918, eight weeks before the armistice.[210] At the beginning of the conflict, the forces involved were composed only of the European powers, including the United Kingdom.[211] Besides, from the beginning to the end of hostilities, all the decisive battles were fought on European soil. After conscription was imposed for the armed services in May 1916,[212] millions of British men took part in the fighting. This deadly and devastating war claimed about 750,000 British lives.[213] This is probably why the Gulf conflict revived the memory of trench warfare in the minds of British journalists and readers.

London that the war was "a crusade on behalf of the 'little five-foot-five nations', like Belgium, flagrantly invaded by the Germans [...]" (Kenneth O. Morgan, ed., *op. cit.*, 2001, p. 584).

210 Frank Welsh, *The Four Nations. A History of the United Kingdom*, London: HarperCollins, 2003, p. 345.

211 But the war was quickly worldwide because it took place not only in Europe but also in the German colonies and on all the seas (Michel Mourre, *op. cit.*, p. 492).

212 Frank Welsh, *op. cit.*, p. 344. Also refer to Kenneth O. Morgan, ed., *op. cit.*, 2001, p. 584.

213 Kenneth O. Morgan, ed., *op. cit.*, 2001, p. 586. Statistics show different results according to the sources. For example, Michel Mourre refers to the amount of 715,000 British soldiers killed in World War I (Michel Mourre, *op. cit.*, p. 493).

The *Sunday Times* differed from other British newspapers in that this war remained in the nation's collective memory as a glorious event in its country's history. Unlike the *Times*, which adopted a moderate tone, and the *Guardian* and *Observer*, journalists and contributors in the *Sunday Times* thus had an essentially positive view about the First World War, despite the suffering it caused. They avoided talking about the scale of human losses,[214] the major sacrifices made by civilian populations and the widespread devastation it left behind.[215] On the whole, the journalistic discourse of the Sunday paper sought to arouse its readers' patriotic fervour by referring to the two world wars.

Finally, the American and British press reminded their readers of World War I although the American president and the British Prime Minister did not often refer to it during the Gulf events.[216]

---

214    The conflict killed over nine million young soldiers (Charles Reed & David Ryall, eds., *op. cit.*, p. 278). The First World War also resulted in over twenty million casualties (Michel Mourre, *op. cit.*, p. 493).

215    In the invaded areas, hundreds of villages, thousands of kilometres of roads and railways were destroyed. Factories were demolished, thousands of fruit trees were cut down, and many hectares of arable land were wrecked. Systematic looting, requisition and destruction impoverished countless people and caused famine, epidemics and increased mortality among children and adults (Marcel Dunan [dir.], *Histoire Universelle, vol. 2*, Paris: Larousse, 1960, pp. 322-339).

216    In a speech delivered to the Federal Assembly in Prague, Czechoslovakia on 17 November 1990, George Bush referred to U.S. isolationism after the First World War (<https://bush41library.tamu.edu/archives/public-papers/2461>, consulted 26 May 2021). Margaret Thatcher also referred to the Great War on several occasions: in a speech to the Aspen Institute, on 5 August 1990 when she stressed the need to maintain a secure defence, which they had failed to do after the First World War (<https://www.margaretthatcher.org/document/108174>). On 1 September 1990, the British Prime Minister, in an interview for TV – AM *Frost on Sunday*, mentioned that Britain went "into the First World War with only 30 per cent of the people having the vote" (<https://www.margaretthatcher.org/

All in all, the American press, as well as, on the British side, the *Guardian* and the *Observer*, revived the traumatic memory of the First World War, to express their opposition, mainly in articles published during the Gulf Crisis, to the possible war against Iraq.

Both wars were dramatic events[217] in the history of the United States and Britain. They united people around their soldiers who had gone through horrific and traumatic experiences. Both conflicts brought with them horrors, misery and moral pain that left an indelible mark on the collective consciousness. Past experiences, however tragic, form the character of a country. It is therefore hardly surprising that, in the face of an impending war, the press reminds its readers of previous conflicts. Since the First and Second World Wars ended in victory for the United States and Britain, it made sense for the proponents of the forthcoming Gulf War to look back on past military successes to reinforce national pride. On the other hand, opponents of a possible war brought back the bloody tragedy of the two world conflicts of the 20th century. This is the twofold observation to which the analysis of articles in American and British newspapers leads us.

---

document/108186>). On 6 September 1990, she alluded to the creation of Iraq in a speech to the House of Commons about the Gulf Crisis (<https://hansard.parliament.uk/Commons/1990-09-06/debates/54db6e15-456e-4257-ba864-cae4950b07f4/TheGulf?highlight=chemical#contribution-c8ad5e14-9ae7-4882-b8c6-836ef88447b7>, consulted 26 May 2021).

217    After the slaughter and devastation caused by the Great War, the Second World War resulted in approximately forty million deaths, more than half of them among the civilian population (Michel Mourre, *op. cit.*, p. 496).

## 3.2 Historical references in the American press

### 3.2.1 The Vietnam War

More recent than the two world wars of the 20th century in which the United States was involved, the memory of Vietnam was still very much in the minds of the Americans in 1990 and 1991. It is therefore logical to find multiple references to this war which "hangs like Marley's ghost"[218] over the Gulf Crisis in the American newspapers. This long and disastrous conflict for the United States, which bitterly divided the Americans, took place from 1964[219] to 1973. On 27 January 1973, the United States signed the Paris Peace Accords, which were "an agreement on ending the war and restoring peace in Vietnam".[220] The *New York Times* devoted more editorials to the Vietnam conflict than the *Washington Post*. However, the *Washington Post* published a

---

218   "Vietnam hangs like Marley's ghost [...]". Anna Quindlen, "The Questions Continue", op-ed, *New York Times*, 25 November 1990, p. E 11. The journalist referred to Charles Dickens' short novel, *A Christmas Carol*, published in 1843 in which Scrooge, a mean old man, receives a visit on Christmas Eve from the ghost of Marley, his late business partner, as well as from ghosts of the past, present and future. They make him feel bad and he realizes that he must make amends for his past behaviour towards people. For the journalist, it was a way of asking the American president to explain clearly to his public opinion the reasons why the lives of American soldiers would have to be sacrificed.

219   The U.S. involvement in Vietnam, which began under President Eisenhower, was gradual. In 1954, the Geneva Accords divided Vietnam, a former French colony, into the Communist North and the anti-Communist South. Under President Kennedy, many military advisors were sent to the South. After the attack of U.S. ships by North Vietnamese torpedo boats near the Gulf of Tonkin in 1964, the U.S. Congress approved the Gulf of Tonkin Resolution which gave President Johnson greater powers to commit troops and fight the war.

220   George Brown Tindall & David Emory Shi, *op. cit.*, p. 1090.

larger number of opinion articles on the subject.[221] While it is difficult to explain these differences, it is worth recalling[222] that the two American newspapers published the Pentagon Papers, which were top-secret documents from the Department of Defense revealing military actions in Vietnam about which the public had not been told.[223] Nevertheless, the *New York Times* began publishing the first instalment of the Pentagon Papers[224] on 13 June 1971, which led to legal action against the newspaper by Nixon's administration and Justice Department.[225]

References to the Vietnam War in the two newspapers were structured around several dominant topics. First of all, editorialists, journalists, contributors and readers, who were opposed to the Gulf War, referred to the American soldiers who were killed in Vietnam.[226] The conflict took a heavy toll on the United States, with 58,220 deaths.[227] These opponents of the

---

221  Among the articles read, ten editorials in the *New York Times* and two editorials in the *Washington Post* referred to the Vietnam War. The opposite is true in the opinion articles as the *New York Times* published twenty-five opinion articles and the *Washington Post* published thirty-one op-eds about the conflict.

222  Refer to the presentation of both newspapers.

223  Jonathan Crowther, ed, *op. cit.*, p. 409; see also George Brown Tindall & David Emory Shi, *op. cit.*, p. 1089; also refer to Howard Zinn, *op.cit.*, pp. 487-488.

224  Michael Schudson, *op. cit.*, p. 88. Also refer to Edwin Diamond, *op. cit.*, pp. 116-119.

225  Michael Emery & Edwin Emery, *op. cit.*, p. 504.

226  For example, the article by Mark Shields, "What Are the Boys Fighting For?", op-ed, *Washington Post*, 28 August 1990, p. A 17, and the letter by Kate Millet, Robin Morgan, Gloria Steinem, Ti-Grace Atkinson, "We Learned the Wrong Lessons in Vietnam. A Feminist Issue Still", letters, *New York Times*, 20 January 1991, p. E 18.

227  Refer to the report on American War and Military Operations Casualties produced by the Congressional Research Service on September 15, 2009:

Gulf conflict thus warned readers of the real possibility of huge casualties for the United States forces in the Gulf region.

In addition, the opponents of the Gulf War did not want their army to engage in a new Vietnam. Numerous articles published in both American newspapers during the Gulf Crisis drew a parallel with the Vietnam conflict[228] to support their opposition to America's entry into the war. For example, the articles addressed threats of escalation,[229] the need for political unity "given the possibility of unforeseen setbacks",[230] the risk of eroding public support,[231] or the possible negative fallout for the U.S. president.[232] Likewise, some journalists, after the outbreak of hostilities, still drew an analogy between the two conflicts. For instance, Anna Quindlen in the *New York Times* recalled the realities of war.[233] Similarly, William Raspberry, in an article from the *Washington Post*, with the ironic title "A Clean War",[234] stressed the fact that

---

<https://www.prisonlegalnews.org/media/publications/congressional_research_service_american_war_casualties_2009.pdf>, consulted 7 June 2021.

228 For instance, the article by Henry F. Graff, professor of history at Columbia University at that time, "The Woolly Pulpit", op-ed, *New York Times*, 15 November 1990, p. A 27.

229 "Escalation, 1990 Style", editorial, *New York Times*, 27 October 1990, p. A 22.

230 "War by Default", editorial, *New York Times*, 16 December 1990, p. E 14.

231 Tom Wicker, "Bush Stands Warned", op-ed, *New York Times*, 2 December 1990, p. E 19.

232 Richard Cohen, "Saving Face – and Lives", op-ed, *Washington Post*, 1 November 1990, p. A 23.

233 Anna Quindlen, "The Back Fence", op-ed, *New York Times*, 20 January 1991, p. E 19.

234 William Raspberry, "A Clean War", op-ed, *Washington Post*, 15 February 1991, p. A 21.

the Americans "want no more My Lais – no more slaughter, intended or not, of non-combatants".[235]

Nonetheless, a minority of journalists and a few readers in the American newspapers[236] criticized the analogy between Vietnam and Iraq. They considered the two conflicts to be very different in military or political terms. These journalists supported U.S. military involvement in the Gulf. In so doing, they were adopting the official rhetoric. The American president in his speeches and press conferences from September 1990 to mid-March 1991 referred to the Vietnam War forty-six times.[237] George Bush also stressed from 30 November 1990 onwards that the Gulf War would in no way be "a new Vietnam".[238] This expression, which he repeated tirelessly, was supposed to touch the deepest sensibilities

---

235   Army Lieutenant William Caley ordered the murder of over 200 Vietnamese civilians in My Lai village in 1968. The massacre was revealed by the American press in November 1969, which aroused public indignation and widespread hostility against the war (George Brown Tindall & David Emory Shi, *op. cit.*, p. 1088; also see André Kaspi, *op. cit.*, 2002, p. 537).

236   For example, Andrew Bennett, "An Air War of Attrition", op-ed, *New York Times*, 11 November 1990, p. E 17; David S. Broder, "The Gulf Debate – Less Disunity than Meets the Eye", op-ed, *Washington Post*, 16 December 1990, p. K 7; Henry Siegman, "Limits of Sanctions", letters, *New York Times*, 24 February 1991, p. E 16.

237   For instance, refer to George Bush's remarks at a Republican fundraising breakfast in Iowa on 16 October 1990 (<https://bush41library.tamu.edu/archives/public-papers/2331>), his news conference on 12 January 1991 (<https://bush41library.tamu.edu/archives/public-papers/2616>), and his exchange with reporters on 17 February 1991 (<https://bush41library.tamu.edu/archives/public-papers/2713>, consulted 1 June 2021).

238   For instance, this expression can be found in the following news conferences by the American president: on 30 November 1990 (<https://bush41library.tamu.edu/archives/public-papers/2516>), and 18 December 1990 (<https://bush41library.tamu.edu/archives/public-papers/2563>), and in his radio Address to the Nation on 5 January 1991 (<https://bush41library.tamu.edu/archives/public-papers/2596>, consulted 1 June 2021).

of American public opinion,[239] still traumatized by the negative experience and reluctant to engage in a new conflict.[240] At the end of hostilities, George Bush stated in the euphoria of the Gulf War victory that "we have kicked the Vietnam syndrome".[241] This argument can for instance be found in a *New York Times* editorial, entitled "Good Morning, Vietnam",[242] in reference to the film of the same name.[243]

The *New York Times* differed from the *Washington Post* by publishing a few opinion articles attacking anti-war activist movements.[244] The Vietnam conflict, which triggered student opposition and protests against the war, became more and more unpopular.[245] Anti-war demonstrations took place in sixty

---

239   Éric Laurent, *op. cit.*, 1991, p. 81.

240   Marcel Merle, *op. cit.*, p. 66.

241   Already anticipating victory, George Bush made this statement on 17 February 1991 (<https://bush41library.tamu.edu/archives/public-papers/2713>), which he reiterated after the conflict on 1 March 1991 (<https://bush41library.tamu.edu/archives/public-papers/2754>), and on 4 March 1991 (<https://bush41library.tamu.edu/archives/public-papers/2759>, consulted on 1 June 2021).

242   "Good Morning, Vietnam", editorial, *New York Times*, 10 March 1991, p. E 14. The editorial argued that "victory in the Gulf War offered an opportunity to bury the bitter legacy" of the Vietnam War.

243   *Good Morning, Vietnam* is a 1987 American film, which was set in Saigon in 1965 during the Vietnam War. The film tells the story of Adrian Cronauer, a radio DJ on Armed Forces Radio Service who is popular with the troops, but who infuriates his superiors.

244   For instance, Casper W. Weinberger, Ronald Reagan's Secretary of Defense, described the anti-war movements as demonstrations organized by "a few moth-eaten relics of the Vietnam peace movements". Casper W. Weinberger, "Bush Has Made the Right Moves, So Far", op-ed, *New York Times*, 2 December 1990, p. E 19.

245   Niall Ferguson, *Colossus. The Rise and Fall of the American Empire*, London: Penguin Books, 2005, pp. 98-101. In 1968 Martin Luther King began speaking out against the Vietnam War as he connected war and

cities[246] from 15 to 17 October 1965. Howard Zinn argued that the anti-war movement "played a critical part in bringing the war to an end".[247] On the whole, it is astonishing how few editorials and opinion articles about the peace protests were published throughout the Gulf Crisis and War. For James Winter, news coverage of war protest rallies was negligible for fear of appearing unpatriotic[248] by giving peace demonstrations what might have seemed excessive attention. For David L. Paletz, when the Gulf War began, the media dismissed the anti-war movement.[249] One could say that the media had to make amends, so to speak, for reporting unfavourably on the Vietnam War.

A few editorials published in the *New York Times*, opinion articles in the two American newspapers, and a letter from a *New York Times* reader referred to the role played by the media in Vietnam.[250] Overall, they deplored the Pentagon's security

poverty (Howard Zinn, *op. cit.*, p. 461). In August 1969, the Woodstock Music Festival became the symbol of young people in rebellion against the 'Establishment' and the Vietnam War (Alan Axelrod, *op. cit.*, p. 120).

246   André Kaspi, *op. cit.*, 2002, p. 526.

247   Howard Zinn, *op. cit.*, p. 531.

248   James Winter, *Common Cents. Media Portrayal of the Gulf War and Other Events*, Montreal; New York: Black Rose Books, 1992, p. 13.

249   David L. Paletz, "Just Deserts?", *in* W. Lance Bennett and David L. Paletz, eds., *Taken by Storm. The Media, Public Opinion and U.S. Foreign Policy in the Gulf War*, Chicago; London: U of Chicago Press, 1994, p. 281. The author explains that the media's difficulty in promoting debate was exemplified in their coverage of the anti-war movement. Although a few opinion articles in the *New York Times* were critical of the peace movements, they encouraged debate because of the plurality of viewpoints which were offered to the reader on other subjects in the articles published in both American newspapers.

250   For instance: "Getting Behind 'Desert Shield'", editorial, *New York Times*, 11 August 1990, p. A 24; Ron Nessen, "The Pentagon's Censors", op-ed, *Washington Post*, 12 January 1991, p. A 21; Francis Shor, "We Learned the

restrictions and censorship in the Gulf and regretted the freedom reporters had in Vietnam. Since there was no censorship[251] and there were no military escorts, correspondents were free to move around on their own and report to American public opinion on their soldiers' actions.[252] The press was blamed by the military for eroding public support for the Vietnam War[253] because of their critical coverage of the conflict and the publication of images of burnt villages, civilians killed by napalm bombs and dead and wounded American soldiers.[254] Moreover, since journalists only had access to one side of the story, the Pentagon accused them of presenting a distorted view of the war and some criticized them for altering a more complex reality.[255] In any case, the lessons of Vietnam were drawn so that American journalists were not allowed to accompany the Marine Corps when they landed on Grenada in 1983.[256] During Operation Desert Storm in 1991, war correspondents, who were stationed in Saudi Arabia, had no direct access to the troops and were organized by the military

Wrong Lessons in Vietnam", letters, *New York Times*, 20 January 1991, p. E 18.

251 Phillip Knightley, *The First Casualty: The War Correspondent as Hero and Myth-Maker from the Crimea to Kosovo*, London: Prion Books, 2000, p. 465.

252 Marie Agnès Combesque & Ibrahim Warde, *op. cit.*, p. 147.

253 Douglas Kellner *in* Bradley S. Greenberg & Walter Gantz, eds., *op. cit.*, p. 42; Edwin Diamond, *op. cit.*, p. 119.

254 André Kaspi, *op. cit.*, 2002, p. 530.

255 *Ibid.*, p. 531. Also refer to R. Michael Schiffer and Michael F. Rinzler, "No News Is No News", op-ed, *New York Times*, 23 January 1991, p. A 19.

256 Marc Kravetz, "Profession: correspondant de guerre", *Écrire la guerre de Homère à Edward Bond*, *Magazine littéraire*, No. 378, juillet-août 1990, p. 101.

into "pools".[257] Therefore, there was really a "before" and an "after" Vietnam[258] for war reporters.

In sum, the numerous references to the Vietnam conflict showed its considerable influence on editorialists, journalists, contributors and readers of the two American newspapers. It is true that Vietnam was the first war in American history to be lost by the United States.[259] One can easily imagine the considerable damage and shock caused by this failure among the American political class[260] and citizens, and therefore journalists. The victory in the Gulf, which seemed like revenge for the United States, probably healed the Americans' wounds and, for them, certainly improved their country's image in the world.

In total, editorials and the majority of opinion articles in the American press addressed several themes in their references to the Vietnam War when expressing their hostility to the involvement of U.S. troops in the Gulf War. Nevertheless, both American newspapers offered their readers a plurality of viewpoints in their opinion articles. Whether opponents or supporters of the looming conflict in January 1991, journalists or contributors in the *New York Times* and the *Washington Post* referred to Vietnam to convince readers of their respective points of view. As in the case

---

257   Douglas Kellner *in* Bradley S. Greenberg & Walter Gantz, eds., *op. cit.*, p. 42.
258   Marc Kravetz, *op. cit.*, p. 101.
259   Edwin Diamond, *op. cit.*, p. 119; André Kaspi, *op. cit.*, 2002, p. 541.
260   According to André Kaspi, the Democrats bore most of the responsibility for the Vietnam War (*Ibid.*, p. 551). Pierre Hassner points out that on the whole the Democrats have both engaged the United States more in wars and put more trust in negotiation and international organizations (Pierre Hassner, "Écoles de pensée et doctrines de politique étrangère", *in* Denis Lacorne [dir.], *Les États-Unis*, Paris: Fayard/CERI, 2006, p. 389).

of the First World War, historical events, such as the Vietnam conflict, were thus used according to the objectives pursued.

Although the war in Vietnam was primarily a U.S. affair, there were several articles – albeit fewer than in American newspapers – on this subject in the British press. The *Times* differed from other British newspapers in that it published a larger number of editorials, which could be explained by its solid reputation built on the strength of its foreign reporting.[261] For example, William Howard Russell, the *Times* reporter, is generally considered to have been the first war correspondent, during the Crimean War.[262] However, this explanation is not completely satisfactory, as the other British newspapers, especially the *Guardian* and the *Observer*, published more opinion articles on this subject than the *Times* and the *Sunday Times*. This may indicate that the Vietnam War had a fairly significant impact in Britain. At the political level, the Vietnam conflict challenged the "special relationship" between Britain and the United States. Harold Wilson, the then British Prime Minister, refused President Lyndon Johnson's request for a British military commitment.[263] While he did not send any British troops to Vietnam, he offered his government's support to the Americans, which caused tensions within his party.[264] Furthermore, British public opinion was largely hostile

---

261    Graham Stewart, *op. cit.*, pp. 617-618.
262    David Loyn, *Frontline. The True Story of the British Mavericks Who Changed the Face of War Reporting*, London: Penguin Books, 2006, p. 395. William Howard Russell reported on the Battle of Balaclava and Charge of the Light Brigade against Russian forces in 1854 (Graham Stewart, *op. cit.*, p. 154).
263    Ritchie Ovendale, ed., *British Defence Policy since 1945*, Manchester: Manchester UP, 1994, p. 132.
264    Paul Vaiss, *Les Relations entre les États-Unis et la Grande-Bretagne depuis 1945*, Paris: Ellipses, 2002, pp. 100, 103.

to American intervention in Vietnam, as evidenced by anti-war demonstrations[265] and student protests on university campuses. Finally, the lessons learnt from this televised war[266] were applied to media coverage of other conflicts, including the Falklands War.[267]

When the Vietnam War was mentioned in the British newspapers, the themes were similar to those addressed in the American press, such as media coverage of the Vietnamese conflict

---

265   Andrew Marr, *A History of Modern Britain*, London: Pan Books, 2008, p. 293. In 1968 there were a number of demonstrations all over the world.

266   While the Second World War was the first radio war, television footage in Vietnam was in colour (Andrew Marr, *op. cit.*, 2005, p. 331).

267   During the Falklands War, there were a number of ways in which the British authorities were able to restrict journalists' coverage of the conflict: the accreditation procedure for journalists, limited access restrictions to the war zone and delays in transmission. During the conflict there were several factors complicating the task of the war correspondents. Access to the task force and the war zone was severely constrained: the Royal Navy was no doubt unenthusiastic about having outsiders on its ships as they sailed to the South Atlantic, and the geographically remote Falklands were out of bounds to all but the very small number of journalists the Ministry of Defence grudgingly agreed to accredit. Moreover, overburdened transmission systems – and perhaps a certain reluctance on the part of the task force – meant that it was difficult for correspondents to get their copy back to London in good time (Michael Parsons, *Le* Times *et la guerre des Malouines – aspects du discours de la guerre*, Thèse, Université Michel de Montaigne, Bordeaux III, 1994, pp. 64-95). Also refer to Philip Seib, *Beyond the Front Lines. How the News Media Cover a World Shaped by War*, New York: Palgrave Macmillan, 2004, pp. 45-46 as well as the article by Michel Morel, "Falklands: Le *Guardian* et la guerre", *La "Civilisation" dans l'enseignement et la recherche*, Lez Valenciennes: Université de Valenciennes, No. 7, hiver 1982, pp. 115-131. Michel Morel writes that "from 31 May to 21 June [1982], 39 collective dispatches [came] from the Falklands. These grouped reports (BBC, ITN, Reuters, *Daily Telegraph*, *Daily Mail*, *Daily Express*, *Sun* and *Yorkshire Post*) ranged from battle reports to reflections on the greatness and constraints of war reporting".

compared to media control in the Gulf War,[268] the rejection of the analogy between the two conflicts,[269] peace movements in the U.S.,[270] or the death of Americans in the Vietnam War.[271] Moreover, the common denominator in British editorials and opinion pieces was that the references to the Vietnam War were primarily about the American people. The information given to British readers was, as it were, a story within a story or a *mise-en-abyme*: it was about an event – the Vietnamese conflict – and various references to the war – reporting, opposition, relevance or not of the parallel between the Vietnam and Gulf Wars – which referred to the United States, but which also indirectly and by a mirror effect concerned British readers involved in the Gulf Crisis and War as the first ally alongside the Americans. For editorialists and journalists, it was therefore important to remind readers of the Vietnam War in the British press. In so doing, they differed from the British Prime Ministers – Thatcher and Major – who did not refer to this conflict in their speeches and press conferences.[272]

---

268　For example: Georgina Henry, "Rights of access to the action", op-ed, *Guardian*, 8 January 1991, p. 17. The journalist stated that Washington was trying to adopt "a more British approach" to controlling the media after its experience in Vietnam. The article thus gave Britain a central role in media management.

269　For example, the numerous articles by Hugo Young in the *Guardian* and an article by Paddy Ashdown, the leader of the Liberal Democrats at that time: Paddy Ashdown, MP, "Why war may still be the least worst option", op-ed, *Guardian*, 10 January 1991, p. 19.

270　For instance: "America, Bush and Munich", editorial, *Sunday Times*, 9 December 1990, Sect. 3, p. 7.

271　For example: Andrew Stephen, "Phew! George's double bluff may yet win through", op-ed, *Observer*, 13 January 1991, p. 10.

272　However, several MPs referred to the Vietnam War during the debates on the Gulf in the House of Commons on 6 September 1990, 15, 17 and 21 January 1991.

Considered a "terrible tragedy"[273] for the Americans, the Vietnam War was omnipresent in editorials, opinion articles and letters from readers in the American press which drew a parallel between that conflict and the Gulf War. The large number of articles published show the importance of this conflict in American history. On the other hand, while the British press also referred to the Vietnam War with similar themes to those covered by American newspapers, it only drew a parallel between the two conflicts in a few editorials and articles that were mainly about the Americans.

## 3.2.2 The Korean War

In addition to its numerous references to the Vietnam War, the American press also referred to the Korean War during the Gulf Crisis and War. The Korean War between North Korean and Chinese forces, on the one hand, and South Korean and U.N. forces, on the other, took place between June 1950 and July 1953. It was the first major manifestation of the Cold War in Asia. The Korean War began on 25 June 1950 after the communist North Korean army had crossed the 38th parallel and invaded South Korea.[274] The fighting ended on 27 July 1953 when an armistice agreement was signed by representatives of the United Nations Command, the North Korean Army and the Chinese People's Volunteer Army.

Articles in the two American newspapers drew identified similarities between the Gulf Crisis and War and the Korean War

---

273    Howard Zinn, *op. cit.*, p. 618.
274    George Brown Tindall & David Emory Shi, *op. cit.*, pp. 972-976.

with regard to several main themes. For example, they referred to the number of American soldiers killed in the Korean War.[275] The war cost the United States more than 33,000 deaths and over 103,000 wounded and missing.[276] The main purpose of editorialists and journalists was to express their opposition to U.S. military involvement in the Gulf by reminding readers that a conflict would necessarily entail American casualties.

Both American newspapers also emphasized the fact that the Korean War, like the Gulf War,[277] had the sanction of the U.N. Security Council.[278] Although the Korean War was waged under the flag of the United Nations,[279] the U.N. forces, which were for the greater part formed by U.S. troops, were under the command of General Douglas MacArthur.[280] A debate on the extent of the

---

275     For example, "Who Will Pay for the Gulf Crisis?", editorial, *New York Times*, 8 October 1990, p. A 16.

276     Refer to the report on American War and Military Operations Casualties produced by the Congressional Research Service on September 15, 2009: <https://www.prisonlegalnews.org/media/publications/congressional_research_service_american_war_casualties_2009.pdf>, consulted 6 July 2021.

277     During the Gulf Crisis, twelve resolutions were adopted by the U.N. Security Council. See appendix 3 for further information.

278     For instance, the article by Jeane Kirkpatrick, "A Puzzle in the Gulf ...", op-ed, *Washington Post*, 1 October 1990, p. A 15. George Brown Tindall & David Emory Shi, *op. cit.*, p. 974. Henry Kissinger explains in his book, *Does America Need a Foreign Policy? Toward a Diplomacy for the 21st Century*, that the Korean War "turned into a U.N. mission juridically although it was in fact orchestrated primarily by the United States" (Henry Kissinger, *Does America Need a Foreign Policy? Toward a Diplomacy for the 21st Century*, New York: Simon & Schuster, 2001, p. 115).

279     Andrew Marr, *op. cit.*, 2008, p. 102.

280     The United States led a fifteen-nation task force. In April 1951 President Truman removed the general from command in Korea. MacArthur had publicly criticized Truman's policy in the war. In addition, he had disobeyed orders, sending his troops beyond the 38th parallel into North Korea,

allies' participation began between editorialists and journalists of the two newspapers.

The consequences of the Korean War for the United States provided the American press with an opportunity to paint a flattering picture of their army and country. For instance, both newspapers argued that the presence of U.S. forces in Korea had kept the peace and made the world better.[281]

The *New York Times* differed from the *Washington Post* in its coverage of the political impact of the Korean War and the possible effect of the Gulf War. Some articles reminded readers that President Truman did not have Congressional authorization to send troops to fight in Korea, which cost him popular support.[282] According to Walter Russell Mead, the limited war in Korea cost President Truman his "job".[283] A few days before the deadline of 15 January 1991 set by the Security Council, the U.S. Congress authorised President Bush on 13 January 1991 to go to war.

---

which had brought communist China into the war. President Truman then feared an escalation that might have expanded into a third world war (Niall Ferguson, *op. cit.*, pp. 88-90; Alan Axelrod, *op. cit.*, p. 111; Joy Hakim, *All the People 1945-2001. A History of US,* New York, Oxford UP, 2003, p. 43).

281 For example, the article by George F. Will, "Stuck in the Sand – For Good", op-ed, *Washington Post*, 9 September 1990, p. D 7.

282 For example, the article by Tom Wicker, "Bush Stands Warned", op-ed, *New York Times*, 2 December 1990, p. E 19. According to Howard Zinn, the Korean War mobilized liberal opinion behind the war and the president (Howard Zinn, *op. cit.*, p. 428). For Walter Russell Mead, the Korean War "lost public support in part because of political decisions not to risk the consequences [...] of all-out war, not necessarily stopping short of the use of nuclear weapons" (Walter Russell Mead, *Special Providence. American Foreign Policy and How It Changed the World,* New York: Alfred A. Knopf, 2001, p. 222).

283 *Ibid.*, p. 257.

Finally, a few *Washington Post* readers compared the invasion of South Korea by North Korea with that of Kuwait by Iraq.[284] In June 1950 North Korean troops, armed with Soviet weapons, invaded South Korea and occupied Seoul, the capital of South Korea, which provoked the United States to condemn the North Korean invasion at the U.N.[285] Like Bush forty years later on the Iraqi invasion of Kuwait, Truman called the invasion of South Korea "an act of unprovoked aggression".[286] The example of these events was therefore significant for those readers.

Although the references to the Korean War in the two U.S. newspapers were not as numerous as those relating to the Vietnam conflict, they nonetheless proved that journalists and readers were interested in it, as was President Bush, who referred to the Korean War in his remarks and exchanges with reporters.[287] In short, this conflict was used as a backdrop by editorialists, some journalists and contributors during the Gulf Crisis to express their fears about the possible death of American soldiers that could result from a war against Iraq. Both newspapers also made an analogy between the two U.N.-sanctioned wars and the formation of a

---

284 E. G. Windchy, "Tale of a Transcript", letters, *Washington Post*, 25 September 1990, p. A 19; Blaine P. Friedlander, "Containing Tyranny", letters, *Washington Post*, 25 November 1990, p. C 6.

285 John Cannon, ed., *op. cit.*, p. 377.

286 Niall Ferguson, *op. cit.*, p. 88.

287 Refer to George Bush's exchange with reporters on the Persian Gulf Crisis on 11 August 1990 (<https://bush41library.tamu.edu/archives/public-papers/2158>), his remarks to officers and troops at Hickam Air Force Base in Hawaii on 28 October 1990 (<https://bush41library.tamu.edu/archives/public-papers/2369>), and to community members at Cherry Point Marine Corps Air Station in North Carolina on 1 February 1991 (<https://bush41library.tamu.edu/archives/public-papers/2670>, consulted 9 July 2021).

coalition. Moreover, while only the *New York Times* recalled the political fallout of the Korean War, which was declared without the authorisation of the American Congress, the two newspapers referred to this conflict to present an admiring portrait of the American army.

To a lesser extent, the British press also covered the Korean War. But it was mainly the two daily newspapers that published the most editorials and opinion pieces referring to this conflict. As in the American press, editorialists and journalists reminded readers during the Gulf Crisis that the Korean War was fought under the aegis of the United Nations.[288] Like the U.S. newspapers, Norman F. Nixon, Emeritus Professor of Psychology at University College, London, warned *Guardian* readers of the loss of life that would result from a conflict in the Gulf, as in the Korean and Vietnam Wars.[289] According to General Sir Anthony Farrar-Hockley, 1,078 British soldiers were killed in the Korean War.[290]

The *Times* stood out from the other British newspapers by stressing in September 1990 that the United States fought for peace and democracy in Korea.[291] The fact that the *Times*

---

288 Michael Howard, "Why UN sanctions are better than a prolonged US war", op-ed, *Times*, 17 August 1990 p. 10; "We cannot afford short cuts", editorial, *Guardian*, 15 August 1990, p. 18. However, the *Guardian* editorial and Michael Howard in the *Times* warned against the U.N. being used as an instrument of U.S. policy and unilateral American action.
289 Norman F. Dixon, "Hindsight that can engulf mankind", op-ed, *Guardian*, 6 November 1990, p. 21.
290 General Sir Anthony Farrar-Hockley, *The British Part in the Korean War*, Vol. II, London: HMSO, 1995, p. 420. The number of U.N. casualties amounted to around 142,000 (Andrew Marr, *op. cit.*, 2008, p. 101).
291 For instance, the following editorial: "Anti-war, Pro-war", editorial, *Times* 10 September 1990, p. 13.

reminded readers of the commitment and merits of the United States was certainly not insignificant given that George Bush's coalition-building was underway. Like some *Washington Post* readers, Ronald Butt in the *Times* also stressed the relevance of the historical parallel between the invasion of South Korea by North Korean troops and that of Kuwait by Iraq.[292] Moreover, both Ronald Butt in the *Times* and Alan Watkins in the *Observer* discussed the effect of the Korean War on British foreign policy by referring to the actions taken by Clement Attlee, the then British Prime Minister of the Labour government. Ronald Butt also recalled the Attlee government's decision in 1950 to send armed forces to fight under the U.N. flag alongside American troops to defend South Korea.[293] Both journalists thus used this conflict to remind readers of the country's past in this area. In the *Observer* article, Alan Watkins mentioned the fact that the Prime Minister persuaded President Truman not to use the atomic bomb.[294] In recalling this event, the journalist evoked

---

292    Ronald Butt, "Our essential battle forum", op-ed, *Times*, 13 August 1990, p. 10.

293    As far as the number of troops were concerned, the American contribution was far larger than that of the allies throughout the war and the British was the next largest (T. O. Lloyd, *op. cit.*, p. 272).

294    "Clement Attlee, in what has become part of Labour's mythology of moral leadership, flew to Washington to persuade President Truman not to use the atomic bomb. He was successful in this, [...]". Alan Watkins, "A crisis that could still spoil things for Neil", op-ed, *Observer*, 30 September 1990, p. 19. There is however little evidence that Truman was ready to authorize MacArthur to use nuclear weapons (See the document: Foreign Relations of the United States, 1950, Korea, Volume VII, Office of the Historian, Foreign Service Institute, United States Department of State, <https://history.state.gov/historicaldocuments/frus1950v07/pg_1261>, consulted 25 May 2023).

Britain's decisive moderating role and its political influence on the United States at that time.[295]

All in all, the two British newspapers, like the American ones, drew a parallel between the conflicts in Korea and the Gulf region. There were similar topics in the British press to those in American newspapers, including the risk of casualties in the Gulf War and the fact that both the Korean War and the Gulf War were fought under the U.N. banner. The *Times* stood out from other British newspapers by presenting a positive image of the United States and especially of Britain about its possible influence on the U.S. government during the Korean War. Although Andrew Marr stated that returning British soldiers in 1953 "found the public largely uninterested in them",[296] the publication of editorials and articles on the Korean War, albeit in smaller numbers in the British press than in the American press, shows that this conflict was still present in the mind of some editorialists and journalists,

---

295    Although the British government "endorsed the American-led UN action" and "agreed to contribute a token force", the Korean War heightened tensions between London and Washington, especially after Truman's talk about the possible use of the atomic bomb against China. The American president's comments elicited an outcry in the House of Commons. In December 1950 Clement Attlee flew to Washington "to play a restraining role" and voice people's concerns in Britain, which resulted in "vague American promises" (David Reynolds, *op. cit.*, p. 172). According to Niall Ferguson, regardless of the opinion of the allies – and therefore of Britain –, "Truman would have opted for limited warfare even if the United States had been acting alone". For T. O. Lloyd, "Truman implied in his memoirs that he had already decided what to do, but when reminiscing, Attlee suggested that his own intervention was decisive" (T. O. Lloyd, *op. cit.*, p. 274; also refer to Niall Ferguson, *op. cit.*, p. 93). There are divergent views in the literature on the degree of Britain's influence on the United States in foreign policy and on whether American or British sources are used.

296    Andrew Marr, *op. cit.*, 2008, p. 103.

particularly in the *Times* and the *Guardian*.[297] Margaret Thatcher also only mentioned the Korean War in the House of Commons on 7 November 1990 when she referred to the "Desert Rats"[298] in Saudi Arabia. Likewise, the publication of editorials and opinion articles in the American newspapers proved that the American public had not forgotten the Korean War.[299] Beyond the apparent uniformity of the subjects covered in the American and British press, U.S. newspapers essentially focused – and this was hardly surprising – on the American army, of which they drew a patriotic portrait. The *New York Times* also remembered the

---

297    The British Sunday newspapers did not publish any editorials on the Korean War. No doubt these newspapers thought that recalling this conflict was not justified. Similarly, there were only a few opinion pieces in each of the Sunday newspapers about this conflict: Norman Stone, "War brings out the mouse in the Continent's wealthy giant", op-ed, *Sunday Times*, 27 January 1991, Sect. 1, p. 11; Barbara Amiel, "Letting a crocodile off the hook", op-ed, *Sunday Times*, 24 February 1991, p. IV; Alan Watkins, "A crisis that could still spoil things for Neil", op-ed, *Observer*, 30 September 1990, p. 19; J. K. Galbraith, "The myth that air power wins war", op-ed, *Observer*, 3 February 1991, p. 18.

298    "Our own 7th Armoured Brigade – the Desert Rats – is in place, commanded by one of the most distinguished and fearless fighting soldiers in the British Army, whose experience goes back to Korea" (<https://hansard. parliament.uk/Commons/1990-11-07/debates/73e4c301-ea20-4785-878d-7c744874e134/FirstDay?highlight=korea#contribution-2257c143-0c2d-4e06-b46d-c2734fb465f4>, consulted 16 July 2021).

299    Marie Agnès Combesque and Ibrahim Warde argue that "unlike the Vietnam War American public opinion has largely forgotten the Korean War" (Marie Agnès Combesque & Ibrahim Warde, *op. cit.*, p. 61). However, it would be necessary to know the studies and criteria that led the authors to draw such a conclusion, especially since they also refer to the Vietnam War, which undoubtedly had a major impact on American public opinion. The Korean War was also called the forgotten war because it only lasted three years, it took place after World War II and "was overshadowed by the Vietnam War" (Carole Bryan Jones, *Twentieth Century USA*, Teach Yourself, London: Hodder Education, 2005, pp. 129-130).

unfortunate consequences for President Truman of the absence of authorization from the American Congress.

The American press and, to a lesser degree, the British press reminded their readers of both the Vietnam Conflict and the Korean War, which were two significant events in their countries. In confirmation of what has been written about the two world wars, editorialists, journalists and contributors on both sides of the Atlantic brought back the past to persuade readers of their views on the merits or otherwise of a new military engagement by their country.

## 3.3 Historical references in the British press[300]

### 3.3.1 The Falklands War

In addition to the previous conflicts, the British press also referred to the Falklands War and drew a historical parallel with the Gulf Crisis. The Falklands War was a conflict between Argentina and Britain over sovereignty of the Falkland Islands, a British overseas territory since 1833.[301] On 2 April 1982 Argentine armed forces under the leadership of President General Leopoldo Galtieri invaded and occupied the Falkland Islands. On the following day, the United Nations Security Council passed Resolution 502, which demanded that Argentina

---

300    Since this section deals with specific references in the British press, it has been decided not to follow the order defined in the introduction and to analyse first the British and then the American newspapers.

301    Andrew Marr, *op. cit.*, 2008, p. 399.

withdraw from the islands.[302] The British government under Prime Minister Margaret Thatcher sent a large task force to retake the islands. The conflict ended on 14 June 1982 with the surrender of the Argentine armed forces and the victory of British troops. The Falklands War, which was hugely popular,[303] transformed Margaret Thatcher's increasing unpopularity "into adulation" as a result of Britain's victory and led to her 1983 election success.[304] Media coverage of the conflict was conditioned by the geographical isolation of the theatre of operations – almost 400 miles off the Argentinian coast in the South Atlantic, thus ensuring that the British military and government had near total control of information.[305] According to Philip M. Taylor, only thirty British journalists were allowed to accompany the troops, and they heavily depended on "the military for information and communications back to Britain". The author adds that "the censorship imperative outweighed the need to inform the public".[306] The numerous references to this conflict in the British press show that the conflict was still very important for editorialists, journalists as well as for readers in 1990.

302    Refer to the following website: <unscr.com/files/1982/00502.pdf>, consulted 28 July 2021.

303    Kenneth O. Morgan, *op. cit.*, 2001, p. 656.

304    Roy Greenslade, *op. cit.*, p. 376. Thatcher moved from being a deeply unpopular leader before the Falklands War to "being an unassailable national heroine" (Andrew Marr, *op. cit.*, 2008, p. 398).

305    Michael Parsons, *op. cit.*, pp. 10-11. Also refer to David Welch, *Propaganda Power and Persuasion*, London: British Library, 2013, p. 27.

306    Philip M. Taylor, *op. cit.*, 1999, p. 252. Roy Greenslade argued that the Ministry of Defence (MoD) sent public relations officers aboard the aircraft carriers *Hermes* and *Invincible* to monitor journalists' activities and established strict rules to be abided by journalists (Roy Greenslade, *op. cit.*, p. 443).

The *Times* referred to the Falklands War to emphasize the fact that Britain had launched its biggest military operation in the Gulf since the Falklands campaign of 1982.[307] Graham Stewart argues that the newspaper and the *Daily Telegraph* unambiguously supported the task force's objectives at that time.[308]

All four British newspapers drew political parallels between the Gulf Crisis and the Falklands War by reminding readers of the impact of that conflict on British domestic politics: from the debates in parliament,[309] to Britain's victory over Argentina that contributed to Margaret Thatcher's electoral success in 1983,[310] to the Labour Party's opposition to the conflict,[311] since its leaders

---

307    For instance: "In a just cause", editorial, *Times*, 13 August 1990, p. 11.
308    Graham Stewart, *op. cit.*, p. 128.
309    For example: "Uniting the nation", editorial, *Times*, 6 September 1990, p. 11. "How hope lies on a fragile foundation", editorial, *Guardian*, 7 September 1990, p. 22.
310    For instance: "Modified magic", editorial, *Guardian*, 16 August 1990, p. 18; Carole and Leonard Bernstein, "The West hell-bent on destruction", letters, *Guardian*, 3 January 1991, p. 14; "Fool's gold", editorial, *Sunday Times*, 23 September 1990, Sect. 3, p. 7; David Hughes, "Will the Gulf factor do for Mr Kinnock?", op-ed, *Sunday Times*, 12 August 1990, Sect. 3, p. 2; Andrew Grice, "Gulf takes heat out of Thatcher's kitchen", op-ed, *Sunday Times*, 26 August 1990, Sect. 3, p. 2; Alan Watkins, "A crisis that could still spoil things for Neil", op-ed, *Observer*, 30 September 1990, p. 19.
311    For example: Martin Jacques, "This fragile Gulf accord", op-ed, *Times*, 5 September 1990, p. 10; "While Britain slumbers", editorial, *Guardian*, 3 January 1991, p. 14. The *Guardian* editorial referred to the Labour's leaders who did not want the Conservative Party to play the patriotic card against them. Also refer to "Fool's gold", editorial, *Sunday Times*, 23 September 1990, Sect. 3, p. 7; Alan Watkins, "A crisis that could still spoil things for Neil", op-ed, *Observer*, 30 September 1990, p. 19. With the exception of the Labour MP Tam Dalyell, a fierce opponent of the Falklands War, the Labour Party, led by Michael Foot, backed Margaret Thatcher's dispatch of military forces to recapture the Falkland Islands (Andrew Marr, *op. cit.*, 2008, p. 401).

feared a "Falklands factor", i.e. appearing unpatriotic in the coming war in the Gulf.

In addition, the two daily newspapers referred to the Falklands War to analyse Margaret Thatcher's personality: the *Times* stressed her "robust attitude to and experience of armed conflict" in 1982 and 1990[312] while for the *Guardian* "her vices (stubbornness, narrowness, bigotry) were transformed into virtues (courage, steadfastness, resolution)" during the Falklands campaign.[313] Unlike the *Times*, some journalists and contributors of opinion pieces in the *Guardian* refuted the analogy drawn between the events in the Gulf and on the Falkland Islands.[314] They reflected the *Guardian's* view as the newspaper had been "the main protest sheet against liberating the Falkland Islands"[315] in 1982.

Finally, British daily and Sunday newspapers also referred to the Falklands War to address the problems of adequate press representation, access to information, limits to journalists' freedom

---

312    "No time for timidity", editorial, *Times*, 10 August 1990, p. 11.
313    "The lady with the iron pump", editorial, *Guardian*, 11 August 1990, p. 18.
314    "There is no resemblance with the Falklands even in military terms". Hugo Young, "Fortunes of war desert the iron lady", op-ed, *Guardian*, 6 September 1990, p. 19. "False comparisons are being made between the Falklands War and the looming conflict in the Gulf. Practically the only things these crises have in common are that British forces have been deployed and that in both cases they face armed forces of dictators who have occupied small countries. There the similarity ends". Paul Wilkinson, "A way to avoid the no-win war", op-ed, *Guardian*, 3 January 1991, p. 15. The professor of international relations at St Andrews University was opposed to war. He argued that a Pyrrhic victory was the best result that the West could expect of a Gulf War. Subsequent events, and in particular the Iraq War in 2003, proved him right in a certain way and especially in terms of the consequences.
315    Graham Stewart, *op. cit.*, p. 128.

and ministry guidelines on media coverage during that conflict.[316] While some journalists pointed to differences in coverage of the Falklands War and a possible conflict in the Gulf, i.e. technological equipment and the presence of journalists from all countries, the majority of editorialists and journalists highlighted the tensions between the media and the military authorities. They were thus concerned about the possible hindrance to their investigations and the potential risks of military censorship in the event of a conflict in the Gulf as in the Falklands War.

While both daily papers published more editorials and articles on the Falklands War than the Sunday newspapers, the *Sunday Times* differed from the *Observer* by printing a larger number of articles on the conflict. For example, editorials and opinion pieces in the *Sunday Times* reminded readers of the British victory in 1982, which Norman Macrae described as "our [...]

---

316 For instance: "War in the open", editorial, *Times*, 21 January 1991, p. 11; "Guidelines for the Experts", editorial, *Guardian*, 14 January 1991, p. 11; Georgina Henry, "Rights of access to the action", op-ed, *Guardian*, 8 January 1991, p. 17; Bridget Wood, "Gotcha and jingoism. Saddam by satellite", letters, *Sunday Times*, 2 September 1990, Sect. 3, p. 8. In addition to those articles and letters, a *Sunday Times* editorial of 10 February 1991, as well as a reader of the newspaper criticized the fact that no member of the royal family was on active service in the Gulf, unlike in the Falklands War: "The Duke of York served bravely in the Falklands but there are no royals [...] in the Gulf". "Royal family at war", editorial, *Sunday Times*, 10 February 1991, Sect. 3, p. 4; G. Kinnear, "Taking the begging bowl to Kuwait. Absence", letters, *Sunday Times*, 10 February 1991, Sect. 1, p. 20. On the one hand, the Sunday paper – certainly by design – published its editorial and the reader's letter on the same day and, on the other, presumably everything about the royal family was – still is – important and newsworthy for the *Sunday Times*. Given the role and place of the monarchy in Britain, it was perhaps expected that one of its members would set an example and go to the front line alongside British soldiers in Saudi Arabia.

Falklands glory".[317] The opinion piece included the first-person plural pronoun "we" as well as the first-person plural possessive "our". As noted earlier, "we" and "our" are often used to collectively represent the entire country and act as a combining element. The *Sunday Times* repeatedly referred to the victory of the British forces over the Argentinians throughout the Gulf Crisis and War. With a deep sense of national greatness, the Sunday paper seemed to believe that the glories of the past, and in this case the Falklands War, strengthened national pride and fostered a sense of belonging to a community of shared values. It revisited history, as it were, and seemed to cling to its memories and rehash them to convince its readers that the events in the Gulf would enable Britain to regain some prestige on the international scene. In so doing, the *Sunday Times* editorials echoed Margaret Thatcher's comments in the House of Commons on 22 November 1990.[318]

Unlike the *Sunday Times*, an *Observer* editorial of 9 September 1990 stated that the Gulf Crisis "is no re-run of the Falklands crisis".[319] On the other hand, the Sunday paper offered a plurality

---

317  "We Britons should stay so proud of our [...] Falklands glory". Norman Macrae, "Short and sharp, here's a case for the Falklands treatment", op-ed, *Sunday Times*, 19 August 1990, Sect. 3, p. 4. The title contains an alliteration that plays on the sound of the expression "short and sharp" and aims to attract the reader's attention.

318  The Prime Minister expressed "pride in the professionalism and courage of our armed forces" and added: "That is a sense of this country's destiny: the centuries of history and experience which ensure that, when principles have to be defended, when good has to be upheld and when evil has to be overcome, Britain will take up arms". See the website: <https://hansard.parliament.uk/Commons/1990-11-22/debates/6c776281-04cb-47fe-afdf-cadd8bb232c3/ConfidenceInHerMajestySGovernment?highlight=falklands#contribution-35208235-95ac-4621-a2f9-25c86d00e7fb>, consulted 4 August 2021.

319  "The questions that remain", editorial, *Observer*, 9 September 1990, p. 12.

of viewpoints diverging from its editorial line in its opinion pieces. For instance, Simon Hoggart underlined Britain's determination when he stated: "we mourn our dead, but we go in prepared for their death" as in the Falklands conflict.[320] As in the *Sunday Times*, the journalist used the first-person plural pronoun "we" and the first-person plural possessive "our".

In general, rhetoric of persuasion was at work in the *Sunday Times*, which endorsed the official discourse. Its editorialists and journalists started with the premise that the past nourished the present and formed the character of a people. It may be astounding that newspapers did not mention the 255 men killed and 777 injured on the British side during the two months of the Falklands conflict.[321] However, by glorifying the latest victory of an economically weakened country in 1990, the editorialists and journalists in question might have wanted to arouse a sense of nostalgia and thus exacerbate readers' patriotism. In addition to the political impact of the Falklands War and the Gulf Crisis the four newspapers referred to in numerous articles, some opinion pieces in the *Guardian* and an editorial in the *Observer* took issue with the comparisons between the events in the Gulf and the Falklands War. There was thus a different interpretation of history between the *Times* and the *Sunday Times* in their articles on the one hand and the *Guardian* in some opinion pieces and the *Observer* in an editorial on the other.

All in all, most of the articles referred to were published in newspapers before the conflict began. It is true that for those

---

320 Simon Hoggart, "Why Bush believes he has God on his side", op-ed, *Observer*, 12 August 1990, p. 11.
321 David Reynolds, *op. cit.*, p. 245.

convinced of the validity of the comparison, the aim was to strike a patriotic chord with readers and awaken nationalist feelings by recalling this military exploit. Readers needed to be convinced that Britain was still capable of embarking on a new adventure alongside the United States and regain its great power status.

Unlike the British press, only a few articles were published on the American side that drew parallels between the Falklands War and the situation in the Gulf. For example, a *New York Times* editorial and Michael Kinsley from the *Washington Post* reminded readers of the resignation of Lord Carrington, the British Foreign Secretary,[322] on 5 April 1982 after the invasion of the Falkland Islands by Argentine troops.[323] Both articles criticized the U.S. president and his Secretary of State for not taking responsibility for their disastrous policies towards Iraq. These examples also show that the *New York Times* and the journalist from the *Washington Post* followed British politics closely. The *Washington Post* also paid tribute to Margaret Thatcher in another editorial in November 1990 and praised her courage when she defended British interests in the Falklands.[324] Although the United States gave significant support to Britain during the Falklands War,[325]

---

322   "No End of Lessons on Iraq", editorial, *New York Times*, 23 September 1990, p. A 20; Michael Kinsley, "James A. Baker, Please Resign", op-ed, *Washington Post*, 18 October 1990, p. A 23.

323   David Reynolds, *op. cit.*, p. 245. Lord Carrington had warned John Nott, the Defence Secretary, three times of the danger of withdrawing the HMS *Endurance*, the only British patrol ship in the South Atlantic. The Argentinians concluded that an invasion of the Falkland Islands would be easy and popular (Andrew Marr, *op. cit.*, 2008, p. 399).

324   "Mrs. Thatcher Departs", editorial, *Washington Post*, 25 November 1990, p. C 6.

325   Before voting on Resolution 502, which demanded an Argentine withdrawal from the Falkland Islands, the United States had tried to avoid a war

it is hardly surprising to find only a minority of articles on the conflict in both American newspapers. On the one hand, the American president[326] did not refer to it and on the other, the Falklands War, which was overwhelmingly supported by British public opinion, essentially marked the history of Britain[327] and as such is part of the identity of the British people.

## 3.3.2 The Suez Crisis

In addition to numerous references to the Falklands War, the British press also referred to the 1956 Suez Crisis, although neither Margaret Thatcher nor John Major made any reference[328] to the event in their speeches from August 1990 to mid-March 1991. On 26 July 1956 Colonel Gamal Abdel Nasser nationalised the Suez Canal and seized control of the Suez Canal Company following Washington's refusal to finance Egypt's construction

---

between Britain and Argentina by brokering a deal through the Secretary of State, General Alexander Haig. It did not want to antagonize its most loyal NATO ally, but at the same time undermine the anti-Communist Argentine regime (Graham Stewart, *op. cit.*, pp. 125, 129; Roy Greenslade, *op. cit.*, p. 443; Philip M. Taylor, *op. cit.*, 1999, p. 251).

326 Nevertheless, when President Bush presented Margaret Thatcher with the presidential Medal of Freedom on 7 March 1991, he referred to the Falklands War (<https://bush41library.tamu.edu/archives/public-papers/2772>, consulted 25 August 2021).

327 The defeat of the Argentinians against Britain led to the fall of the military regime and the advent of a liberal regime in Argentina (Maurice Vaïsse, *Les Relations internationales depuis 1945*, 10e éd., Paris: Armand Colin, 2005, p. 152).

328 However, several MPs referred to the Suez Crisis during the debates on the Gulf in the House of Commons on 6 September 1990, 7 November 1990 and 15 January 1991.

of the projected Aswan Dam on the Nile.[329] The Suez Canal was a major artery of world trade and a crucial waterway by which oil was shipped to Britain, which thus represented "a vital national interest".[330] According to Robert Fisk,[331] Anthony Eden, the British Prime Minister at the time, wanted to topple Nasser. In October 1956 the British, the French and the Israelis agreed at a secret meeting at Sèvres, outside Paris, to mount "Operation Musketeer", which involved an Israeli attack on Egypt and an Anglo-French intervention force in the Canal Zone around Port Said.[332] Under pressure from the United States and when the U.N. passed the motion for a ceasefire, the attack was called off, and "the British troops withdrew ignominiously".[333] Prime Minister Eden, who suffered from poor health after an operation, resigned in early 1957.[334] The Suez Crisis, which was a complete failure for Britain, marked the end of the country's influence in the region and the advent of the United States as the new "big power" in the Middle East.[335]

It is worth recalling that the *Manchester Guardian* and the *Observer* opposed the military intervention in Egypt in 1956 while the *Sunday Times* unconditionally supported the British

---

329   Robert Fisk, *op. cit.*, p. 1128; T. O. Lloyd, *op. cit.*, p. 297; Niall Ferguson, *op. cit.*, p. 111. The Suez Canal Company was controlled by British and French interests.

330   Jeremy Paxman, *Empire*, London: Penguin Books, 2012, p. 265; Andrew Marr, *op. cit.*, 2008, p. 151.

331   Robert Fisk, *op. cit.*, p. 1129.

332   T. O. Lloyd, *op. cit.*, pp. 297, 299.

333   Kenneth O. Morgan, ed., *op. cit.*, 2001, p. 642. Andrew Marr refers to Britain's humiliation by the United States (Andrew Marr, *op. cit.*, 2008, p. 157).

334   Jeremy Paxman, *op. cit.*, p. 268.

335   Robert Fisk, *op. cit.*, p. 1137.

Prime Minister, and the *Times* changed its mind three times.[336] In confirmation of what has already been written, British newspapers, the *Sunday Times*[337] in particular, compared the Iraqi leader with Nasser. Some journalists and contributors also referred to the disastrous consequences of the Suez episode for Britain as a result of failing to act in concert with the United States. For example, Harold James in the *Times* stressed the importance of economic power when the Americans exerted financial pressure to force Eden's government to back down.[338] The Suez operation temporarily compromised the "special relationship" between both countries.[339] President Eisenhower was outraged by the allies' invasion as Eden had failed to consult the United States.[340] Besides, he was standing for re-election and was worried about the simultaneous Russian invasion of Hungary.[341] According to Ritchie Ovendale, the U.S. president later described "his handling of the Suez Crisis as his major foreign policy mistake".[342] In May 1982, Henry Kissinger publicly regretted the American government's action over Suez, when Washington had humiliated Britain and France.[343]

---

336  Roy Greenslade, *op. cit.*, pp. 123, 131.
337  For example: "The defeat of Saddam", editorial, *Sunday Times*, 24 February 1991, p. V.
338  Harold James, "Mirage of dominance", op-ed, *Times*, 1 October 1990, p. 14. The currency markets began selling the UK pound sterling, and the Bank of England could not stop the currency plummeting "without the help of the Americans, who refused to act until there was a ceasefire" (Jeremy Paxman, *op. cit.*, p. 267).
339  John Cannon, ed., *op. cit.*, p. 266.
340  Niall Ferguson, *op. cit.*, p. 111; Andrew Marr, *op. cit.*, 2008, p. 152.
341  Richard Cockett, *op. cit.*, p. 225.
342  Ritchie Ovendale, ed., *op. cit.*, 1994, p. 10.
343  Ritchie Ovendale, *Britain, the United States and the Transfer of Power in the Middle East*, London: Leicester UP, 1996, p. 140.

Unlike journalists in the *Times*, Fred Halliday in the *Guardian* found the application of economic sanctions, imposed by the United States against Britain in 1956, successful and justified.[344] A *Guardian* editorial compared the invasion of Kuwait by Iraq with that of Suez, which it also described as an "act of aggression".[345] Another *Guardian* editorial and some journalists looked at the impact of the two crises on Britain's domestic policy and argued that, in contrast to the Suez Crisis, the Labour Party was willing to support the government for its action in the Gulf.[346] This subject was also covered in the *Sunday Times*[347] and the *Observer*.[348] The Suez conflict tore Britain apart. Huge demonstrations took place in London to challenge Eden's government going to war.[349] Labour's opposition in Parliament and the lack of domestic support undermined the government's actions.[350]

The *Sunday Times* found the Nasser analogy "apt in several respects".[351] Likewise, Robert Harris wrote in the Sunday paper about "several uncanny similarities between the Gulf Crisis

---

344    Fred Halliday, "Biting the hand that helped them", op-ed, *Guardian*, 13 August 1990, p. 19.

345    "Paying the price for past errors", editorial, *Guardian*, 3 August 1990, p. 18.

346    "Why don't they defend their rights?", editorial, *Guardian*, 20 August 1990, p. 18; Michael White, "No rocking the warship", op-ed, *Guardian*, 12 January 1991, p. 23. However, the Labour Party was initially prepared to support the Conservative government and the use of force against Egypt before opposing the operation.

347    For example: Andrew Grice, "Gulf takes heat out of Thatcher's kitchen", op-ed, *Sunday Times*, 26 August 1990, Sect. 3, p. 2.

348    For instance: Alan Watkins, "A crisis that could still spoil things for Neil", op-ed, *Observer*, 30 September 1990, p. 19.

349    Andrew Marr, *op. cit.*, 2008, p. 155.

350    David Reynolds, *op. cit.*, p. 193.

351    For instance: "The defeat of Saddam", editorial, *Sunday Times*, 24 February 1991, p. V.

and that which erupted in 1956".[352] On the other hand, Simon Hoggart in the *Observer* highlighted the military humiliation suffered by Britain in the Suez venture.[353] For Jeremy Paxman, the Suez debacle was a great imperial humiliation.[354] While some people questioned Eden's use of military force, others thought that the government's armed intervention in the Suez Canal was right and necessary as it also showed that Britain was still a strong country. However, the United Nations General Assembly condemned Britain and France, which were seen as aggressors by the international community. A resolution requiring foreign troops to be withdrawn from Egypt[355] was passed by 64 votes to 5.

To sum up, the references to the Suez Crisis were mainly mentioned in editorials and opinion pieces published during the Gulf Crisis. They elicited various reactions. The *Times* drew bitter lessons from the Suez episode about Britain's strained relationship with the United States. The *Guardian* put the Suez adventure and the Gulf Crisis on an equal footing. While the *Times* focused on the influence of the Suez military operation on Britain's foreign policy, the *Guardian* and some journalists in both Sunday newspapers drew attention to domestic political problems due to Labour's opposition in 1956. Nevertheless, these journalists conveyed a positive message, given that the Labour

---

352 "[...] the basic issue is the same: oil, and the West's dependence upon it. In 1956, two-thirds of Europe's oil came through the canal giving Nasser in Eden's words, 'a thumb on our windpipe'. In 1990, two-thirds of the West's oil comes from a region menaced by Saddam. Same windpipe; different thumb". Robert Harris, "Eerie echoes of Suez debacle as Bush dons Eden mantle", op-ed, *Sunday Times*, 12 August 1990, Sect. 3, p. 4.

353 Simon Hoggart, Column, op-ed, *Observer*, 3 March 1991, p. 22.

354 Jeremy Paxman, *op. cit.*, p. 269.

355 T. O. Lloyd, *op. cit.*, p. 299.

Party endorsed the Conservative government's action in 1990. Finally, as noticed earlier, the discourse of the *Sunday Times*, carried away by patriotic fervour, suggested nostalgia for Britain's former splendour in the context of the analogy between Saddam Hussein and Nasser. On the whole, references to the Suez Crisis showed that the ghost of that debacle for Britain haunted British editorialists and journalists in 1990 and continues to do so with each new crisis.

On the American side, in addition to the comparison between Nasser and Saddam Hussein, a few opinion articles published in the two newspapers drew an analogy between the 1956 Suez Crisis and the Gulf Crisis. For instance, Robert J. Samuelson in the *Washington Post* focused on the difference between Suez and the Persian Gulf in that the United States was far more powerful economically and militarily in 1990 than Britain in the 1950s.[356] The journalist thus referred to the Suez Crisis to reassure its readers about the state of his country. William Bragg Ewald Jr., in the *New York Times*, and Charles Krauthammer, in the *Washington Post*, reminded their readers of the events in Suez to emphasize that "the age of imperialism" ended in 1956[357] for "the two great imperial forces, Britain and France, that had dominated the Middle East for half a century".[358] The two articles explained the United States' attitude at that time. Washington

---

356    Robert J. Samuelson, "The Shadow of Isolationism", op-ed, *Washington Post*, 5 September 1990, p. A 19.

357    William Bragg Ewald Jr., author of *Eisenhower the President: Crucial Days, 1951-1960*, "What Ike Would Do in the Gulf", op-ed, *New York Times*, 30 September 1990, p. E 21.

358    Charles Krauthammer, "… And Why Saddam Fights", op-ed, *Washington Post*, 17 January 1991, p. A 21.

dissociated itself from its British ally's "last imperial adventure"[359] in the Suez Canal, which was deemed "a colonial relic".[360] With the exception of these few articles, the American press was not particularly interested in the Suez event. Like the British Prime Ministers, President Bush did not refer to it in his speeches. It is true that any mention of the Suez Crisis could only remind British readers of its damaging effects on Britain's "national self-esteem and international prestige".[361] The Suez episode thus continued to plague the British press, as evidenced by the publication of numerous editorials and opinion pieces on the subject.

## Conclusion

One cannot build one's identity and understand the present without referring to the past that has marked the destiny of a nation. This is why editorials, opinion articles and letters in the American and British press mentioned events that had affected their countries' histories and therefore their readers to some extent. The selection of some specific events and the importance given to them reflect a particular approach to History. They result from an ideological choice and indicate the bias of editorialists, journalists and contributors, who looked back at the past to draw parallels between previous crises and conflicts and that of the Gulf in order to explain what was happening there but also to anticipate the future. In a way, their approach reassured readers

---

359  Robert Fisk, *op. cit.*, p. 1136.
360  David Reynolds, *op. cit.*, p. 192. Andrew Marr argues that "Washington was pursuing a vigorous policy of trying to turf out the old colonial powers from the Middle East in favour of America herself" (Andrew Marr, *op. cit.*, 2008, p. 151).
361  David Reynolds, *op. cit.*, p. 193.

in that they were referring to known things and gave them the impression that they were in control of the course of events to come.

Nonetheless, since memory is selective and subjective, editorialists, journalists and contributors summoned the past according to the message they wanted to convey and objectives they had set for themselves. The historical account thus interpreted past events and was therefore biased and partial in the American and British press. In the context of references to past conflicts, editorialists and journalists commented on a variety of topics, such as the policy of 'appeasement' or the political impact of past events. While opinion articles in the press on both sides of the Atlantic offered a range of viewpoints that might sometimes differ and diverge from the editorial line of the newspaper that published them, this was not the case in editorials. For example, on the British side, the *Sunday Times*, which followed the official rhetoric, used Britain's military successes in the two world wars and the Falklands War to draw a laudatory portrait of its country and convince its readers of the need for war against Iraq. In contrast, the Gulf Crisis and War brought back the traumas of History for the two American newspapers and, in the British press, for the *Guardian* and the *Observer*. In their editorials, these newspapers drew lessons from the past and commemorated its dramatic episodes in order to inform their readers, before the beginning of the Gulf War, that they were opposed to a military engagement of their country. For these newspapers, which read History according to criteria different from those of the *Sunday Times* and to a lesser degree of the *Times*, History is not only the memory of States, as Henry Kissinger[362] wrote, but also that of individuals, especially soldiers who lay down their lives for their country. All in all, the way newspapers recalled historical precedents showed that the events of the past still resonated in the collective consciousness of the United States and Britain.

---

362    Quoted by Howard Zinn, *op. cit.*, p. 9.

# Part V:

## Image of the Other: The allies

### Differences and similarities between the American press and the British press during the Gulf Crisis and War

# Introduction

As discussed in the previous chapters, a country's military power, its role at the international level, especially in times of crisis and war, as well as its victories in past conflicts strengthen national pride and contribute to the identity of the nation, which also manifests itself in the country's relations with other states. For Carl Schmitt and Julien Freund, the essence of politics is relationships of friendship and hostility between states, and this is particularly true in foreign policy, which often designates official enemies.[1] According to Julien Freund, other states are either real or virtual enemies or else friends, that is, allies,[2] and a state can adjust its bonds of friendship with other states. The extent of its trade preferences and financial aid as much as the actions specific to its foreign policy enable a state to signify the degree of friendship or coldness in its foreign relations.

Julien Freund defines two aspects of friendship in politics: on the one hand, concord and on the other hand, the kind of alliance which can be established within a multilateral agreement, such as a coalition, league, community or confederation.[3] Since alliances are primarily presented as political friendships, they only really make sense insofar as they create a common front against an enemy or tilt the balance of power in favour of the allies.[4] As in the Gulf War, the formation of alliances and coalitions makes it possible in particular to balance hegemonic attempts, which are

---

1     Edward W. Said, *op. cit.*, p. 332.
2     Julien Freund, *op. cit.*, p. 568.
3     *Ibid.*, p. 465.
4     *Ibid.*, pp. 469, 466.

constant in international relations.[5] It thus appears that there is no alliance without interest. Moreover, there does not seem to be such a thing as a perpetual alliance given that yesterday's enemy can become tomorrow's friend and vice versa.[6] For example, this was the case with the non-aggression treaty between Hitler and Stalin signed on 23 August 1939 and also with the alliance between Soviet Russia and the United States[7] and Britain during World War II.

A few centuries earlier, Machiavelli attributed geographical causes to alliances. In *The Prince*, he postulated that "the neighbour is my enemy" and "therefore the neighbour's neighbour will be my friend".[8] Aristotle, on the other hand, considered friendship a virtue;[9] political friendship being the link between cities.[10] For the Greek philosopher, if the enemy represents what one is not, the friend is the mirror of what one is or would like to be.[11] As already mentioned, the Other, friend or foe, helps shape our identity. The way in which we describe this Other informs us about the way we see ourselves.

---

5    Max Gounelle, *Relations internationales*, 6e éd., Paris: Dalloz, 2004, p. 67.

6    Julien Freund, *op. cit.*, p. 470.

7    *Ibid.*, pp. 466, 545.

8    Quoted by Thomas Lindemann *in* "Les Images dans la politique internationale: l'image de l'autre". See the Institute of Comparative Strategy's website: <http://www.stratisc.org/strat72_Lindemann.html>, 2005, consulted 21 October 2021.

9    Élisabeth Clément, et al., *op. cit.*, p. 15.

10   Philippe Raynaud & Stéphane Rials (dir.), *op. cit.*, p. 30.

11   Quoted by Edgardo Carosella and Thomas Pradeu *in* "L'Identité: la part de l'autre". See the Canal Académie's website: <http://www.canalacademie.com/ida5575-L-identite-la-part-de-l-autre.html>, consulted 21 October 2021.

While the second and third parts of this study have analysed the image of the enemy, this part will endeavour to show how editorials, opinion articles and letters from readers in the American and British press described the allies – the friends – of the United States and Britain.

# Chapter I:
# The alliance as a whole

## 1.1  The alliance as a whole in the American press

Like George Bush who referred seventy-five times to the allies of the United States and two hundred and three times to the coalition in his speeches and remarks during the Gulf Crisis and War,[12] the American press extensively mentioned the allies and the coalition in its editorials and opinion articles. For both the U.S. president and the two American newspapers, the term "ally" seemed deeply nostalgic in that it appeared to evoke historical resonances harking back to the two world wars of the 20th century.[13] The word "ally" was used at the beginning of the crisis[14] whereas the term "coalition" was only employed in the *Washington Post*[15] from the end of August 1990 and in the *New York Times*[16] from the beginning of September 1990. American editorialists thus preceded the U.S. president who mentioned the

---

12    These numbers do not include the references to the allied forces and armed coalition forces, but the generic terms "ally" and "coalition" used by George Bush in his speeches from August 1990 to mid-March 1991 have been taken into account. See the George Bush's library website: <http://bushlibrary.tamu.edu/research/public_papers.php?>, consulted 2 October 2021.

13    John Ayto, *20th Century Words*, Oxford: Oxford UP, 1999, p. 68.

14    For example: "Its European allies". Gary Sick, "Hussein Must Be Stopped …", op-ed, *New York Times*, 3 August 1990, p. A 20; "our allies". Charles Krauthammer, "A Festival of Appeasement", op-ed, *Washington Post*, 3 August 1990, p. A 23.

15    For instance: "The extraordinary coalition". "Talk with Iraq?", editorial, *Washington Post*, 28 August 1990, p. A 16.

16    For example: "The coalition partners". "The Month That Shook the World", editorial, *New York Times*, 2 September 1990, p. E 12.

term "coalition" for the first time in his press conference on 21 September 1990.[17]

In addition to the two words "allies" and "coalition", American newspapers often used equivalent nouns, such as "consensus", "alliance", "community", "unity" as well as the adjectives "international" and "collective". Furthermore, these terms were often repeated several times in the same article. Numerous references to the allies and the coalition thus show the importance of this topic for American journalists. While the *New York Times* devoted more editorials to this subject,[18] the *Washington Post* published a slightly larger number of opinion articles about it.[19]

Beyond the large number of articles published in the American press on the allies and the coalition, a few remarks should be raised. While the majority of editorials[20] appreciated the support of the allies and agreed that George Bush's coalition against Iraq was valid, this was not the case for some editorials and most opinion articles in the American newspapers. These few editorials as well as 82% of opinion articles in the *New York Times* and 69% in the *Washington Post* were critical of the allies and the coalition. For example, the coalition was described as "fragile" by William

17    Cf. George Bush's news conference of 21 September 1990 (<https://bush41library.tamu.edu/archives/public-papers/2244>, consulted 2 October 2021).
18    There were twenty-two editorials in the *New York Times* and ten in the *Washington Post* referring to the allies and the coalition.
19    The *New York Times* published twenty-five opinion articles and twenty-nine were published in the *Washington Post*.
20    64% of editorials published in the *New York Times* and 67% in the *Washington Post* approved of the allies' help within the coalition.

Safire[21] in the *New York Times*, by a reader[22] of the newspaper and by Charles Krauthammer[23] in the *Washington Post*.

Editorials unfavourable to the allies were published in the *New York Times* as early as August 1990 and in the *Washington Post* from early September 1990. Thus, on the one hand, editorialists of both newspapers approved of the help of the allies and the formation of a coalition, while on the other hand they expressed reservations about them. They presented nuanced viewpoints that might have been confusing to readers as they might have seemed contradictory. It can be assumed that the diversity of apparently paradoxical positions in editorials reflected the evolution of public opinion in the period under consideration.[24] In any case, the publication of critical editorials in the *New York Times* from the

---

21 "The fragile coalition". William Safire, "Trusting Our Allies", op-ed, *New York Times*, 6 December 1990, p. A 27.

22 "Our fragile 'coalition'". John Bovey, "Too Much Openness Will Doom Iraq", letters, *New York Times*, 30 December 1990, p. E 10.

23 "The coalition is fragile". Charles Krauthammer, "The Ground War: Hold It Off", op-ed, *Washington Post*, 1 February 1991, p. A 21.

24 This is only a hypothesis since there are no surveys available on this subject. The opinion polls to which the two American newspapers and their journalists referred concerned the public support for sending American soldiers to Saudi Arabia (for example in the articles by Tom Wicker, "Politics and the Gulf", op-ed, *New York Times*, 9 September 1990, p. E 10 or Robert J. Samuelson, "Tax Energy to Show Saddam We're Serious", op-ed, *Washington Post*, 20 August 1990, p. A 13), or the entry of the United States into the war (see the following articles: "Once Again: What's the Rush?", editorial, *New York Times*, 29 November 1990, p. A 28; Charles Krauthammer, "War and Public Opinion", op-ed, *Washington Post*, 11 January 1991, p. A 21). Polls conducted by the Gallup Institute showed for example that George Bush's approval rating rose from 64% on 11 January 1991 to 89% on 3 March 1991 (refer to the article by Jeffrey M. Jones, "Only 3 in 10 Americans Believe War Is Over", 18 April 2003, <http://www.gallup.com/poll/8212/Only-Americans-Believe-War-Over.aspx>, consulted 4 October 2021).

beginning of the Gulf Crisis and the higher percentage of negative opinion articles about the allies seemed to display a more hostile attitude from the *New York Times*[25] towards coalition forces than the *Washington Post*.

Some editorialists and many journalists in both newspapers questioned the military participation and especially the financial contribution of the allies to the Gulf operations while reminding readers at the same time of the heavy responsibilities borne by the United States as the coalition leader. For example, an editorial of 30 August 1990 in the *New York Times* wondered whether the allies were carrying "their fair share of the military and economic burden" and blamed them for "making little more than a token contribution".[26] This disapproval of the allies' derisory contribution can also be found in other editorials in the newspaper and in those of the *Washington Post* published during the Gulf Crisis while opinion articles from August 1990 to mid-March 1991 – i.e. until after the hostilities – echoed the criticism levelled at the allies in the editorials. For instance, Hobart Rowen demanded in the *Washington Post* that "our allies share the monetary burden of the confrontation with Saddam".[27] Even after the hostilities, Leslie H. Gelb in the *New York Times* ironically accused "our loyal allies" of owing "us about $40 billion for their share of war expenses" as "they've paid only a fraction of their pledges, which

---

25  Nevertheless, one cannot be absolutely sure: either it was a deliberate choice by the *New York Times* to publish a larger number of articles by journalists opposed to the allies, or most of the opinion articles sent to the newspaper were negative towards the coalition as a whole.

26  "Loose Ends in Gulf Policy", editorial, *New York Times*, 30 August 1990, p. A 22.

27  Hobart Rowen, "The Gulf Crisis. No Excuse …", op-ed, *Washington Post*, 6 September 1990, p. A 27.

were far too low to begin with".[28] Journalists might have relied on the cost estimates of the military authorities during the Gulf Crisis and the war itself to make their case for allied financial participation. Nevertheless, André Nouschi[29] argues that the Gulf War was rather beneficial for the United States as its war expenses were reimbursed by Kuwait and Saudi Arabia. According to Niall Ferguson, the Gulf War had been free to Americans since the allies "had paid between 80 and 90 percent of its total military costs".[30] For William Engdahl, informed estimates claimed that when all allied war contributions were taken into account, the United States "had come out of the entire Gulf War with a net 'profit' of perhaps $19 billion".[31] Finally, Emil Vlajki contends that the Gulf War also enabled the United States to sign most arms contracts with Mideastern countries.[32]

At any rate, the recurring questions of editorialists and journalists about the allies' financial support – which was considered modest – suggest a more general and direct criticism of the coalition members. For example, an editorial in the *New York Times* on 8 October 1990 emphasized their lack of willingness

---

28    Leslie H. Gelb, "Dear Mr. President …", op-ed, *New York Times*, 3 March 1991, p. E 17.
29    André Nouschi, *op. cit.*, 1999, pp. 174, 238.
30    Niall Ferguson, *op. cit.*, p. 263.
31    William Engdahl, *op. cit.*, p. 245. The report of 29 June 2010 presented to Congress on, inter alia, the costs of military operations in the Gulf mentioned an amount of 61 billion dollars. However, a footnote specified that these expenses were offset by allied contributions. See the report by Stephen Daggett about the costs of the major wars waged by the United States: <http://www.fas.org/sgp/crs/natsec/RS22926.pdf>, 29 June 2010, consulted 9 October 2021.
32    Emil Vlajki, *La Terreur américaine*, Paris: François-Xavier de Guibert, 2003, p. 202.

and sense of responsibility[33] although the allies were better off economically than the United States for the *Washington Post*.[34] William Safire in the *New York Times* even questioned their trustworthiness in his article of 6 December 1990,[35] ironically titled "Trusting Our Allies", whose behaviour was described as "almost shameful"[36] by Robert J. Samuelson in the *Washington Post* in December 1990 because of their "hollow rhetoric", the modest financial contribution of some coalition members and the fatal risks to American soldiers in the forthcoming fighting.

These observations call for several comments. On the one hand, the caustic remarks in the articles on the allies diverged from the official and neutral, or even kind, words of the American president in his speeches towards the coalition members. On the other hand, the question of the insignificant financial contribution of some allies, which was at the heart of the reflections of the American newspapers, masked a bitter resentment and even, so to speak, pure jealousy towards some allies who, according to the journalists concerned, benefited from a stronger economy than that of the United States. These journalists thus dismantled the deceptive unity of the coalition, of which George Bush was proud, with their often ironic and sometimes scathing comments about the allies. Alongside the relentless verbal onslaught against the enemy, a more subtle discourse of disparagement was at work among these

---

33    "Who Will Pay for the Gulf Crisis?", editorial, *New York Times*, 8 October 1990, p. A 16.

34    "Paying for Desert Shield", editorial, *Washington Post*, 2 September 1990, p. B 6.

35    William Safire, "Trusting Our Allies", op-ed, *New York Times*, 6 December 1990, p. A 27.

36    Robert J. Samuelson, "Tired of Being the Superpower", op-ed, *Washington Post*, 19 December 1990, p. A 23.

journalists. But the purpose remained the same: amid the bitter accusations levelled at the coalition members, these journalists sought to re-establish the supremacy of national interests and reaffirm the identity of their country, which, despite being the coalition leader, might have lost visibility when presented as part of the allied group. In this way, they made the United States emerge from the mass of allies not only because of its military power and its vital role in the Gulf, but also because of its qualities and skills.

As is the case in states of crisis and war, the main aim is above all to strengthen national identity in the face of adversaries and allies. According to Samuel P. Huntington, a common enemy creates a common interest in politics. Economic associations and military alliances therefore require cooperation among their members which depends on their trust in one another.[37] The comments of the editorialists and journalists in question did not reflect this sense of security and openness to allies. Although they did not adopt a Manichean approach and did not use a rhetoric as belligerent and virulent as that used against Saddam Hussein, their arguments were mainly based on the difference between the United States on the one hand and the allied countries on the other. In other words, those editorials (a minority) and opinion articles (a clear majority) in the two newspapers which launched an uncompromising indictment against the allies emphasized the sense of moral duty dictating U.S. conduct in this crisis. As already noted, it would appear that the United States, unlike

---

37    Samuel P. Huntington, *The Clash of Civilizations and the Remaking of World Order*, New York: Simon & Schuster, 1996, pp. 131, 185. Samuel P. Huntington adds that trust among allies is built on shared values and culture. This was not the case with George Bush's broad and heterogeneous coalition composed of Arab and Western countries.

its allies, defined itself as a chosen people with an exceptional destiny and felt invested with a civilizing mission: "the sacred duty of Americans to impose democracy on the world" according to François Thual.[38] Finally, regardless of the fact that the majority of editorials and some opinion articles, like the American president, appreciated the support of the coalition members, articles, whether critical or not of the allies, thus portrayed the United States as an exemplary country that met its obligations, thus playing to the readers' patriotic tune.

## 1.2   The alliance as a whole in the British press

As on the American side – but to a lesser extent[39] – the British press also referred to the allies and the coalition in articles and letters published during the Gulf Crisis and War. Editorialists and journalists also used equivalent terms such as "community", "alliance", and the adjectives "international" and "collective" in their articles. The *Times* and the *Observer* stood out from the other British newspapers in this respect, with the *Times* devoting the most editorials and the *Observer* the most opinion pieces to all the allies. The larger number of editorials in the *Times* shows the newspaper's keen interest in the commitment of British troops to the coalition forces in the Gulf. As for the many opinion pieces published in the *Observer*, it turns out that more journalists decided to write articles about the coalition in the Sunday newspaper. It was also only in these two newspapers that letters about the allies

---

38   François Thual, *op. cit.*, p. 140.
39   The British press published fewer articles about the coalition as a whole than the American press, which could be explained by the fact that Britain was part of the coalition while the United States was leading it.

and the coalition could be found. While it is difficult to draw any conclusions on this point, it could at most be suggested that either readers did not send letters about the coalition to the *Guardian* and the *Sunday Times*, or the newspapers chose not to publish them.

In general, the *Times* published editorials favourable to the allies and the coalition which was described in January 1991 as "the most powerful coalition ever mustered in peacetime".[40] While the newspaper in January 1991 praised "the unprecedented solidarity"[41] among the allies, an editorial of 22 August 1990 had emphasized the fact that Britain, Canada and Australia were the only Western allies to "provide unequivocal support"[42] to the United States from the beginning of the formation of the coalition. With this statement, the *Times* thus underlined the importance of Britain's role[43] in the coalition alongside the United States. Opinion pieces and letters echoed the newspaper's editorials. For instance, Martin Fletcher wrote from the outset of the Gulf Crisis that "international unity is holding up".[44]

Unlike the *Times*, the *Guardian* considered the coalition "flaky"[45] in an editorial published on 11 January 1991. Martin Walker stressed the fact in February 1991 that "the other allies

---

40    "Deadlock in Geneva", editorial, *Times*, 10 January 1991, p. 13.

41    "No holy war", editorial, *Times*, 17 January 1991, p. 13.

42    "Holding together", editorial, *Times*, 22 August 1990, p. 11.

43    See Chapter II in Part IV, point 2.2 about Britain's role.

44    Martin Fletcher, "Glory restored, but what of the cost?", op-ed, *Times*, 23 August 1990, p. 8.

45    "When the masters lose control", editorial, *Guardian*, 11 January 1991, p. 20.

impose their own priorities on the peace".[46] Like the *Times*, the *Sunday Times* emphasized in an editorial in September 1990 that "America and its allies are resolute in their determination to liberate Kuwait"[47] and in another editorial published in February 1991 the Sunday paper underlined "the allied willpower".[48] While editorialists from the Sunday newspaper lauded the coalition, Michael Jones[49] and Norman Macrae[50] took great care to remind their readers of Britain's vital role in the coalition.

Viewpoints were divided in the *Observer*. While the Sunday newspaper hailed "an impressive display of international co-operation"[51] in an editorial of August 1990, it changed its mind seven months later and suggested in early March 1991 that the interests of the coalition members were bound to diverge after the war.[52] In addition, the majority of opinion pieces were rather negative towards the allies and the coalition, which was described as "fragile"[53] by David Owen and which, according to Andrew Stephen, risked "disintegrating".[54]

46    Martin Walker, "A world without Saddam", op-ed, *Guardian*, 26 February 1991, p. 23.

47    "The Russian card", editorial, *Sunday Times*, 30 September 1990, Sect. 3, p. 7.

48    "Saddam blinks", editorial, *Sunday Times*, 17 February 1991, p. V.

49    Michael Jones, "War sounds a retreat from Brussels", op-ed, *Sunday Times*, 20 January 1991, Sect. 3, p. 2.

50    Norman Macrae, "We've got the right stuff to prove dictators dead wrong", op-ed, *Sunday Times*, 3 March 1991, p. VIII.

51    "The logic of war and peace in the Gulf", editorial, *Observer*, 26 August 1990, p. 10.

52    "Now for the harder task of peace", editorial, *Observer*, 3 March 1991, p. 22.

53    David Owen, "A deadly game of chicken", op-ed, *Observer*, 13 January 1991, p. 14.

54    Andrew Stephen, "Jittery George tries to keep mum happy", op-ed, *Observer*, 6 January 1991, p. 18.

In summary, the *Times* articles and most of those in the *Sunday Times,* as well as a few editorials in the *Observer* were in favour of the coalition assembled by the American president. In so doing, they followed the official rhetoric of the British Prime Minister, be it Margaret Thatcher[55] or John Major.[56] The *Times,* in an editorial, and two journalists from the *Sunday Times* also highlighted Britain's key position in the coalition. In contrast, an editorial in the *Guardian* and the *Observer* as well as opinion pieces in these newspapers were disparaging of the coalition, as were numerous opinion articles in the two American newspapers. The British press thus offered a plurality of viewpoints about the allies and the coalition depending on the newspaper.

## Conclusion

The American press published more articles about the alliance as a whole than the British press, and the support or lack of support for the allies depended on the type of articles published:

---

55    For example, refer to the House of Commons debates on the Gulf and the allies on 6 September 1990 (<https://hansard.parliament. uk/Commons/1990-09-06/debates/54db6e15-456e-4257-ba864-cae4950b07f4/TheGulf?highlight=chemical#contribution-c8ad5e14-9ae7-4882-b8c6-836ef88447b7>), or to Margaret Thatcher's speech at Lord Mayor's Banquet on 12 November 1990 about the greatest international coalition in history (<https://www.margaretthatcher.org/document/108241>, consulted 15 October 2021).

56    For instance, John Major referred to Britain's allies on 15 January 1991 (<https://hansard.parliament.uk/Commons/1991-01-15/debates/3498d88e-f437-47bc-bdc6-cd0c78a0fee8/TheGulf?highlight=chemic al#contribution-93c27615-93f1-43c2-b05e-395509d2>), and to "our coalition partners" on 26 February 1991 (<https://johnmajorarchive.org. uk/1991/02/26/pmqt-written-answers-26-february-1991/>, consulted 15 October 2021).

most editorials in the *New York Times* and the *Washington Post* were favourable to the allies whereas the majority of opinion articles in the American newspapers criticized them. While the articles published on the American side – whether kind or not towards the allies – painted a favourable portrait of the United States, the situation was more contrasted on the British side: the *Times* and two journalists in the *Sunday Times* stressed Britain's essential role in the coalition while the *Guardian* and above all the *Observer* downplayed their country's position.

# Chapter II:
# The main allies[57]

In addition to the newspapers' comments on the coalition in general and whether or not they were consistent with official statements, it is now time to analyse how each ally in particular was described. American and British newspapers referred extensively to the coalition members, though in many different ways.

## 2.1  Arab countries

### 2.1.1  Arab countries in the American press

The Arab countries were above all the allies to which the American press repeatedly referred as a large number of editorials and opinion articles were published on them. Some articles favourable to the Arab states concerned, for example, their support for the coalition assembled by the American president[58] or their sending of armed forces to Saudi Arabia.[59] However, the majority of editorials and opinion articles were critical, sometimes

---

57   This chapter focuses on the most mentioned allies in the articles published in the two American newspapers and the four British ones. This is an arbitrary choice, but it makes it possible to better characterize the reactions at work.

58   For example: "Found: A New Treasure in the Gulf", editorial, *New York Times*, 23 August 1990, p. A 22.

59   For instance: "Iraq's Isolation", editorial, *Washington Post*, 12 August 1990, p. C 6.

virulently. Several major criticisms dominated editorials and articles in both American newspapers.

The most widespread criticism concerned the absence of democracy[60] in Middle Eastern countries. This argument, which was repeated on many occasions during the Gulf Crisis and War, was used by some journalists, mostly from the *Washington Post*, to criticize American policy in the Middle East. For example, Jim Wallis, senior editor of *Sojourners Magazine* at the time, wrote in the newspaper on 30 October 1990 that "U.S. policy in the region has served to protect feudalism and gas-guzzling more than democracy".[61]

The *New York Times* differed from the *Washington Post* by publishing articles[62] and more letters[63] devoted to the plight of Arab people in the Gulf countries and their support for the Iraqi leader. However, it is difficult to conclude that the *New York Times* showed more empathy towards the Arab population than the

---

60    For example: Flora Lewis, "Old-Think for the Gulf", op-ed, *New York Times*, 8 September 1990, p. A 23; Richard Cohen, "Nations Built on Sand", op-ed, *Washington Post*, 17 August 1990, p. A 27.

61    Jim Wallis, "Killing in the Name of God", op-ed, *Washington Post*, 30 October 1990, p. A 21.

62    For instance, the article by Flora Lewis, "Steady Against Saddam", op-ed, *New York Times*, 21 August 1990, p. A 27.

63    For example, the letter by M. T. Mehdi, "The New Saladin?", letters, *New York Times*, 23 September 1990, p. E 20. The president of the American-Arab Relations Committee in 1990 referred to demonstrations in support of Saddam Hussein among Arab people through the Arab and Muslim worlds. According to Samuel P. Huntington, "the Gulf War became a civilization war because the West intervened militarily in a Muslim conflict", and Arab and Muslim public opinion saw the intervention as a war against them and "one more instance of Western imperialism" (Samuel P. Huntington, *op. cit.*, p. 247).

*Washington Post* as these were not its editorials, but its articles and letters.

Moreover, as was found in the description of the enemy, editorialists and journalists in both newspapers also speculated about the future and possible – but above all negative – actions of their Middle Eastern allies, resorting extensively to auxiliaries and circumlocutions to emphasize the possibility or degree of probability or certainty of the planned actions.[64]

In general, the criticisms aimed at the Arab countries and their leaders were reminiscent of the damning indictment against Saddam Hussein in the two American newspapers. For example, an editorial in the *New York Times* in September 1990 referred to "the Persian Gulf's autocratic regimes".[65] But it was mainly in opinion articles in both American newspapers that vehement attacks on "the puny military forces of the Gulf countries",[66] the "feudal Arab tyrannies",[67] the dangerous Arab nations led by

---

64    This remark also applies to the treatment of all allies. The auxiliaries *may*, *would*, *should*, *ought to*, *will*, *might* and the circumlocutions such as *likely to* and *bound to* were used extensively. The verb *expect* was also used in the articles.

65    "A Good Gulf Pep Rally", editorial, *New York Times*, 13 September 1990, p. A 26.

66    Gary Sick, "Hussein Must Be Stopped ...", op-ed, *New York Times*, 3 August 1990, p. A 27.

67    "Feudal tyrannies". A. M. Rosenthal, "Soldiers in the Sands", op-ed, *New York Times*, 12 August 1990, p. E 21. Likewise, a reader described "Arabs" as "repressive feudal aristocracies". Thornton S. Sanders, "Oil Sheiks Will Fight to the Last American", letters, *New York Times*, 22 November 1990, p. A 26. "Arab tyrannies". A. M. Rosenthal, "Making a Killer", op-ed, *New York Times*, 5 August 1990, p. E 19.

"dictators",[68] and "an Arab world driven by ethnic xenophobia and religious fanaticism"[69] could be found. In the *Washington Post*, for instance, Jim Hoagland, in his article with the eloquent title "The Tyrants on Our Side in the Gulf", blamed Morocco and Turkey, "key partners in the coalition against Iraq", for having "a free ride of human rights abuses at home in return for support for human rights in Kuwait".[70] The two newspapers also emphasized that the Gulf region was inherently unstable[71] and stressed, like Henry Kissinger, that "upheavals in the Middle East are a way of life".[72]

Nevertheless, a few contributors distanced themselves from the scathing comments of these journalists and other commentators. For example, Cyrus Vance, Secretary of State for Foreign Affairs from 1977 to 1980, in the *Washington Post* wanted Arab states

---

68     "The Arab nations are dangerous, [...] only dictators rule". A. M. Rosenthal, "From Mirage to War", op-ed, *New York Times*, 19 August 1990, p. E 19. The journalist used the terms "dictator" or "dictatorship" to describe Arab leaders and countries in other articles (For example: "Making a Killer", op-ed, *New York Times*, 5 August 1990, p. E 19; "The Goals of War", op-ed, *New York Times*, 23 August 1990, p. A 23; "Our Ally, the Killer", op-ed, *New York Times*, 2 October 1990, p. A 27). William Safire also referred to "the hypocrisy of duplicitous dictatorships [...]" in Tehran and Baghdad in his article of 7 February 1991 (William Safire, "Friends, More Than Interests", op-ed, *New York Times*, 7 February 1991, p. A 25). Echoing these articles, a letter also referred to "friendly dictators" (Carl Stein, "Buildup of U.S. Troops Alarms the Arab World. Friendly Dictators", letters, *New York Times*, 26 August 1990, p. A 18).

69     Rowland Evans and Robert Novak, "What Bush Has Opened", op-ed, *Washington Post*, 13 August 1990, p. A 11.

70     Jim Hoagland, "The Tyrants on Our Side in the Gulf", op-ed, *Washington Post*, 1 November 1990, p. A 23.

71     For example: Zbigniew Brzezinski, "Patience in the Persian Gulf, Not War", op-ed, *New York Times*, 7 October 1990, p. E 19; "More Saudi Oil", editorial, *Washington Post*, 14 October 1990, p. C 6.

72     Henry Kissinger, "A Dangerous Mirage", op-ed, *Washington Post*, 11 November 1990, p. B 7.

to play a central role in negotiations to end Iraq's occupation of Kuwait.[73] However, apart from a few minority comments, the bitter arguments and expressive vocabulary used by the majority of journalists and contributors from August 1990 to March 1991 to depict the Arab countries, their attitudes and behaviour created an atmosphere of distrust towards the Middle Eastern states. Furthermore, by highlighting the propensity of "Arabs from the Persian Gulf" to dicker with Saddam Hussein,[74] the political instability of the region described as a "powder keg"[75] and the brutality of the regimes, journalists opposed the Arab states on the one hand to the United States and Israel on the other. Some articles in the American press indeed painted a favourable picture of Israel, which was described among other things as the only democracy in the Middle East.[76] The flattering representation of Israel might perhaps be attributed to the Jewish origin of some journalists, such as A. M. Rosenthal or Flora Lewis. Like the portrait of the Iraqi leader in the American newspapers, most journalists, regardless of their political affinities and origin, resorted to simplistic binary rhetoric between the United States and Israel on the one hand – in some articles – and the Arab countries on the other.

In contrast to the harsh description of Arab countries, many journalists also presented a reassuring and empowering picture

---

73   Cyrus Vance, "Pressure on Iraq Can Work", op-ed, *Washington Post*, 21 October 1990, p. C 7.
74   Les Aspin, "Define Our Goals in the Gulf", op-ed, *Washington Post*, 10 August 1990, p. A 15.
75   Jack Anderson and Dale Van Atta, "Lots of Energy in the U.S.A.", op-ed, *Washington Post*, 16 September 1990, p. B 7.
76   For example: George F. Will, "Wolf Out of Babylon", op-ed, *Washington Post*, 3 August 1990, p. A 23.

of the United States[77] given that the USA protected[78] Saudi Arabia from a possible invasion by Iraq, and only the United States was capable of opposing Saddam Hussein.[79] The United States thus appeared in the editorials and opinion articles published in the American newspapers as the saviour[80] of the Persian Gulf, evoking the idea of the messianic character of an American nation determined to spread civilization and save the world.[81] Christophe Kuntz argues that, with regard to the "Great Game" in the Middle East, the underlying objective of the United States is to establish its lasting political and economic domination in the long term.[82] According to Bruno Carton, the oil-producing countries are subservient to America,[83] which is "by far the greatest economic and political influence in the region".[84]

The journalistic discourse differed from George Bush's remarks. For example, the American president welcomed the

---

77 For instance: "Resistance and Appeasement", editorial, *Washington Post*, 7 August 1990, p. A 18.
78 For example: "War? Make the Case", editorial, *New York Times*, 4 November 1990, p. E 18.
79 For instance: Jim Hoagland, "Force Hussein to Withdraw", op-ed, *Washington Post*, 7 August 1990, p. A 19. Refer to Part IV, Chapter I, point 1.1 on the military power of the United States which was described in the American press.
80 For Bruno Carton from the GRESEA (Research Group for an Alternative Economic Strategy – Brussels), the United States was the only protection for the regimes of oil-producing countries in the Persian Gulf (Bruno Carton *in* Gérard de Selys & Bogdan van Doninck [dir.], *op. cit.*, p. 52).
81 Cf. Aurélie Lorrain and François Thual, *op. cit.*, pp. 140, 173.
82 Christophe Kuntz, "*Syria Accountability Act* et grand Moyen-Orient américain", *in Géopolitique des États-Unis. Culture, intérêts, stratégies. Revue Française de Géopolitique*, Paris: Ellipses, 2005, p. 314.
83 Bruno Carton *in* Gérard de Selys & Bogdan van Doninck (dir.), *op. cit.*, p. 52.
84 Edward W. Said, *op. cit.*, p. 324.

Arab League's condemnation of Saddam Hussein's invasion;[85] its diplomatic efforts as well as those initiated by the United States, the European Community and the United Nations to achieve a peaceful solution to the Gulf Crisis;[86] the fact that many Arab states stood up to "Iraqi aggression" and were on the side of the United States,[87] and that their armed forces stood "shoulder to shoulder" with U.S. military forces against Saddam Hussein.[88] The U.S. president also called the Arab leaders "our Arab friends".[89] In contrast, the articles of most journalists seemed to ignore the fact that the Arab states, located in a region rich in energy resources and vital to American interests,[90] were part of the U.S.-led coalition. On the whole, the rhetoric of these journalists thus reinforced prejudices and stereotypes against the Arab countries and their leaders. These preconceptions were also denounced by some readers in their letters,[91] stating for instance that "most of

---

85    For example, refer to the joint news conference of President Bush and Soviet President Mikhail Gorbachev in Helsinki, Finland on 9 September 1990 (<https://bush41library.tamu.edu/archives/public-papers/2207>, consulted 4 November 2021).

86    For instance, refer to  Bush's remarks to the Reserve Officers Association on 23 January 1991 (<https://bush41library.tamu.edu/archives/public-papers/2648>, consulted 4 November 2021).

87    For instance, refer to Bush's remarks at a Rally for Senatorial Candidate Lynn Martin in Chicago, Illinois on 26 September 1990 (<https://bush41library.tamu.edu/archives/public-papers/2263>, consulted 4 November 2021).

88    Cf. George Bush's Address to the Nation announcing allied military action in the Persian Gulf on 16 January 1991 (<https://bush41library.tamu.edu/archives/public-papers/2625>, consulted 4 November 2021).

89    Cf. Bush's interview with Middle Eastern journalists on 8 March 1991 (<https://bush41library.tamu.edu/archives/public-papers/2778>, consulted 4 November 2021).

90    Refer to Part III, Chapter IV, point 4.4 on the oil issue.

91    Joseph Elias, "We Need More Than a Big Stick in Mideast", letters, *New York Times*, 17 February 1991, p. E 12.

those in Congress who voted for war were ignorant of Islamic culture"[92] and condemning the stereotypes perpetuated in the media which portrayed the Arab people as Terrorists. Finally, the fact that the two American newspapers published letters with viewpoints that differed from their editorial line as well as conflicting opinion articles is evidence of their pluralism.

In summary, more journalists from the *Washington Post* were critical of U.S. policy in the Middle East, and articles and numerous letters published in the *New York Times* were sympathetic towards Arab people. All in all, the contemptuous comments made by most journalists about Arab countries and leaders in both American newspapers differed from official discourses. The ethnocentric rhetoric of the journalists concerned also confirmed that events such as crises or wars tend to constrain international relations by shaping and reinforcing a bipolar and reductive world view. These incidents lead to a hardening of the tone of journalistic discourse and positions towards the Other – friend or foe – and increase the positive feeling of superiority of Western identity[93] over Arab countries in an ideological context that is marked in particular in the West by discourses of respect for human rights and democratic values. Similarly, the stereotypical judgments of the journalists in question appeared to be a factor of social cohesion, a constituent element in the relationship with the Other[94] and sparked a resurgence of patriotism, and even nationalism.

---

92     For example: Walter A. Fairservis Jr., "Silence of Discourse", letters, *New York Times*, 10 March 1991, p. E 14; Gail A. Nolan, "Debunking the Myth of the 'Ugly Arab'", letters, *Washington Post*, 28 August 1990, p. A 16.

93     Margarita Sanchez-Mazas et Laurent Licata (dir.), *L'Autre: regards psychosociaux*, Grenoble: PU de Grenoble, 2005, pp. 95-97.

94     Ruth Amossy & Anne Herschberg Pierrot, *op. cit.*, p. 43.

## 2.1.2 Arab countries in the British press

Like the American press, the British press published many articles on Arab countries during the Gulf Crisis and War. This could be explained by the fact that Britain, a large Western colonial power,[95] once dominated the Middle East, where it had settled during the 19th century[96] and whose overland and sea routes between the home country and India had been vital for the British Empire.[97] While the four British newspapers published a more or less comparable number of articles about the Arab states, the *Times* devoted the most editorials to them, perhaps because of the importance of international news for the paper, especially when it comes to events in that region.[98] On the other hand, the *Times* published fewer opinion pieces than the *Guardian* and the Sunday papers because these newspapers may have decided to devote a large proportion of their opinion pieces to Middle Eastern countries.

Some editorials and articles published in the four newspapers,[99] mostly before the outbreak of hostilities, paid tribute to Arab countries, particularly for their opposition to Saddam Hussein following the invasion of Kuwait, their diplomatic initiatives to

---

95    Kenneth O. Morgan, ed., *op. cit.*, p. 593.
96    Alain Gresh & Dominique Vidal, *op. cit.*, p. 217.
97    *Ibid.*, p. 218.
98    The *Times*'s Richard Beeston was one of the first journalists to go to the Iraqi town of Halabja in 1988, after it had been bombed with nerve gas by the Iraqi army (Graham Stewart, *op. cit.*, p. 387).
99    For example: "No holy war", editorial, *Times*, 17 January 1991, p. 13; "At the eleventh hour, and beyond", editorial, *Guardian*, 10 January 1991, p. 18; "Lest we forget", editorial, *Sunday Times*, 16 September 1990, Sect. 3, p. 7; David Owen, "A deadly game of chicken", op-ed, *Observer*, 13 January 1991, p. 14.

resolve the crisis in a peaceful manner, and the presence of their troops in the coalition. These editorials and articles echoed what Margaret Thatcher and John Major said in their statements[100] about the support of many Arab countries for the international coalition, their sending of armed forces to Saudi Arabia, and their participation in the conflict against Iraq. Finally, and as noted earlier, Michael Jones[101] in the *Sunday Times* emphasized the importance of Britain's role[102] in the coalition alongside that of the Arab allies, proof for this journalist of the primacy of the national interest.

However, as in the American press, the majority of articles in the British press were unfavourable to Arab allies. Similar arguments can be found in the four newspapers, such as criticisms

---

100    For example, refer to Margaret Thatcher's statements on the Gulf to the House of Commons on 6 September 1990 (<https://hansard.parliament. uk/Commons/1990-09-06/debates/54db6e15-456e-4257-ba864-cae4950b07f4/TheGulf?highlight=chemical#contribution-c8ad5e14-9ae7-4882-b8c6-836ef88447b7>), as well as John Major's statements on the Gulf War to the House of Commons on 15 January 1991 (<https://hansard. parliament.uk/Commons/1991-01-15/debates/3498d88e-f437-47bc-bdc6-cd0c78a0fee8/TheGulf?highlight=chemical#contribution-93c27615-93f1-43c2-b05e-395509d2>, consulted 16 November 2021). Both Prime Ministers also referred to the Arab-Israeli problem, which needed to be solved for Margaret Thatcher (see her interview for TV-AM *Frost on Sunday* on 1 September 1990) and John Major (refer to his statements on the Gulf War on 17, 21 and 31 January 1991). A peace conference, which was sponsored by the United States and the Soviet Union, took place in Madrid from 30 October 1991 to 1 November 1991. Negotiations between Israel and its Arab neighbours were conducted in an attempt to resolve the Israeli-Palestinian conflict (Alain Gresh & Dominique Vidal, *op. cit.*, pp. 30, 143, 316).

101    Michael Jones, "War sounds a retreat from Brussels", op-ed, *Sunday Times*, 20 January 1991, Sect. 3, p. 2.

102    Reference is made to Part IV, Chapter II, point 2.2 concerning Britain's role during the Gulf Crisis and War.

of the lack of democracy[103] in the Gulf countries. While the *Times* described the "Arab solution to the confrontation in the Gulf" as a "mirage"[104] in an editorial of 3 January 1991, an editorial in the *Sunday Times* referred in a less moderate tone to the "many predators in the Middle East"[105] in December 1990. Opinion pieces in British newspapers confirmed the partisan and negative views about the Arab countries that were expressed in most of their editorials. For instance, Conor Cruise O'Brien in the *Times* wrote in August 1990 that "the Middle East remains a highly unstable and unpredictable area".[106] In the *Sunday Times*, Norman Macrae stood out from other journalists by the sarcastic tone of his articles and his verbal attacks on some Arab states ruled by "Third World thugs",[107] and against "some ignorant Arabs" who "think that a Saddamite single Arab nation could raise oil prices to any height, and make the infidels' pips squeak".[108]

The majority of letters, which were published in both dailies from August 1990 to March 1991 and mainly during the Gulf Crisis in the Sunday papers, repeated the negative attitude of commentators. For example, a reader of the *Guardian* described

103   For example: "Patience depends on more than hardware", editorial, *Guardian*, 13 September 1990, p. 18; Brian Walden, "Arab aspirations cry out for constant care and attention", op-ed, *Sunday Times*, 12 August 1990, Sect. 3, p. 4; Edward W. Said, "Fuelling the Arab fire next time", op-ed, *Observer*, 12 August 1990, p. 12.

104   "The Arab dimension", editorial, *Times*, 3 January 1991, p. 11.

105   "The dark clouds gather", editorial, *Sunday Times*, 30 December 1990, Sect. 1, p. 13.

106   Conor Cruise O'Brien, "Why Bush is treating Kuwait as a modern Pearl Harbour", op-ed, *Times*, 9 August 1990, p. 12.

107   Norman Macrae, "Disarm dictators to save us from the next Saddam", op-ed, *Sunday Times*, 10 February 1991, Sect. 1, p. 12.

108   Norman Macrae, "Short and sharp, here's a case for the Falklands treatment", op-ed, *Sunday Times*, 19 August 1990, Sect. 3, p. 4.

the Arab political regimes in the Gulf as "nasty" and "repressive".[109] However, a letter published in the *Observer* in August 1990 was instructive in that the reader referred to the construction of all Middle Eastern states after the First World War.[110] With the exception of a minority of editorials, opinion pieces and letters, there was thus a predominantly unfavourable position against Arab countries in the British press even if the *Times* and the *Guardian* adopted a less virulent tone than the *Sunday Times* in particular.

Unlike the *Washington Post*, British newspapers distinguished Arab leaders from their oppressed peoples.[111] By making readers aware of the plight of the Arab population, editorialists and journalists thus emphasized the moral and social aspects in their articles. The British press was thus more sympathetic towards the people of Arab countries than the American newspaper.

The four British newspapers also differed from the two American newspapers in that they published numerous opinion pieces and letters criticizing Western hypocrisy,[112] and particularly

---

109   Tony Greenstein, "The rules that Stalin knew – and Saddam doesn't", letters, *Guardian*, 11 August 1990, p. 18.

110   Vernon Hamilton, "Saddam and the Israeli myth", letters, *Observer*, 19 August 1990, p. 42.

111   For instance: "Saddam's bogus appeal", editorial, *Times*, 7 February 1991, p. 11; Barbara Amiel, "Let Iraq's true voice be heard", op-ed, *Sunday Times*, 3 March 1991, p. VIII; Adrian Hamilton, "Arabs will pay price of mixing oil and politics", op-ed, *Observer*, 19 August 1990, p. 15.

112   For example: Jim Sillars, "Keeping a grip on Gulf war aims", letters, *Times*, 24 January 1991, p. 15; Martin Woollacott, "The next move in the game", op-ed, *Guardian*, 13 August 1990, p. 19; Barbara Amiel, "Let Iraq's true voice be heard", op-ed, *Sunday Times*, 3 March 1991, p. VIII; Helga Graham, "Catherine wheel of calamity", op-ed, *Observer*, 26 August 1990, p. 10.

Britain's[113] foreign policy towards Arab countries and their arms sales to Middle Eastern states.[114] Nevertheless, the *New York Times* published articles by A. M. Rosenthal[115] about the sale of weapons to the Arab "tyrannies" and their "dictators" as well as the inertia of Western governments despite atrocity reports from the Middle East. The *Washington Post* also published articles by Jim Hoagland and Rowland Evans and Robert Novak on this subject.[116] However, on the whole, there were fewer articles on this topic published on the other side of the Atlantic than in the British press, which was thus more critical of Western power than the American press.

Moreover, some articles and letters in British newspapers also referred to Britain's colonial past and recounted the history of

---

113     For instance: Bernard Levin, "To lie, to creep, perchance to smarm, ay, there's the rub", op-ed, *Times*, 23 August 1990, p. 8; Frank Hooley, "Ceasefire sought to secure the Middle East", letters, *Guardian*, 24 January 1991, p. 20; Adrian Hamilton, "No future for FO yes men who got it wrong", op-ed, *Observer*, 5 August 1990, p. 18. Only the *Sunday Times* did not criticize its country on this subject.

114     Refer to Benedict Yeoman, "The crucial Palestinian link", letters, *Guardian*, 17 January 1991, p. 18; Denis MacShane, "Gotcha and jingoism", letters, *Sunday Times*, 2 September 1990, Sect. 3, p. 8; Denis Healy, "There's still time to escape Armageddon", op-ed, *Observer*, 6 January 1991, p. 16.

115     For example, A. M. Rosenthal, "Making a Killer", op-ed, *New York Times*, 5 August 1990, p. E 19; "The Goals of War", op-ed, *New York Times*, 23 August 1990, p. A 23. The *New York Times* also published the letter from M. T. Mehdi, President of American-Arab Relations Committee, "The New Saladin?", letters, *New York Times*, 23 September 1990, p. E 20. The author criticized American hypocrisy and wrote that "Arabs and Muslims view the American build-up as the continuation of traditional Western colonialism".

116     Refer to the following articles: Jim Hoagland, "The Tyrants on Our Side", op-ed, *Washington Post*, 1 November 1990, p. A 23; Rowland Evans and Robert Novak, "What Bush Has Opened", op-ed, *Washington Post*, 13 August 1990, p. A 11.

strained relations between the West and the Middle East.[117] For example, David Hirst argued in the *Guardian* that every Arab regime was the inheritor of the colonial order and that "existing policies of the region [...] have clung to the frontiers which their former colonial masters drew for them".[118] Likewise, a reader in the *Times* considered "former colonial Britain at the root of most of the present and past trouble in the Middle East".[119] British newspapers thus provided readers with a moral reflection on Britain's and the West's responsibility for the troubled situation in the Gulf States. By the same token, two journalists from the *Sunday Times* described Westerners' attitudes towards Arabs as racist: the former wrote that "many Westerners see Arabs as an inconsequential people, with unpleasant habits and beliefs";[120] the latter suggested that Westerners were not very enthusiastic about going to war to defend Arab countries, which "is a mild case of armchair racism".[121]

To sum up, with the exception of a few positive articles towards the Arab states, and despite a difference in the tone of the articles between the *Sunday Times* on the one hand and the other

---

117   For instance: "No holy war", editorial, *Times*, 17 January 1991, p. 13; Abdelrahman Munif, "Bitter fruit of power politics", op-ed, *Guardian*, 27 December 1990, p. 19; J. Mayers, "Gas-mask children get a lesson in courage. Beyond the pale", letters, *Sunday Times*, 17 February 1991, Sect. 1, p. 23; Vernon Hamilton, "Saddam and the Israeli myth", letters, *Observer*, 19 August 1990, p. 42.

118   David Hirst, "A lion among the gazelles", op-ed, *Guardian*, 3 August 1990, p. 17.

119   Tamara Adler, "UN diplomacy as Gulf option", letters, *Times*, 30 August 1990, p. 11.

120   Brian Walden, "How truth bites the dust when politicians go into the front line", op-ed, *Sunday Times*, 19 August 1990, Sect. 3, p. 4.

121   Barbara Amiel, "Letting a crocodile off the hook", op-ed, *Sunday Times*, 24 February 1991, p. 7.

newspapers on the other, most attitudes towards Arab countries in the American and British press were essentially negative. The unflattering portrait of Arab allies in the majority of articles seemed to be underpinned by an ethnocentric conception of Western superiority. The publication of contradictory opinions, which were mostly unfavourable to Arab countries, showed the pluralism of the newspapers. However, these points of view in the Gulf Crisis reinforced a range of standard ideological clichés about the Arab allies reminiscent of those about Saddam Hussein. These opinions showed journalists' negative attitudes towards Arab countries – towards the Other – and at the same time projected a positive image of the United States and Britain. Unlike the American press and in particular the *Washington Post*, British newspapers nevertheless invited their readers recall the colonial background. They distinguished the rulers of Arab countries from their people, and they above all railed against British and Western foreign policy towards Middle Eastern states.

## 2.2 The Soviet Union

### 2.2.1 The Soviet Union in the American press

As with the Arab countries, editorials, opinion articles and letters to the editor repeatedly referred to the Soviet Union. This is hardly surprising given that this country had been the United States' number one enemy during the Cold War confrontation[122]

---

122 These were geopolitical confrontations over Berlin, for example, or during the Korean and Indochina wars. During the East-West antagonism, the entire planet was used as a battleground between the indirect strategies of the United States and the Soviet Union, by setting up bases or alliances

between the two superpowers. And yet, like George Bush,[123] some editorials and opinion articles, which were published in both American newspapers from the beginning of August 1990, highlighted Soviet support for economic sanctions against Iraq,[124] its condemnation of the Iraqi invasion[125] and U.S. – Soviet cooperation.[126] They also emphasized the Soviet vote on resolutions on the U.N. Security Council.[127] The *New York Times* differed from the *Washington Post* by publishing more pro-Soviet editorials. In so doing, the newspaper seemed to agree with the American president's comments on the subject.

A few articles in the two American newspapers noted the "near-disintegration of the Soviet economy"[128] and stated in a

---

with various Third World states (Philippe Moreau Defarges, *op. cit.*, pp. 68, 173).

123    For example, refer to George Bush's news conference on 14 August 1990 about the Soviet condemnation of Iraq's "aggression" (<https://bush41library.tamu.edu/archives/public-papers/2162>); his remarks about the cooperation between the United States and the Soviet Union at a Fundraising Luncheon for Governor Mike Hayden in Topeka, Kansas (<https://bush41library.tamu.edu/archives/public-papers/2196>), and the Soviet Union-United States joint statement on the Persian Gulf Crisis of 9 September 1990 (<https://bush41library.tamu.edu/archives/public-papers/2206>, consulted 7 December 2021).

124    For example: "The Month that Shook the World", editorial, *New York Times*, 2 September 1990, p. E 12.

125    For instance: Robert D. Hormats, "A Bush Doctrine for the '90s'", op-ed, *Washington Post*, 28 August 1990, p. A 17.

126    For example: Gary Sick, "Hussein Must Be Stopped ...", op-ed, *New York Times*, 3 August 1990, p. A 27; "On a U.S. – Soviet Track", editorial, *Washington Post*, 31 January 1991, p. A 18.

127    Refer for example to the following article: "Use the *United* United Nations", editorial, *New York Times*, 15 August 1990, p. A 26.

128    Hobart Rowen, "Bush's Shift on Soviet Aid", op-ed, *Washington Post*, 20 December 1990, p. A 23.

neutral tone that the Soviet Union, "is no longer a superpower".[129] In contrast, a few editorials in the *New York Times*, the majority of those published in the *Washington Post* and most opinion articles published in both newspapers, especially from the beginning of September 1990, were particularly critical of the Soviet Union. For example, journalists reminded readers that Moscow had been Iraq's long-time ally.[130] Likewise, Paul H. Nitze, who was diplomat-in-residence at the John Hopkins University's School of Advanced International Studies at that time and had been a special adviser to the president and secretary of state on arms control in the Reagan administration, argued that the Soviet Union owned "strategic nuclear weapons targeted primarily against the U.S".[131] He also considered the collaboration between the United States and the USSR as "thin and uncertain". William Safire from the *New York Times* stood out with his biting remarks as he tried to revive the deep-seated distrust of the Soviet Union, which he accused of breaching the embargo against Iraq[132] and double gaming,[133] or when he described the Gorbachev regime as "mischievous".[134] There was also a hint of the Cold War in Henry Kissinger's ironic arguments in the *Washington Post* in September

129   Tom Wicker, "Politics and the Gulf", op-ed, *New York Times*, 9 September 1990, p. A 23.
130   "The World v. Saddam Hussein", editorial, *New York Times*, 25 August 1990, p. A 22.
131   Paul H. Nitze, "Leapfrog into Start II", op-ed, *New York Times*, 25 October 1990, p. A 27; Paul H. Nitze, "Getting the Good of this Crisis", op-ed, *Washington Post*, 26 August 1990, p. C 7. His articles were published in both American newspapers.
132   William Safire, "The Letter Rejected", op-ed, *New York Times*, 10 January 1991, p. A 25.
133   William Safire, "Forget about Gulfo", op-ed, *New York Times*, 6 September 1990, p. A 27.
134   William Safire, "Friends, More Than Interests", op-ed, *New York Times*, 7 February 1991, p. A 25.

1990 when he wondered whether it was "really wise to tempt a Soviet military role in the Middle East" and asked if that was "not like handing a drink to a reformed alcoholic".[135]

The two American newspapers thus presented readers with a range of different viewpoints in editorials and opinion articles and offered a rather acerbic portrait of the Soviet Union. Readers echoed this diversity of positions in their letters, either by praising the Soviet tough stand on Iraq,[136] or criticizing the Soviet Union.[137] Despite a few favourable editorials and opinion articles, it is surprising that there were so many negative comments about the country. Following the thawing of U.S.-Soviet relations thanks to Mikhail Gorbachev,[138] the Soviet leader at that time, a new geopolitical situation emerged and the Soviet Union ceased to be viewed as a major threat to the United States from then on.[139] The American president in his statements[140] emphasized the

---

135   Henry Kissinger, "The Dangers of Stalemate", op-ed, *Washington Post*, 30 September 1990, p. D 7.

136   For instance: Eduard Ryabtsev, "Why Moscow Must Walk the Tightrope in Iraq", letters, *New York Times*, 2 September 1990, p. E 12.

137   For example: Raju G. C. Thomas, "Let Arms-Sale Profits Aid Poor Countries", letters, *New York Times*, 14 October 1990, p. E 18.

138   Michel Mourre, *op. cit.*, pp. 993-994. Mikhail Gorbachev (1931-2022) had been the general secretary of the Communist Party of the Soviet Union from 1985 to 1991 before becoming president of the Soviet Union in 1990-91. He undertook radical reforms in the Soviet Union and agreed to the reunification of East with West Germany. He played a crucial role in ending the Cold War. Gorbachev was awarded the Nobel Peace Prize in October 1990. On 25 December 1991, Mikhail Gorbachev resigned as president of the Soviet Union, which was dissolved.

139   Unfortunately, the geopolitical situation in the world has completely changed since the Russian invasion of Ukraine on 24 February 2022.

140   Cf. Bush's remarks on the Soviet military intervention in Lithuania and a question-and-answer session with reporters on 13 January 1991 (<https://bush41library.tamu.edu/archives/public-papers/2619>). The American

unprecedented cooperation and partnership between the United States and the Soviet Union despite his concern about Soviet repression and use of force against the Baltic States in January 1991 and Gorbachev's peace proposal to Iraq in February 1991. However, most editorials and opinion articles took the opposite view. They chose to ignore the evolution of relations between the two superpowers. The events in the Gulf thus only served to revive the anxieties of the Cold War "Red Scare"[141] and to perpetuate ideological prejudices against the Soviet Union.

## 2.2.2 The Soviet Union in the British press

As in the American press, British newspapers published many articles about the Soviet Union. Since past events mark the history of a nation, it is possible that historical reasons, such as

---

president was "deeply concerned by the violence in the Baltics". Also refer to his exchange with reporters on the Soviet peace proposal for the Persian Gulf conflict on 19 February 1991 (<https://bush41library.tamu.edu/archives/public-papers/2715>, consulted 10 December 2021). On 18 February 1991 President Gorbachev offered a Soviet peace proposal to Iraqi foreign minister Tariq Aziz, which the Bush administration rejected (Susan Jeffords & Lauren Rabinovitz, eds., *op. cit.*, p. 318).

141    The "Red Scare" amounts to the fear of the rise of communism. The phrase is mostly used to refer to two periods in the history of the United States. The First Red Scare, which occurred after World War I, was prompted by the Russian Bolshevik revolution of 1917. The Second Red Scare took place during the early years of the Cold War and is known as McCarthyism, named after the Republican Senator Joseph R. McCarthy, who accused communists of infiltrating U.S. society and the federal government (David Weigall, *op. cit.*, pp. 190-191).

the Crimean War,[142] the Triple Entente,[143] the two World Wars of the 20th century or the Cold War, may explain the large number of articles about the Soviet Union. As in the case of the Arab countries on the British side, the *Times* stood out from other newspapers by publishing the most editorials about the USSR, which again shows the newspaper's interest in events taking place abroad. In addition, it was in the *Times* that more favourable editorials on the Soviet Union were published. For example, an editorial of 27 September 1990 described Moscow as "a vital partner in the Gulf".[144]

On the other hand, a larger number of opinion pieces about the Soviet Union were published in the *Guardian* and the *Observer*. The fact that both newspapers decided to devote numerous articles to the USSR during the Gulf Crisis and War, or that a significant number of journalists chose to take a stand about the country indicate the persistence of past and present obsessive fears about the Soviet Union. That also shows how much the collective unconscious remains fixed in its past certainties, especially in times of crisis, and also how difficult it is to change them.

In general, opinions about the Soviet Union were mixed in the editorials of the *Guardian* and the Sunday papers as well as in the opinion pieces of the four British newspapers. While there

---

142    From 1853 to 1856, this conflict opposed Russia on the one hand and Turkey, Britain, France and Sardinia on the other hand (Kenneth O. Morgan, ed., *op. cit.*, p. 562. Also refer to John Cannon, ed., *op. cit.*, p. 185).

143    In 1907 an agreement – an *entente* – was reached between Britain, Russia and France (David Reynolds, *op. cit.*, pp. 69, 72-73, 75, 80).

144    "The mood hardens", editorial, *Times*, 27 September 1990, p. 13.

were positive comments[145] about the USSR as in most editorials in the *Times*, a majority of unfavourable opinions were expressed in articles published in the British press. The assault by the Soviet army on "Baltic nationalism" in January 1991[146] and the Soviet peace plan to Iraq[147] attracted widespread criticism. Some articles reminded readers that the Soviet Union, "a waning superpower",[148] had been "Iraq's most important ally"[149] and "the biggest supplier of arms to Iraq".[150] Moreover, some journalists argued that the Soviet Union had not sent any soldiers to join the allied coalition forces.[151]

It was above all the resignation of Eduard Shevardnadze, the Foreign Minister of the Soviet Union in December 1990,[152] which triggered the most significant change in the attitude of some journalists and contributors towards the Soviet Union in the British press. For example, Jonathan Eyal, the director of

---

145    For instance, Paul Wilkinson in the *Guardian* referred to the "new spirit of co-operation between Washington and Moscow". Paul Wilkinson, "Olive branch over the abyss", op-ed, *Guardian*, 1 December 1990, p. 27.

146    "The Kremlin's deaf ear", editorial, *Times*, 12 January 1991, p. 11.

147    "Fighting for justice, not for power", editorial, *Observer*, 24 February 1991, p. 24.

148    "The UN is the fulcrum", editorial, *Guardian*, 4 October 1990, p. 18.

149    "The Russian card", editorial, *Sunday Times*, 30 September 1990, Sect. 3, p. 7.

150    David Owen, "Beware of a partial settlement", op-ed, *Observer*, 17 February 1991, p. 20.

151    For example, the article by Hugo Young, "What the war is still about", op-ed, *Guardian*, 21 February 1991, p. 20.

152    Eduard Shevardnadze was an effective proponent of the reform policies of glasnost and perestroika alongside President Gorbachev. He had forged a close working relationship with U.S. Secretary of State James Baker before the Gulf Crisis. Refer to the article by David Hoffman, "After the Fall of Shevardnadze – Resignation Leaves Superpowers with Unfinished Business", *Washington Post*, 21 December 1990 (<http://archive.seattletimes.com/arc hive/?date=19901221&slug=1110814>, consulted 18 December 2021).

studies at the Royal Services Institute in London at the time, speculated in the *Guardian* on the possible negative impact of Shevardnadze's resignation on U.S.-Soviet relations[153] and the solidarity of the international anti-Iraq coalition. The journalistic discourse thus returned to the dualistic rhetoric of the Cold War: the Soviet Union, an ally during the Persian Gulf Crisis, was once again perceived as a certainly diminished but very real threat whose influence could perhaps be strengthened in the Middle East after the war.

Favourable opinions towards the Soviet Union, particularly in the *Times* editorials and in a minority of articles in other newspapers, relayed the official position of the British government. Margaret Thatcher welcomed the Soviet Union's condemnation of the Iraqi invasion of Kuwait, the close U.S.-Soviet cooperation through Jim Baker and Eduard Shevardnadze, and, as a permanent member of the Security Council, its firm support for the United Nations resolutions.[154]

In summary, the British press presented readers with a plurality of viewpoints, the majority of which, with the exception of most

---

153    Jonathan Eyal, "Gorbachev sits on his fences", op-ed, *Guardian*, 28 February 1991, p. 21.

154    For example, refer to the Prime Minister's press conference in Washington on 6 August 1990 (<https://www.margaretthatcher.org/document/108175>), and her press conference on the Gulf situation on 21 August 1990 (<https://www.margaretthatcher.org/document/108176>, consulted 18 December 2021). Likewise, John Major praised the economic reforms brought about in the Soviet Union under Gorbachev's presidency (<https://johnmajorarchive.org.uk/1990/12/08/pmqt-4-december-1990/>). However, the Prime Minister deplored the Soviet repression in Vilnius (<https://johnmajorarchive.org.uk/1991/01/15/pmqt-15-january-1991/>, consulted 19 December 2021).

editorials in the *Times*, reinforced prejudices against the Soviet Union. On the other hand, echoing the official rhetoric, the *New York Times*, on the American side, and the *Times*, on the British side, seemed less hostile in their editorials to the Soviet Union – to the Other – than other commentators.

## 2.3 China

### 2.3.1 China in the American press

In contrast to the numerous articles published about the Soviet Union's attitude, there were few articles about China's conduct in the two American newspapers during the Gulf events. The bloody repression by the Chinese regime of student demonstrations in Tiananmen Square in 1989,[155] which undermined domestic American support for U.S. policy towards China, might explain the limited number of articles. Given the repressive nature of the Chinese government, which contrasted with U.S. concern for human rights in democracies, journalists might have decided not to focus on Sino-American relations[156] in the context of Gulf operations. It is also difficult to understand the reason for the absence of editorials on this subject in the *Washington Post*. Nevertheless, the newspaper published a larger number of opinion articles than the *New York Times* about China.

---

155 Henry Kissinger, *op. cit.*, 2001, pp. 141-142.
156 Diplomatic contact between the United States and China was restored in 1971 (*Ibid.*, p. 138). President Richard Nixon arrived in Beijing on 21 February 1972 for an eight-day visit to China. A joint communiqué, which was released on 27 February 1972, called for increased Sino-US contacts (Sarah Janssen, executive ed., *The World Almanac and Book of Facts 2021*, New York: World Almanac Books, 2020, p. 480).

Although President Bush "was offended [...] by the human rights abuse at Tiananmen Square",[157] he sought to keep the relationship between the United States and China "on some sort of even keel"[158] after the Tiananmen incident. This was reflected in his remarks on 1 March 1991[159] when he welcomed China's support for the U.N. resolutions against Iraq.[160] In contrast to the American president's comments, and with the exception of a minority of articles favourable to China,[161] the few articles published in the two newspapers were mostly critical of the country.[162] For example, an editorial in the *New York Times* described China as "a potentially hostile power".[163] Both newspapers also criticized the country for its nuclear arsenal[164] and took the American government to task

157   The American president referred to the events in Tiananmen Square in his exchange with reporters on 30 November 1990 (<https://bush41library.tamu.edu/archives/public-papers/2517>), and in a question-and-answer session on 6 February 1991 (<https://bush41library.tamu.edu/archives/public-papers/2691>, consulted 27 December 2021).

158   Henry Kissinger, *op. cit.*, 2001, p. 144.

159   Refer to the President's news conference on the Persian Gulf Conflict on 1 March 1991 (<https://bush41library.tamu.edu/archives/public-papers/2755>, consulted on 27 December 2021).

160   However, China abstained from voting on Resolution 678 of 29 November 1990. The resolution permitted members of the United Nations to use "all means necessary" to enforce the previous U.N. resolutions concerning Iraq if Iraq did not withdraw from Kuwait by 15 January 1991. See the United Nations document: <http://undocs.org/S/RES/678(1990)>, consulted 27 December 2021.

161   For example: "A U.S. Strategy for the Gulf Crisis", editorial, *New York Times*, 7 August 1990, p. A 18.

162   For instance: Jim Hoagland, "The Tyrants on Our Side", op-ed, *Washington Post*, 1 November 1990, p. A 23.

163   "Patriots Work. Star Wars Won't", editorial, *New York Times*, 3 February 1991, p. E 18.

164   For example: "War? Make the Case", editorial, *New York Times*, 4 November 1990, p. E 18; Richard Cohen, "Heading Off Iraq's Bomb", op-ed, *Washington Post*, 23 August 1990, p. A 25.

for its relations with China despite "the massacres in Tiananmen Square and Tibet".[165] Although this period was marked by China's economic expansion,[166] the small number of editorials and articles did not comment on this situation. On the other hand, the morality of its regime and that of the U.S. government were questioned in the American press. In addition to China's negative portrayal, most editorialists and journalists also projected the U.S. in a negative light, deviating from the positive image of the United States that they generally imposed on their readers in articles about the allies.

## 2.3.2 China in the British press

There were even fewer articles and letters in the British press than in the American press about China's conduct during the Gulf events which were published before the outbreak of hostilities in January 1991. They included an article in the *Guardian* by Rowan Williams, Professor of Divinity at Oxford at that time, and a letter from a reader of the *Times*, questioning the moral credibility of the Chinese government at the U.N. because of its

---

165 For instance: "Good Morning, Vietnam", editorial, *New York Times*, 10 March 1991, p. E 14. Also refer to the article by George F. Will, "Selective Morality", op-ed, *Washington Post*, 3 February 1991, p. C 7.

166 As early as 1979, China began decentralization and modernization reforms. It allowed foreign investment to boost its economy from the 1980s onwards. The Communist government expanded commercial ties to the West and the role of market forces. In 1986 negotiations to join the World Trade Organization (WTO) started (Pierre Bezbakh & Sophie Gherardi [dir.], *op. cit.*, p. 129; also refer to Sarah Janssen, executive ed., *op. cit.*, p. 676). "In the late 1980s, China began converting its growing economic resources into military power and political influence" (Samuel P. Huntington, *op. cit.*, p. 229).

actions in Tibet.[167] In his letter of 13 September 1990, the reader also referred to the Chinese government's behaviour "towards its own tragically brave students" in Tiananmen Square, which was also a topic addressed in the American press. Some editorialists and readers also criticized China for being an arms-exporting country.[168]

In contrast to these negative moral views, Norman Stone[169] in the *Sunday Times* noted Peking's opposition to Saddam Hussein, and David Owen[170] in the *Observer* recalled China's approval for the U.S. president's actions since the beginning of the Gulf Crisis. The journalist and the British politician thus relayed the position of Margaret Thatcher, who, on 1 and 17 September 1990,[171] emphasized that the five permanent members of the Security Council, including China, were able to work and act together.

These articles and letters thus offered readers a diversity of opinions about China with opposing views between the *Guardian* and the *Times* readers on the one hand, the *Sunday Times* and the

---

167    Rowan Williams, the 104th Archbishop of Canterbury from 2002 to 2012, "Onward Christian soldiers?", op-ed, *Guardian*, 1 November 1990, p. 19; H. J. Cross, "UN resolution", letters, *Times*, 13 September 1990, p. 15.

168    For instance: "Paying the price for past error", editorial, *Guardian*, 3 August 1990, p. 16; Ann Feltham, Janet Williamson, "Keeping up world pressure on Iraq", letters, *Times*, 23 August 1990, p. 9.

169    Norman Stone, "Heath, isolated and wrong, a clear essay in ineptitude", op-ed, *Sunday Times*, 23 September 1990, Sect. 3, p. 7.

170    David Owen, "A deadly game of chicken", op-ed, *Observer*, 13 January 1991, p. 14.

171    Refer to the Prime Minister's TV interview for AM *Frost on Sunday* on 1 September 1990 (<https://www.margaretthatcher.org/document/108186>), and her joint press conference with Czechoslovak President Vaclav Havel on 17 September 1990 (<https://www.margaretthatcher.org/document/108193>, consulted 30 December 2021).

*Observer* on the other. Nevertheless, due to the limited number of these articles and letters, it is not possible to draw any conclusions about the resulting image of Britain or whether the viewpoints expressed corresponded to the editorial lines of the newspapers – except for the *Guardian* – about China during the Gulf events.[172]

However, these few articles and letters show that the British press was interested in China not only because of its status as a member of the U.N. Security Council, but also for historical reasons: Macartney's trade mission to China at the end of the 18th century;[173] the Chinese Wars, also known as the Opium Wars in 1839-42 and 1856-60; the resulting Treaty of Nanking of 1842, which gave Britain Hong Kong and opened up five Chinese ports to British trade, as well as the Treaty of Tien-Tsin in 1858, which forced the Chinese authorities to open up more treaty ports and legalize the opium trade.[174] During the Korean War, Communist China helped North Korea by sending several hundred thousand "volunteers" in October 1950.[175] Finally, Queen Elizabeth II was the first British monarch to make a state visit to the People's Republic of China in 1986. These facts may help explain the presence, in the British press, of some articles and readers' reactions to China in the context of Gulf events.

---

172    Since there were no editorials in the *Times* and in the Sunday papers on China's attitude during the Gulf Crisis, it was difficult to draw any conclusions on this subject.

173    Jeremy Paxman, *op. cit.*, pp. 58-61.

174    John Cannon, ed., *op. cit.*, pp. 142-143, 452, 630.

175    General Sir Anthony Farrar-Hockley, *op. cit.*, pp. 1, 11-13, 21.

## 2.4    Japan and Europe

### 2.4.1  Japan and Europe[176] in the American press

Although articles on Japan and Europe were less numerous than those on the Arab countries, they were well represented in the American press during the Gulf Crisis and War and as such deserve attention. Some editorials and opinion articles praised the support of Japan[177] and the European countries[178] for Operation Desert Shield. But apart from these articles, the majority of editorials and opinion articles in the two American newspapers were vehemently critical of Japan and Europe in general and of Germany and France in particular. The arguments centred around several main themes.

First, in confirmation of what has been written about the strategic importance of oil[179] for the United States as well as for Japan and Europe, numerous editorials and opinion articles, mostly published before the outbreak of hostilities in both newspapers, highlighted the heavy dependence of Japan,[180]

---

176    This section does not refer to Britain, whose treatment in the American press will be covered in point 2.5.

177    For instance: "The Month that Shook the World", editorial, *New York Times*, 2 September 1990, p. E 12.

178    For example: Rowland Evans and Robert Novak, "Bush Backs Off …", op-ed, *Washington Post*, 5 October 1990, p. A 25.

179    Refer to point 4.4 in Chapter IV, Part III on the oil issue and more particularly to the dependence of Japan and Europe on imported oil.

180    While Jim Sasser, Democrat of Tennessee and chairman of the Senate Budget Committee in 1990, claimed in the *New York Times* that Japan imported 70% of its oil from the Persian Gulf, Robert J. Samuelson mentioned 63% in the *Washington Post* (see the following articles: Jim Sasser, "Is Uncle Sam Getting Stiffed?", op-ed, *New York Times*, 19 December 1990, p. A 25; Robert J. Samuelson, "Beyond the Price of Oil", op-ed, *Washington Post*,

Germany[181] and France[182] on oil imported from the Middle East, compared to the United States. These editorials and opinion articles recalled the major role played by the United States and deplored the fact that it had to assume a disproportionate share of the burden of protecting the oil that these countries[183] needed, accusing them of shirking their responsibilities in the Gulf despite their oil dependence.

In addition to this recurrent criticism against the European and Japanese allies, there was also the question of their military contribution and the accusation that they did not share this burden. In their articles published from the end of August to December 1990, editorialists[184] and journalists in both newspapers[185] demanded that European members of the coalition, and in particular France, should increase their military commitment by sending more ships and planes as well as more forces to Saudi Arabia alongside the American troops already deployed. It is doubtful whether the

---

7 August 1990, p. A 19). Since the senator and the journalist did not quote their sources, readers were not able to be sure of the accuracy of these percentages. According to the final report to Congress published in April 1992 on the conduct of the Persian Gulf War, Japan imported 12% of its annual oil needs from Iraq and Kuwait (p. 62, <http://www.globalsecurity. org/military/library/report/1992/cpgw.pdf>, consulted 9 January 2022). In other words, the percentages mentioned in both newspapers were not correct.

181    For example: Irving Kristol, "The Gulf: Born-Again Isolationists ...", op-ed, *Washington Post*, 22 August 1990, p. A 21.

182    For instance: Robert J. Samuelson, "Why We Should Stay in the Gulf", op-ed, *Washington Post*, 14 August 1990, p. A 21.

183    "Where's their Fair Share?", editorial, *New York Times*, 6 September 1990, p. A 26.

184    For example: "Loose Ends in Gulf Policy", editorial, *New York Times*, 30 August 1990, p. A 22.

185    For instance: Robert J. Samuelson, "Tired of Being the Superpower", op-ed, *Washington Post*, 19 December 1990, p. A 23.

journalists' reproaches to France were relevant given that as early as August 1990 this country had committed an aircraft carrier and the first units of the French Navy.[186]

On the other hand, and like George Bush,[187] both newspapers also referred to the constitutional constraints imposed on Japan and Germany by the Allies in 1945,[188] which prevented them from sending troops during the Gulf events.[189] For example, James Q. Wilson, Collins Professor of management and political science at UCLA at the time, reminded readers in the *Washington Post*[190] of the "powerful political and constitutional constraints" Japan and Germany faced "against sending military forces outside their borders".[191] In contrast to the neutral tone of the article in the *Washington Post*, a *New York Times* editorial ironically described this situation as "cynical kind of hair-splitting".[192] William Safire

---

186 The French troops that participated in Operation 'Daguet', which was led by General Roquejeoffre, were composed of 16,400 soldiers. The war materiel consisted of sixty fighter-bombers, one hundred and twenty helicopters, four hundred and forty-two armoured vehicles and fourteen ships (Yann le Pichon, *Guerre éclair dans le Golfe*, Paris: Jean-Claude Lattès/ADDIM, 1991, pp. 179, 190, 209).

187 Cf. George Bush's remarks and a question-and-answer session at a meeting of the Economic Club in New York on 6 February 1991 (<https://bush41library.tamu.edu/archives/public-papers/2691>, consulted 11 January 2022).

188 In July 1994 the German Constitutional Court approved the participation of Bundeswehr soldiers in peacekeeping missions. Similarly, Prime Minister Miyazawa (1991-1993) passed a law that allowed Japan to send troops to U.N.-led peace missions (Michel Mourre, *op. cit.*, pp. 37, 605).

189 Jean-Baptiste Duroselle & André Kaspi, *op. cit.*, p. 547.

190 James Q. Wilson, "Why We Are Fighting …", op-ed, *Washington Post*, 17 January 1991, p. A 21.

191 However, Germany sent military equipment, especially to Israel (Yann le Pichon, *op. cit.*, p. 186).

192 "Where's their Fair Share?", editorial, *New York Times*, 6 September 1990, p. A 26.

went further in the newspaper by blaming the two countries for hiding "behind a web of legalisms left over from defeat after World War II".[193]

It was mainly the economic argument, as noted earlier about the coalition, which was constantly repeated in articles published in the American newspapers. Editorialists, journalists and contributors criticized[194] Germany, Europe in general and Japan for their modest financial contribution despite their economic prosperity, arguing that the United States seemed to be paying "a disproportionate share of the costs of Desert Shield".[195] Editorials in the *New York Times* in particular echoed Americans' deep resentment against Japan's hesitation, "hemming and hawing",[196] and above all because of its financial and technological rise in 1990 as the United States's economic rival.[197] At that time, the

193 "The excuse offered [...]". William Safire, "Pacifism in the Pacific", op-ed, *New York Times*, 27 September 1990, p. A 23.

194 For example: "Where's their Fair Share?", editorial, *New York Times*, 6 September 1990, p. A 26; Lawrence J. Korb, "We Can Afford to Fight Iraq", op-ed, *New York Times*, 21 August 1990, p. A 27; Robert J. Samuelson, "Tired of Being the Superpower", op-ed, *Washington Post*, 19 December 1990, p. A 23.

195 "Paying for Desert Shield", editorial, *Washington Post*, 2 September 1990, p. B 6.

196 "Japan's leaders are hesitating". "Loose Ends in Gulf Policy", editorial, *New York Times*, 30 August 1990, p. A 22. "Faced with Washington's wrath, Japan stopped some of its hemming and hawing yesterday and pledged at least $1 billion for the multilateral effort in the Persian Gulf. But regrettably, Tokyo remains vague about its promises to help beleaguered frontline gulf states". "Tokyo's Share of World Leadership", editorial, *New York Times*, 31 August 1990, p. A 26.

197 Germany maintained a strong economic position due the quality and diversity of its industrial production despite the costs of the reunification in 1990 (Pierre Bezbakh & Sophie Gherardi [dir.], *op. cit.*, p. 62). As for Japan, "for nearly half a century after its defeat in the Second World War, [it] has concentrated on its economic revival, leaving security policy largely

United States was in the grip of serious economic difficulties. This fact could in part explain the scathing criticism levelled by editorialists and journalists at European and Japanese competitors who, in their opinion, were economically stronger than the United States, but who, according to the comments, contributed the least to the war effort. According to William Engdahl, U.S. Secretary of State James Baker went on a financial fund-raising mission, "extracting pledges from Germany, Japan, Kuwait and Saudi Arabia to guarantee a total of $54.5 billion to pay the costs" of Operation Desert Storm.[198] Given that Japan and Germany[199] paid one third of the war costs for Operations Desert Shield and Desert Storm,[200] it is questionable whether the arguments developed by these editorialists and journalists on this subject were valid. In their defence, it can be assumed that they were not in possession of the final figures and all the necessary information when they wrote their articles.

What is noteworthy is that all journalists' caustic comments on both the small financial and military contribution of the coalition members referred above all to the behaviour of these allies. For example, many journalists in the American press described the

---

to the United States [...]" (Henry Kissinger, *op. cit.*, 2001, p. 119). In 1991 Japan became the world's second largest economy behind the United States (Samuel P. Huntington, *op. cit.*, p. 87).

198    William Engdahl, *op. cit.*, p. 220.

199    The German contribution to the Gulf operations amounted to eighteen billion Deutsche Mark (Heinrich August Winkler, *Der Lange Weg nach Westen. Vom "Dritten Reich" bis zur Wiedervereinigung*, 2. Band, München: C. H. Beck, 2001, p. 626).

200    Refer to the final report to Congress on the Persian Gulf War, *op. cit.*, p. 725.

attitude of Japan, Germany, France and Europe as "reluctant"[201] during the Gulf events. Leslie H. Gelb in the *New York Times* argued that Japan, Germany and France ought to be ashamed of their insignificant war effort.[202] While William Safire in the *New York Times* blamed Japan and Germany for their unwillingness to contribute significantly,[203] the *Washington Post* emphasized Europe's lack of cohesion and in particular "the scattered and disorganized European response to the invasion of Kuwait [...]".[204] Finally, Robert J. Samuelson in the *Washington Post* judged the U.S. allies' behaviour in the Gulf crisis "shameful" and wondered whether Europe and Japan were really "our allies".[205]

As in the case of the USSR, the editorialists and journalists' attacks in the two American newspapers implicitly portrayed the United States as a country of valour that assumed its military and

---

201    For instance: "[...] the traditional reluctance of the Europeans and Japanese [...]". Kimberly Ann Elliott, "... And Sanctions Can Do the Trick", op-ed, *New York Times*, 3 August 1990, p. A 27. "Contrast this deep alliance with the off-and-on, reluctant, laced-with-conditions support of the French. Appeasement offered right up to the deadline; [...]". William Safire, "Friends, More Than Interests", op-ed, *New York Times*, 7 February 1991, p. A 25. "The reluctant industrial democracies – Japan and Germany included – [...]". Richard Harwood, "Pilgrims and the Gulf", op-ed, *Washington Post*, 26 August 1990, p. C 6.

202    Leslie H. Gelb, "To Fight in the Gulf?", op-ed, *New York Times*, 2 January 1991, p. A 17.

203    "At first it offered a billion-dollar tip for our trouble; when that was deemed niggardly, the Japanese begrudged three million more". William Safire, "Pacifism in the Pacific", op-ed, *New York Times*, 27 September 1990, p. A 23. "Germany has [...] skinflintily mailed in its pledge [...]". William Safire, "Friends, More Than Interests", op-ed, *New York Times*, 7 February 1991, p. A 25.

204    "Europe Rising", editorial, *Washington Post*, 24 December 1990, p. A 14.

205    Robert J. Samuelson, "Tired of Being the Superpower", op-ed, *Washington Post*, 19 December 1990, p. A 23.

moral obligations and supported the full weight of operations in the Gulf. The journalistic discourse reveals a simplistic dualism based on an oversimplified conception of relations between the United States and its allies. The Gulf Crisis thus reinforced prejudices against the allies. The antagonism between the United States, on the one hand, and Japan and Germany, on the other, can be explained by historical reasons since both countries were America's enemies during the Second World War and Germany was its enemy in the First World War. However, it seems more difficult to justify the hostile criticism of Europe in general and France in particular. In addition to the economic rivalry between the United States and Europe in 1990 and 1991, the enmity of editorialists and journalists[206] could be explained by the fact that the Europeans[207] and especially France[208] offered last-minute concessions and diplomatic solutions to Iraq. For example,

---

206 The following articles criticized European and French diplomatic initiatives: "The Larger Patriotism", editorial, *New York Times*, 10 January 1991, p. A 24; William Safire, "Don't Throw Away Victory", op-ed, *New York Times*, 31 January 1991, p. A 23; "No Tonkin Vote", editorial, *Washington Post*, 13 January 1991, p. C 6; Henry Kissinger, "A Dangerous Mirage", op-ed, *Washington Post*, 11 November 1990, p. B 7.

207 On 31 December 1990, the EEC "declared its readiness to resume dialogue with Iraq, which refused". On 4 January 1991, the EEC proposed the date of the 10th to meet the Iraqi minister. But Iraq refused to meet the twelve members. Nevertheless, on 18 December 1990, the EEC had replied in the negative to the Iraqi proposal to engage in dialogue (Yann le Pichon, *op. cit.*, p. 180-181, 183).

208 On 3 October 1990 François Mitterrand was the first head of state to go to the Gulf. At the Franco-Italian summit on 8 October 1990, the French president promoted the idea of an international conference on all the problems in the Gulf region, including the Palestinian question. On 4 December 1990, France said that it was in favour of an international conference for a comprehensive settlement of all the issues in the Gulf area. At the press conference of 9 January 1991, President Mitterrand declared that France would be seeking a diplomatic solution until the last hours of the ultimatum. On 14 January 1991, a six-point peace plan was proposed

Henry Siegman, the Executive Director of the American Jewish Congress, blamed the Europeans, including the French, in a letter to the *New York Times* for trying "to cut a Munich-like deal with Saddam Hussein at Israel's expense",[209] referring to the concept of 'appeasement' and the drama of the upcoming war. Moreover, the hostility of journalists[210] towards France might also have stemmed from the fact that France had been Iraq's second largest arms supplier after the Soviet Union.[211]

Unlike most editorials, opinion articles and letters published in both newspapers, the American president praised the attitude of Japan[212] and Europe[213] towards the application of economic sanctions against Iraq as well as the financial contribution of Japan and Germany[214] to the operations in the Gulf. In general, George

---

by France and rejected by the United States. This plan irritated London and Jerusalem (*Ibid.*, pp. 182-183).

209　Henry Siegman, "Limits of Sanctions", letters, *New York Times*, 24 February 1991, p. E 16. The reader's accusation against France's diplomatic initiative echoed the newspaper's unfavourable editorial on the subject in January 1991 ("The Larger Patriotism", editorial, *New York Times*, 10 January 1991, p. A 24). In any case, the Bush administration did not want to link the resolution of the Gulf Crisis to the Israeli Palestinian issue.

210　For instance: Henry Kissinger, "The Game Has Just Begun", op-ed, *Washington Post*, 19 August 1990, p. C 7.

211　William Engdahl, *op. cit.*, p. 214. Also refer to Alain Gresh & Dominique Vidal, *op. cit.*, pp. 25, 187. France had also sold two nuclear reactors to Iraq, one of which, Osirak, was destroyed by Israeli aircraft in June 1981.

212　For instance, refer to Bush's remarks and exchange with reporters on 6 August 1990 (<https://bush41library.tamu.edu/archives/public-papers/2144>, consulted 21 January 2022).

213　For example, refer to his remarks at a White House Briefing on the Persian Gulf Crisis on 28 August 1990 (<https://bush41library.tamu.edu/archives/public-papers/2185>, consulted 21 January 2022).

214　Cf. Bush's remarks and session with members of the regional news media on 17 September 1990 (<https://bush41library.tamu.edu/archives/public-papers/2231>, consulted 20 January 2022).

Bush paid tribute to the support of the European countries[215] and the diplomatic initiatives of the European Community[216] to find a peaceful solution to the Gulf Crisis. Similarly, in contrast to the comments in the American press, George Bush was unstinting in his praise of France[217] and in particular its steadfast position on Iraq, its financial contribution and military participation. The U.S. president also thanked President Mitterrand for the "extraordinary cooperation"[218] between the two countries and the major leadership role that the French played in the coalition. In summary, most editorials, opinion articles and letters published in both American newspapers diverged from the official rhetoric by their unfavourable comments on the Japanese, European, German and French allies.

---

215  For example, refer to the President's news conference on the Persian Gulf Crisis on 22 August 1990 (<https://bush41library.tamu.edu/archives/public-papers/2177>), as well as George Bush's address before a joint session of the Congress on the Persian Gulf Crisis on 11 September 1990 (<https://bush41library.tamu.edu/archives/public-papers/2217>, consulted 22 January 2012).

216  Cf. George Bush's news conference on the Persian Gulf Crisis on 9 January 1991 (<https://bush41library.tamu.edu/archives/public-papers/25605>, consulted 21 January 2022).

217  For instance, refer to Bush's news conference on 14 August 1990 (<https://bush41library.tamu.edu/archives/public-papers/2162>, consulted 22 January 2022).

218  For instance, refer to Bush's remarks prior to discussions with Foreign Minister Roland Dumas of France on 28 February 1991 (<https://bush41library.tamu.edu/archives/public-papers/2747>, consulted 22 January 2022).

## 2.4.2 Japan and Europe[219] in the British press

On the British side, newspapers were as negative as in the American press about Japan and Europe in general, Germany and France in particular. Nevertheless, some articles highlighted the support of Bonn and Paris for American policy in the Gulf.[220] They thus partly echoed the speeches of Margaret Thatcher and John

---

219 On 1 January 1973 Britain joined the European Community. In 1975 the referendum on Europe overwhelmingly confirmed British membership. However, British attitudes to the Common Market were governed after 1975 by "sullen hostility". By the late eighties, anti-Europeanism was diminishing. Nevertheless, the economic and political relationship with Europe remained a divisive issue within British public opinion and political parties (Kenneth O. Morgan, ed., *op. cit.*, pp. 654-655). Favourable to a Europe conceived as an area of free economic exchange, Margaret Thatcher was hostile to the project of a federal Europe, which was seen as a threat to Britain's sovereignty and independence. Her speech in Bruges on 20 September 1988, in which she set out her vision of Europe, was seen as a turning point and led to the birth of Eurosceptics in Britain. Margaret Thatcher's hostility to Britain's participation in the Exchange Rate Mechanism (ERM), or European Monetary Union (EMU) led to the resignation of Nigel Lawson on 26 October 1989 and Geoffrey Howe on 1 November 1990 (John Cannon, ed., *op. cit.*, p. 248). In contrast to Margaret Thatcher's negative attitude, John Major seemed to make progress in reconciling the divisions in the Conservative party over Europe (Kenneth O. Morgan, ed., *op. cit.*, p. 663).

220 For example, "History begins again", editorial, *Times*, 13 September 1990, p. 15.

Major about Japan, Europe,[221] Germany[222] and France[223] during the Gulf Crisis and War. Apart from this minority of articles, the majority of editorials, opinion pieces and letters in the British press were highly critical of these countries.

The British press covered more or less the same topics as the two American newspapers. For example, British newspapers,

221    For instance, at the press conference of 6 August 1990 ending Margaret Thatcher's visit to the U.S., the Prime Minister welcomed the strong support and condemnation of the European countries and Japan of the Iraqi invasion (<https://www.margaretthatcher.org/document/108175>, consulted 12 February 2022). On 18 December 1990 John Major also emphasized the degree of European unity on the application of economic sanctions against Iraq (<https://hansard.parliament.uk/Commons/1990-12-18/debates/d7161181-8d19-4533-a513-4054d6cc43c8/EuropeanCouncil(Rome)?highlight=sanctions#contribution-264644e8-5a3f-4929-8eb5-4fe587515ba5>; also refer to the Prime Minister's website: <http://www.johnmajor.co.uk/>, consulted 12 February 2022).

222    Refer for example to Margaret Thatcher's TV interview for TV-AM *Frost on Sunday* of 1 September 1990 about Germany's financial help in the Gulf (<https://www.margaretthatcher.org/document/108186>, consulted 14 February 2022). John Major also addressed the issue of Germany's financial contribution towards the cost of the forces in the Gulf (refer to the Prime Minister's Question Time from 29 January 1991 (<https://johnmajorarchive.org.uk/1991/01/29/pmqt-29-january-1991/>, consulted 12 February 2022).

223    Cf. Margaret Thatcher's statement in an article for *Inside the New Europe* on 19 October 1990 about the "rapid and decisive action" taken by Britain and France when it came to sending troops to the Gulf (<https://www.margaretthatcher.org/document/108225>, consulted 14 February 2022). John Major's statement on the European Council from 18 December 1990 referred to French ground forces stationed in the Gulf (<https://hansard.parliament.uk/Commons/1990-12-18/debates/d7161181-8d19-4533-a513-4054d6cc43c8/EuropeanCouncil(Rome)?highlight=sanctions#contribution-264644e8-5a3f-4929-8eb5-4fe587515ba5>, consulted 14 February 2022).

repeating Margaret Thatcher's remarks about Europe,[224] stigmatized "Europe's weak-kneed response in the Gulf"[225] and the lack of joint action and coherence of the various European countries. The *Sunday Times* differed from other newspapers in its more vehement attacks on Europe in a few editorials and opinion pieces. For instance, an editorial of 27 January 1991 referred to "the flabby European response" to the Iraqi invasion and argued that "Europe is lumbered with governments unable to rise to the demands of the Gulf Crisis".[226] Regardless of the virulent tone of the *Sunday Times*, British newspapers implied likewise that, unlike European countries, Britain was taking its responsibilities alongside the United States in the coalition against Iraq.

With the exception of the *Observer*,[227] British newspapers also emphasized the dependence of Japan,[228] Europe[229] and especially Germany[230] on imported oil from the Middle East. In so doing, the journalists concerned took their cue from Margaret Thatcher's

---

224 Despite her positive comments on European countries' support, the Prime Minister deplored the much slower and more patchy European response on 30 August 1990 (<https://www.margaretthatcher.org/document/108183>), as well as the lack of cohesion of Europe on 1 September 1990 (<https://www.margaretthatcher.org/document/108186>, consulted 21 February 2022).

225 For instance: "Summit without a cause", editorial, *Times*, 25 October 1990, p. 17.

226 "The shame of Europe", editorial, *Sunday Times*, 27 January 1991, Sect. 1, p. 11.

227 However, it cannot be argued that the oil dependence of European countries is not a major issue worthy of publication for the *Observer* since the Sunday paper discussed the extent of the Iraqi threat to the West's oil reserves.

228 For example: "Japanese jitters", editorial, *Times*, 23 August 1990, p. 9.

229 For instance: Hella Pick, "Sheltering behind a political fig-leaf", op-ed, *Guardian*, 21 August 1990, p. 15.

230 For example: Norman Stone, "War brings out the mouse in the Continent's wealthy giant", op-ed, *Sunday Times*, 27 January 1991, Sect. 1, p. 11.

comments on the subject.[231] In this context, Norman Stone in the *Sunday Times* stressed the "enormous burden" carried by the United States "for the sake of an oil-producing region that mainly benefits Germany and Japan".[232] As usual, the journalist's articles in the Sunday paper differed from editorials and opinion pieces in other newspapers in the mocking tone of their comments about both countries. British newspapers also referred to the financial contribution of Germany and Japan, which some editorials and opinion pieces in the *Times* and the *Sunday Times* considered too small.[233]

In addition, the British press also emphasized the economic power of Germany, described as "an ungrateful economic giant"[234] and that of Japan, considered as a commercial threat by the United States.[235] Journalists used the argument of the economic dominance of these two countries to further highlight the inadequacy of their financial contribution. Moreover, some journalists from the *Times* and the *Sunday Times* criticized

---

231 The Prime Minister underlined the fact that "Europe is much more dependent than the United States on oil from the Gulf for its industries and its prosperity" in an article for *Inside the New Europe* on 19 October 1990 (<https://www.margaretthatcher.org/document/108225>, consulted 22 February 2022).
232 Norman Stone, "Will the new Germany play in tune with its old enemies?", op-ed, *Sunday Times*, 16 September 1990, Sect. 3, p. 7.
233 For example: "Europe engulfed", editorial, *Times*, 24 January 1991, p. 15; Martin Fletcher, "Glory restored, but what of the cost?", op-ed, *Times*, 23 August 1990, p. 8.
234 For instance: "Economic giant". Hella Pick, "Gulf angst in Germany", op-ed, *Guardian*, 31 January 1991, p. 19.
235 For example: "Renaissance in danger. Mutual suspicion", editorial, *Observer*, 9 December 1990, p. 18.

Germany for having sent "obsolete East German military equipment".[236]

As in the American press, British newspapers referred to the institutional constraints on Germany and Japan forbidding them to deploy troops abroad. While most comments conveyed this information to their readers in a neutral tone,[237] the *Times* accused both countries of being "glad to shelter behind [their] constitutional difficulty in sending troops overseas".[238]

In addition to the legal argument concerning Germany and Japan, the British Sunday papers in particular blamed Germany[239] for having sold chemical weapons and nuclear technology to Iraq, as well as France[240] for its "sleazy" arms sales and for having supplied nuclear material to Saddam Hussein.

But it is above all the attitude of France and Germany that the British press criticized strongly. Several themes emerge from the review of articles and letters. For example, the *Times* argued that both countries did not like to be seen "to support American policy

---

236     For instance: Daniel Johnson, "Old fires lick at Germany", op-ed, *Times*, 24 January 1991, p. 14; Norman Stone, "War brings out the mouse in the Continent's wealthy giant", op-ed, *Sunday Times*, 27 January 1991, Sect. 1, p. 11.
237     For instance: "Patience is still the best course", editorial, *Guardian*, 23 August 1990, p. 18.
238     "Europe engulfed", editorial, *Times*, 24 January 1991, p. 15.
239     For instance: Adrian Hamilton, "The Axis should be powers of peace, not war", op-ed, *Observer*, 11 November 1990, p. 18.
240     For example: Norman Macrae, "Western gun-peddlers hold the key to a lasting peace in Araby", op-ed, *Sunday Times*, 20 January 1991, Sect. 2, p. 4; Simon Hoggart, Column, op-ed, *Observer*, 13 January 1991, p. 14.

too readily".[241] Likewise, David Hughes in the *Sunday Times* described Germany's response in the Gulf as slow and small.[242] On the whole, most articles in the *Sunday Times* were hostile to Germany and France.

Furthermore, some journalists speculated about the possible behaviour of France. For instance, David Owen in the *Observer* described the country as "a very unreliable ally" and argued that "every day after 15 January that the military option is delayed, it is more likely that the French will equivocate".[243] Editorials in British newspapers were generally moderate in tone. However, some journalists like Michael Jones and Norman Macrae in the *Sunday Times* made some derogatory and contemptuous remarks about France. For example, Michael Jones ironically described Mitterrand's peace initiative as "an opera bouffe"[244] in an article of 20 January 1991. Similarly, Norman Macrae criticized France for wanting to organize a "Saddam-rewarding Middle East peace conference" and accused the country of having sought to "escape from a domestic military shame by seeking to sell a few more Jews down the river. Dreyfus, Laval, Mitterrand".[245] This

---

241 "Pusillanimous partners", editorial, *Times*, 31 January 1991, p. 13.

242 David Hughes, "Will the Gulf factor do for Mr Kinnock?", op-ed, *Sunday Times*, 12 August 1990, Sect. 3, p. 2.

243 David Owen, "A deadly game of chicken", op-ed, *Observer*, 13 January 1991, p. 14.

244 Michael Jones, "War sounds a retreat from Brussels", op-ed, *Sunday Times*, 20 January 1991, Sect. 3, p. 2.

245 Norman Macrae, "Western gun-peddlers hold the key to lasting peace in Araby", op-ed, *Sunday Times*, 20 January 1991, Sect. 2, p. 4. In 1894 Alfred Dreyfus (1859-1935), a French army officer of Jewish origin, was wrongly accused of selling military secrets to the Germans. He was convicted and sentenced to life imprisonment. The Dreyfus Affair became an extremely divisive issue in France. In 1906 a civilian court of appeals overturned Dreyfus's previous convictions and exonerated him. Pierre

historical reminder enabled the journalist to express his disdain for France and, implicitly and in contrast, to highlight the heroic behaviour of Britain, particularly during the Second World War and the events in the Gulf, as a country that did not accept any compromise with the enemy.

In connection with the hostages case, which was widely reported in the American and British press,[246] a few articles in the *Guardian* and the *Observer* referred to French and German initiatives to free their nationals used as "human shields" at strategic sites. These interventions gave rise to mixed comments. For example, Hella Pick in the *Guardian* questioned France's action and the Brandt mission to Iraq, which angered Britain.[247] By contrast, readers of the newspaper praised both countries for their efforts.[248] While readers' comments were an exception, the journalist's remarks were consistent with Margaret Thatcher's disapproval of some European countries for sending emissaries to Iraq to obtain the release of their nationals.[249]

---

Laval (1883-1945), a French politician and statesman, served in Pétain's collaborationist government during World War II. In 1945 he was tried for treason and executed. François Mitterrand (1916-1996), the president of France from 1981 to 1995, was captured by the Germans in 1940. After escaping in late 1941, he served under the collaborationist Vichy Regime before joining the Resistance in 1943 (Michel Mourre, *op. cit.*, p. 748).

246    Refer to point 1.8 in Chapter I, Part III on this subject.

247    Hella Pick, "Sheltering behind a political fig-leaf", op-ed, *Guardian*, 21 August 1990, p. 21; Hella Pick, "Hurd following the instinct to roam", op-ed, *Guardian*, 8 November 1990, p. 21.

248    For example: T. Kaliski, P. J. Barr, G. Loretan, G. R. Sims, "British hostages paying the president's price", letters, *Guardian*, 6 December 1990, p. 18.

249    Cf. Thatcher's interview for the *Sunday Times* on 15 November 1990 (<https://www.margaretthatcher.org/document/107868>, consulted 28 February 2022).

Lastly, some articles in the *Times* and the *Sunday Times* reported on the protest demonstrations in Germany against the war. For example, Norman Stone in the *Sunday Times* accused the country of having let down the allies and advised its protesters "to wake up and grow up".[250] That the *Sunday Times* condemned the German protesters was hardly surprising since both the Sunday paper and the *Times* supported the British government's policy[251] during the Gulf events. It is also possible that the *Sunday Times* could not imagine anyone daring to question the wisdom of the American and British operations in Kuwait. As in the American press, the reference to the protests that took place in Europe remained marginal as only these two newspapers devoted several articles to it.[252] Unlike the *Times* and the *Sunday Times*, the *Guardian* and the *Observer* did not seem to be interested in the demonstrations in their editorials and opinion pieces, perhaps to avoid making things even more confrontational.

In summary, apart from a few positive articles on Europe, France, Germany and Japan, the majority of articles in the four British newspapers were unfavourable to these allies in the press on this side of the Atlantic. The *Sunday Times* differed from other newspapers as its language was catchier and its attacks more virulent. However, British newspapers generally covered similar themes: the lack of cohesion and unanimity among the various European countries; their dependence, as well as that of Japan, on oil from the Middle East; the financial contribution

---

250   Norman Stone, "War brings out the mouse in the Continent's wealthy giant", op-ed, *Sunday Times*, 27 January 1991, Sect. 1, p. 11.
251   Both newspapers also supported the Thatcher's government throughout the miners' strike in 1984-85 (Roy Greenslade, *op. cit.*, pp. 384, 388).
252   Only a few articles, most of which were published in the *New York Times*, referred to anti-war demonstrations in the United States.

of Germany and Japan, which was deemed insufficient despite their flourishing economies; the arms sales to Iraq by German and French firms, or even the delayed and diffuse reactions of the European allies. Journalists from the *Times* and the *Sunday Times* castigated Germany for sending obsolete military equipment and accused both Germany and Japan for invoking constitutional restrictions to avoid sending military forces. The Sunday papers blamed France for having delivered military technology to Iraq. Moreover, some journalists from the *Guardian* and the *Observer* criticized France and Germany for their diplomatic initiatives in favour of the hostages. There was a common denominator about the topics addressed either in the four British newspapers or only in the Sunday papers, namely their repetition in articles published throughout the Gulf Crisis and the hostilities, which thus increased the persuasive force of the journalistic narrative. The positions taken by the newspapers, and in particular the sometimes hypothetical and at times ironic opinions of the *Sunday Times* towards Europe as a whole,[253] followed the editorial line of each of the newspapers.

---

253  According to Roy Greenslade, the four British newspapers each in their own way were in favour of Britain's entry into the European Economic Community (EEC) in 1973. The *Times* was "overtly, massively, and sometimes broodingly pro-entry". The *Guardian* was among the first to urge British entry into the EEC. The *Sunday Times* and the *Observer* were "all ashamed Common Market fans" (Roy Greenslade, *op. cit.*, pp. 292-293). The British referendum on whether to remain in the European Economic Community took place on 5 June 1975. Jeremy Tunstall argues that "every single daily newspaper [...] carried more positive than negative EEC stories" (Jeremy Tunstall, *op. cit.*, p. 344). As Europe changed over the years, it became a bone of contention in Britain. Just as political parties' views changed, so too did the newspapers' stance, which realigned after Margaret Thatcher's Bruges speech in September 1988. Several newspaper owners like Rupert Murdoch, Conrad Black and Lord Rothermere were strongly opposed to further European integration of Britain and to the

Finally, there were similar subjects in the American and British press. The economic, energy-related, legal and military comments were mostly aggressive towards Japan, Europe, Germany and France, such as, for example, on the American side, in the articles by William Safire in the *New York Times*, and, on the British side, in the *Sunday Times*, and therefore they diverged from the official statements on both sides of the Atlantic. The critical arguments of the newspapers in question were thus akin to subjective moral judgments that confirmed prejudice against these countries.[254] Above all, they enabled the editorialists and journalists concerned to reinforce, in the American press, the image of the United States as an exemplary and responsible country and, on the other hand, to highlight, in the British press, the role and importance of Britain compared to those of their allies within the coalition.[255]

---

Maastricht Treaty negotiated in December 1991 (Roy Greenslade, *op. cit.*, p. 613). The *Times* under Charles Douglas-Home took a "sharp right-wing turn". He was the editor-in-chief of the daily paper from 1982 to 1985 and a Tory, who endorsed Thatcher's policies (*Ibid.*, p. 384). When Nigel Lawson, the Chancellor of the Exchequer who favoured joining the European Monetary System, resigned in October 1989, the *Times* "in its leading column" displayed its loyalty to Margaret Thatcher "before sensible analysis of what had happened" (Graham Stewart, *op. cit.*, p. 345). A few years later, the *Guardian* expressed reservations about Britain's joining monetary union and endorsement of the Euro (see the leader of 31 December 1998, "The Euro has landed", published on 31 December 1998: <http://www.guardian.co.uk/world/1998/dec/31/euro.eu>, consulted 18 February 2022).

254  Many editorialists and journalists might have felt that the United States was carrying out a role which should have been more strongly supported by its allies. See part IV on the subject.

255  Reference is made to Part IV, Chapter II, point 2.2 on Britain's role during the Gulf Crisis and War.

## 2.5 Britain in the American press

In contrast to the many critical remarks about the European countries in the U.S. press, the majority of editorials and opinion articles about Britain in the two American newspapers were positive. Articles thus showed a trend away from negative articles on the other European allies. Favourable comments on Britain, which had plainly sided with the United States, addressed several dominant themes.

First of all, a number of opinion articles and a few letters[256] published especially in the *Washington Post* set the issue in its historical context. These articles and letters reminded readers of Britain's role in the Middle East in the colonial era and in particular the division of the territories of the Ottoman Empire and the establishment of most existing borders by the British.[257] Most articles on this subject referred to these historical facts in a neutral tone. Nevertheless, a few journalists in the *Washington Post* used them to shed some harsh light on Britain's policy in the early 20th century, described by Rowland Evans and Robert Novak as "the hated colonial era",[258] with the partition of the

---

256    For instance: Erwin Knoll, "Why the Rush to War?", op-ed, *New York Times*, 8 November 1990, p. A 35; Jim Hoagland, "Force Hussein to Withdraw", op-ed, *Washington Post*, 7 August 1990, p. A 19; Vera Beaudin Saeedpour, "What Britain Sowed, Iraq and U.S. Now Reap", letters, *New York Times*, 23 September 1990, p. E 20.
257    Throughout the 19th century, Britain settled in the Middle East. The Sykes-Picot Agreement, which was a 1916 secret convention between Britain and France, dismembered the Ottoman Empire into areas of British and French control (Alain Gresh & Dominique Vidal, *op. cit.*, p. 218; also refer to Fred Halliday, *100 Myths about the Middle East*, London: SAQI, 2005, p. 102).
258    Rowland Evans and Robert Novak, "The Arab Solution", op-ed, *Washington Post*, 29 August 1990, p. A 25.

region by Britain and France having, according to Jim Hoagland, frustrated Arabs.[259] The negative remarks of these journalists were, however, the exception in the published articles.

In addition to these articles, some editorials and opinion articles echoed the U.S. president's words[260] and paid tribute to Margaret Thatcher[261] when she was ousted by the Conservative Party in November 1990 as Prime Minister and to the "special relationship" between the United States and Britain.[262] Numerous articles praised Britain as a loyal ally of the United States.[263] Editorialists and journalists also emphasised the significant military contribution of the British.[264]

---

259    Jim Hoagland, "A Real Arab Reawakening", op-ed, *Washington Post*, 16 August 1990, p. A 23.
260    For example, refer to Bush's exchange with reporters near Dharan, Saudi Arabia on 22 November 1990 (<https://bush41library.tamu.edu/archives/public-papers/2486>, consulted 8 March 2022).
261    For instance: "After Mrs. Thatcher", editorial, *New York Times*, 23 November 1990, p. A 36; "Mrs. Thatcher Departs", editorial, *Washington Post*, 25 November 1990, p. C 6. Refer to point 3.3.1 in Chapter III, Part IV concerning the Falklands War and more particularly to the articles in the American press about Margaret Thatcher and the conflict.
262    For instance: William Safire, "Friends, More Than Interests", op-ed, *New York Times*, 7 February 1991, p. A 25; Henry Kissinger, "Thatcher Still Leads the Way", op-ed, *Washington Post*, 2 December 1990, p. C 7.
263    For example: "Mrs. Thatcher's Lengthened Shadow", editorial, *New York Times*, 28 November 1990, p. A 20; Jeane Kirkpatrick, "A Puzzle in the Gulf ...", op-ed, *Washington Post*, 1 October 1990, p. A 15.
264    For instance: "Escalation, 1990 Style", editorial, *New York Times*, 27 October 1990, p. A 22; John Keegan, "How the War Was Won", op-ed, *Washington Post*, 3 March 1991, p. C 7. According to the National Army Museum, the Gulf War saw the "largest single deployment of British troops" since World War II. About 35,000 British servicemen and women with 13,000 vehicles served in the war against Iraq (<www.nam.ac.uk/explore/gulf-war>, consulted 10 March 2022).

These observations deserve some additional comments. On the one hand, there is a correspondence between the laudatory articles in both American newspapers about Britain and what the U.S. president said about the country.[265] On the other hand, in addition to a majority of editorials and opinion articles praising Britain, the American press put Britain and the United States on an equal footing. This confirms the explanations advanced in this study for the parallelism in the description of the enemy in American and British editorials.[266] In addition to sharing a common language and culture, the existence of historical ties between the two countries and the close relationships between the leaders of the United States and Britain, which have certainly amplified the strength of the "special relationship",[267] it could be suggested that the fact that Margaret Thatcher was the first to declare her support for George Bush in the campaign against Saddam Hussein[268] strengthened the "special relationship" more concretely than in ordinary times. According to Paul Vaiss, Margaret Thatcher impressed the President and his administration so much that they invited her to the White House for a meeting on measures to take against Iraq.[269] The British Prime Minister – Margaret Thatcher through her attitude and John Major because of Britain's strong military involvement – cemented Anglo-American relations. While German reunification had led to a rapprochement between

---

265  For example, refer to George Bush's remarks on the Persian Gulf Crisis on 14 September 1990 (<https://bush41library.tamu.edu/archives/public-papers/2229>, consulted 11 March 2022).

266  Refer to the conclusion about the enemy.

267  Paul Vaiss, *op. cit.*, p. 164.

268  Margaret Thatcher was in Aspen, Colorado at the time of the announcement of the invasion of Kuwait. She had been invited "to give a lecture on defence issues" (*Ibid.*, p. 149).

269  *Ibid.*, p. 149.

the United States and Germany[270] and as there was no longer a Soviet threat "requiring Britain to be the alliance standard-bearer in Europe for the Americans",[271] the principal reason for the special relationship had gone. However, the events in the Gulf revived the privileged link between the United States and Britain.[272] To sum up, because of their common interests and shared enemy, the United States treated Britain as an equal partner during the Gulf Crisis and War, which was reflected in most articles in the two American newspapers.

## 2.6    The United States in the British press

The British press published more articles about the United States than about any other ally from August 1990 to mid-March 1991. American leadership of the coalition and operations in the Gulf as well as British interest in the United States by virtue of the ties between the two countries and the "special relationship" largely explain the considerable number of articles about the United States in British newspapers.[273] These articles were as

---

270    Jérôme Élie, "L'Unification allemande et les relations anglo-américaines: première crise d'après-guerre froide de la relation spéciale", *Relations Internationales*, No. 120, hiver 2004, p. 434. While Margaret Thatcher was reluctant to accept the prospect of German unification because of a possible downgrading of British influence (p. 438), the United States was in favour of German unification while ensuring the preservation of its interests (p. 439).

271    John Dickie, *"Special" No More. Anglo-American Relations: Rhetoric and Reality*, London: Weidenfeld & Nicholson, 1994, p. xiv.

272    *Ibid.*, p. xiv. Nevertheless, Washington informed London of its decision to end the Gulf War without prior consultation (Ritchie Ovendale, *op. cit.*, 1998, p. 154).

273    For example, Andrew Stephen's column in the *Observer* referred to the United States, reflecting the importance of American politics and society to

much about U.S. foreign policy decisions in the Middle East before and during the events as they were about the U.S. economy and domestic policy, such as the mid-term elections in November 1990.[274]

In contrast to the negative attitudes towards the European, French, German and Japanese allies, the majority of editorials and opinion pieces published in the daily newspapers and the *Sunday Times* were favourable to the United States. In the *Observer*, however, although the editorials were also supportive of the Americans, most of its opinion pieces were critical of the United States. This was also the case of letters published in newspapers, which were on the whole unfavourable to the Americans and therefore opposed to the editorial line of British newspapers, thus providing further proof of their readiness to publish dissenting views.[275] Only the *Sunday Times* published as many positive as negative letters about the United States during the Gulf Crisis and War.

Articles in favour of the United States were organized around several main themes. From the beginning of the crisis until after the hostilities, editorials and opinion pieces emphasized the military power of the United States,[276] which was described for example

---

 the newspaper and its readers. It was also in the *Observer* that most articles about the United States were published from August 1990 to mid-March 1991.

274 The vote for the renewal of one third of the U.S. Senate and House of Representatives took place on 6 November 1990.

275 Michael Parsons wonders whether "pluralism is always genuine and fair" and whether "there are not sometimes cases where a few contrary articles are included just to pay lip service to the idea of impartiality".

276 For instance, Peter Stothard argued that the United States was "the world's greatest military power". Peter Stothard, "Is the real George Bush resolute

as the "reigning global superpower"[277] in the *Sunday Times* and "the most powerful nation in the world"[278] in the *Guardian*. Many articles also praised America's leadership[279] and its handling of the Gulf Crisis and War. In the same vein, a large number of articles paid tribute to Bush's "quiet determination" in countering Iraqi aggression, his firm leadership of the international coalition as well as his statesmanlike decisions in the Gulf.[280] Since the leader of a nation represents the country and the people who have elected him, he therefore promotes the image of his country.[281]

In addition, there were a few comments that lauded the quick reaction of the United States following the invasion of Kuwait,[282] American diplomacy,[283] public debates and Congressional hearings

---

enough for war?", op-ed, *Times*, 21 September 1990, p. 12.

277    For example: "The thief of Baghdad", editorial, *Sunday Times*, 5 August 1990, Sect. 3, p. 7.

278    "No easy options", editorial, *Guardian*, 21 August 1990, p. 14.

279    For example: "Regional peace in Africa", editorial, *Times*, 13 August 1990, p. 11.

280    For instance: "When to stop", editorial, *Times*, 28 February 1991, p. 13; "Patience depends on more than hardware", editorial, *Guardian*, 13 September 1990, p. 18; "Stopping Saddam", editorial, *Sunday Times*, 12 August 1990, Sect. 3, p. 5; "Squeeze the man, not the trigger", editorial, *Observer*, 12 August 1990, p. 12.

281    Similarly, the personality of a nation's leader determines the relationships between his or her country with other countries. For example, Adrian Hamilton noted in the *Observer* that Margaret Thatcher had taken to President Ronald Reagan rather than President Bush, who did not know how to flatter her (Adrian Hamilton, "No Future for future FO yes men who got it wrong", op-ed, *Observer*, 5 August 1990, p. 18).

282    For instance: Norman Macrae, "Freedom could drown in a sea of sand", op-ed, *Sunday Times*, 21 October 1990, Sect. 3, p. 6.

283    For example: "Withdraw or fight", editorial, *Times*, 1 December 1990, p. 17.

in the United States on its involvement in the Gulf,[284] as well as its management of the media[285] during the hostilities. These articles presented the United States as a model for the British government and readers to follow. The systematic repetition of arguments in favour of the United States was part of a real rhetoric of persuasion. It goes without saying that articles in the British press endorsing the war against Iraq supported U.S. actions in the Gulf for seven months. In addition, positive comments in the newspapers about the United States in part echoed what Margaret Thatcher[286] and John Major[287] had said.

On the whole, numerous articles in the *Times* and the *Sunday Times*,[288] as well as a few articles in the *Guardian* and the *Observer*[289] that presented an ideal image of the coalition leader,

---

284    For instance: Hugo Young, "One man and world tragedy", op-ed, *Guardian*, 3 January 1991, p. 15.

285    "War in the open", editorial, *Times*, 21 January 1991, p. 11; Georgina Henry, "Rights of access to the action", op-ed, *Guardian*, 8 January 1991, p. 17.

286    Refer for example to her speech to the European Democrat Union Conference on 30 August 1990 (<https://www.margaretthatcher.org/document/108183>, consulted 7 April 2022).

287    Cf. John Major's statement on the Gulf War to the House of Commons on 17 January 1991 (<https://hansard.parliament.uk/Commons/1991-01-17/debates/e77492a9-dee0-487f-8964-6824f654845e/The Gulf?highlight=just%20war#contribution-ce2c66f9-61bb-472e-bddd-155232931ec9>, consulted 7 April 2022).

288    For example: "Desert calm", editorial, *Times*, 1 March 1991, p. 15; "Britain at war", editorial, *Sunday Times*, 20 January 1991, Sect. 2, p. 5; Peter Stothard, "Hard facts for the special relation", op-ed, *Times*, 20 December 1990, p. 10; David Hughes, "Will the Gulf factor do for Mr Kinnock?", op-ed, *Sunday Times*, 12 August 1990, Sect. 3, p. 2.

289    For instance: Douglas Hurd, "Why Kuwait isn't Lithuania", op-ed, *Guardian*, 24 January 1991, p. 21; Andrew Stephen, "Bush caught in jam as conflict hits gridlock", op-ed, *Observer*, 30 September 1990, p. 17.

put Britain on a par with the United States and, as noted earlier,[290] emphasized the importance of Britain's role as its staunch ally. In this way, British editorialists and journalists were able to convince readers of the need to support the United States, asserting the wisdom of sending British soldiers to Saudi Arabia to fight alongside American troops and affirming the strength and value of the Anglo-American "special relationship".

In contrast, most opinion pieces in the *Observer*,[291] but also the majority of readers' letters in all four newspapers,[292] as well as a few articles in the *Times*,[293] the *Guardian*[294] and the *Sunday Times*[295] were critical of the decisions taken by George Bush and the American government in the Gulf from August 1990 to mid-March 1991. For example, Andrew Stephen in the *Observer* described George Bush in October 1990 as arrogant and

---

290 Refer to the perception of Britain's role in British newspapers alongside the United States during the Gulf Crisis and War.

291 For example: Andrew Stephen, "You ain't seen nothing yet – more's the pity", op-ed, *Observer*, 28 October 1990, p. 15.

292 For instance: E. P. Carlisle, Captain, "Limits of UN resolution on embargo against Iraq", letters, *Times*, 16 August 1990, p. 11; Sir Frederic Bennett, "Morality and legality on trial in the Gulf crisis", letters, *Guardian*, 30 August 1990, p. 18; L. P. Watkinson, "Broken beat from the drums of war", letters, *Observer*, 16 December 1990, p. 66. However, the *Sunday Times* only published a letter by John Whitbeck criticizing American policy in the Gulf: John Whitbeck, "Gotcha and jingoism. Aggression", letters, *Sunday Times*, 2 September 1990, Sect. 3, p. 8.

293 For instance: Michael Howard, "Gulf: no time for sanctions to bite", op-ed, *Times*, 2 January 1991, p. 10.

294 For example: "A sensible matter for real debate", editorial, *Guardian*, 5 December 1990, p. 20.

295 Refer to "A president adrift", editorial, *Sunday Times*, 21 October 1990, Sect. 3, p. 7.

"dangerous".[296] Similarly, John Berger in the *Guardian* denounced "Washington's deafness concerning the Middle East" and the fact that since the beginning of the Gulf Crisis, "American power" had been "deaf to the experience of the Arab peoples".[297] In addition to these comments, which also opposed armed intervention against Iraq, there were some articles and letters in the *Guardian*[298] and the *Observer*[299] that blamed the British government for dancing to Washington's tune.

Some journalists advanced apparently contradictory arguments that could lead to confusion. For example, Adrian Hamilton described George Bush's approach of the crisis as confused while emphasizing "America's good intentions"[300] and arguing that the American president was not a warmonger even though he had imposed a deadline for war. But above all journalists wanted to report various aspects of the leaders' actions and shed light on the developments of the Gulf Crisis and War. Providing a forum for an enlightened debate on the attitude of the American president and the United States during this period, British newspapers sought to foster the kind of constructive criticism that underpins a healthy

---

296   Andrew Stephen, "'Read my hips' Bush gave US a bum steer", op-ed, *Observer*, 21 October 1990, p. 12 and "Bush men beat the war drums", op-ed, *Observer*, 14 October 1990, p. 13.

297   John Berger, "In the land of the deaf", op-ed, *Guardian*, 2 March 1991, p. 23.

298   For example: "When the masters lose control", editorial, *Guardian*, 11 January 1991, p. 20; Paul Wilkinson, "A way to avoid the no-win war", op-ed, *Guardian*, 3 January 1991, p. 15.

299   For instance: Andrew Stephen, "Self-delusion and escapism grip America's poodle", op-ed, *Observer*, 17 February 1991, p. 15; Andy Gregg, "Former Baghdad hostage speaks out", letters, *Observer*, 24 February 1991, p. 54.

300   Adrian Hamilton, "The deadly dangers of playing peace games", op-ed, *Observer*, 2 December 1990, p. 16.

democracy. Finally, like the coverage of other allies in the British press, some comments speculated on the possible U.S. reaction and attitude to the events by the use of modals and especially the conjunction "if".[301]

## Conclusion

In summary, the four British newspapers provided readers with a diversity of viewpoints approving or disapproving of U.S. actions during the Gulf Crisis and War: editorials in the four newspapers and opinion pieces in the *Times*, the *Guardian* and the *Sunday Times* were predominantly positive whereas articles in the *Observer* and letters published in all newspapers were mainly negative. Comments critical of the United States also questioned its role and the "special relationship" between the two countries. Conversely, articles in favour of the United States, which repeated official arguments, implicitly portrayed Britain in a favourable light because of its status as a privileged partner of the Americans during the events in the Gulf.

All in all, articles in the American and British press sympathetic towards the allies – which were in the minority except those about the United States on the British side and Britain on the American side – generally echoed the rhetoric of the U.S. and British governments. While they offered a variety of viewpoints to readers, articles in the press on both sides of the Atlantic were mostly unfavourable to the European, French, German, Chinese

---

301    For instance: Ben Lowe, "Time for Western powers to leave the Gulf in sight of peace", letters, *Guardian*, 25 October 1990, p. 20.

and Russian allies although the *New York Times* on the American side and the *Times* on the British side published positive editorials on the Soviet Union. Virulent comments by some journalists about Arab countries – particularly in the *Sunday Times* – were reminiscent of those made on Saddam Hussein. They conveyed an ethnocentric, even racist, vision of the Other by the journalists in question. Nevertheless, the British press differed from the American press, the *Washington Post* in particular, in being more sensitive to the plight of the Arab peoples, whom they did not equate with their leaders, and in questioning the colonial policy of Western countries and Britain in the Middle East. On balance, the predominantly negative comments about the coalition members in articles and letters presented, in contrast, a positive image of the United States in the American press and of Britain in the British press.

# Chapter III:
# Foreign policy

## 3.1 The concept of *realpolitik* in the American and British press

According to Thomas Lindemann,[302] images of friends and foes result from the distribution of power within the international system. He points out that when taken to its extreme, this paradigm, favoured by realists, reduces these images to a mere reflection of power interests in relations between states. Lord Palmerston's famous remark to the House of Commons on 1 March 1848 that Britain had neither eternal allies nor perpetual enemies but eternal and perpetual interests reflects this view and the usually pragmatic nature of British foreign policy.[303] Hence the notion of *realpolitik*, namely realism in international relations which are based on power relations, and that emphasizes pragmatism over principle.[304] During the Gulf Crisis and War, newspapers – admittedly mostly British – referred to this notion

---

302  Thomas Lindemann, *op. cit.*, <http://www.stratisc.org/strat72_Lindemann. html>, 2005, consulted 26 April 2022.

303  <https://api.parliament.uk/historic-hansard/commons/1848/mar/01/ treaty-of-adrianople-charges-against#S3V0097PO_18480301_HOC_8>, consulted 29 April 2022. Henry John Temple, 3rd Viscount Palmerston (1784-1865) was twice Prime Minister. As foreign secretary from 1830 to 1841, he defended British political, strategic, and economic interests in Europe and overseas (John Cannon, ed., *op. cit.*, p. 490). Gladstone, and Robin Cook in Tony Blair's government, expressed on occasions their intention to pursue an "ethical foreign policy".

304  Chris Rohman, *op. cit.*, p. 336. *Realpolitik* is a German term which was coined in 1853 to describe the politics of realism. It involves a willingness to use force where necessary (David Weigall, *op. cit.*, p. 89). State security is central to the realist view of international relations which are dominated by

especially in editorials and opinion pieces about both the coalition and each individual ally in the context of U.S. and British foreign policy. This point thus deserves further attention.

American foreign policy has been shaped both by idealists, traditionally referred to as "Wilsonians", who base their approach to international relations on moral principles and values, and "realists".[305] There were very few articles on the concept of *realpolitik* in the press on the other side of the Atlantic.[306] For example, Michael Kinsley criticized U.S. Iraq policy, which he described as "a foolish *realpolitik*, a soft-headed, a failed attempt to play geo-chess like Henry Kissinger".[307] Why were there not many articles on this subject in the *New York Times* and the *Washington Post*? One could suggest that this notion no longer really prevailed at that time, or that both newspapers did not think that it applied to American foreign policy in 1990-91. Like Michael Kinsley, the American press in 1990 might have disavowed the *realpolitik* of Nixon and Kissinger. Moreover, following the collapse of the

---

war and the risks of war in a situation of anarchy (Marie-Claude Smouts, Dario Battistella & Pascal Venesson, *op. cit.*, pp. 452, 454, 457).

305   David Weigall, *op. cit.*, p. 241.

306   Articles on this concept were published in other sections of the American newspapers.

307   Michael Kinsley, "James A. Baker, Please Resign", op-ed, *Washington Post*, 18 October 1990, p. A 23. According to Walter Russel Mead, Kissinger recommended to take "distasteful but necessary measures of amoral realpolitik". Ronald Reagan had been chafed as Nixon and Kissinger "attempted to manage U.S.-Soviet relations on the basis of realpolitik" (Walter Russell Mead, *op. cit.*, pp. 63, 75). Rejecting ideologies, the former Secretary of State and adviser for national security to Presidents Richard Nixon and Gerald Ford had placed American national interests as the primary criterion for U.S. relations with other states, making him a proponent of *realpolitik* (Alexis Chabot, *op. cit.*, p. 248; also see Éric Nguyen, *op. cit.*, p. 90).

USSR, some hoped that the *Pax Americana*, which corresponded to the dominant military and economic position of the United States, would take on a global dimension.[308] Finally, although for Pierre Hassner the realistic tradition has been present throughout American history,[309] it is also possible that neither editorialists nor other American journalists and contributors wished to devote articles to *realpolitik* since George Bush did not refer to this concept in his speeches during the Gulf events.

In contrast to the American press, British newspapers referred more to this concept in their articles. For instance, the *Times* argued at the beginning of the crisis that "quarantining Iraq is now an obligation of *realpolitik*".[310] The newspaper thus seemed to favour a realistic vision of politics, in other words a policy of firmness. On the other hand, the *Guardian* reminded readers in December 1990 of "the *realpolitik* of backyard intervention in Panama".[311] Likewise, Hugo Young, opposed to going to war against Iraq, alerted readers in the *Guardian* in November 1990 to "the human results to be weighed in the balance against the demands of *realpolitik*".[312] The journalist's comments confirmed

---

308    Pierre Melandri, "*Pax Americana*. Rendre le monde sûr pour la démocratie et le marché", *in* Denis Lacorne (dir.), *op. cit.*, p. 374. In 1989 Francis Fukuyama published an article in the conservative magazine *The National Interest,* whose ideas he developed in his book *The End of History* in 1992. Fukuyama predicted the eventual supremacy of liberal democracies in the world and in particular the liberal model embodied by the United States (Francis Fukuyama, "The End of History?", *The National Interest*, No. 16, summer 1989, pp. 3-18).

309    Pierre Hassner, *in* Denis Lacorne (dir.), *op. cit.*, p. 382.

310    "Iraq's naked villainy", editorial, *Times*, 3 August 1990, p. 11.

311    "Remember Panama", editorial, *Guardian*, 19 December 1990, p. 20.

312    Hugo Young, "Averting our gaze from the blood of war", op-ed, *Guardian*, 13 November 1990, p. 23.

the *Guardian's* stance, which was not in favour of Britain's entry into war.

What is striking is that both American and British newspapers did not explain the concept of *realpolitik* to their readers, who were expected to know its definition and have sufficient knowledge of foreign policy to understand editorialists' and journalists' arguments. In addition, British daily newspapers took opposing positions on *realpolitik*: the *Times* advocated it and the *Guardian* opposed it. Why did British newspapers publish articles on this notion when neither Margaret Thatcher nor John Major referred to it in their speeches throughout the events? It was perhaps because of the European tradition of *raison d'État* that inspired *realpolitik*.[313] Finally, there were no articles about this concept in British Sunday newspapers. These newspapers might have not considered *realpolitik* as a topic of interest to their readers.

---

313 Pierre Hassner *in* Denis Lacorne (dir.), *op. cit.*, p. 382. "The Machiavellian tradition of *raison d'état* is essentially based on a theory about the conduct of foreign policy" (Ken Booth, ed., *Realism and World Politics*, London: Routledge, 2001, p. 148). Jack Donnelly quotes Haslam (2002, p. 12) on the doctrine of *raison d'état* that "holds that where international relations are concerned, the interests of the state predominate over all other interests and values". He also argues that national interests and values, which are held by nations, may limit a state's foreign policy (Jack Donnelly, *The Ethics of Realism, in The Oxford Handbook of International Relations*, Oxford: Oxford UP, 2008, pp. 154, 156). In addition, the fact that neither Margaret Thatcher nor John Major referred to this notion might be that neither Prime Minister considered it useful to define the principles behind their foreign policy decisions.

## 3.2 Multilateralism in the American press[314]

The American press actually seemed to have another objective. The two American newspapers presented the United States as a non-isolationist country that led a coalition of thirty-four countries engaged in military action against Saddam Hussein. The *Washington Post*, in its editorials during the Gulf Crisis and after the hostilities, advised the U.S. government not to act alone and to give "American post-Cold War policy a vigorous and principled internationalist cast" that could win the support of U.S. allies.[315]

Opinion articles in the *New York Times* were more nuanced. For example, Richard Spielmann, who was assistant professor of international affairs at Lewis and Clark College in Portland, Oregon at that time, defended a unipolar world dominated by a single power, i.e. the United States, but argued that America had not become the world's hegemon.[316] While most journalists in the *Washington Post* favoured a multilateral approach,[317] Charles Krauthammer in October 1990 disapproved of Bush's "erratic performance" and drew the readers' attention to the "hidden

---

314   The British press did not seem to cover this point, which could be explained by the fact that it was the United States that had assembled a coalition and oversaw military operations in the Gulf.

315   For instance: "Mr. Bush at the U.N.", editorial, *Washington Post*, 2 October 1990, p. A 18. The *New York Times*, on the other hand, did not seem to have published editorials on this subject.

316   Richard Spielmann, "The Emerging Unipolar World", op-ed, *New York Times*, 21 August 1990, p. A 27.

317   For example: Jim Wallis, "Killing in the Name of God", op-ed, *Washington Post*, 30 October 1990, p. A 21.

costs of such expansive multilateralism",[318] which must take into account the national interests of each country in the coalition. On a more prosaic level, the American political columnist did not refer to the costs of a military operation, namely those of deploying the armed forces. It is true that the United States' expenses generated by the Gulf War were reimbursed by Kuwait and Saudi Arabia and that, even if this had not been the case, a great power like the United States could undoubtedly have borne the financial costs of such a conflict alone.

As Charles Krauthammer explained in his article, George Bush was criticized for having been too sensitive to the wishes of the international community during the Gulf events.[319] For Henry Kissinger, however, "American diplomacy since the end of the Cold War has turned more and more into a series of proposals for adherence to an American agenda".[320] In other words, the so-called multilateralism only served to legitimize the domination of the United States, as the only military, economic and political superpower.[321]

---

318    Charles Krauthammer, "The Great Cooperator", op-ed, *Washington Post*, 19 October 1990, p. A 23. The journalist argued that "one cost of coalition is that it inhibits you from doing what you might want to do unilaterally. The other [...] cost is that it makes you do things you wouldn't ordinarily do".

319    Niall Ferguson, *op. cit.*, p. 132. Charles Krauthammer also argued about the idea of American unipolarity that for domestic reasons, "American political leaders make sure to dress unilateral action in multilateral clothing" (Charles Krauthammer, "The Unipolar Moment", *Foreign Affairs: America and the World (1990/91)*, quoted *in* "The Unipolar Moment Revisited", December 2002, (<https://nationalinterest.org/article/the-unipolar-moment-revisited-391>, consulted 16 May 2022).

320    Henry Kissinger, *op. cit.*, 2001, p. 30.

321    According to William Engdahl, the Pentagon used the expression *full spectrum dominance*, which meant that the United States "should control

Letters in the American press followed the editorial line of both newspapers as readers recommended a multilateral approach, i.e. the United States working with its partners.[322] To sum up, the United States was described in the *Washington Post* editorials and by readers of both newspapers as a country pursuing a multilateral policy during the Gulf events. Apart from Charles Krauthammer in the *Washington Post*, most journalists and readers of both newspapers painted the same positive picture of the United States.

## 3.3    The U.N. in the American and British press

The positive image of the United States was also reinforced by references to the United Nations[323] in the American press. Both American newspapers referred, in their articles, either to the United Nations as a whole or to the Security Council, without

---

military, economic and political developments, everywhere" (William Engdahl, *op. cit.*, p. 269).

322    For example: Sam Nunn, Senator, "Emphasize Air Power", letters, *New York Times*, 9 September 1990, p. E 24; J. Robert Schaetzel, "Crisis in the Gulf: The International Response", letters, *Washington Post*, 21 August 1990, p. A 22.

323    The United Nations, headquartered in New York, is an international organization established on 24 October 1945. The United Nations has six principal organs: the General Assembly, the Security Council, the Economic and Social Council, the Trusteeship Council, the International Court of Justice, and the Secretariat. The U.N. Charter assigns to the Security Council primary responsibility for the maintenance of international peace and security in the world. It consists of fifteen members, five of whom (China, France, Russia, the United Kingdom, the U.S.) have permanent seats. Javier Pérez de Cuéllar from Peru was the Secretary General of the United Nations during the Gulf Crisis and War (David Weigall, *op. cit.*, pp. 229, 231-232; also see the U.N. website: <http://www.un.org/en/sections/about-un/main-organs/index.html>, consulted 5 June 2022).

giving more details to the reader, who was undoubtedly expected to know about the subtleties of the organization. While most editorials in the U.S. press praised the "impressive" performance of the United Nations in the Gulf Crisis,[324] a few editorials in the *New York Times* reminded readers of the way the international organization was described before the Gulf Crisis, such as "a body once scorned as a dithering talk-shop".[325] Likewise, some editorials in the *Washington Post* published between August 1990 and January 1991 expressed certain reservations about the United Nations. For instance, an editorial of 15 August 1990 in the daily paper referred to the U.N.'s familiar dithering.[326] In November 1990, another editorial advised Congress to weigh in since "it is its political duty and its constitutional obligation".[327]

Opinion articles published in the two American newspapers offered readers a plurality of views: half of them adopted the editorial line of both newspapers and emphasized the crucial role assigned to the United Nations by the Gulf crisis.[328] In contrast, some journalists and contributors criticized the institution. For example, Henry Kissinger argued in the *Washington Post*

---

324   For instance: "The U.N.'s Biggest Deadbeat", editorial, *New York Times*, 11 September 1990, p. A 24; "Iraq's Double Grab", editorial, *Washington Post*, 21 August 1990, p. A 22.

325   "Getting Serious about the U.N.", editorial, *New York Times*, 24 September 1990, p. A 18. "The often-toothless United Nations". "Isolate Iraq", editorial, *New York Times*, 5 August 1990, p. E 18.

326   "Enforcing the Embargo", editorial, *Washington Post*, 15 August 1990, p. A 20.

327   "U.N. Logic", editorial, *Washington Post*, 29 November 1990, p. A 22. The *Washington Post* expressed rather inconsistent opinions on the U.N. in its editorials between August 1990 and January 1991.

328   For example: Flora Lewis, "Old-Think for the Gulf", op-ed, *New York Times*, 8 September 1990, p. A 23; Cyrus Vance, "Pressure on Iraq Can Work", op-ed, *Washington Post*, 21 October 1990, p. C 7.

that "U.N. debates are certain to be protracted".[329] Similarly, Jeane Kirkpatrick claimed that the process of consultation and consensus among the Security Council members "has proved cumbersome, time-consuming and [...] irrational".[330] What these authors seemed to reject was the transfer of U.S. leadership to the United Nations. In this regard, Paul H. Nitze, a diplomat-in-residence at the Johns Hopkins University's School of Advanced International Studies at that time, explained in the *New York Times* in October 1990: "Our reliance on the U.N. Security Council to sanction the response to Iraq ties our actions to those of the Soviets through the vote".[331] William W. Van Alstyne, Perkins Professor of Law at Duke University in 1990, went even further, vehemently challenging the United Nations which, he said, had no power under the American Constitution "to substitute itself for Congress in determining whether this country is to go to war".[332] As implied in the editorial of 29 November 1990 in the *Washington Post* and the article by William W. Van Alstyne, it is Congress that has the power to start a war. During the events in the Gulf, President Bush, as Commander-in-Chief of the armed

---

329    Henry Kissinger, "A Dangerous Mirage", op-ed, *Washington Post*, 11 November 1990, p. B 7.

330    Jeane Kirkpatrick, "Not Just the Gulf, but the Globe", op-ed, *Washington Post*, 3 December 1990, p. A 15.

331    Paul H. Nitze, "Leapfrog into Start II", op-ed, *New York Times*, 25 October 1990, p. A 27. However, the former special adviser and Secretary of State on arms control in the Reagan administration had advocated a solution to the Gulf Crisis under the auspices of the United Nations in the *Washington Post* on 26 August 1990 (Paul H. Nitze, "Getting the Good of this Crisis", op-ed, *Washington Post*, 26 August 1990, p. C 7). In other words, Paul H. Nitze changed his opinion between August and October 1990. In addition, it is worth noting that the two newspapers published the viewpoints of the same authoritative person.

332    William W. Van Alstyne, "Letting Slip the Dogs of War", op-ed, *Washington Post*, 23 December 1990, p. C 7.

forces, had the intervention of the U.S. armed forces authorized by Congress in accordance with U.N. resolutions; the Gulf War, like the Vietnam War, had not been the subject of a formal declaration of hostilities.[333] In general, the endorsement of the United Nations makes it easier for a government to convince its public opinion of the need to go to war.[334] Its endorsement is therefore an asset for a state and in particular for the United States since it is this organization that authorizes the use of force and, in the event of failure, the responsibility for the action can then be shared with the international community.[335]

Readers' letters in the *New York Times* expressed a range of different opinions. For example, while a reader described the United Nations forces as "protean and usually inadequate",[336] another blamed the Administration for disparaging the United Nations and refusing to pay the "country's assessed dues"[337] to

---

333   Pierre Lagayette, *Les États-Unis contemporains*, Rosny s/Bois: Bréal, 2002, p. 193.
334   Marie-Claude Smouts, Dario Battistella & Pascal Venesson, *op. cit.*, p. 370.
335   See Vincent Troin and Aurélie Lorrain, *op. cit.*, pp. 167, 175.
336   Harvard Hollenberg, "Defeating Iraq Would Create Worse Problems", letters, *New York Times*, 6 January 1991, p. E 18.
337   Douglas Mattern, "On the Eve of Drifting into War, Once Again", letters, *New York Times*, 13 January 1991, p. E 18. The U.N. General Assembly determines the basis for payment of the expenses of the organization. A Committee on Contributions meets annually to review the scale of assessment based on each member state's gross national product (GNP). The United States has been the largest contributor to the U.N. budget since its inception in 1945. Prior to 1 January 2001 its assessment level was 25%, but it was reduced to 22% of the U.N. regular budget after that date to pay its arrearages. Refer to the report by Marjorie Ann Browne and Luisa Blanchfield about the United Nations regular budget contributions by members from 1990 to 2010: <https://sgp.fas.org/crs/row/RL30605.pdf>, consulted 13 June 2022. For Brett D. Schaefer, Jay Kingham Fellow in International Regulatory Affairs in Heritage's Margaret Thatcher Center

the institution. It is true that at the time of the Gulf Crisis the United States owed the United Nations several hundred million dollars.[338] On the other hand, readers of the *Washington Post* were full of praise for the United Nations,[339] whose unanimous condemnation of Iraq's belligerent actions was "a landmark decision, worthy of note".[340] The viewpoints of the *Washington Post* readers were thus largely consistent with most opinions expressed in the newspaper's editorials.

As expected, most editorials, opinion articles and letters to the editor referring to the U.N. were published before the outbreak of hostilities. To sum up, the majority of editorials in both newspapers, fifty percent of the journalists as well as most readers of the *Washington Post* paid tribute to the work of the United Nations in the Gulf crisis.[341] In doing so, they followed

---

for Freedom, "the U.S. should seek to adjust the U.N. scale of assessment to more equitably distribute the costs of the organization among the member states [...]". Refer to his report "The History of the Bloated U.N. Budget: How the U.S. Can Rein It In" published on 2 April 2012: <https://www. heritage.org/report/the-history-the-bloated-un-budget-how-the-us-can-rein-it>, consulted 14 June 2022.

338 Richard Keeble, *op. cit.*, 1997, p. 98. The U.S. contributions outstanding as of 31 December 1990 amounted to $296,169,865 (Marjorie Ann Browne & Luisa Blanchfield, <https://sgp.fas.org/crs/row/RL30605.pdf>, consulted 13 June 2022). According to Niall Ferguson, "the United States suspended the payment of its dues to the United Nations in 1996". However, the U.S. contributions "were resumed and arrears partially paid in 1999" (Niall Ferguson, *op. cit.*, p. 133).

339 For example: Anthony Allen, "Crisis in the Gulf: The International Response", letters, *Washington Post*, 21 August 1990, p. A 22.

340 Timothy Cooper, "Crisis in the Gulf: The International Response", letters, *Washington Post*, 21 August 1990, p. A 22.

341 One of the consequences of the Gulf Crisis was that the U.N.' s credibility, which had been undermined by the Yugoslav and Rwandan conflicts, was restored (Pascal Boniface [dir.], *op. cit.*, p. 36).

the official rhetoric. George Bush multiplied his references to the United Nations in his speeches from August 1990 to March 1991,[342] which certainly created an impression of widespread agreement among the American public.[343] Given that the rise of multilateralism in the 20th century was accompanied by a proliferation of international organizations,[344] editorialists, journalists and readers who advocated the involvement of the U.N. and its Security Council, particularly in conflict situations such as those in the Gulf, therefore supported a multilateral U.S. policy. They thus presented a positive image of the United States that implemented its foreign policy in conjunction with international bodies[345] and took into account the views of other coalition members. However, for Pascal Boniface, the U.N. is perpetually held hostage by the United States[346] which wants to impose its own agenda unilaterally and above all according to its own interests.[347] Niall Ferguson even claims that the United Nations is a "creature of the United States".[348] This then raises the question of whether the U.N. really represents a form of multilateralism or whether this organization is only what powerful states, the United States in particular, want it to be.[349] Because of its predominant position in the U.N., the United States has the capacity to influence the

---

342    For instance, refer to the President's news conference on the Persian Gulf Crisis on 22 August 1990 (<https://bush41library.tamu.edu/archives/public-papers/2177>, consulted 21 June 2022).

343    Aurélie Lorrain, *op. cit.*, p. 175.

344    Marie-Claude Smouts, Dario Battistella & Pascal Venesson, *op. cit.*, p. 357.

345    It should be recalled that in 1920, following the Senate's refusal, the United States remained outside the League of Nations that President Wilson had helped to found (René Rémond, *op. cit.*, pp. 92-93).

346    Pascal Boniface (dir.), *op. cit.*, p. 36.

347    Christophe Kuntz, *op. cit.*, p. 314.

348    Niall Ferguson, *op. cit.*, p. 134.

349    Pascal Boniface (dir.), *op. cit.*, p. 36.

decisions taken by this world organization as well as by the large economic, financial, political or strategic bodies that depend on it.

In the British press, numerous editorials, opinion pieces and letters to the editor also referred to the United Nations and the Security Council resolutions. While most editorials in the two British daily newspapers and the *Observer* praised the international body,[350] it is not surprising that a few editorials in the *Sunday Times* criticized it. For example, the editorial of 2 September 1990 blamed the U.N. for vacillating "for ten days before it could even summon up the collective will to give its own sanctions teeth".[351] The Sunday newspaper was inconsistent in its stance, publishing both negative and positive editorials[352] on the U.N. from August 1990 to February 1991.

Opinion pieces in the British press offered readers a range of opinions. Most of them were in favour of the international organization.[353] For instance, Hugo Young in the *Guardian*

---

350 "When to stop", editorial, *Times*, 28 February 1990, p. 13; "The UN is the fulcrum", editorial, *Guardian*, 4 October 1990, p. 18; "Shun the siren voices", editorial, *Sunday Times*, 6 January 1991, Sect. 3, p. 7; "The logic of war and peace in the Gulf", editorial, *Observer*, 26 August 1990, p. 10.

351 "The Peace party", editorial, *Sunday Times*, 2 September 1990, Sect. 3, p. 7.

352 For instance, "Finishing Saddam", editorial, *Sunday Times*, 3 February 1991, Sect. 1, p. 11. The editorial argued that relying on the U.N. was an imprudent policy. On the other hand, the following editorial paid tribute to the United Nations for having backed "resolutions with force if need be". "Christmas in the desert", editorial, *Sunday Times*, 23 December 1990, Sect. 1, p. 11.

353 For example: David Fairhall, "The temptations of option one and a half", op-ed, *Guardian*, 4 September 1990, p. 19; Brian Walden, "Arab aspirations cry out for constant care and attention", op-ed, *Sunday Times*, 12 August 1990, Sect. 3, p. 4; Philip Crowe, Rev., "The case against a 'just war' in the Gulf", op-ed, *Observer*, 11 November 1990, p. 22.

stressed the rehabilitation of the United Nations after having been a "discredited world body".[354] However, Norman Macrae in the *Sunday Times* blamed the United Nations for five months of "meandering".[355] In the *Guardian*, Richard Falk, professor of International Law at Princeton University at that time, questioned the future credibility of the United Nations as he had the impression that the organization had been converted "into a virtual tool of U.S. foreign policy".[356] One may wonder why the American press did not publish similar articles. In contrast, some American journalists and contributors argued against the loss of U.S. national sovereignty to the U.N. This can be seen as indirect evidence of U.S. reluctance towards the U.N. While the United States wanted to keep itself out of international decisions, Britain was more internationalist, except in the *Sunday Times*.

Letters to the editor about the United Nations were only published in the British daily newspapers and not in the Sunday newspapers.[357] Readers of the *Times* approved of the U.N.'s action,[358] suggesting that there was a correspondence between the views of the *Times* and its readers. However, readers of the

---

354    Hugo Young, "Fortunes of war desert the iron lady", op-ed, *Guardian*, 6 September 1990, p. 19.

355    Norman Macrae, "Gazing in a crystal hazy with mumbo-jumbo and Gulf sand", op-ed, *Sunday Times*, 30 December 1990, Sect. 1, p. 13.

356    Richard Falk, "A war built on grand illusions", op-ed, *Guardian*, 17 January 1991, p. 19.

357    Why were there no letters from readers about the United Nations in the *Sunday Times* and the *Observer*? The negative comments about the U.N. in the *Sunday Times* could explain it. While the answer is not quite as straightforward for the *Observer*, it may be that both Sunday papers left aside what they did not like.

358    For instance: Ivor Richard, "Limits of UN resolution on embargo against Iraq", letters, *Times*, 16 August 1990, p. 11.

*Guardian* were divided. For example, one reader welcomed the resolutions passed by the United Nations Security Council about the crisis in the Gulf.[359] By contrast, another argued that what went on in the Security Council was "horse-trading of the most cynical kind" and that the U.N. was "a cruel hoax".[360] This reader also stated that U.N. resolutions were only enforced when they suited the United States, thereby echoing Richard Falk's criticism of the U.N. in a *Guardian* opinion piece. In short, some of the *Guardian's* readers did not follow the editorial line of the newspaper.

As with the American press, editorials, opinion pieces and letters about the United Nations were mostly published in the British press before the conflict began. In short, most editorials in the daily newspapers and the *Observer* – with the exception of a few in the *Sunday Times* – as well as readers of the *Times* approved of the work of the United Nations during the Gulf operations. On the other hand, opinion pieces and letters in the *Guardian* offered a variety of viewpoints on this subject. The editorialists, journalists and contributors who supported the implementation of the Security Council resolutions echoed the Prime Minister, be it Margaret Thatcher or John Major.[361]

---

359 Muriel Davies, "Let's cast a net over the whole Middle East when seeking peace for Kuwait", letters, *Guardian*, 23 August 1990, p. 18.

360 Howard Senter, "West's capabilities for waging the peace", letters, *Guardian*, 28 February 1991, p. 20.

361 For instance, refer to Margaret Thatcher's press conference on the Gulf situation on 21 August 1990 (<https://www.margaretthatcher.org/document/108176>), and John Major's Question Time on the Gulf in the House of Commons on 15 January 1991 (<https://hansard.parliament.uk/Commons/1991-01-15/debates/3498d88e-f437-47bc-bdc6-cd0c78a0fee8/TheGulf?highlight=chemical#contribution-93c27615-93f1-43c2-b05e-395509d2>, consulted 9 July 2022).

In summary, editorials, opinion articles and letters in the American press overwhelmingly endorsed the recourse to the U.N. and painted a glowing picture of the United States as a multilateral policy-making state. In the British press, references to the U.N. in editorials, opinion pieces and letters were not directly relevant to Britain's image, perhaps because of its place as a staunch ally, but nonetheless second in the international coalition alongside the United States. However, it was in this less explicit and less directly conflict-related area that the reactions, or lack thereof, were the most interesting. What was left unsaid spoke volumes and showed the true attitudes, as well as the divergence between the press on both sides of the Atlantic.

## Conclusion

Although realism has often been considered a hallmark of U.S. foreign policy, there was little mention of the concept of *realpolitik* in the American press during the Gulf Crisis and War. Regardless of this situation, most articles in the American press – with the exception of a few opinion articles – praised the multilateral approach taken by the U.S. president in his consultation with allied countries under the auspices of the U.N. These articles therefore painted a flattering picture of the United States. On the British side, the two daily newspapers offered readers opposing views on the concept of *realpolitik* according to their position on the war against Iraq – the *Times* being in favour and the *Guardian* being against it.

All in all, given that a country's foreign policy is underpinned by its relations with other countries, American and British newspapers published a large number of articles about the coalition in general and the allies in particular during the Gulf Crisis and the war itself. Two tables – one concerning the American press and the other the British press – summarize the attitudes of the American and British press towards the members of the coalition. The first table shows which allies were most often mentioned in the two American newspapers and also specifies the number of favourable and unfavourable articles – editorials and opinion articles – per ally:

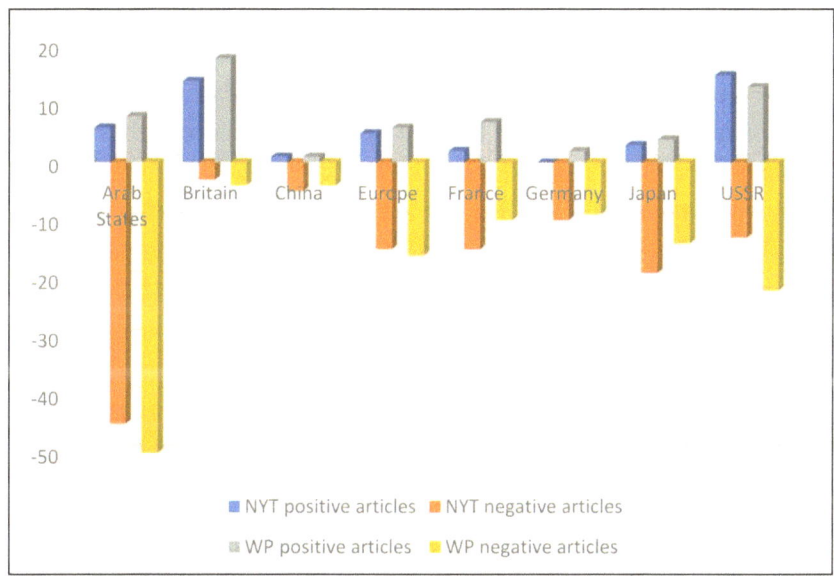

As this table shows, both American newspapers published a large number of editorials and opinion articles about the Arab countries. That could be explained by the fact that they were part of the coalition, and the theatre of operations was located in the Persian Gulf region. While both newspapers considered the

Arab states as key allies of the United States in the coalition, their journalists' comments were often contemptuous and reminiscent of those directed against the Iraqi leader. On the other hand, the two newspapers dealt mostly negatively with China in only a few articles, which, as a reminder, might be because of the incidents in Tiananmen Square, or due to the limited interest of the American press in China's attitude during the Gulf events.

Japan, Europe, France and, to a lesser extent, Germany represented allies of equivalent level for the U.S. press if one takes into account the comparable number of articles published which were primarily critical of these allies. There is little explanation for the fact that the *New York Times* did not publish any positive articles about Germany.[362] On the other hand, comments on the Soviet Union were more divided: there were a number of articles favourable to the USSR in both newspapers – especially in the *New York Times* – due in part to its support for U.S. government decisions during the Gulf Crisis and War. Nevertheless, the *Washington Post* published many more articles hostile to the country than the *New York Times*. It is difficult to explain this difference between the two American newspapers. Nonetheless, it is likely that the publication by the newspapers – above all in the *Washington Post* – of a large number of negative articles against the Soviet Union reinforced, in readers' mind, the status of the USSR as an adversary despite the significant changes in that country at that time. Ultimately, only Britain was consistently

---

362    Would it be greatly exaggerated to claim that the Gulf Crisis might have awakened old grudges against Germany in the daily newspaper? Without being able to answer this question, it is worth noting that the *New York Times* published 8,800 columns of war coverage during World War II, which was more than any other U.S. newspaper (Edwin Diamond, *op. cit.*, p. 48).

favoured by American journalists, notably because of the special relationship between the United States and Britain and due to the fact that it was the most active ally.

What stands out in the table is the greater number of negative articles about the allies – with the exception of Britain – published in both American newspapers compared to the number of positive articles. The portrait of each ally in the newspapers hardly changed from August 1990 to mid-March 1991: it remained either favourable or negative throughout this period. The journalists' arguments were indeed constantly repeated in articles, which were marked by a rhetoric of persuasion and self-persuasion. In addition, the journalistic discourse of the articles unfavourable to the allies also diverged from the American president's remarks and referred to a kind of Manicheism between the United States on the one hand and each of the allies in question on the other. This dichotomy can be seen in readers' letters, which echoed the sympathetic or disapproving articles about the allies. However, most of the letters, which criticized the allies and in particular the Arab countries, were published in the *Washington Post*. In confirmation of what has been written in this study about individual allies, the Gulf Crisis and War served as a catalyst – as in the case of Saddam Hussein – and gave free rein to journalists' resentments and prejudices towards the allies. Since international relations also determine the image of a nation, criticism of the allies in question went hand in hand with support for the United States.

The second table also lists the positive and negative articles published in the British press about each ally:

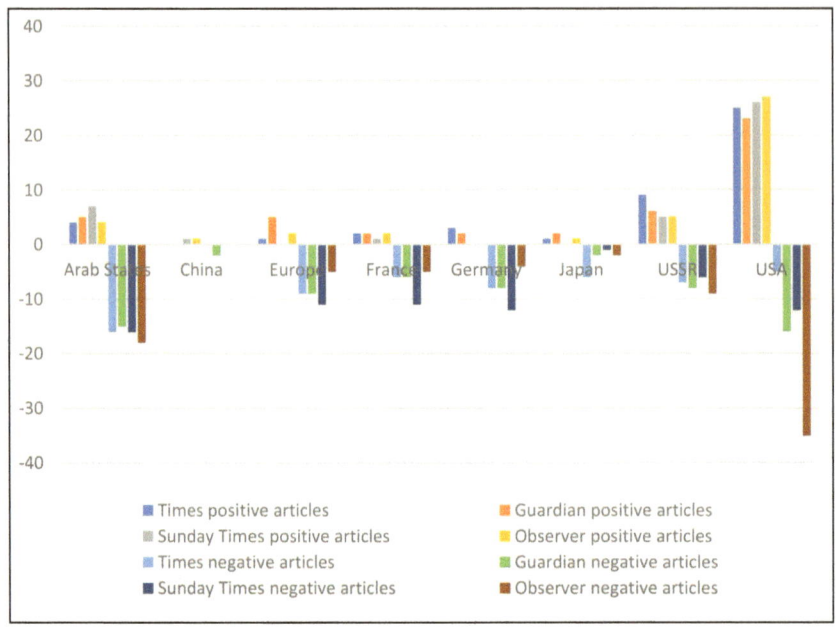

- Times positive articles
- Sunday Times positive articles
- Times negative articles
- Sunday Times negative articles
- Guardian positive articles
- Observer positive articles
- Guardian negative articles
- Observer negative articles

The high number of articles about the United States reflects both its status as the coalition leader as well as the importance of the ties between the two nations. As we have seen, the *Observer* stood out from the other newspapers by publishing a majority of articles unfavourable to the United States. The Sunday paper was an exception, however, as the other newspapers published articles that were generally supportive of U.S. actions in the Gulf. The same cannot be said about readers' letters in British newspapers since most of them were unfavourable to American decisions in the Gulf, contrary to the editorial line of the *Times*, the *Guardian* and the *Sunday Times*.

As in the American press, there were a large number of negative articles against the Arab countries. In addition, the *Sunday Times*

482

stood out for its negative comments, particularly on Germany, Europe and France, thus reaffirming the importance of Britain and thereby also showing its nationalism. Like the *New York Times*, the *Times* published the most pro-USSR articles because of the Soviet support for U.S. policy. Although British newspapers allowed journalists and contributors to express different opinions, which were sometimes opposed to their editorial lines, it is worth noting that all the articles analysed were rather critical of the allies other than the United States. Similarly, letters echoed the negative views of editorials and opinion pieces towards coalition members. This attitude could prove that in a crisis or war national interests still prevail, and that countries, even allies in conflict, continue to see each other as rivals. Likewise, it would appear that extraordinary events generate mistrust of others and ultimately serve only to reinforce prejudices and clichés against them. In general, unusual circumstances also facilitate the making of subjective judgments about others and moreover offer some journalists – such as, on the American side, William Safire from the *New York Times* or, on the British side, those from the *Sunday Times,* the opportunity to give free rein to sometimes violent comments on other countries – friends or enemies.

# General conclusion

The objective of this study has been to analyse the image of the Other and the Self in editorials, opinion articles and letters to the editor published in both the American and British press throughout the Gulf Crisis and War.

### *The image of the Other – the Enemy*

The enemy facing the United States, Britain and their allies was Saddam Hussein, the president of Iraq. His uncompromising portrait was defined in the press on both sides of the Atlantic as early as August 1990 and remained unchanged until after the end of hostilities. Repeating the qualifiers used by the American president and the British Prime Minister, editorialists, journalists and readers described the Iraqi leader virulently with expressions from the lexical fields of crime in editorials and of war in opinion articles. They portrayed a terrifying and dangerous adversary to be defeated.

As part of their strategy of stigmatizing the enemy leader, American and British journalists called Saddam Hussein by his first name, downgrading his presidential status in this way. Although marginal in his portrayal, the Iraqi leader's alleged madness appeared in some articles in the press on both sides of the Atlantic. A few editorials and opinion articles also compared him with wild animals during the Gulf Crisis and depicted the Iraqi ruler as the embodiment of Evil.

To further denigrate Saddam Hussein's personality, numerous

articles in the American and British press compared him to Hitler, following the Bush administration. American and British newspapers referred to other vilified statesmen, such as Nebuchadnezzar, Saladin, Mussolini, Stalin, Nasser, Bismarck, Mao and Noriega to emphasize the Iraqi ruler's ruthless character.

The press on both sides of the Atlantic tarnished Saddam Hussein's image even more by highlighting the main exactions perpetrated by the Iraqi ruler before 2 August 1990 such as the Iran-Iraq war. They also referred to the abuses committed during the Gulf Crisis and War by describing Iraq's invasion of Kuwait as a criminal and illegal act of aggression. Above all, they condemned Saddam Hussein inter alia for taking foreign civilians hostage, looting in Kuwait, the launch of Iraqi Scuds on Israel, and for mistreating allied soldiers.

Subscribing to the official rhetoric of the U.S. president and the British Prime Minister, American and British newspapers also speculated upon the military, nuclear, economic and geopolitical threat Iraq's president posed to the Western world. To this end, they stressed and overestimated the military power of Iraq. They emphasized the risks entailed by Iraq's nuclear ambitions and those inherent in its possession of chemical and biological weapons. They echoed George Bush's and Margaret Thatcher's major worries about Saddam Hussein's possible control over oil reserves following his invasion of Kuwait, and the risks of supply disruption and subsequent economic instability for the West. Finally, they fuelled speculation on the risk of regional instability, presenting Saddam Hussein as a danger to Israel's security and Western interests.

By exaggerating the portrait of an aggressive adversary, journalists' scathing and alarming comments perpetuated the usual stereotype of the enemy. They presented a Manichean view of the events between "Good", namely the coalition, American and British journalists and their readers on the one hand, and "Evil", i.e. Saddam Hussein on the other. Most journalists adopted a rhetoric of persuasion based on the same official arguments to persuade their readers of the need for war against Iraq.

*Similarities between the American and British press*

Beyond the characteristics of each newspaper, there was a common denominator in the image of the enemy: many editorialists and journalists caricatured Saddam Hussein's personality and his behaviour through repetitions and exaggerations. The journalistic discourse, which was classic in terms of the themes addressed, consisted of virulent and moralizing semantic charges against the foe. Articles in the American and British press were adorned with clichés and stereotypes to represent a caricature Other and develop aversion to him.

To include readers, articles used the pronoun "we" and the possessive adjective "our" as unifying elements, which made it also possible to distinguish between the opposite sides and differentiate them from the Other. In the British press, the two opposition newspapers, the *Guardian* and the *Observer*, whose positions were quite radically different from those of the pro-American *Times*, nevertheless followed an almost identical line in their description of the Iraqi leader. In this area, the same was true of the American and British press, suggesting that this was an approach that went far beyond national belonging.

Appealing to the emotions, editorialists and journalists repeated words or used synonyms to the point of exaggeration to strike the reader's mind. Terms overloaded with affect were used to describe Saddam Hussein, playing not only on feelings, but also on fear. The emotion linked to a moralising discourse was given free rein in the newspapers on both sides of the Atlantic with regard to the hostage case or the bombing of the Amiriyah shelter.

Another element of Saddam Hussein's portrait was the fact that the enemy was presented as uncivilized. The qualifiers used to describe his personality and his behaviour – his past, present and future abuses – reinforced the antagonism between the Iraqi leader and the Western moral values to which journalists referred. In general, articles in both the American and British press were full of cultural references – literary, musical and cinematographic – and historical and political allusions, but often different for American and British readers, to ensure cultural relevance.

*Differences between the American and British press*

There were some differences between the American press and the British press in the portrayal of Saddam Hussein. While numerous articles attested to the high media profile to the Gulf Crisis in both countries, the American press was more outspoken than the British press, as evidenced by the large number of articles referring to the invasion as an act of aggression.

As for the comparison of the Iraqi leader with Hitler, part of the British press – the *Guardian*, the *Sunday Times* and the *Observer* – retained it in its editorials and thus appeared more sectarian than the American press, which criticized, in a limited number of editorials, the fact that the Bush administration used the comparison. American and British journalists also differed in their views on equating the Iraqi president with Nebuchadnezzar or about parallels between Saddam Hussein and Nasser.

Although the American and British press speculated alarmingly about the risk of Iraq's use of its nuclear arsenal – a hypothesis that was later proven wrong –, the U.S. newspapers differed from British dailies by emphasizing the need to reduce the proliferation of nuclear weapons. The publication of more editorials and opinion articles on Saddam Hussein's destruction of oil wells and the impact on the environment also showed that the American press appeared to be more sensitive to environmental issues.

While the press on both sides of the Atlantic, like George Bush and Margaret Thatcher, highlighted the West's oil dependence on the countries of the Middle East, it was only in the American newspapers that the means required to reduce this dependence were specified. The American press therefore took a more concrete approach on this point.

On the hostage issue, each country was only thinking of its own hostages. In the American press, the *Washington Post* was cautious about the hostages and seemed to focus on U.S. nationals held hostage while the *New York Times* was less isolationist in this area and referred to the British and other Western hostages. On the British side, opinion pieces referred above all to the British hostages.

The parallel with the conflict in Israel was a sensitive subject for the press on both sides of the Atlantic. The American newspapers as well as the *Times* and the *Sunday Times* questioned the correlation established by the Iraqi leader between the withdrawal of his troops from Kuwait and the Palestinian issue, showing the ideological side of these newspapers that did not want to put Israel on the same level as Iraq.

The specificity of each newspaper and the individual style of each journalist also influenced the way in which the enemy was portrayed: for example, William Safire's emphatic and very often simplistic comments in the *New York Times*. On the British side, the use of catchy and even slang qualifiers to describe the Iraqi leader characterized the articles of the *Sunday Times*. By contrast, the *Times* focused on factual information devoid of pathos.

*Did the American and British press comply with the official line?*

Both the *New York Times* and the *Washington Post* adopted a critical approach towards the authorities (e.g. about the lack of an energy policy; the rejection of Bush's comparison between Saddam Hussein and Hitler; the inaction of the U.S. government towards the Iraqi leader before the Gulf Crisis). They thus acted as a watchdog in a critical and distanced reflection of events. On the British side, the *Guardian* and the *Observer* were critical of the government on several points, unlike the *Times* and the *Sunday Times*. Nevertheless, similar arguments can be found in the discourse of government authorities and newspapers on both sides of the Atlantic. For instance, American and British newspapers used the same qualifiers employed by politicians from both countries to describe the Iraqi leader and bring out an identical portrait of the enemy.

In general, the American and British press followed the official rhetoric about the description of Saddam Hussein and his abuses before 2 August 1990 and during the Gulf Crisis and War. They thus amplified the threat that official statements insisted was posed by Saddam Hussein. In the U.S., of the two major newspapers, the *New York Times* seemed more willing to repeat the official line but only on a few points. In Britain, it was the *Times* and the *Sunday Times* whereas the *Guardian* and the *Observer* tended not to follow that official line.

Most editorials and many opinion articles, the speeches of the U.S. president and the British Prime Minister concurred on the military, nuclear, economic and geopolitical threat represented by the Iraqi leader. Echoing the authorities, the press focused on the atrocities of the Iraqi regime during the Iran-Iraq war and especially against the Kurds. The newspapers did on occasion act on their role as the Fourth Estate by addressing subjects the governments ignored.

Environmental pollution caused by Saddam Hussein's army was reported whereas the ecological impact of the coalition's Gulf War on the environment was not. Likewise, the damage and deaths caused by allied missiles were not mentioned in the press on both sides of the Atlantic – except in the *Guardian*. It is, perhaps, not surprising that the press adopted a patriotic discourse, modelled on the official ideology, of support for the allied troops engaged in combat.

To sum up, the almost unanimous image of an enemy whose negative characteristics were continually repeated by the six newspapers seems to indicate an adherence, or even a more or less voluntary submission, of a part of the American and British press to the arguments of the authorities. The strategy of demonization of the Iraqi leader can be seen as a classic propaganda process. According to Noam Chomsky, propaganda is to a democracy what violence is to dictatorships. The term "propaganda" is used here in the sense given by Jean-Michel Domenach and Anne Morelli, i.e. suggesting that an adversary is associated with notions of evil, the enemy country's leader is infantilized, and terrible atrocities are credited to the enemy. This was the case in the American press and the British press albeit to a varying degree according to each newspaper but was especially true of the *Sunday Times*. The Sunday paper was the champion of this type of discourse as a number of strong and simple ideas were repeated. It used effective phrases that created mistrust of the Other on the one hand and a surge of patriotism on the other. Within a few months, certain journalists became the heralds of a culture of war insofar as they advocated jingoistic warmongering.[1] What was once "propaganda" is now "communication" since it is as important for the military and governments to not just be seen to be winning the war on the ground but also to be doing so with the backing of public opinion. Hence the overriding need to influence the messaging in the press and even try to control it.

### *The image of the allies*

The Other is not only the enemy but can also be the friend, i.e. the allies. Since a country's relations with other states determines its own identity, the way in which editorials, opinion articles and

---

1    Annette Becker, "14-18 Écrire la Grande Guerre", *Écrire la guerre de Homère à Edward Bond*, Magazine littéraire, n° 378, juillet-août 1999, p. 49.

492

letters to the editor on both sides of the Atlantic described the allies showed how they perceived their own country.

Most editorials in the two American newspapers endorsed George Bush's formation of the coalition and were in favour of the allies. However, numerous opinion articles, especially in the *New York Times*, questioned their military participation and their financial contribution, which was deemed too modest. American editorialists and journalists, critical or not of the allies, stressed the United States' sense of moral duty, as the leader of the coalition. On the British side, the situation was more nuanced: articles in the *Times* and most of those published in the *Sunday Times* were in favour of the alliance, thereby following the British Prime Ministers' rhetoric and highlighting Britain's key role in the coalition. In contrast, many opinion pieces in the *Guardian* and the *Observer* were disparaging of the coalition and downplayed their country's position.

American and British newspapers referred widely to the coalition members. Unlike the official narrative, most editorials and opinion articles and letters criticized the European, French, German, Chinese and Russian allies. In this respect, the press on both sides of the Atlantic was thus playing its role as the Fourth Estate, guaranteeing democratic debate, by analysing the actions, decisions and attitudes of their government towards their allies during the period under study. Among the members of the coalition, it was the Arab states who received the most negative, even virulent, criticism in the American and British press, which was similar to the dualistic approach to the Iraqi leader.

While the *New York Times,* in the American press, and the

*Times,* in the British press, published positive editorials about the Soviet Union, echoing the official line, most comments perpetuated unfavourable ideological prejudices against this country, making it appear to the reader as a still very real threat and thus reinforcing its status as an adversary. As already mentioned, the Gulf Crisis and War enabled many journalists – including William Safire of the *New York Times* and a few from the *Sunday Times* – to give free rein to their prejudices towards the Other, Enemy or Friend. By contrast, Britain in the American press and the United States on the British side received positive, even laudatory, comments from editorialists and journalists – apart from those in the *Observer.* The British press differed from the American press in the large number of articles on the United States, reflecting the interest of British newspapers in the U.S. and the asymmetric nature of the special relationship. The British press, nostalgic for its country's former power, wanted to give events in the Gulf an epic feel.

*Other differences between the American and British press*

The American press published more articles than the British press about the coalition as a whole, probably due to the position of the United States as the leader of the coalition. The British press was more critical than the American press as it questioned the colonial policy of the West and Britain in the Gulf States. This provided readers with a moral reflexion on the historical responsibility of Western countries and in particular Britain in the Middle East. Likewise, on the American side, a few opinion articles, mostly published in the *Washington Post* and some of them in very harsh terms, reminded their readers of Britain's role in the history of the Gulf States.

On the other hand, some journalists from the *New York Times* and especially the *Washington Post* criticized U.S. foreign policy in the Gulf countries. On the British side, it was above all the articles in the *Guardian* and the *Observer* that blamed the British government for submitting to Washington's orders. Based on these four newspapers (two in each country), it cannot be concluded that one country's press was more critical of the government than the other. Another difference between the press on both sides of the Atlantic was the reference to the notion of *realpolitik*, which was discussed more in the British press and to which the American press devoted few articles, perhaps because journalists did not consider this concept to be applicable to U.S. foreign policy during the Gulf events.

As for the more specific differences between the newspapers, the *Washington Post* advocated an internationalist approach in order to gain the support of U.S. allies while the *New York Times* did not devote editorials to this subject, showing that the national interest was much more important to the paper. The *New York Times* published editorials and numerous opinion articles that were negative about the allies, which seemed to indicate a more hostile attitude to the coalition forces than that of the *Washington Post*. The *Washington Post* published many more hostile articles, in particular against the Soviet Union while most of the letters published criticized the allies, especially the Arab countries. On balance, there did not seem to be any fundamental difference between the two newspapers in their attitude towards the allies. The *New York Times* and the British newspapers, on the other hand, differed from the *Washington Post* by publishing articles and letters more sympathetic to the Arab peoples, whom they did not equate with their leaders, thus reflecting a more ethical stance.

On the British side, the *Times* published the most editorials about the alliance as a whole, the Arab countries and the Soviet Union, showing the newspaper's focus on the involvement of British troops in the coalition and events abroad, especially in the Middle East. In particular, its positive editorials on the Soviet Union relayed what the authorities were saying.

It is hardly surprising, given the stance the *Sunday Times* took during the Gulf events, that it was the only one of the other British newspapers not to incriminate its country's foreign policy in the Middle East. Nor was it astonishing that its editorials were critical of the United Nations. As with the description of the enemy, the *Sunday Times* differed from other newspapers in its more colloquial language, its scathing attacks on Europe in general and its hostile comments on France and Germany. Its remarks on the Arab states reflected an ethnocentric and even racist view of the Other. The negative trend in its comments showed that British national interest was of paramount importance to the Sunday paper, which was truly nationalistic. The *Observer* differed from other British newspapers in publishing a majority of articles criticizing the decisions taken by the U.S. president between August 1990 and mid-March 1991. The Sunday paper was also inconsistent in its stance on the co-operation of the coalition members. The same applied to the *Washington Post*, on the American side, which changed its opinion in its editorials on the U.N.

The favourable remarks towards Britain in the American newspapers and conversely towards the United States in the British press, allied to the negative comments about the Iraqi leader – the Enemy – and the other allies, painted a flattering portrait of both Britain and the United States. That referred to the duality between the Self and the Other.

### *The image of the Self*

While describing the enemy and the coalition members, the American and British press projected their countries' self-image regarding their armed forces and military equipment; the role played by the United States and Britain during the Gulf events; the previous crises and conflicts that influenced their countries' histories.

First, on the American side, most editorials, opinion articles and readers' letters glorified the military power of the United States and its high-technology weaponry, following George Bush's rhetoric. The British press, however, was more nuanced: echoing the Prime Minister's comments, the *Times* and the *Sunday Times* praised the British armed forces and emphasized the fighting spirit of their country. They thus portrayed Britain as a determined and combative nation. The *Guardian* and the *Observer* painted a contrasting picture of the British army by publishing contradictory positions. Like George Bush and Margaret Thatcher, a few articles in the American press and numerous editorials and opinion pieces in the British press addressed the notion of "just war" to validate the legitimacy of the Gulf War. That the two American newspapers published few articles on this concept could be explained by the fact that both newspapers might have been convinced of their good faith and moral superiority as, for them, the cause they were defending could not be disputed.

Second, most editorials in both American newspapers welcomed U.S. leadership of the coalition during the Gulf Crisis and hostilities, following the U.S. president's rhetoric and thus painting a glowing picture of their country. By contrast, opinion articles expressed mixed viewpoints. There were some differences in the image of the United States between the two American newspapers: because of financial costs and the possible loss of life, the *New York Times* appeared to be more hostile than the *Washington Post* to the United States' leading role in the coalition. This perspective was reflected in a few editorials, a large number of opinion articles and in letters. On the British side, the four newspapers variously assessed Britain's role: repeating the British Prime Ministers' remarks, the *Times* and the *Sunday Times* inflated its role, which was put on an equal footing with the United States especially in the Sunday paper. In contrast, the *Guardian* and particularly the *Observer* belittled Britain's position vis-à-vis the United States. Britain's image was thus more mixed in the British press.

Third, editorials, opinion articles and letters in the press on both sides of the Atlantic drew parallels between earlier crises and wars and that of the Gulf. They reminded their readers of the First and Second World Wars in the American and British press; the Vietnam War and the Korean War above all in the U.S. press and the Falklands War and the Suez Crisis in the British press. Editorialists and journalists, who opposed the entry of their country into the Gulf War, referred to past conflicts before the outbreak of hostilities to warn their readers of the possible risk of high casualties. By contrast, those who favoured the military engagement of their country indulged in nostalgia for their nation's past victories to convince their readers of the need to go to war against Iraq. Newspapers thus engaged in a relatively multifaceted but biased reading of History depending on the message they wanted to convey to their readers.

While the tone of journalistic comments in each newspaper differed – from moderate in the *Times* to aggressive with some journalists from the *New York Times* and the *Sunday Times* – the objective was the same: the restoration of the supremacy of national interests and the reassertion of the country's identity. As we have seen, crises and wars immobilise international relations, harden the tone of journalistic discourse and confirm stereotypes and subjective moral judgments about the Other – Enemy or Friend.

Newspapers in the press on both sides of the Atlantic more or less followed the official narrative regarding the description of the enemy and deviated from it concerning that of the allies. A rhetoric of persuasion was at work in the press about the image of the Enemy, the allies and their country. Editorials, opinion articles and letters in both U.S. newspapers used the same lexical and semantic field as well as laudatory arguments that were repeated over and over again to depict the leading role of the United States in the coalition and its power against that of the enemy. British newspapers also kept repeating the same themes in articles throughout the Gulf Crisis and hostilities (i.e. the lack of cohesion and unanimity among the various European countries; their dependence on Middle Eastern oil and that of Japan; the financial contribution of Germany and Japan, which was deemed insufficient despite their flourishing economies; the arms sales of French and German firms to Iraq and the delayed and diffuse reactions of the various European allies).

Finally, the American and British press offered readers a

range of different viewpoints in opinion articles and letters to the editor concerning the portrayal of Saddam Hussein or the allies and regarding their country's military might, its role in the Gulf and references to previous conflicts. By publishing articles and letters diverging from their editorial line, American and British newspapers enabled the reader to refine his or her opinion and eventually to endorse, or otherwise, the editorial line of his or her newspaper. In other words, the press on both sides of the Atlantic demonstrated journalistic pluralism and fuelled democratic debate.

To sum up, editorialists and journalists promoted and enhanced the image of the United States in the American press and that of Britain in the British press. References to the United Nations and to the USA's multilateral approach as the leader of the coalition further reinforced the United States' positive image in the American press. Journalists in the American and British press portrayed the United States as an exemplary country as it took its moral and military responsibilities seriously during the events. On the British side, the majority of opinions – especially in the *Times* and the *Sunday Times* – projected a positive image of Britain, stressing the importance of its own role in the Gulf Crisis and War. Britain was described as a country that assumed its obligations alongside the United States in the coalition against Iraq. The press on both sides of the Atlantic adopted a patriotic discourse, coupled with ethnocentric rhetoric that reinforced reductive and bipolar world views.

### *The press in perspective*

Even though the press on both sides of the Atlantic reproduced the official line by repeating the stereotype of the Enemy – of the Other – and thus conveying a dualist vision of the world, can we condemn the newspapers in question for being the faithful interpreters of their respective governments? Whereas a dictatorial regime does not ask the opinion of its people to go to war, the same is not true of a democracy. The leaders of a democratic nation have a duty to explain to the citizens who elected them the reasons – sometimes far remote from the everyday concerns of the people – for the envisaged military intervention, which is more essential when the conflict is taking place in a distant country that is little known or even unknown to citizens. The government of a democratic country will aim to convince its citizens of the merits of sending its armed troops to participate in the war by issuing a series of official explanatory communiqués. In wartime, journalists are torn between their duty to inform their readers and their sense of responsibility for the lives of soldiers on the ground. Beyond the question of self-censorship influencing the content of articles, the problem arises of how freedom of information and of the press and the security of the armed forces can be reconciled.

Although it was not necessary to go to great lengths to blacken Saddam Hussein's image, the written press was required to strive to inform readers in an objective manner despite the pressure of time constraints on writing news articles for timely and regular transmission. The press is indeed expected to be highly professional, to distance itself from the information provided by military and government authorities, and above all to question and dismantle propaganda techniques, political speeches and official decisions, especially if they involve the nation's troops in a conflict. In this context, American and British newspapers could be criticized for not having taken enough distance from the media hype caused by the invasion of Kuwait since other countries have been invaded and abuses perpetrated in other parts of the world without attracting the same level of interest from the media on both sides of the Atlantic.

While editorialists and journalists, on the American side, gave a flattering image of the United States based on the belief in their destiny as a leader country and a chosen nation, some journalists on the British side clung to nostalgia for a once great but now vanished power. But should we really blame editorialists and journalists for overestimating and exaggerating the role of their country and for developing a patriotic narrative? In wartime it is hardly possible for journalists to criticize soldiers of their country's army who are risking their lives. In a conflict opposing its country's army and enemy soldiers, the media is compelled to adhere to the government's policy and support the war effort or risk offending its readers' sensibilities and thus losing them. If a newspaper loses its readers, it loses its raison d'être. On the other hand, it should not be forgotten that media companies are private enterprises subject to the diktats of the market economy. Since media power is subordinate to economic interests, the newspaper, whatever its editorial line, depends on its owners or shareholders who want their investments to be profitable. In this context, while journalists must aim for objectivity and truth in their articles, they must above all write what the editors and their readers expect of them and produce information of relevance and/ or interest to their readers. Thus, journalists have little room for manoeuvre between their investigative work on the one hand, and the norms and unspoken requirements of their newspaper on the other. They must comply with economic constraints, especially the expectations of shareholders and the powerful.

This work on the press on both sides of the Atlantic during the selected period leads to several more general conclusions. For the 20th-century historian Fernand Braudel, who contrasts the short-term event with the long-term historical view, the press deals primarily with facts that are in the "short term" of the immediate present.[2] Journalists, subject to the reign of immediacy and the constraints of time and competition, find it difficult to keep the required distance in the very moment of war. They cannot take the time to check and reflect. Writing from day to day and without a long-term plan, journalists are therefore in a sense the historians of the immediacy, which raises the problem of their reliability. This study, carried out more than twenty years after the Gulf events, was instead undertaken at a distance in time, which enabled us to take the necessary distance from the facts to ensure an analytical perspective. Moreover, examining the journalistic treatment – herein the American and British press – of past events, such as those of 1990 and 1991 allows for a better understanding of the events that unfolded afterwards. This thesis is thus a case study of what was repeated during the Second Gulf War in 2003.

During a war, the press is not only under the constraint of the short term because of the lack of time for reflection but also tends to continuous journalistic repetition of facts, thus transforming them into events. The event, which is seen as a fact that disrupts order and ordinary life, is perceived as extraordinary and thus becomes worthy of interest for the journalist. Defined in this way, the Gulf Crisis and War are significant events. Thanks to technical progress in the instant dissemination of information, these events are quickly known throughout the world, the "global village" so

---

2    Thomas Ferenczi, *op. cit.*, p. 16.

named by Marshall McLuhan. Since events never cease to follow one another, History is written continuously, first by journalists and then by historians who base their work among other things on available material, including newspaper articles. History – often that of the victors – is therefore also made, not just by events but also by the contributions of journalists. Journalism is often called "the first rough draft of history".

Anchored in their time and the situation of the moment, journalists urgently make an arbitrary selection of what then may contribute to the collective memory. This choice, imposed upon the reader, is often made according to their convictions and above all those of their newspaper. In this way, journalists give the reader their perception of reality and offer their representation of the world. This study therefore raises the question about the interpretation of events by journalists as well as their writing and immediate production of the first version of History. In the same vein, this work can also lead to question the way in which the individual as a citizen interprets the information provided by newspapers and in particular the event of crisis and war. This thus raises the question about the construction of our own world view and production of ideas and, more generally, how our sense of History is developed.

This study also shows a case of bringing to the fore simplistic evidence, such as the polarisation between the West and the Middle East. It is thus a textbook case of the state of war and the consensus on the enemy between journalists on the one hand and authorities on the other. The state of war feeds prejudice and a good versus evil ideology. For Plato, cities are in a continuous state of war with each other. Hobbes, meanwhile, considers the state of nature as a permanent state of war of all against all, a characteristic of humanity and of the individual. This work provides food for thought on the consequences of war on the functioning of the press in a contemporary democracy. As we have seen, journalists are torn between the need to inform their readers on the one hand, and *reasons of state* and the compassion for the lives of their fellow citizens engaged in the armed forces on the other; *reasons of state* impose military supervision of reporters and therefore limit access to sources of information and freedom of expression. This phenomenon increased during the Second Gulf War in 2003.

In addition to learning the ethical standards inherent to their profession, journalists must be rigorous in all circumstances and self-critical about their journalistic practice, even and above all in times of war. Adopting a constructive approach, they must not only inform their readers, but also set the issues in context to provide better understanding of the origins of events and stimulate critical thinking. Like the task of philosophy for Nietzsche, the mission of journalists should consist in trying to harm stupidity. It would also be necessary that newspapers in general do not only publish catastrophic and anxiety-provoking articles, which arouse a sick feeling in the collective consciousness and only fuel fear, even hatred, towards the Other.

Finally, there is also the question of what kind of press is desirable in a democracy in wartime but also in peacetime. The first condition is that the press should be free and independent in order to be able to contribute to the democratic debate of ideas and thus play its role as the Fourth Estate. To do so, the press must be vigilant especially during conflict, to guard against subtle attempts at manipulation by military and government authorities. By providing a contrary perspective, the press must also challenge the uniform dominant thinking of the established power and that of the shareholders or owners of newspapers who are mostly motivated by profit. Since they, owners or shareholders, often decide the business strategy of newspapers considered as commercial enterprises, they aim to ensure that nothing is published that could harm advertising revenues. In the existing market order, the press must seek to maintain its profitability and increase its sales as much as possible to ensure its existence.

Although readers of "quality" newspapers are supposed to be informed and educated, it is, however, difficult for them not to be influenced by the repetitive style of their newspapers and question the arguments developed. During a conflict, readers should of course aim to maintain a critical and emotional distance from the events. They could apply Henry David Thoreau's concept of "civil disobedience"[3] and practise a kind of "media disobedience" by diversifying their sources of information and reading different newspapers with opposite editorial lines.

Because of the multiple constraints in which they have to operate, it is difficult for journalists in time of war to remain as impartial as they might like. They are often obliged to write under pressure: they usually have tight deadlines to respect and have little time to reflect. War correspondents find that their relationships with the men and women whose lives they share can affect their perception of the events they witness, while

---

3    David Henry Thoreau (1817-1862) was an American thinker and transcendentalist who wrote an essay called "Civil Disobedience".

journalists at home may be influenced by the polarization of opinion that war inevitably generates. Even if journalists are able to resist any tendency to introduce involuntary bias into their reports and comments, they lack the critical distance that time can help provide, and they may well only see a small part of events taking place on a much larger scale than anything they can themselves observe. This is at least what this study has sought to show by focusing on these tensions during the Gulf events and finding numerous examples of the perils of journalistic writing in wartime. Whether these reflections bear fruit in this area would be desirable but remains unlikely.

# Appendices

## Appendix 1: Chronology of the Gulf Crisis and War

### *August 1990*

| | |
|---|---|
| 2 August: | Iraqi forces invade Kuwait at 2 a.m. local time. The U.N. Security Council passes Resolution 660, condemning the invasion and demanding the withdrawal of Iraqi forces. |
| 3 August: | A puppet government is set up in Kuwait. The Council of Foreign Ministers of the Arab League states condemn the Iraqi invasion. Iraq masses its troops on Saudi Arabian border. |
| 5 August: | The European Community, Japan and the United States ban imports of Iraqi and Kuwaiti crude oil and petrol. President Bush declares that Iraq's invasion of Kuwait "will not stand". |
| 6 August: | The U.N. adopts Resolution 661, imposing a trade embargo against Iraq. The Saudi Arabian government requests U.S. troops to help protect the country from an Iraqi attack. Iraq begins to move Westerners in Kuwait to Iraq. |
| 7 August: | 4,000 U.S. troops from 82nd Airborne Division are sent to Saudi Arabia. |
| 8 August: | Saddam Hussein proclaims the annexation of Kuwait. |

|  | The United States launches Operation Desert Shield. |
|---|---|
| 9 August: | U.N. Resolution 662 declares Iraq's annexation of Kuwait null and void. |
|  | Iraq seals its borders. |
| 10 August: | Iraq orders foreign governments to close their embassies in Kuwait. |
|  | The Arab League votes 12-9 to send Arab troops to Saudi Arabia. |
| 12 August: | Saddam Hussein connects Iraqi withdrawal from Kuwait with Israeli withdrawal from occupied territories. This becomes known as the issue of "linkage". |
|  | President Bush orders naval blockade of Iraq. |
| 16 August: | Iraq begins detaining all foreign nationals in both Iraq and Kuwait. |
| 18 August: | Iraq threatens to use foreign hostages as "human shields" at key installations. |
|  | United Nations Security Council Resolution 664 demands the immediate release of all foreign nationals in Iraq and Kuwait. |
|  | Oil prices climb to about $28 per barrel. |
| 19 August: | Iraq offers to release all foreign nationals if the United States withdraws its forces from the Gulf region. |
| 23 August: | The Iraqi leader appears on Iraqi television with a group of hostages, including little children. |
| 24 August: | Iraqi troops surround any embassies in Kuwait that have not complied with Iraq's order to close. |
| 25 August: | U.N. Resolution 665 authorises naval blockade to enforce economic sanctions. |

|  | BBC and CNN crews enter Iraq. |
| 28 August: | The Iraqi leader declares Kuwait to be its 19th province. |
|  | Iraq offers to free women and children detained. |

## *September 1990*

---

| 1 September: | 200 British women and children are allowed to leave Iraq. |
| 9 September: | At the Helsinki summit, Presidents Bush and Gorbachev issue a joint statement, calling for an immediate withdrawal of Iraq from Kuwait. They pledge cooperation but acknowledge that there are still differences in the American and Soviet positions. |
| 11 September: | The United Kingdom commits ground forces to the Gulf. |
|  | President Bush addresses Congress on his actions and states his concept of a new world order. |
| 13 September: | U.N. Resolution 666 authorises humanitarian food shipments if distributed through international aid agencies. |
| 14 September: | The United Kingdom announces it is sending its 7th Armoured Brigade to the Gulf region. |
|  | Iraqi troops entered the Belgian Embassy and the residences of the French and Canadian ambassadors to Kuwait. |
| 16 September: | U.N. Resolution 667 condemns Iraqi aggressive acts against diplomatic premises and personnel in Kuwait. |

| 17 September: | EC countries order the expulsion of all military staff from Iraqi embassies after the invasion by Iraqi troops of the residences of foreign diplomats in Kuwait. |
| 24 September: | The U.N. Security Council unanimously passes Resolution 669, requesting Security Council to assist other nations affected by trade sanctions. |
| 25 September: | U.N. Resolution 670 bans all cargo flights to Iraq. |

## October 1990

| 1 October: | President Bush addresses the United Nations. |
| 8 October: | Israeli police fire on Palestinians at Temple Mount in Jerusalem (21 killed and over 100 wounded). |
| 9 October: | Oil prices jump to $40 a barrel. |
| 23 October: | Edward Heath, the former British Prime Minister (1970-74), returns from Baghdad with 37 freed British hostages. Iraq releases 330 French hostages. |
| 29 October: | U.N. Resolution 674 calls for an immediate end to Iraqi hostage taking and demands reparations for war crimes in Kuwait. |

## November 1990

| 3 November: | James Baker, the American Secretary of State, starts a seven-nation tour to form large coalition force. |

| 8 November: | President Bush announces that the number of U.S. troops will be doubled in Saudi Arabia. |
| 18 November: | Iraq announces that it will release all foreign hostages over a three-month period starting on Christmas Day. |
| 19 November: | Iraq mobilizes 250,000 more soldiers. |
| | At a meeting of the Conference of Security and Cooperation in Europe (CSCE), Prime Minister Thatcher declares that the use of military force will become necessary if Iraqi forces do not withdraw. |
| 22 November: | Prime Minister Thatcher resigns. |
| | The United Kingdom announces that it will send 14,000 more troops to the Gulf region. |
| 28 November: | John Major becomes Britain's new Prime Minister. |
| | U.N. Resolution 677 condemns Iraq for attempting to alter the demographic records of Kuwait. |
| 29 November: | The U.N. Security Council passes Resolution 678, requiring Iraq to withdraw from Kuwait by 15 January 1991 and authorizing allies to use "all means necessary" to evict Iraq thereafter. |

### December 1990

| 6 December: | Saddam Hussein announces the release of all hostages still held in Iraq and Kuwait. |
| 24 December: | The Iraqi leader threatens that Israel will be the first target if war breaks out in the Gulf. |

| | |
|---|---|
| 6 January: | Saddam Hussein announces "the mother of all battles" if war breaks out. |
| 9 January: | Talks between U.S. Secretary of State James Baker and Iraqi Foreign Minister Tariq Aziz in Geneva fail. |
| 12 January: | The U.S. Congress approves the use of military force against Iraq. |
| 13 January: | Unsuccessful talks between U.N. Secretary General Perez de Cuellar and Iraq's leader take place. |
| | The Iraqi parliament approves Saddam Hussein's rejection of the U.N. deadline. |
| 14 January: | France submits a peace proposal, which is rejected by the United States. |
| | The Pentagon issues official ground rules and guidelines to the media (12 categories of information cannot be reported; pool coverage is mandatory). |
| 15 January: | Both the last-minute E.C. and French peace proposals collapse. |
| | U.N. Secretary General Perez de Cuellar makes a final appeal to prevent the conflict before the expiry of the U.N. deadline. |
| | Operation Desert Shield comes to an end. |
| 16-17 January: | Operation Desert Storm begins with air warfare. |
| | The price of oil drops from $30 to $18 a barrel. |
| | CNN broadcast live from Baghdad for 17 hours. |
| | Press pools officially spring into action. |
| 18 January: | Iraq fires Scud missiles at Israel and Saudi |

|  | Arabia. The United States warns Israel against retaliation. One Scud missile struck at Saudi Arabia is intercepted by a U.S. Patriot missile. |
|---|---|
| 19 January: | Iraq expels most foreign journalists, except Peter Arnett from CNN and some Jordanian reporters. |
| 20 January: | Iraqi television displays seven captured allied pilots. |
| 22 January: | The Iraqi leader orders the destruction of Kuwaiti oil wells. |
| 23 January: | Iraq publishes photographs of civilian damage. U.S. planes bomb an Iraqi plant described as a "baby-milk" factory by the Iraqis and as a military site by U.S. officials. |
| 24 January: | Iraq releases oil into the Persian Gulf. |
| 28 January: | The Iraqi president warns that worldwide terrorist attacks will be carried out. |
| 29 January: | Iraqi troops invade the town of Khafji in Saudi Arabia near the Kuwaiti border. |
| 30 January: | The first U.S. soldiers are killed in ground combat. |
| 31 January: | Allied forces recapture Khafji. |

### February 1991

| 13 February: | Over 300 Iraqi civilians are killed in an air raid shelter at Amiriyah in Baghdad, which U.S. military officials identified as a military command bunker. |
|---|---|
| 15 February: | Iraq offers to withdraw from Kuwait but adds |

|                |                                                    |
| -------------- | -------------------------------------------------- |
|                | many conditions to his proposal, which coalition leaders reject. |
| 24 February:   | The allied ground offensive, dubbed Operation Desert Sabre, begins at 4 a.m. local time. |
| 26 February:   | Saddam Hussein announces that Iraqi forces have been ordered to retreat from Kuwait, but he does not renounce his claims to Kuwait. |
| 27 February:   | Iraqi Foreign Minister Aziz informs the United Nations that Iraq will comply with all Security Council resolutions on Kuwait. Iraqi forces are defeated. President Bush announces the liberation of Kuwait and declares the end of hostilities, which will be effective the following day. |
| 28 February:   | A ceasefire comes into effect after a 100-hour ground war. |

## *March 1991*

---

|            |                                                         |
| ---------- | ------------------------------------------------------- |
| 3 March:   | Iraq agrees to comply with U.N. Resolution 686. Iraqi commanders accept the military terms of a permanent ceasefire. |

**References:**

Blair, Arthur H., *At War in the Gulf: A Chronology*, Texas: Texas A & M University Press, 1992, Appendix B.

Fialka, John J., *Hotel Warriors: Covering the Gulf War*, Washington, DC: Woodrow Wilson Center Press, 1992, pp. 67-71.

Jeffords, Susan and Lauren Rabinovitz, eds., *Seeing through the Media: The Persian Gulf War*, New Brunswick; NJ: Rutgers University Press, 1994, pp. 307-321.

Mueller, John, *Policy and Opinion in the Gulf War*, Chicago: University of Chicago Press, 1994, pp. 15-16.

Smith, Hedrick, ed., *The Media and the Gulf War: The Press and Democacy in Wartime*, Washington, DC: Seven Locks Press, 1992, pp. 424-429.

Taylor, Philip M., *War and the Media: Propaganda and Persuasion in the Gulf War*, 2nd ed., Manchester; New York: Manchester University Press, 1998, pp. 320-325.

# Appendix 2: Coalition nations

The following countries participated in Operation Desert Storm:

Afghanistan, Argentina, Australia, Bahrain, Bangladesh, Belgium, Canada, Czechoslovakia, Denmark, Egypt, France, Germany, Greece, Honduras, Hungary, Italy, Kuwait, Morocco, the Netherlands, Niger, Norway, New Zealand, Oman, Pakistan, Poland, Portugal, Qatar, Saudi Arabia, Senegal, Spain, Syria, Turkey, the United Arab Emirates, the United Kingdom, the United States.

**References:**

Blair, Arthur H., *At War in the Gulf: A Chronology*, Texas: Texas A & M University Press, 1992, Appendix B.

Taylor, Philip M., *War and the Media: Propaganda and Persuasion in the Gulf War*, 2nd ed., Manchester; New York: Manchester University Press, 1998, p. 325.

# Appendix 3: Summary of the twelve U.N. Security Council Resolutions

**Resolution 660** adopted by the Security Council at its 2932nd meeting, on 2 August 1990:

Condemns the Iraqi invasion of Kuwait; demands that Iraq withdraw immediately and unconditionally all its forces to the positions in which they were located on 1 Aug. 1990; calls upon Iraq and Kuwait to begin immediately intensive negotiations for the resolution of their differences and supports all efforts in this regard, and especially those of the League of Arab States; decides to meet again as necessary to consider further steps to ensure compliance with the resolution.

**Resolution 661** adopted by the Security Council at its 2933rd meeting, on 6 August 1990:

Decides that all States shall prevent: (a) the import into their territories of all commodities and products originating in Iraq or Kuwait exported therefrom after the date of the present resolution; (b) any activities by their nationals or in their territories which would promote the export or trans-shipment of any commodities or products from Iraq or Kuwait; (c) the sale or supply by their nationals or from their territories or using their flag vessels of any commodities or products but not including supplies intended strictly for medical purposes, and in humanitarian circumstances, foodstuffs, to any person or body in Iraq or Kuwait; decides that all States shall not make available to the Government of Iraq or to any commercial, industrial or public utility undertaking in Iraq or Kuwait, any funds or any other financial or economic resources;

decides to establish a Committee of the Security Council consisting of all the members of the Council: (a) to examine the reports on the progress of the implementation of the present resolution; (b) to seek from all States information regarding the action taken by them concerning the implementation of the present resolution; calls upon all States: (a) to take appropriate measures to protect assets of the legitimate Government of Kuwait and its agencies; (b) not to recognize any régime set up by the occupying Power; requests the Secretary-General to report to the Council on the resolution, the 1st report to be submitted within 30 days.

**Resolution 662** adopted by the Security Council at its 2934th meeting, on 9 August 1990:

Decides that annexation of Kuwait by Iraq under any form and whatever pretext has no legal validity, and is considered null and void; calls upon all States, international organizations and specialized agencies not to recognize that annexation, and to refrain from any action or dealing that might be interpreted as an indirect recognition of the annexation; further demands that Iraq rescind its actions purporting to annex Kuwait; decides to keep this item on its agenda and to continue its efforts to put an early end to the occupation.

**Resolution 664** adopted by the Security Council at its 2937th meeting, on 18 August 1990:

Demands that Iraq permit and facilitate the immediate departure from Kuwait and Iraq of the nationals of third countries and grant immediate and continuing access of consular officials to such nationals; further demands that Iraq take no action to jeopardize the safety, security or health of such nationals; reaffirms its decision in Resolution 662 (1990) that annexation of Kuwait by Iraq is null and void, and therefore demands that the Government of Iraq rescind its orders for the closure of diplomatic and consular missions in Kuwait and the withdrawal of the immunity of their personnel, and refrain from any such actions in the future.

**Resolution 665** adopted by the Security Council at its 2938th meeting, on 25 August 1990:

Calls upon those Member States cooperating with the Government of Kuwait which are deploying maritime forces to the area to use such measures commensurate to the specific circumstances as may be necessary under the authority of the Security Council to halt all inward and outward maritime shipping in order to inspect and verify their cargoes and destinations and to ensure strict implementation of the provisions related to such shipping laid down in Resolution 661 (1990); invites Member States to cooperate to ensure compliance with the provisions of Resolution 661 (1990) with maximum use of political and diplomatic measures; requests all States to provide such assistance as may be required by the States referred to in paragraph 1 of this resolution; requests the States concerned to coordinate their actions using as appropriate mechanisms of the Military Staff Committee and after consultation with the Secretary-General to submit reports to the Security Council and its Committee established under Resolution 661 (1990).

**Resolution 666** adopted by the Security Council at its 2939th meeting, on 13 September 1990:

Decides that in order to make the necessary determination whether or not for the purposes of paragraph 3 (c) and paragraph 4 of Resolution 661 (1990) humanitarian circumstances have arisen, the Committee shall keep the situation regarding foodstuffs in Iraq and Kuwait under constant review; requests, for the purposes of paragraphs 1 and 2 of this resolution, that the Secretary-General seek urgently, and on a continuing basis, information from relevant UN and other appropriate humanitarian agencies and all other sources on the availability of food in Iraq and Kuwait, such information to be communicated by the Secretary-General to the Committee regularly; requests further that in seeking and supplying such information particular attention will be paid to such categories of persons who might suffer specially, such as children under 15 years of age, expectant mothers, maternity cases, the sick and the elderly; decides that if the Committee, after receiving the reports from the Secretary-General, determines that circumstances have arisen in which there is an urgent humanitarian need to supply foodstuffs to Iraq or Kuwait in order to relieve human suffering, it will report promptly to the Council its decision as to how such need should be met; directs the Committee that in formulating its decisions it should bear in mind that foodstuffs should be provided through the UN in cooperation with the International Committee of the Red Cross or other appropriate humanitarian agencies and distributed by them or under their supervision in order to ensure that they reach the intended beneficiaries.

**Resolution 667** adopted by the Security Council at its 2940th meeting, on 16 September 1990:

Strongly condemns aggressive acts perpetrated by Iraq against diplomatic premises and personnel in Kuwait, including the abduction of foreign nationals who were present in those premises; demands the immediate release of those foreign nationals as well as all nationals mentioned in Resolution 664 (1990); further demands that Iraq immediately and fully comply with its international obligations under Resolutions 660 (1990) and 664 (1990) of the Security Council, the Vienna Conventions on diplomatic and consular relations and international law; further demands that Iraq immediately protect the safety and well-being of diplomatic and consular personnel and premises in Kuwait and in Iraq and take no action to hinder the diplomatic and consular missions in the performance of their functions, including access to their nationals and the protection of their person and interests.

**Resolution 669** adopted by the Security Council at its 2942nd meeting, on 24 September 1990:

Conscious of the fact that an increasing number of requests for assistance have been received under the provisions of Article 50 of the Charter of the UN, entrusts the Committee established under Resolution 661 (1990) concerning the situation between Iraq and Kuwait with the task of examining requests for assistance under the provisions of Art. 50 of the Charter of the UN and making recommendations to the President of the Security Council for appropriate action.

**Resolution 670** adopted by the Security Council at its 2943rd meeting, on 25 September 1990:

Confirms that Resolution 661 (1990) applies to all means of transport, including aircraft; decides further that all States shall deny permission to any aircraft destined to land in Iraq or Kuwait, whatever its State of registration, to overfly its territory unless: (a) the aircraft lands at an airfield designated by that State outside Iraq or Kuwait in order to permit its inspection to ensure that there is no cargo on board in violation of Resolution 661 (1990) or the present resolution, and for this purpose the aircraft may be detained for as long as necessary; or (b) the particular flight has been approved by the Committee established by Resolution 661 (1990); or (c) the flight is certified by the UN as solely for the purposes of UNIIMOG; decides that each State shall take all necessary measures to ensure that any aircraft registered in its territory or operated by an operator who has his principal place of business or permanent residence in its territory complies with the provisions of Resolution 661 (1990) and the present resolution; decides further that all States shall notify in a timely fashion the Committee established by Resolution 661 (1990) of any flight between its territory and Iraq or Kuwait to which the requirement to land in paragraph 4 above does not apply, and the purpose for such a flight.

**Resolution 674** adopted by the Security Council at its 2951st meeting, on 29 October 1990:

Demands that the Iraqi authorities and occupying forces immediately cease and desist from taking third State nationals hostage, and mistreating and oppressing Kuwaiti and third-State nationals; invites States to collate substantiated information in their possession or submitted to them on the grave breaches by Iraq and to make this information available to the Security Council; reaffirms its demand that Iraq permit and facilitate the immediate departure from Kuwait and Iraq of those third-State nations, including diplomatic and consular personnel, who wish to leave; demands that Iraq ensure the immediate access to food, water and basic services necessary to the protection and well-being of Kuwaiti nationals and of nationals of third States in Kuwait and Iraq, including the personnel of diplomatic and consular missions in Kuwait; reaffirms its demand that Iraq takes no action to hinder diplomatic and consular missions in the performance of their functions, including access to their nationals and the protection of their person and interests and rescind its orders for the closure of diplomatic and consular missions in Kuwait and the withdrawal of the immunity of their personnel; invites States to collect relevant information regarding their claims, and those of their nationals and corporations, for restitution or financial compensation by Iraq; requires that Iraq comply with the provisions of the resolution and its previous resolutions, failing which the Security Council will need to take further measures under the Charter; decides to remain actively and permanently seized of the matter until Kuwait has regained its independence and peace has been restored; reposes its trust in the Security Council to make available his good offices, to pursue them and to undertake diplomatic efforts in order to reach a peaceful solution to the crisis caused by the Iraqi invasion and occupation of Kuwait.

**Resolution 677** adopted by the Security Council at its 2962nd meeting, on 28 November 1990:

Condemns the attempts by Iraq to alter the demographic composition of the population of Kuwait and to destroy the civil records maintained by the legitimate Government of Kuwait; mandates the Secretary-General to take custody of a copy of the population register of Kuwait, the authenticity of which has been certified by the legitimate Government of Kuwait and which covers the registration of the population up to 1 Aug. 1990; requests the Secretary-General to establish, in cooperation with the legitimate Government of Kuwait, an Order of Rules and Regulations governing access to and use of the said copy of the population register.

**Resolution 678** adopted by the Security Council at its 2963rd meeting, on 29 November 1990:

Demands that Iraq comply fully with Resolution 660 (1990) and all subsequent relevant resolutions, and decides, while maintaining all its decisions, to allow Iraq one final opportunity, as a pause of goodwill, to do so; authorizes Member States cooperating with the Government of Kuwait, unless Iraq on or before 15 Jan. 1991 fully implements the foregoing resolutions, to use all necessary means to uphold and implement Resolution 660 (1990) and all subsequent relevant resolutions and to restore international peace and security in the area; requests all States to provide appropriate support for the actions undertaken in pursuance of paragraph 2 of the resolution; requests the States concerned to keep the Security Council regularly informed on the progress of actions undertaken pursuant to paragraphs 2 and 3 of the resolution; decides to remain seized of the matter.

**Reference:**

United Nations Digital Library, <https://digitallibrary.un.org/record/>, consulted 15 March 2023.

# Appendix 4: United Nations Charter, Chapter VII

ACTION WITH RESPECT TO THREATS TO THE PEACE,
BREACHES OF THE PEACE, AND ACTS OF AGGRESSION.

## *Article 39*

The Security Council shall determine the existence of any
threat to the peace, breach of the peace, or act of aggression and
shall make recommendations, or decide what measures shall be
taken in accordance with Articles 41 and 42 to maintain or restore
international peace and security.

## *Article 40*

In order to prevent an aggravation of the situation, the Security
Council may, before making the recommendations or deciding
upon the measures provided for in Article 39, call upon the
parties concerned to comply with such provisional measures as it
deems necessary or desirable. Such provisional measures shall be
without prejudice to the rights, claims, or position of the parties
concerned. The Security Council shall duly take account of failure
to comply with such provisional measures.

## *Article 41*

The Security Council may decide what measures not involving
the use of armed force are to be employed to give effect to
decisions, and it may call upon the Members of the United Nations
to apply such measures. These may include complete or partial
interruption of economic relations and of rail, sea, air, postal,

telegraphic, radio, and other means of communication, and the severance of diplomatic relations.

### *Article 42*

Should the Security Council consider that measures provided for in Article 41 would be inadequate or have proved to be inadequate, it may take such action by air, sea, or land forces as may be necessary to maintain or restore international peace and security. Such action may include demonstrations, blockade, and other operations by air, sea or land forces of Members of the United Nations.

### *Article 43*

1. All Members of the United Nations, in order to contribute to the maintenance of international peace and security, undertake to make available to the Security Council, on its call and in accordance with a special agreement or agreements, armed forces, assistance, and facilities, including rights of passage, necessary for the purpose of maintaining international peace and security.

2. Such agreement or agreements shall govern the numbers and types of forces, their degree of readiness and general location, and the nature of the facilities and assistance to be provided.

3. The agreement or agreements shall be negotiated as soon as possible on the initiative of the Security Council. They shall be concluded between the Security Council and Members or between the Security Council and groups of Members and shall be subject

to ratification by the signatory states in accordance with their respective constitutional processes.

### *Article 44*

When the Security Council has decided to use force it shall, before calling upon a Member not represented on it to provide armed forces in fulfilment of the obligations assumed under Article 43, invite that Member so desires, to participate in the decisions of the Security Council concerning the employment of contingents of that Member's armed forces.

### *Article 45*

In order to enable the United Nations to take military measures, Members shall hold immediately available national air force contingents for combined international enforcement action. The strength and degree of readiness of these contingents and plans for their combined action shall be determined within the limits laid down in the special agreement or agreements referred to in Article 43, by the Security Council with the assistance of the Military Staff Committee.

### *Article 46*

Plans for the application of armed force shall be made by the Security Council with the assistance of the Military Staff Committee.

*Article 47*

1. There shall be established a Military Staff Committee to advise and assist the Security Council on all questions relating to the Security Council's military requirements for the maintenance of international peace and security, the employment and command of forces placed at its disposal, the regulation of armaments, and possible disarmament.

2. The Military Staff Committee shall consist of the Chiefs of Staff of the permanent members of the Security Council or their representatives. Any Member of the United Nations not permanently represented on the Committee shall be invited by the Committee to be associated with it when the efficient discharge of the Committee's responsibilities requires the participation of that Member in its work.

3. The Military Staff Committee shall be responsible under the Security Council for the strategic direction of any armed forces placed at the disposal of the Security Council. Questions relating to the command of such forces shall be worked out subsequently.

4. The Military Staff Committee, with the authorization of the Security Council and after consultation with appropriate regional agencies, may establish regional sub-committees.

*Article 48*

1. The action required to carry out the decisions of the Security Council for the maintenance of international peace and security

shall be taken by all the Members of the United Nations or by some of them, as the Security Council may determine.

2. Such decisions shall be carried out by the Members of the United Nations directly and through their action in the appropriate international agencies of which they are members.

### *Article 49*

The Members of the United Nations shall join in affording mutual assistance in carrying out the measures decided upon by the Security Council.

### *Article 50*

If preventive or enforcement measures against any state are taken by the Security Council, any other state, whether a Member of the United Nations or not, which finds itself confronted with special economic problems arising from the carrying out of those measures shall have the right to consult the Security Council with regard to a solution of those problems.

### *Article 51*

Nothing in the present Charter shall impair the inherent right of individual or collective self-defence if an attack occurs against a Member of the United Nations, until the Security Council has taken measures necessary to maintain international peace and security. Measures taken by Members in the exercise of this right of self-defence shall be immediately reported to the Security Council and shall not in any way affect the authority and responsibility of the Security Council under the present Charter to take at any time such action as it deems necessary in order to maintain or restore international peace and security.

**Reference:**

Charter of the United Nations, Chapter VII, <https://www.un.org/en/about-us/un-charter/chapter-7>, consulted 15 March 2023.

# Bibliography

## Media sources (2 August 1990 – 15 March 1991)

The American press: the *New York Times* and the *Washington Post*

The British press: the *Times*, the *Guardian*, the *Sunday Times* and the *Observer*

## Works cited

Abercrombie, Nicholas and Brian Longhurst. *Dictionary of Media Studies*. London: Penguin Books, 2007.

Albert, Pierre. *La Presse*. Que sais-je? 10e éd. Paris: PUF, 1994.

Amossy, Ruth et Anne Herschberg Pierrot. *Stéréotypes et clichés*. Paris: Nathan/SEYER, 2004.

Anstey, Joanna and John Silverlight, eds. The Observer *Observed. 200 Years of Distinguished Writing from One of the World's Great Newspapers*. London: Barrie & Jenkins, 1991.

Arquié, Marie-José. *A Key to Contemporary British Civilisation*. Paris: Vuibert, 1999.

Aubenas, Florence et Miguel Benasayag. *La Fabrication de l'information. Les journalistes et l'idéologie de la communication*. Paris: La Découverte, 1999.

Axelrod, Alan. *Ace Your Midterms & Finals. U.S. History.* New York: McGraw-Hill, 1999.

Ayerst, David. *Guardian. Biography of a Newspaper.* London: Collins, 1971.

Ayto, John. *Twentieth Century Words.* Oxford: Oxford University Press, 1999.

Bacon, Jean. *Les Saigneurs de la guerre. Brève histoire de la guerre et de ceux qui la font.* Paris: Phébus, 2003.

Balakrishnan, Gopal. *L'Ennemi. Un portrait intellectuel de Carl Schmitt.* Paris: Amsterdam, 2006.

Baudrillard, Jean. *La Guerre du Golfe n'a pas eu lieu.* Paris: Galilée, 1991.

Bennett, W. Lance and David L. Paletz, eds. *Taken by Storm. The Media, Public Opinion, and U.S. Foreign Policy in the Gulf War.* Chicago; London: University of Chicago Press, 1994.

Bertrand, Claude-Jean. *Les Médias aux États-Unis.* Que sais-je? 3e éd. Paris: PUF, 1987.

Bezbakh, Pierre et Sophie Gherardi (sous la dir. de). *Dictionnaire de l'économie.* Paris: Larousse/HER, 2000.

Blair, Arthur H. *At War in the Gulf: A Chronology.* Texas: Texas A & M University Press, 1992.

Blin, Louis. *Le Pétrole du Golfe. Guerre et paix au Moyen-Orient.* Paris: Maisonneuve & Larose, 1996.

Boniface, Pascal (sous la dir. de). *Atlas des relations internationales.* Paris: Hatier, 2003.

Booth, Ken, ed. *Realism and World Politics.* London: Routledge, 2001.

Campagna, Norbert. *Carl Schmitt. Eine Einführung.* Berlin: Parerga, 2004.

Cannon, John, ed. *Dictionary of British History.* Oxford: Oxford University Press, 2001.

Chabot, Alexis. *Cours particulier de culture générale.* Paris: Ellipses, 2009.

Chaliand, Gérard et Annie Jafalian (dir.). *La Dépendance pétrolière. Mythes et réalités d'un enjeu stratégique.* Paris: Encyclopaedia Universalis, 2005.

Chalton, Nicola, ed. *Who Wrote What When?* London: Simon & Schuster UK, 1999.

Chartier, Delphine. *La Traduction journalistique, Anglais-Français.* Toulouse: Presses Universitaires du Mirail, 2000.

Chautard, Sophie. *Géopolitique et pétrole.* Levallois-Perret: Studyrama, 2007.

Chautard, Sophie. *Guerres et conflits du XXe siècle.* Paris: E.J.L., 2004.

Chesnais, Robert. *Médias et politique. William Randolph Hearst à la conquête du pouvoir.* Paris: Dagorno, 1996.

Chevalier, Jean et Alain Gheerbrant. *Dictionnaire des symboles: mythes, rêves, coutumes, gestes, formes, figures, couleurs, nombres.* Paris: Robert Laffont, 2004.

Clément, Élisabeth, et al. *La Philosophie de A à Z.* Paris: Hatier, 2000.

Cockett, Richard. *David Astor and* The Observer. London: André Deutsch, 1991.

Colman, Jonathan. *A 'special relationship'? Harold Wilson, Lyndon B. Johnson and Anglo-American relations 'at the summit', 1964–68.* Manchester: Manchester University Press, 2004.

Combesque, Marie Agnès et Ibrahim Warde. *Mythologies américaines.* Paris: Félin, 2002.

Cottret, Bernard. *Histoire de l'Angleterre. De Guillaume le Conquérant à nos jours.* Paris: Tallandier, 2007.

Crowther, Jonathan, ed. *Oxford Guide to British and American Culture.* Oxford; New York: Oxford University Press, 2001.

Cumin, David. *Carl Schmitt. Biographie politique et intellectuelle.* Paris: Cerf, 2005.

Daiches, David. *A Critical History of English Literature.* 4 vol. 2nd ed. London: Secker & Warburg, 1972.

Delmotte, Axel. *L'Indispensable de la culture anglo-saxonne.* Levallois-Perret: Jeunes éditions/Studyrama, 2003.

De Selys, Gérard et Bogdan van Doninck (sous la dir. de). *La Guerre du pétrole.* Bruxelles, EPO, 1991.

Diamond, Edwin. *Behind the Times. Inside the New* New York Times. New York: Villard Books, 1993.

Dickie, John. *"Special" No More. Anglo-American Relations: Rhetoric and Reality.* London: Weidenfeld & Nicholson, 1994.

Domenach, Jean-Marie. *La Propagande politique.* Que sais-je? 7e éd. Paris: PUF, 1973.

Drabble, Margaret, ed. *The Oxford Companion to English literature.* Oxford: Oxford University Press, 1995.

Duccini, Hélène. *Faire voir, faire croire. L'opinion publique sous Louis XIII.* Seyssel: Champ Vallon, 2003.

Dufour, Jean-Louis. *Les Crises internationales. De Pékin (1900) à Bagdad (2004).* Bruxelles: Complexe, 2004.

Dunan, Marcel (sous la dir. de). *Histoire Universelle. Vol. 2.* Paris: Larousse, 1960.

Duroselle, Jean-Baptiste et André Kaspi. *Histoire des relations internationales de 1945 à nos jours.* Tome 2. 13e éd. Paris: Armand Colin, 2002.

Eco, Umberto. *Il Superuomo Di Massa*. Milano: Fabbri & Bompiani Sonzoguo, 1978.

Emery, Michael and Edwin Emery. *The Press and America. An Interpretive History of the Mass Media*. 6th ed. Englewood Cliffs, NJ: Prentice-Hall, 1988.

Engdahl, William. *A Century of War: Anglo-American Oil Politics and the New World Order*. Rev. ed. London: Pluto Press, 2004.

Fabijanić, Darija, Christian Spahr, Vladimir Zlatarsky, eds. *Conflict Reporting in the Smartphone Era*. Berlin: Konrad-Adenauer-Stiftung, 2016.

(General Sir) Farrar-Hockley, Anthony. *The British Part in the Korean War*. Vol. II. An Honourable Discharge. London: HMSO, 1995.

Ferenczi, Thomas. *Le Journalisme*. Que sais-je? Paris: PUF, 2005.

Ferguson, Niall. *Colossus. The Rise and Fall of the American Empire*. London: Penguin Books, 2005.

Fialka, John J. *Hotel Warriors: Covering the Gulf War*. Washington, DC: Woodrow Wilson Center Press, 1992.

Fisher, David. *Morality and War. Can War be Just in the Twenty-first Century?* Oxford: Oxford University Press, 2011.

Fisk, Robert. *The Great War for Civilization. The Conquest of the Middle East*. Rev. ed. London: Harper Perennial, 2006.

Fleury-Vilatte, Béatrice (sous la dir. de). *Les Médias et la guerre du Golfe.* Nancy: Presses Universitaires de Nancy, 1992.

Foucault, Michel. *Histoire de la folie à l'âge classique.* Paris: Gallimard, 1976.

Fox, Kate. *Watching the English. The Hidden Rules of English Behaviour.* London: Hodder and Stoughton, 2005.

Freund, Julien. *L'Essence du politique.* 3e éd. Paris: Dalloz, 2004.

Gallo, Max. *Les Clés de l'Histoire contemporaine.* Paris: Libraires Arthème Fayard, 2005.

Gammal, Denise Lohrey. *Relations between British Government Sources and the Media in Wartime.* Dissertation. Cambridge: Cambridge University, 1997.

Géré, François. *Pourquoi les guerres? Un siècle de géopolitique.* Paris: Larousse, 2003.

Germond, Jack W. and Jules Witcover. *Whose Broad Stripes and Bright Stars? The Trivial Pursuit of the Presidency 1988.* New York: Warner Books, 1989.

Gernelle, Étienne. *Les Nouveaux défis du pétrole.* Toulouse: Les Essentiels Milan, 2006.

Golding, William. *Lord of the Flies.* London: Faber and Faber, 2005.

Gounelle, Max. *Relations internationales.* 6e éd. Paris: Dalloz, 2004.

Greenberg, Bradley S. and Walter Gantz, eds. *Desert Storm and the Mass Media*. 2nd ed. Cresskill, NJ: Hampton Press, 1993.

Greenslade, Roy. *Press Gang. How Newspapers Make Profits from Propaganda*. London: Pan Books, 2004.

Gresh, Alain et Dominique Vidal. *Les 100 clés du Proche-Orient*. Paris: Hachette Littératures, 2003.

Griffiths, Dennis, ed. *The Encyclopedia of the British Press 1422-1992*. Basingstroke: Macmillan Press, 1992.

Gros, Frédéric. *Michel Foucault*. Que sais-je? 3e éd. Paris: PUF, 2005.

Guët, Alain et Philippe Laruelle. *The US in a Nutshell*. Paris: PUF, 1996.

Hakim, Joy. *All the People 1945-2001. A History of US*. New York: Oxford University Press, 2003.

Hakim, Joy. *Freedom. A History of US*. Oxford; New York: Oxford University Press, 2003.

Halliday, Fred. *100 Myths about the Middle East*. London: SAQI, 2005.

Hargreaves, Ian. *Journalism. A Very Short Introduction*. Oxford: Oxford University Press, 2005.

Herman, Edward S. and Noam Chomsky. *Manufacturing Consent. The Political Economy of the Mass Media*. New York: Pantheon Books, 1988.

Hocmard, Gérard (sous la dir. de). *What's What. Dictionnaire culturel du monde anglophone.* Paris: Ellipses, 2004.

Hope, Tim and Richard Sparks, eds. *Crime, Risk and Insecurity. Law and Order in Everyday Life and Political Discourse.* London: Routledge, 2000.

Huntington, Samuel P. *The Clash of Civilizations and the Remaking of World Order.* New York: Simon & Schuster, 1996.

*Hutchinson: The Encyclopedia of Britain.* Oxford: Helicon Publishing, 1999.

Jacquard, Albert. *Petite philosophie à l'égard des non-philosophes.* Paris: Calmann-Lévy, 1997.

Janssen, Sarah, executive ed. *The World Almanac and Book of Facts 2021.* New York: World Almanac Books, 2020.

Jeffords, Susan and Lauren Rabinovitz, eds. *Seeing through the Media. The Persian Gulf War.* New Brunswick, NJ: Rutgers University Press, 1994.

Jones, Carole Bryan. *Twentieth Century USA.* Teach Yourself. London: Hodder Education, 2005.

Kaminsky, Catherine. *La Géopolitique et ses enjeux.* Toulouse: Les Essentiels Milan, 2002.

Kaspi, André. *Les Américains. 2. Les États-Unis de 1945 à nos jours.* Paris: Seuil, 2002.

Kaspi, André. *Les Américains. 1. Naissance et essor des États-Unis 1607-1945.* Paris: Seuil, 1986.

Keeble, Richard. *The Newspapers Handbook.* 4th ed. London: Routledge, 2006.

Keeble, Richard. *Secret State, Silent Press. New militarism, the Gulf and the Modern Image of Warfare.* Luton: University of Luton Press, 1997.

Kissinger, Henry. *Does America Need a Foreign Policy? Toward a Diplomacy for the 21st Century.* New York: Simon & Schuster, 2001.

Knightley, Phillip. *The First Casualty: The War Correspondent as Hero and Myth-Maker from the Crimea to Kosovo.* London: Prion Books, 2000.

Lacorne, Denis (sous la dir. de). *Les États-Unis.* Paris: Fayard/CERI, 2006.

Lagayette, Pierre. *Les États-Unis contemporains.* Rosny s/Bois: Bréal, 2002.

Laupies, Frédéric (sous la dir. de). *Dictionnaire de culture générale.* 2e éd. Paris: PUF, 2005.

Laurent, Éric. *La Face cachée du pétrole.* Paris: Plon, 2006.

Laurent, Éric. *Tempête du désert. Les secrets de la Maison-Blanche.* Paris: Olivier Orban, 1991.

Le Goff, Jacques. *Un Autre Moyen Âge.* Paris: Gallimard, 1999.

Lemonnier, Bertrand, et al. *Médias et culture de masse en Grande-Bretagne depuis 1945.* Paris: Armand Colin, 1999.

Lévi-Strauss, Claude. *Race and History.* Paris: Unesco, 1952.

Lieberman, Trudy. *Slanting the Story. The Forces That Shape the News.* New York: New Press, 2000.

Lloyd, T. O. *Empire, Welfare State, Europe. History of the United Kingdom 1906-2001.* 5th ed. Oxford: Oxford University Press, 2002.

Loyn, David. *Frontline. The True Story of the British Mavericks Who Changed the Face of War Reporting.* London: Penguin Books, 2006.

Luizard, Pierre-Jean. *La Question irakienne.* Paris: Fayard, 2002.

Lurbe, Pierre. *Le Royaume-Uni aujourd'hui.* Paris: Hachette, 2000.

MacArthur, Brian. *Deadline Sunday. A Life in the Week of the Sunday Times.* London: Hodder & Stoughton, 1991.

MacMillan, Margaret. *War – How Conflict Shaped Us.* London: Profile Books, 2020.

Marr, Andrew. *A History of Modern Britain.* London: Pan Books, 2008.

Marr, Andrew. *My Trade. A Short History of British Journalism.* London: Pan Books, 2005.

Martinière, Nathalie. *Décrypter les médias américains.* Paris: PUF, 1998.

Marx, Roland. *Histoire de la Grande-Bretagne*. Paris: Perrin, 2004.

McGeveran, William A. Jr., ed. *The World Almanac and Book of Facts 2004*. New York: World Almanac Books, 2004.

McNair, Brian. *Journalism and Democracy*. London: Routledge, 2000.

McNair, Brian. *News and Journalism in the UK*. London: Routledge, 1994.

Mead, Walter Russell. *Special Providence. American Foreign Policy and How It Changed the World*. New York: Alfred A. Knopf, 2001.

Merle, Marcel. *La Crise du Golfe et le nouvel ordre international*. Paris: Economica, 1991.

Moreau Defarges, Philippe. *Introduction à la géopolitique*. Paris: Seuil, 2005.

Morelli, Anne. *Principes élémentaires de propagande de guerre*. Bruxelles: Labor, 2001.

Morgan, Kenneth O., ed. *The Oxford History of Britain*. Rev. ed. Oxford: Oxford University Press, 2001.

Morgan, Kenneth O. *Twentieth-Century Britain: A Very Short Introduction*. Oxford: Oxford University Press, 2000.

Mouriquand, Jacques. *L'Écriture journalistique*. Que sais-je? Paris: PUF, 1997.

Mourre, Michel. *Le Petit Mourre. Dictionnaire de l'Histoire.* Paris: Larousse-Bordas, 1998.

Mowlana, Hamid, George Gerbner and Herbert I. Schiller, eds. *Triumph of the Image. The Media's War in the Persian Gulf – A Global Perspective.* Boulder; San Francisco; Oxford: Westview Press, 1992.

Mueller, John. *Policy and Opinion in the Gulf War.* Chicago: University of Chicago Press, 1994.

Nguyen, Éric. *La Politique étrangère des États-Unis depuis 1945.* Levallois-Perret: Studyrama, 2004.

Nouschi, André. *Pétrole et relations internationales depuis 1945.* Paris: Armand Colin, 1999.

Ostermann, Änne und Hans Nicklas. *Vorurteile und Feindbilder.* Basel: Beltz, 1984.

Ovendale, Ritchie. *Anglo-American Relations in the Twentieth Century.* Basingstoke: Macmillan Press, 1998.

Ovendale, Ritchie. *Britain, the United States, and the Transfer of Power in the Middle East.* London: Leicester University Press, 1996.

Ovendale, Ritchie, ed. *British Defence Policy since 1945.* Manchester: Manchester University Press, 1994.

*(The) Oxford Handbook of International Relations.* Oxford: Oxford University Press, 2008.

Parsons, Michael. *Le* Times *et la guerre des Malouines – aspects du discours de guerre*. Thèse. Université Michel de Montaigne, Bordeaux III. 1994.

Paugam, Serge (sous la dir. de). *Les 100 Mots de la sociologie*. Que sais-je? Paris: PUF, 2010.

Pauwels, Marie-Christine. *Civilisation américaine*. Paris: Hachette Livre, 1994.

Paxman, Jeremy. *Empire*. London: Penguin Books, 2012.

Picard, Robert G. and Jeffrey H. Brody. *The Newspaper Publishing Industry*. Boston, MA; London: Allyn & Bacon, 1997.

Pichon, Yann le. *Guerre éclair dans le Golfe*. Paris: Jean-Claude Lattès/ ADDIM, 1991.

Pigeat, Henri et Jean Huteau. *Déontologie des médias. Institutions, pratiques et nouvelles approches dans le monde*. Paris: Economica/ Unesco, 2000.

Pouvelle, Jean, Mark Niemeyer et Adrian Park. *Repères de civilisation: Grande-Bretagne, États-Unis*. Paris: Ellipses, 2003.

Quandt, William B. *Peace Process. American Diplomacy and the Arab-Israeli Conflict since 1967*. 3rd ed. Washington, DC: Brookings Institution Press, 2005.

Randall, David. *The Universal Journalist*. 3rd ed. London: Pluto Press, 2007.

Raynaud, Philippe et Stéphane Rials (sous la dir. de). *Dictionnaire de philosophie politique.* 3e éd. Paris: Quadrige/PUF, 2005.

Reed, Charles and David Ryall, eds. *The Price of Peace. Just War in the Twenty-First Century.* Cambridge: Cambridge University Press, 2007.

Reimen, Jacqueline (sous la dir. de). *Méthodes et sources. Manuel bilingue à l'usage des étudiants de civilisation américaine et britannique.* Nancy: Presses Universitaires de Nancy, 1989.

Rémond, René. *Histoire des États-Unis.* Que sais-je? 19e éd. Paris: PUF, 2003.

Reynolds, David. *Britannia Overruled. British Policy and World Power in the Twentieth Century.* 2nd ed. London: Pearson Education, 2000.

Rezé, Michel and Ralph Bowen. *Key Words in American Life: Understanding the United States.* 4th ed. Paris: Armand Colin, 1998.

Rezé, Michel and Ralph Bowen. *Introduction à la vie américaine.* 2e éd. Paris: Armand Colin, 1997.

Rohmann, Chris. *The Dictionary of Important Ideas and Thinkers.* London: Arrow Books, 2002.

Room, Adrian, rev. *Brewer's Dictionary of Phrase & Fable.* London: Cassell & Co, 2002.

Said, Edward W. *Orientalism.* London: Penguin Books, 2003.

Sampson, Anthony. *Who Runs this Place? The Anatomy of Britain in the 21st Century.* London: John Murray, 2005.

Sanchez-Mazas, Margarita et Laurent Licata (dir.). *L'Autre: regards psychosociaux.* Grenoble: Presses Universitaires de Grenoble, 2005.

Schmitt, Carl. *The Concept of the Political.* Chicago: University of Chicago Press, 2007.

Scholes, David. *La Grande-Bretagne contemporaine.* 3e éd. Rosny s/Bois: Bréal, 2000.

Schudson, Michael. *The Power of News.* Cambridge, MA; London: Harvard University Press, 1995.

Seib, Philip. *Beyond the Front Lines. How the News Media Cover a World Shaped by War.* New York: Palgrave Macmillan, 2004.

Sergeant, Jean-Claude. *Les Médias britanniques.* Paris: Ophrys, 2004.

Sergeant, Jean-Claude (sous la dir. de). *Visages de la presse britannique.* Nancy: Presses Universitaires de Nancy, 1987.

Serres, Michel. *Hominescence.* Paris: Le Pommier, 2001.

Smith, Hedrick, ed. *The Media and the Gulf War: The Press and Democracy in Wartime.* Washington, DC: Seven Locks Press, 1992.

Smouts, Marie-Claude, Dario Battistella et Pascal Vennesson. *Dictionnaire des relations internationales.* 2e éd. Paris: Dalloz, 2006.

Soulas, Christine. *Les États-Unis d'aujourd'hui en QCM*. Paris: Ellipses, 2000.

Steiner, Zara S. *Britain and the Origins of the First World War*. London: Macmillan Education, 1987.

Stewart, Graham. *The History of* The Times. *Volume VII 1981-2002. The Murdoch Years*. London: HarperCollins, 2005.

Taylor, Philip M. *British Propaganda in the Twentieth Century. Selling Democracy*. Edinburgh: Edinburgh University Press, 1999.

Taylor, Philip M. *War and the Media: Propaganda and Persuasion in the Gulf War*. 2nd ed. Manchester; New York: Manchester University Press, 1998.

Tindall, George Brown and David Emory Shi. *America. A Narrative History*. 4th ed. New York; London: W.W. Norton & Co, 1997.

Tunstall, Jeremy. *Newspaper Power. The New National Press in Britain*. Oxford: Clarendon Press, 1996.

Vaiss, Paul. *Les Relations entre les États-Unis et la Grande-Bretagne depuis 1945*. Paris: Ellipses, 2002.

Vaïsse, Maurice. *Les Relations internationales depuis 1945*. 10e éd. Paris: Armand Colin, 2005.

Vartier, Jean. *Les Procès d'animaux du Moyen Âge à nos jours*. Paris: Hachette, 1970.

Vlajki, Emil. *La Terreur américaine.* Paris: François-Xavier de Guibert, 2003.

Waelhens, Alphonse De. *La Psychose. Essai d'interprétation analytique et existentiale.* Louvain: Nauwelaerts, 1972.

Weigall, David. *International Relations. A Concise Companion.* London: Arnold, 2002.

Welch, David. *Propaganda Power and Persuasion.* London: British Library, 2013.

Welsh, Frank. *The Four Nations. A History of the United Kingdom.* London: HarperCollins, 2003.

Whittaker, Andrew, ed. *Speak the Culture. Britain.* London: Thorogood Publishing, 2009.

Winkler, Heinrich August. *Der Lange Weg nach Westen. Vom "Dritten Reich" bis zur Wiedervereinigung.* 2. Band. München: C. H. Beck, 2001.

Winter, James. *Common Cents. Media Portrayal of the Gulf War and Other Events.* Montreal; New York: Black Rose Books, 1992.

Wolfsfeld, Gadi. *Media and Political Conflict. News from the Middle East.* Cambridge: Cambridge University Press, 1997.

Zinn, Howard. *A People's History of the United States.* New York: Harper Perennial, 2015.

## Articles and reports cited

Browne, Marjorie Ann and Luisa Blanchfield. Report about the United Nations Regular Budget Contributions by Members from 1990 to 2010. Congressional Research Service. 15 January 2013. <https://sgp.fas.org/crs/row/RL30605.pdf>.

Carosella, Edgardo et Thomas Pradeu. "L'Identité: la part de l'autre". Canal Académie. 2 mai 2010. <http://www.canalacademie.com/ida5575-L-identite-la-part-de-l-autre.html>.

Crowther, Mel and/or Nick Thomas. "Ipsos Reveals British Business Habits". *Daily Research News Online*. 11 October 2005. <http://www.mrweb.com/drno/news4670.htm>.

Cumin, David. "L'Ennemi dans les relations internationales. Le point de vue de Carl Schmitt". *Institut de Stratégie Comparée*. 2005. <www.stratisc.org/strat72_Cumin2-_tdm.html>.

Daggett, Stephen. Report about the Costs of Major U.S. Wars. Congressional Research Service. 29 June 2010. <http://www.fas.org/sgp/crs/natsec/RS22926.pdf>.

Djalli, Mohammad-Reza. "Le Golfe Persique 1971 – 1991: de l'ordre colonial à un nouvel ordre mondial?". *Relations internationales*, No. 66. Été 1991.

Dowd, Vincent. "The birth of Oh! What a Lovely War". *BBC*. 12 November 2011. <http://www.bbc.co.uk/news/magazine-15691707>.

Duguid, Mark. "The Life and Death of Colonel Blimp". BFI Screenonline. 2003-2014. <http://www.screenonline.org.uk/film/id/438362/>.

Élie, Jérôme. "L'Unification allemande et les relations anglo-américaines: première crise d'après-guerre froide de la relation spéciale". *Relations Internationales*, No. 120. Hiver 2004.

"(The) Euro has landed". *Guardian*. Editorial. 31 December 1998. <http://www.guardian.co.uk/world/1998/dec/31/euro.eu>.

Foreign Relations of the United States, 1950, Korea, Volume VII. Office of the Historian, Foreign Service Institute, United States Department of State. <https://history.state.gov/historicaldocuments/frus1950v07/pg_1261>.

Frachon, Alain et Daniel Vernet. "Messianisme à l'américaine. Voyage chez les idéologues de 'W'". *Le Monde 2*. 22 Octobre 2002.

Fukuyama, Francis. "The End of History?". *The National Interest*, No. 16. Summer 1989.

Hall, Ben, Tim Burt and Fiona Symon. "Election 2005: What the papers said". *Financial Times*. 3 May 2005. <http://www.ft.com/cms/s/2/417fa1a2-ab60-11d9-893c-00000e2511c8,dwp_uuid=fdb2b318-aa9e-11d9-98d7-00000e2511c8.html>.

Heisbourg, François. "Quelles leçons stratégiques de la guerre du Golfe?". *Politique Étrangère*, No. 2. Eté 1991.

Hoffman, David. "After the Fall of Shevardnadze – Resignation Leaves Superpowers with Unfinished Business". *Washington Post*. 21 December 1990. <http://archive.seattletimes.com/archive/?date=19901221&slug=1110814>.

Ishow, Habib. "Le Koweït: un État vulnérable". *Relations internationales*, No. 66. Eté 1991.

Jones, Jeffrey M. "Only 3 in 10 Americans Believe War Is Over". Gallup News Service. 18 April 2003. <http://www.gallup.com/poll/8212/Only-Americans-Believe-War-Over.aspx>.

Kelly, John B. "L'Après – Saddam Hussein". *Politique internationale*, No. 49. Automne 1990.

Klein, Jean. "La Réglementation des armements après la guerre du Golfe". *Politique étrangère*, No. 3. Automne 1991.

Krauthammer, Charles. "The Unipolar Moment". *Foreign Affairs: America and the World (1990/91)*. 1 December 2002. <https://nationalinterest.org/article/the-unipolar-moment-revisited-391>.

Kravetz, Marc. "Profession: correspondant de guerre". Écrire la guerre de Homère à Edward Bond. *Magazine littéraire*, No. 378. Juillet – Août 1990.

Kuntz, Christophe. "*Syria Accountability Act* et grand Moyen-Orient américain". *Géopolitique des États-Unis. Culture, intérêts, stratégies. Revue Française de Géopolitique*. Paris: Ellipses, 2005.

"Le Guide mondial de la presse en ligne". *Courrier International*. Hors-série. Octobre – Novembre – Décembre 2003.

Lindemann, Thomas. "Les Images dans la politique internationale: l'image de l'autre". Institut de Stratégie Comparée, 2005. <http://www.stratisc.org/strat72_Lindemann.html>.

Lorrain, Aurélie. "Les États-Unis et la stigmatisation de l'ennemi". *Géopolitique des États-Unis. Culture, intérêts, stratégies. Revue Française de Géopolitique*. Paris: Ellipses, 2005.

MacAskill, Ewen. "Conrad Black freed on $2m bail". *Guardian*. 21 July 2010. <http://www.guardian.co.uk/business/2010/jul/21/conrad-black-released-on-bail>.

Maynes, Charles William. "Les Défis de l'Administration Bush". *Politique étrangère,* No. 1. Printemps 1989.

McFadden, Robert D. "A. M. Rosenthal, Editor of The Times, Dies at 84". *New York Times*. 11 May 2006. <http://www.nytimes.com/2006/05/11/nyregion/11rosenthal.html>.

McFadden, Robert D. "Lelyveld Will Succeed Frankel as the Times's Executive Editor". *New York Times.* 8 April 1994. <http://www.nytimes.com/1994/04/08/nyregion/lelyveld-will-succeed-frankel-as-the-times-s-executive-editor.html>.

Mercier, Arnaud. "Médias et violence durant la guerre du Golfe". *Cultures & Conflits*. Nos 09-10. Printemps – Eté 1993. 4 Mars 2005. <http://conflits.revues.org/index296.html>.

Moïsi, Dominique. "Forces et faiblesses des États-Unis". *Politique étrangère*, No. 1. Printemps 1989.

Morel, Michel. "Howard Barker: la disposition de spectacle et de lecture mise à nu". *Études anglaises*. 2002/3. Tome 55. <http://www.cairn.info/revue-etudes-anglaises-2002-3-page-344.htm>.

Morel, Michel. "Falklands: Le *Guardian* et la guerre". *La "Civilisation" dans l'enseignement et la recherche*, No. 7. Hiver 1982. Lez Valenciennes: Université de Valenciennes.

Newens, Stan. Ray Challinor Obituary. *Guardian*. 24 March 2011. <https://www.guardian.co.uk/theguardian/2011/mar/24/ray-challinor-obituary>.

Norton-Taylor, Richard and Tracy McVeigh. "'It would be bad for our interest': why Thatcher ignored the murder of an *Observer* journalist". *Guardian*. 1 January 2017. <https://theguardian.com/world/2017/jan/01/fazad-bazoft-journalist-iraq-executed-saddam-hussein-thatcher>.

Nouschi, André. "Le Golfe et le pétrole: d'un impérialisme à l'autre?" *Relations internationales*, No. 66. Eté 1991.

(Sir) Parsons, Anthony. "La Crise du Golfe et l'avenir du Moyen-Orient". *Politique étrangère*, No. 4. Hiver 1990.

Peck, Robert S. "Constitutional Protection". *An Unfettered Press*. InfoUSA, U.S. Department of State. 2001. <http://usinfo.org/enus/media/overview/press02.html>.

Peters, Jeremy. "Newspaper Circulation Falls Broadly but at Slower Pace". *New York Times.* 25 October 2010. <https://archive.nytimes.com/ mediadecoder.blogs.nytimes.com/2010/10/25/newspaper-circulation-falls-broadly-but-at-slower-pace/>.

Pew Research Center. "Divided Public Focused on Gulf News; Braced for Bloody War". Report. 10 January 1991. <https://www.pewresearch.org/politics/1991/01/10/divided-public-focused-on-gulf-news-braced-for-bloody-war/>.

Powell, john a. and Stephen Menendian. "The Problem of Othering: Towards Inclusiveness and Belonging". *Othering & Belonging: Expanding the Circle of Human Concern.* Issue 1. Summer 2016. University of California, Berkeley. <http://live-otheringandbelonging. pantheon.berkeley.edu/the-problem-of-othering/>.

Quandt, William B. "L'Amérique et le conflit israélo-arabe". *Politique étrangère*, No. 2. Eté 1990.

Report to Congress. Conduct of the Persian Gulf War. April 1992. <http://www.globalsecurity.org/military/library/report/1992/cpgw. pdf>.

Resche, Catherine. "*The Economist*: discours de spécialité économique ou discours sur l'économie?", *ILCEA*, 11. 30 Avril 2009. <http://journals.openedition.org/ilcea/64>; <https://doi.org/10.4000/ ilcea.64>.

"Return from Munich". *Guardian.* 1 October 1938. <http:// www.theguardian.com/world/1938/oct/01/secondworldwar. fromthearchive>.

Rudick, Marilynne. "Editing the Washington Post". *An Unfettered Press*. InfoUSA, U.S. Department of State. 2001. <http://usinfo.org/enus/media/overview/press01.html>.

Salamé, Ghassan. "Le Golfe: nuages après la tempête". *Politique étrangère*, No. 2. Eté 1991.

Salamé, Ghassan. "Est/ Ouest/ (Proche) Orient". *Politique étrangère*, No. 2. Eté 1990.

Schaefer, Brett D. The History of the Bloated U.N. Budget: How the U.S. Can Rein It In. Report. 2 April 2012. <https://www.heritage.org/report/the-history-the-bloated-un-budget-how-the-us-can-rein-it>.

"Seven nationals each suffer double digit drop". *Press Gazette*. 12 November 2010. <http://pressgazette.co.uk/seven-nationals-each-suffer-double-digit-drop/>.

Taheri, Amir. "Golfe Persique: Tempête sur l'Eldorado". *Politique internationale*, No. 49. Automne 1990.

Targonski, Rosalie and Suzanne Dawkins, eds. "The American Press". *An Unfettered Press*. InfoUSA, U.S. Department of State. 2001. <http://usinfo.org/enus/media/overview/press01.html>.

Thual, François. "L'Impact du puritanisme anglais". *Géopolitique des États-Unis. Culture, intérêts, stratégies. Revue Française de Géopolitique*. Paris: Ellipses, 2005.

Troin, Vincent. "La maîtrise de l'information: naissance et essor d'une doctrine stratégique". *Géopolitique des États-Unis. Culture, intérêts, stratégies. Revue Française de Géopolitique*. Paris: Ellipses, 2005.


**Websites cited**

Advertising & Marketing Technology News. Paid weekday circulation 1990-2008.
<https://adage.com/images/random/0309/4-1990s-030909.pdf>.

(The) American Presidency Project. George Bush, Statement by Press Secretary Fitzwater on Allied Bombing in Baghdad. 13 February 1991.
<https://www.presidency.ucsb.edu/node/264918>.

American War and Military Operations Casualties: Lists and Statistics. CRS Report for Congress. 15 September 2009.
<https://www.prisonlegalnews.org/media/publications/congressional_research_service_american_war_casualties_2009.pdf>.

Bush, George H.W. Collected papers and speeches. Presidential Library & Museum. <https://bush41library.tamu.edu/archives/public-papers/>.

Charter of the United Nations, Chapter VII.
<https://www.un.org/en/about-us/un-charter/chapter-7>.

(The) Desert Rats. Brief History of the British 7th Armoured Division. 24 October 2001. <desertrats.org.uk/history.htm>.

Deweweire, Ingrid. *Image de l'Autre, image de Soi. Ressemblances et divergences thématiques entre la presse américaine et britannique pendant la crise et la guerre du Golfe*. Thèse. Université de Pau et des Pays de l'Adour. 2013. <http://www.theses.fr/178570982>.

(The) European Environment Agency.
<http://www.eea.europa.eu/about-us/who>.

Hansard. UK Parliament. The official report of all Parliamentary debates. <https://hansard.parliament.uk/>.

International Churchill Society. "The War Situation: House of Many Mansions". 20 January 1940.
<https://winstonchurchill.org/resources/speeches/1940-the-finest-hour/the-war-situation-house-of-many-mansions/>.

King's College London. Liddle Hart Military Archives. September 1996. <https://www.kingscollections.org/catalogues/lhcma/collection/l/li30-001/>. February 1997.
<https://www.kingscollections.org/catalogues/lhcma/collection/f/fu20-001/>.

Major, John. Speeches and statements. The Rt. Hon. Sir John Major KG CH. <https://johnmajorarchive.org/uk/>.

Military Resources: Classified/declassified Records. National Archives. <https://www.archives.gov/research/alic/reference/military/records-declassification.html>.

Morrell, David. <https://www.davidmorrell.net/rambo/>.

National Army Museum. Gulf War. <www.nam.ac.uk/explore/gulf-war>.

(The) National Security Archive at the George Washington University. <https://nsarchive2.gwu.edu/NSAEBB/NSAEBB39/>.

Statista. Unemployment rate in the United Kingdom from 1971. <https://statista.com/statistics/279898/unemployment-rate-in-the-united-kingdom-uk/>.

Thatcher, Margaret. Speeches, interviews and statements. The Margaret Thatcher Foundation. <https://www.margaretthatcher.org/speeches>.

UK Parliament. Publications & records. <https://www.parliament.uk/business/publications/>.

United Nations Digital Library. <https://digitallibrary.un.org/record/>.

United Nations (Main Bodies). <http://www.un.org/en/sections/about-un/main-organs/index.html>.

U.N. Resolution 502. <unscr.com/files/1982/00502.pdf>.

U.N. Resolution 678. <http://undocs.org/S/RES/678(1990)>.

(The) U.S. Department of Justice Archives. <https://www.justice.gov/archives/open/declassification>.

U.S. Bureau of Labor Statistics. Household survey data. 2021 annual averages. <https://www.bls.gov/cps/cpsaat01.pdf>.

## Short biography

 After graduating as a teacher in Belgium, the author worked in the financial sector in Luxembourg before returning to teaching. She has a PhD in Foreign Languages and Literature.